Venetia

Earl of Beaconsfield Benjamin Disraeli

Alpha Editions

This edition published in 2024

ISBN : 9789362928511

Design and Setting By
Alpha Editions
www.alphaedis.com
Email - info@alphaedis.com

As per information held with us this book is in Public Domain.
This book is a reproduction of an important historical work. Alpha Editions uses the best technology to reproduce historical work in the same manner it was first published to preserve its original nature. Any marks or number seen are left intentionally to preserve its true form.

Contents

BOOK I. .... - 1 -
CHAPTER I. .... - 3 -
CHAPTER II. .... - 5 -
CHAPTER III. .... - 10 -
CHAPTER IV. .... - 12 -
CHAPTER V. .... - 16 -
CHAPTER VI. .... - 20 -
CHAPTER VII. .... - 28 -
CHAPTER VIII. .... - 32 -
CHAPTER IX. .... - 35 -
CHAPTER X. .... - 40 -
CHAPTER XI. .... - 44 -
CHAPTER XII. .... - 48 -
CHAPTER XIII. .... - 52 -
CHAPTER XIV. .... - 57 -
CHAPTER XV. .... - 62 -
CHAPTER XVI. .... - 67 -
CHAPTER XVII. .... - 72 -
CHAPTER XVIII. .... - 77 -
CHAPTER XIX. .... - 81 -
CHAPTER XX. .... - 86 -
BOOK II. .... - 89 -
CHAPTER I. .... - 91 -
CHAPTER II. .... - 95 -
CHAPTER III. .... - 101 -
CHAPTER IV. .... - 104 -

CHAPTER V.	- 110 -
CHAPTER VI.	- 114 -
CHAPTER VII.	- 119 -
CHAPTER VIII.	- 122 -
CHAPTER IX.	- 126 -
CHAPTER X.	- 130 -
CHAPTER XI.	- 135 -
BOOK III.	- 139 -
CHAPTER I.	- 141 -
CHAPTER II.	- 148 -
CHAPTER III.	- 152 -
CHAPTER IV.	- 155 -
CHAPTER V.	- 159 -
CHAPTER VI.	- 163 -
CHAPTER VII.	- 167 -
CHAPTER VIII.	- 175 -
BOOK IV.	- 179 -
CHAPTER I.	- 181 -
CHAPTER II.	- 186 -
CHAPTER III.	- 195 -
CHAPTER IV.	- 200 -
CHAPTER V.	- 209 -
CHAPTER VI.	- 211 -
CHAPTER VII.	- 213 -
CHAPTER VIII.	- 217 -
CHAPTER IX.	- 221 -
CHAPTER X.	- 226 -
CHAPTER XI.	- 236 -

CHAPTER XII.	- 241 -
CHAPTER XIII.	- 245 -
CHAPTER XIV.	- 249 -
CHAPTER XV.	- 257 -
CHAPTER XVI.	- 264 -
CHAPTER XVII.	- 270 -
CHAPTER XVIII.	- 274 -
CHAPTER XIX.	- 280 -
BOOK V.	- 283 -
CHAPTER I.	- 285 -
CHAPTER II.	- 289 -
CHAPTER III.	- 295 -
CHAPTER IV.	- 298 -
CHAPTER V.	- 305 -
CHAPTER VI.	- 310 -
CHAPTER VII.	- 314 -
CHAPTER VIII	- 318 -
CHAPTER IX.	- 322 -
CHAPTER X.	- 324 -
BOOK VI.	- 331 -
CHAPTER I.	- 333 -
CHAPTER II.	- 339 -
CHAPTER III.	- 348 -
CHAPTER IV.	- 353 -
CHAPTER V.	- 359 -
CHAPTER VI.	- 364 -
CHAPTER VII.	- 367 -
CHAPTER VIII.	- 370 -

CHAPTER IX. ....- 374 -
CHAPTER X. ....- 380 -
CHAPTER XI. ....- 384 -
CHAPTER XII. ....- 389 -
BOOK VII..- 393 -
CHAPTER I. ....- 395 -
CHAPTER II. ....- 400 -
CHAPTER III. ....- 403 -
CHAPTER IV. ....- 406 -
CHAPTER V. ....- 409 -

BOOK I.

CHAPTER I.

Some ten years before the revolt of our American colonies, there was situate in one of our midland counties, on the borders of an extensive forest, an ancient hall that belonged to the Herberts, but which, though ever well preserved, had not until that period been visited by any member of the family, since the exile of the Stuarts. It was an edifice of considerable size, built of grey stone, much covered with ivy, and placed upon the last gentle elevation of a long ridge of hills, in the centre of a crescent of woods, that far overtopped its clusters of tall chimneys and turreted gables. Although the principal chambers were on the first story, you could nevertheless step forth from their windows on a broad terrace, whence you descended into the gardens by a double flight of stone steps, exactly in the middle of its length. These gardens were of some extent, and filled with evergreen shrubberies of remarkable overgrowth, while occasionally turfy vistas, cut in the distant woods, came sloping down to the south, as if they opened to receive the sunbeam that greeted the genial aspect of the mansion, The ground-floor was principally occupied by the hall itself, which was of great dimensions, hung round with many a family portrait and rural picture, furnished with long oaken seats covered with scarlet cushions, and ornamented with a particoloured floor of alternate diamonds of black and white marble. From the centre of the roof of the mansion, which was always covered with pigeons, rose the clock-tower of the chapel, surmounted by a vane; and before the mansion itself was a large plot of grass, with a fountain in the centre, surrounded by a hedge of honeysuckle.

This plot of grass was separated from an extensive park, that opened in front of the hall, by tall iron gates, on each of the pillars of which was a lion rampant supporting the escutcheon of the family. The deer wandered in this enclosed and well-wooded demesne, and about a mile from the mansion, in a direct line with the iron gates, was an old-fashioned lodge, which marked the limit of the park, and from which you emerged into a fine avenue of limes bounded on both sides by fields. At the termination of this avenue was a strong but simple gate, and a woodman's cottage; and then spread before you a vast landscape of open, wild lands, which seemed on one side interminable, while on the other the eye rested on the dark heights of the neighbouring forest.

This picturesque and secluded abode was the residence of Lady Annabel Herbert and her daughter, the young and beautiful Venetia, a child, at the time when our history commences, of very tender age. It was nearly seven years since Lady Annabel and her infant daughter had sought the retired shades of Cherbury, which they had never since quitted. They lived alone and for each other; the mother educated her child, and the child interested her mother by her affectionate disposition, the development of a mind of no ordinary promise, and a sort of captivating grace and charming playfulness of temper, which were extremely delightful. Lady Annabel was still young and lovely. That she was wealthy her establishment clearly denoted, and she was a daughter of one of the haughtiest houses in the kingdom. It was strange then that, with all the brilliant accidents of birth, and beauty, and fortune, she should still, as it were in the morning of her life, have withdrawn to this secluded mansion, in a county where she was personally unknown, distant from the metropolis, estranged from all her own relatives and connexions, and without resource of even a single neighbour, for the only place of importance in her vicinity was uninhabited. The general impression of the villagers was that Lady Annabel was a widow; and yet there were some speculators who would shrewdly remark, that her ladyship had never worn weeds, although her husband could not have been long dead when she first arrived at Cherbury. On the whole, however, these good people were not very inquisitive; and it was fortunate for them, for there was little chance and slight means of gratifying their curiosity. The whole of the establishment had been formed at Cherbury, with the exception of her ladyship's waiting-woman, Mistress Pauncefort, and she was by far too great a personage to condescend to reply to any question which was not made to her by Lady Annabel herself.

The beauty of the young Venetia was not the hereditary gift of her beautiful mother. It was not from Lady Annabel that Venetia Herbert had derived those seraphic locks that fell over her shoulders and down her neck in golden streams, nor that clear grey eye even, whose childish glance might perplex the gaze of manhood, nor that little aquiline nose, that gave a haughty expression to a countenance that had never yet dreamed of pride, nor that radiant complexion, that dazzled with its brilliancy, like some winged minister of Raffael or Correggio. The peasants that passed the lady and her daughter in their walks, and who blessed her as they passed, for all her grace and goodness, often marvelled why so fair a mother and so fair a child should be so dissimilar, that one indeed might be compared to a starry night, and the other to a sunny day.

CHAPTER II.

It was a bright and soft spring morning: the dewy vistas of Cherbury sparkled in the sun, the cooing of the pigeons sounded around, the peacocks strutted about the terrace and spread their tails with infinite enjoyment and conscious pride, and Lady Annabel came forth with her little daughter, to breathe the renovating odours of the season. The air was scented with the violet, tufts of daffodils were scattered all about, and though the snowdrop had vanished, and the primroses were fast disappearing, their wild and shaggy leaves still looked picturesque and glad.

'Mamma,' said the little Venetia, 'is this spring?'

'This is spring, my child,' replied Lady Annabel, 'beautiful spring! The year is young and happy, like my little girl.'

'If Venetia be like the spring, mamma is like the summer!' replied the child; and the mother smiled. 'And is not the summer young and happy?' resumed Venetia.

'It is not quite so young as the spring,' said Lady Annabel, looking down with fondness on her little companion, 'and, I fear, not quite so happy.'

'But it is as beautiful,' said Venetia.

'It is not beauty that makes us happy,' said Lady Annabel; 'to be happy, my love, we must be good.'

'Am I good?' said Venetia.

'Very good,' said Lady Annabel

'I am very happy,' said Venetia; 'I wonder whether, if I be always good, I shall always be happy?'

'You cannot be happy without being good, my love; but happiness depends upon the will of God. If you be good he will guard over you.'

'What can make me unhappy, mamma?' inquired Venetia.

'An evil conscience, my love.'

'Conscience!' said Venetia: 'what is conscience?'

'You are not yet quite old enough to understand,' said Lady Annabel, 'but some day I will teach you. Mamma is now going to take a long walk, and Venetia shall walk with her.'

So saying, the Lady Annabel summoned Mistress Pauncefort, a gentlewoman of not more discreet years than might have been expected in the attendant of so young a mistress; but one well qualified for her office, very zealous and devoted, somewhat consequential, full of energy and decision, capable of directing, fond of giving advice, and habituated to command. The Lady Annabel, leading her daughter, and accompanied by her faithful bloodhound, Marmion, ascended one of those sloping vistas that we have noticed, Mistress Pauncefort following them about a pace behind, and after her a groom, at a respectful distance, leading Miss Herbert's donkey.

They soon entered a winding path through the wood which was the background of their dwelling. Lady Annabel was silent, and lost in her reflections; Venetia plucked the beautiful wild hyacinths that then abounded in the wood in such profusion, that their beds spread like patches of blue enamel, and gave them to Mistress Pauncefort, who, as the collection increased, handed them over to the groom; who, in turn, deposited them in the wicker seat prepared for his young mistress. The bright sun bursting through the tender foliage of the year, the clear and genial air, the singing of the birds, and the wild and joyous exclamations of Venetia, as she gathered her flowers, made it a cheerful party, notwithstanding the silence of its mistress.

When they emerged from the wood, they found themselves on the brow of the hill, a small down, over which Venetia ran, exulting in the healthy breeze which, at this exposed height, was strong and fresh. As they advanced to the opposite declivity to that which they had ascended, a wide and peculiar landscape opened before them. The extreme distance was formed by an undulating ridge of lofty and savage hills; nearer than these were gentler elevations, partially wooded; and at their base was a rich valley, its green meads fed by a clear and rapid stream, which glittered in the sun as it coursed on, losing itself at length in a wild and sedgy lake that formed the furthest limit of a widely-spreading park. In the centre of this park, and not very remote from the banks of the rivulet, was an ancient gothic building, that had once been an abbey of great repute and wealth, and had not much suffered in its external character, by having served for nearly two centuries and a half as the principal dwelling of an old baronial family.

Descending the downy hill, that here and there was studded with fine old trees, enriching by their presence the view from the abbey, Lady Annabel and her party entered the meads, and, skirting the lake, approached the venerable walls without crossing the stream.

It was difficult to conceive a scene more silent and more desolate. There was no sign of life, and not a sound save the occasional cawing of a rook. Advancing towards the abbey, they passed a pile of buildings that, in the summer, might be screened from sight by the foliage of a group of elms, too scanty at present to veil their desolation. Wide gaps in the roof proved that the vast and dreary stables were no longer used; there were empty granaries, whose doors had fallen from their hinges; the gate of the courtyard was prostrate on the ground; and the silent clock that once adorned the cupola over the noble entrance arch, had long lost its index. Even the litter of the yard appeared dusty and grey with age. You felt sure no human foot could have disturbed it for years. At the back of these buildings were nailed the trophies of the gamekeeper: hundreds of wild cats, dried to blackness, stretched their downward heads and legs from the mouldering wall; hawks, magpies, and jays hung in tattered remnants! but all grey, and even green, with age; and the heads of birds in plenteous rows, nailed beak upward, and so dried and shrivelled by the suns and winds and frosts of many seasons, that their distinctive characters were lost.

'Do you know, my good Pauncefort,' said Lady Annabel, 'that I have an odd fancy to-day to force an entrance into the old abbey. It is strange, fond as I am of this walk, that we have never yet entered it. Do you recollect our last vain efforts? Shall we be more fortunate this time, think you?'

Mistress Pauncefort smiled and smirked, and, advancing to the old gloomy porch, gave a determined ring at the bell. Its sound might be heard echoing through the old cloisters, but a considerable time elapsed without any other effect being produced. Perhaps Lady Annabel would have now given up the attempt, but the little Venetia expressed so much regret at the disappointment, that her mother directed the groom to reconnoitre in the neighbourhood, and see if it were possible to discover any person connected with the mansion.

'I doubt our luck, my lady,' said Mistress Pauncefort, 'for they do say that the abbey is quite uninhabited.'

''Tis a pity,' said Lady Annabel, 'for, with all its desolation, there is something about this spot which ever greatly interests me.'

'Mamma, why does no one live here?' said Venetia.

'The master of the abbey lives abroad, my child.'

'Why does he, mamma?'

'Never ask questions, Miss Venetia,' said Mistress Pauncefort, in a hushed and solemn tone; 'it is not pretty.' Lady Annabel had moved away.

The groom returned, and said he had met an old man, picking water-cresses, and he was the only person who lived in the abbey, except his wife, and she was bedridden. The old man had promised to admit them when he had completed his task, but not before, and the groom feared it would be some time before he arrived.

'Come, Pauncefort, rest yourself on this bench,' said Lady Annabel, seating herself in the porch; 'and Venetia, my child, come hither to me.'

'Mamma,' said Venetia, 'what is the name of the gentleman to whom this abbey belongs?'

'Lord Cadurcis, love.'

'I should like to know why Lord Cadurcis lives abroad?' said Venetia, musingly.

'There are many reasons why persons may choose to quit their native country, and dwell in another, my love,' said Lady Annabel, very quietly; 'some change the climate for their health.'

'Did Lord Cadurcis, mamma?' asked Venetia.

'I do not know Lord Cadurcis, dear, or anything of him, except that he is a very old man, and has no family.'

At this moment there was a sound of bars and bolts withdrawn, and the falling of a chain, and at length the massy door slowly opened, and the old man appeared and beckoned to them to enter.

"Tis eight years, come Martinmas, since I opened this door,' said the old man, 'and it sticks a bit. You must walk about by yourselves, for I have no breath, and my mistress is bedridden. There, straight down the cloister, you can't miss your way; there is not much to see.'

The interior of the abbey formed a quadrangle, surrounded by the cloisters, and in this inner court was a curious fountain, carved with exquisite skill by some gothic artist in one of those capricious moods of sportive invention that produced those grotesque medleys for which the feudal sculptor was celebrated. Not a sound was heard except the fall of the fountain and the light echoes that its voice called up.

The staircase led Lady Annabel and her party through several small rooms, scantily garnished with ancient furniture, in some of which were portraits of the family, until they at length entered a noble saloon, once the refectory of the abbey, and not deficient in splendour, though sadly soiled and worm-eaten. It was hung with tapestry representing the Cartoons of Raffael, and their still vivid colours contrasted with the faded hangings and the dingy damask of the chairs and sofas. A mass of Cromwellian armour was huddled together in a corner of a long monkish gallery, with a standard, encrusted with dust, and a couple of old drums, one broken. From one of the windows they had a good view of the old walled garden, which did not tempt them to enter it; it was a wilderness, the walks no longer distinguishable from the rank vegetation of the once cultivated lawns; the terraces choked up with the unchecked shrubberies; and here and there a leaden statue, a goddess or a satyr, prostrate, and covered with moss and lichen.

'It makes me melancholy,' said Lady Annabel; 'let us return.'

'Mamma,' said Venetia, 'are there any ghosts in this abbey?'

'You may well ask me, love,' replied Lady Annabel; 'it seems a spell-bound place. But, Venetia, I have often told you there are no such things as ghosts.'

'Is it naughty to believe in ghosts, mamma, for I cannot help believing in them?'

'When you are older, and have more knowledge, you will not believe in them, Venetia,' replied Lady Annabel.

Our friends left Cadurcis Abbey. Venetia mounted her donkey, her mother walked by her side; the sun was beginning to decline when they again reached Cherbury, and the air was brisk. Lady Annabel was glad to find herself by her fireside in her little terrace-room, and Venetia fetching her book, read to her mother until their dinner hour.

CHAPTER III.

Two serene and innocent years had glided away at Cherbury since this morning ramble to Cadurcis Abbey, and Venetia had grown in loveliness, in goodness, and intelligence. Her lively and somewhat precocious mind had become greatly developed; and, though she was only nine years of age, it scarcely needed the affection of a mother to find in her an interesting and engaging companion. Although feminine education was little regarded in those days, that of Lady Annabel had been an exception to the general practice of society. She had been brought up with the consciousness of other objects of female attainment and accomplishment than embroidery, 'the complete art of making pastry,' and reading 'The Whole Duty of Man.' She had profited, when a child, by the guidance of her brother's tutor, who had bestowed no unfruitful pains upon no ordinary capacity. She was a good linguist, a fine musician, was well read in our elder poets and their Italian originals, was no unskilful artist, and had acquired some knowledge of botany when wandering, as a girl, in her native woods. Since her retirement to Cherbury, reading had been her chief resource. The hall contained a library whose shelves, indeed, were more full than choice; but, amid folios of theological controversy and civil law, there might be found the first editions of most of the celebrated writers of the reign of Anne, which the contemporary proprietor of Cherbury, a man of wit and fashion in his day, had duly collected in his yearly visits to the metropolis, and finally deposited in the family book-room.

The education of her daughter was not only the principal duty of Lady Annabel, but her chief delight. To cultivate the nascent intelligence of a child, in those days, was not the mere piece of scientific mechanism that the admirable labours of so many ingenious writers have since permitted it comparatively to become. In those days there was no Mrs. Barbauld, no Madame de Genlis, no Miss Edgeworth; no 'Evenings at Home,' no 'Children's Friend,' no 'Parent's Assistant.' Venetia loved her book; indeed, she was never happier than when reading; but she soon recoiled from the gilt and Lilliputian volumes of the good Mr. Newbury, and her mind required some more substantial excitement than 'Tom Thumb,' or even 'Goody Two-Shoes.' 'The Seven Champions' was a great resource and a great favourite; but it required all the vigilance of a mother to eradicate the false impressions which such studies were continually making on so tender a student; and to disenchant, by rational discussion, the fascinated imagination of her child. Lady Annabel endeavoured to find some substitute in the essays of Addison and Steele; but they required more knowledge of the every-day world for their enjoyment than an infant, bred in such seclusion, could at present afford; and at last Venetia lost herself in the wildering pages of Clelia and the

Arcadia, which she pored over with a rapt and ecstatic spirit, that would not comprehend the warning scepticism of her parent. Let us picture to ourselves the high-bred Lady Annabel in the terrace-room of her ancient hall, working at her tapestry, and, seated at her feet, her little daughter Venetia, reading aloud the Arcadia! The peacocks have jumped up on the window-sill, to look at their friends, who love to feed them, and by their pecking have aroused the bloodhound crouching at Lady Annabel's feet. And Venetia looks up from her folio with a flushed and smiling face to catch the sympathy of her mother, who rewards her daughter's study with a kiss. Ah! there are no such mothers and no such daughters now!

Thus it will be seen that the life and studies of Venetia tended rather dangerously, in spite of all the care of her mother, to the development of her imagination, in case indeed she possessed that terrible and fatal gift. She passed her days in unbroken solitude, or broken only by affections which softened her heart, and in a scene which itself might well promote any predisposition of the kind; beautiful and picturesque objects surrounded her on all sides; she wandered, at it were, in an enchanted wilderness, and watched the deer reposing under the green shadow of stately trees; the old hall itself was calculated to excite mysterious curiosity; one wing was uninhabited and shut up; each morning and evening she repaired with her mother and the household through long galleries to the chapel, where she knelt to her devotions, illumined by a window blazoned with the arms of that illustrious family of which she was a member, and of which she knew nothing. She had an indefinite and painful consciousness that she had been early checked in the natural inquiries which occur to every child; she had insensibly been trained to speak only of what she saw; and when she listened, at night, to the long ivy rustling about the windows, and the wild owls hooting about the mansion, with their pining, melancholy voices, she might have been excused for believing in those spirits, which her mother warned her to discredit; or she forgot these mournful impressions in dreams, caught from her romantic volumes, of bright knights and beautiful damsels.

Only one event of importance had occurred at Cherbury during these two years, if indeed that be not too strong a phrase to use in reference to an occurrence which occasioned so slight and passing an interest. Lord Cadurcis had died. He had left his considerable property to his natural children, but the abbey had descended with the title to a very distant relative. The circle at Cherbury had heard, and that was all, that the new lord was a minor, a little boy, indeed very little older than Venetia herself; but this information produced no impression. The abbey was still deserted and desolate as ever.

CHAPTER IV.

Every Sunday afternoon, the rector of a neighbouring though still somewhat distant parish, of which the rich living was in the gift of the Herberts, came to perform divine service at Cherbury. It was a subject of deep regret to Lady Annabel that herself and her family were debarred from the advantage of more frequent and convenient spiritual consolation; but, at this time, the parochial discipline of the Church of England was not so strict as it fortunately is at present. Cherbury, though a vicarage, possessed neither parish church, nor a residence for the clergyman; nor was there indeed a village. The peasants on the estate, or labourers as they are now styled, a term whose introduction into our rural world is much to be lamented, lived in the respective farmhouses on the lands which they cultivated. These were scattered about at considerable distances, and many of their inmates found it more convenient to attend the church of the contiguous parish than to repair to the hall chapel, where the household and the dwellers in the few cottages scattered about the park and woods always assembled. The Lady Annabel, whose lot it had been in life to find her best consolation in religion, and who was influenced by not only a sincere but even a severe piety, had no other alternative, therefore, but engaging a chaplain; but this, after much consideration, she had resolved not to do. She was indeed her own chaplain, herself performing each day such parts of our morning and evening service whose celebration becomes a laic, and reading portions from the writings of those eminent divines who, from the Restoration to the conclusion of the last reign, have so eminently distinguished the communion of our national Church.

Each Sunday, after the performance of divine service, the Rev. Dr. Masham dined with the family, and he was the only guest at Cherbury Venetia ever remembered seeing. The Doctor was a regular orthodox divine of the eighteenth century; with a large cauliflower wig, shovel-hat, and huge knee-buckles, barely covered by his top-boots; learned, jovial, humorous, and somewhat courtly; truly pious, but not enthusiastic; not forgetful of his tithes, but generous and charitable when they were once paid; never neglecting the sick, yet occasionally following a fox; a fine scholar, an active magistrate, and a good shot; dreading the Pope, and hating the Presbyterians.

The Doctor was attached to the Herbert family not merely because they had given him a good living. He had a great reverence for an old English race, and turned up his nose at the Walpolian loanmongers. Lady Annabel, too, so beautiful, so dignified, so amiable, and highly bred, and, above all, so pious, had won his regard. He was not a little proud, too, that he was the only person in the county who had the honour of her acquaintance, and yet was disinterested enough to regret that he led so secluded a life, and often lamented that nothing would induce her to show her elegant person on a racecourse, or to attend an assize ball, an assembly which was then becoming much the fashion. The little Venetia was a charming child, and the kind-hearted Doctor, though a bachelor, loved children.

O! matre pulchrâ, filia pulchrior,

was the Rev. Dr. Masham's apposite and favourite quotation after his weekly visit to Cherbury.

Divine service was concluded; the Doctor had preached a capital sermon; for he had been one of the shining lights of his university until his rich but isolating preferment had apparently closed the great career which it was once supposed awaited him. The accustomed walk on the terrace was completed, and dinner was announced. This meal was always celebrated at Cherbury, where new fashions stole down with a lingering pace, in the great hall itself. An ample table was placed in the centre on a mat of rushes, sheltered by a large screen covered with huge maps of the shire and the neighbouring counties. The Lady Annabel and her good pastor seated themselves at each end of the table, while Venetia, mounted on a high chair, was waited on by Mistress Pauncefort, who never condescended by any chance attention to notice the presence of any other individual but her little charge, on whose chair she just leaned with an air of condescending devotion. The butler stood behind his lady, and two other servants watched the Doctor; rural bodies all, but decked on this day in gorgeous livery coats of blue and silver, which had been made originally for men of very different size and bearing. Simple as was the usual diet at Cherbury the cook was permitted on Sunday full play to her art, which, in the eighteenth century, indulged in the production of dishes more numerous and substantial than our refined tastes could at present tolerate. The Doctor appreciated a good dinner, and his countenance glistened with approbation as he surveyed the ample tureen of potage royal, with a boned duck swimming in its centre. Before him still scowled in death the grim countenance of a huge roast pike, flanked on one side by a leg of mutton *à-la-daube*, and on the other by the tempting delicacies of bombarded veal. To these succeeded that masterpiece of the culinary art, a grand battalia pie, in which the bodies of chickens, pigeons, and rabbits were embalmed in spices, cocks' combs, and savoury balls, and well bedewed with one of those rich sauces of claret, anchovy, and sweet herbs, in which our great-grandfathers delighted, and which was technically termed a Lear. But the grand essay of skill was the cover of this pasty, whereon the curious cook had contrived to represent all the once-living forms that were now entombed in that gorgeous sepulchre. A Florentine tourte, or tansy, an old English custard, a more refined blamango, and a riband jelly of many colours, offered a pleasant relief after these vaster inventions, and the repast closed with a dish of oyster loaves and a pompetone of larks.

Notwithstanding the abstemiousness of his hostess, the Doctor was never deterred from doing justice to her hospitality. Few were the dishes that ever escaped him. The demon dyspepsia had not waved its fell wings over the eighteenth century, and wonderful were the feats then achieved by a country gentleman with the united aid of a good digestion and a good conscience.

The servants had retired, and Dr. Masham had taken his last glass of port, and then he rang a bell on the table, and, I trust my fair readers will not be frightened from proceeding with this history, a servant brought him his pipe. The pipe was well stuffed, duly lighted, and duly puffed; and then, taking it from his mouth, the Doctor spoke.

'And so, my honoured lady, you have got a neighbour at last.'

'Indeed!' exclaimed Lady Annabel.

But the claims of the pipe prevented the good Doctor from too quickly satisfying her natural curiosity. Another puff or two, and he then continued.

'Yes,' said he, 'the old abbey has at last found a tenant.'

'A tenant, Doctor?'

'Ay! the best tenant in the world: its proprietor.'

'You quite surprise me. When did this occur?'

'They have been there these three days; I have paid them a visit. Mrs. Cadurcis has come to live at the abbey with the little lord.'

'This is indeed news to us,' said Lady Annabel; 'and what kind of people are they?'

'You know, my dear madam,' said the Doctor, just touching the ash of his pipe with his tobacco-stopper of chased silver, 'that the present lord is a very distant relative of the late one?'

Lady Annabel bowed assent.

'The late lord,' continued the Doctor, 'who was as strange and wrong-headed a man as ever breathed, though I trust he is in the kingdom of heaven for all that, left all his property to his unlawful children, with the exception of this estate entailed on the title, as all estates should be, 'Tis a fine place, but no great rental. I doubt whether 'tis more than a clear twelve hundred a-year.'

'And Mrs. Cadurcis?' inquired Lady Annabel.

'Was an heiress,' replied the Doctor, 'and the late Mr. Cadurcis a spendrift. He was a bad manager, and, worse, a bad husband. Providence was pleased to summon him suddenly from this mortal scene, but not before he had dissipated the greater part of his wife's means. Mrs. Cadurcis, since she was a widow, has lived in strict seclusion with her little boy, as you may, my dear lady, with your dear little girl. But I am afraid,' said the Doctor, shaking his head, 'she has not been in the habit of dining so well as we have to-day. A very limited income, my dear madam; a very limited income indeed. And the guardians, I am told, will only allow the little lord a hundred a-year; but, on her own income, whatever it may be, and that addition, she has resolved to live at the abbey; and I believe, I believe she has it rent-free; but I don't know.'

'Poor woman!' said Lady Annabel, and not without a sigh. 'I trust her child is her consolation.'

Venetia had not spoken during this conversation, but she had listened to it very attentively. At length she said, 'Mamma, is not a widow a wife that has lost her husband?'

'You are right, my dear,' said Lady Annabel, rather gravely.

Venetia mused a moment, and then replied, 'Pray, mamma, are you a widow?'

'My dear little girl,' said Dr. Masham, 'go and give that beautiful peacock a pretty piece of cake.'

Lady Annabel and the Doctor rose from the table with Venetia, and took a turn in the park, while the Doctor's horses were getting ready.

'I think, my good lady,' said the Doctor, 'it would be but an act of Christian charity to call upon Mrs. Cadurcis.'

'I was thinking the same,' said Lady Annabel; 'I am interested by what you have told me of her history and fortunes. We have some woes in common; I hope some joys. It seems that this case should indeed be an exception to my rule.'

'I would not ask you to sacrifice your inclinations to the mere pleasures of the world,' said the Doctor: 'but duties, my dear lady, duties; there are such things as duties to our neighbour; and here is a case where, believe me, they might be fulfilled.'

The Doctor's horses now appeared. Both master and groom wore their pistols in their holsters. The Doctor shook hands warmly with Lady Annabel, and patted Venetia on her head, as she ran up from a little distance, with an eager countenance, to receive her accustomed blessing. Then mounting his stout mare, he once more waived his hand with an air of courtliness to his hostess, and was soon out of sight. Lady Annabel and Venetia returned to the terrace-room.

CHAPTER V.

'And so I would, my lady,' said Mistress Pauncefort, when Lady Annabel communicated to her faithful attendant, at night, the news of the arrival of the Cadurcis family at the abbey, and her intention of paying Mrs. Cadurcis a visit; 'and so I would, my lady,' said Mistress Pauncefort, 'and it would be but an act of Christian charity after all, as the Doctor says; for although it is not for me to complain when my betters are satisfied, and after all I am always content, if your ladyship be; still there is no denying the fact, that this is a terrible lonesome life after all. And I cannot help thinking your ladyship has not been looking so well of late, and a little society would do your ladyship good; and Miss Venetia too, after all, she wants a playfellow; I am certain sure that I was as tired of playing at ball with her this morning as if I had never sat down in my born days; and I dare say the little lord will play with her all day long.'

'If I thought that this visit would lead to what is understood by the word society, my good Pauncefort, I certainly should refrain from paying it,' said Lady Annabel, very quietly.

'Oh! Lord, dear my lady, I was not for a moment dreaming of any such thing,' replied Mistress Pauncefort; 'society, I know as well as any one, means grand balls, Ranelagh, and the masquerades. I can't abide the thought of them, I do assure your ladyship; all I meant was that a quiet dinner now and then with a few friends, a dance perhaps in the evening, or a hand of whist, or a game of romps at Christmas, when the abbey will of course be quite full, a—'

'I believe there is as little chance of the abbey being full at Christmas, or any other time, as there is of Cherbury.' said Lady Annabel. 'Mrs. Cadurcis is a widow, with a very slender fortune. Her son will not enjoy his estate until he is of age, and its rental is small. I am led to believe that they will live quite as quietly as ourselves; and when I spoke of Christian charity, I was thinking only of kindness towards them, and not of amusement for ourselves.'

'Well, my lady, your la'ship knows best,' replied Mistress Pauncefort, evidently very disappointed; for she had indulged in momentary visions of noble visitors and noble valets; 'I am always content, you know, when your la'ship is; but, I must say, I think it is very odd for a lord to be so poor. I never heard of such a thing. I think they will turn out richer than you have an idea, my lady. Your la'ship knows 'tis quite a saying, "As rich as a lord."'

Lady Annabel smiled, but did not reply.

The next morning the fawn-coloured chariot, which had rarely been used since Lady Annabel's arrival at Cherbury, and four black long-tailed coach-horses, that from absolute necessity had been degraded, in the interval, to the service of the cart and the plough, made their appearance, after much bustle and effort, before the hall-door. Although a morning's stroll from Cherbury through the woods, Cadurcis was distant nearly ten miles by the road, and that road was in great part impassable, save in favourable seasons. This visit, therefore, was an expedition; and Lady Annabel, fearing the fatigue for a child, determined to leave Venetia at home, from whom she had actually never been separated one hour in her life. Venetia could not refrain from shedding a tear when her mother embraced and quitted her, and begged, as a last favour, that she might accompany her through the park to the avenue lodge. So Pauncefort and herself entered the chariot, that rocked like a ship, in spite of all the skill of the coachman and the postilion.

Venetia walked home with Mistress Pauncefort, but Lady Annabel's little daughter was not in her usual lively spirits; many a butterfly glanced around without attracting her pursuit, and the deer trooped by without eliciting a single observation. At length she said, in a thoughtful tone, 'Mistress Pauncefort, I should have liked to have gone and seen the little boy.'

'You shall go and see him another day, Miss,' replied her attendant.

'Mistress Pauncefort,' said Venetia, 'are you a widow?'

Mistress Pauncefort almost started; had the inquiry been made by a man, she would almost have supposed he was going to be very rude. She was indeed much surprised.

'And pray, Miss Venetia, what could put it in your head to ask such an odd question?' exclaimed Mistress Pauncefort. 'A widow! Miss Venetia; I have never yet changed my name, and I shall not in a hurry, that I can tell you.'

'Do widows change their names?' said Venetia.

'All women change their names when they marry,' responded Mistress Pauncefort.

'Is mamma married?' inquired Venetia.

'La! Miss Venetia. Well, to be sure, you do ask the strangest questions. Married! to be sure she is married,' said Mistress Pauncefort, exceedingly flustered.

'And whom is she married to?' pursued the unwearied Venetia.

'Your papa, to be sure,' said Mistress Pauncefort, blushing up to her eyes, and looking very confused; 'that is to say, Miss Venetia, you are never to ask questions about such subjects. Have not I often told you it is not pretty?'

'Why is it not pretty?' said Venetia.

'Because it is not proper,' said Mistress Pauncefort; 'because your mamma does not like you to ask such questions, and she will be very angry with me for answering them, I can tell you that.'

'I tell you what, Mistress Pauncefort,' said Venetia, 'I think mamma is a widow.'

'And what then, Miss Venetia? There is no shame in that.'

'Shame!' exclaimed Venetia. 'What is shame?'

'Look, there is a pretty butterfly!' exclaimed Mistress Pauncefort. 'Did you ever see such a pretty butterfly, Miss?'

'I do not care about butterflies to-day, Mistress Pauncefort; I like to talk about widows.'

'Was there ever such a child!' exclaimed Mistress Pauncefort, with a wondering glance.

'I must have had a papa,' said Venetia; 'all the ladies I read about had papas, and married husbands. Then whom did my mamma marry?'

'Lord! Miss Venetia, you know very well your mamma always tells you that all those books you read are a pack of stories,' observed Mistress Pauncefort, with an air of triumphant art.

'There never were such persons, perhaps,' said Venetia, 'but it is not true that there never were such things as papas and husbands, for all people have papas; you must have had a papa, Mistress Pauncefort?'

'To be sure I had,' said Mistress Pauncefort, bridling up.

'And a mamma too?' said Venetia.

'As honest a woman as ever lived,' said Mistress Pauncefort.

'Then if I have no papa, mamma must be a wife that has lost her husband, and that, mamma told me at dinner yesterday, was a widow.'

'Was the like ever seen!' exclaimed Mistress Pauncefort. 'And what then, Miss Venetia?'

'It seems to me so odd that only two people should live here, and both be widows,' said Venetia, 'and both have a little child; the only difference is, that one is a little boy, and I am a little girl.'

'When ladies lose their husbands, they do not like to have their names mentioned,' said Mistress Pauncefort; 'and so you must never talk of your papa to my lady, and that is the truth.'

'I will not now,' said Venetia.

When they returned home, Mistress Pauncefort brought her work, and seated herself on the terrace, that she might not lose sight of her charge. Venetia played about for some little time; she made a castle behind a tree, and fancied she was a knight, and then a lady, and conjured up an ogre in the neighbouring shrubbery; but these daydreams did not amuse her as much as usual. She went and fetched her book, but even 'The Seven Champions' could not interest her. Her eye was fixed upon the page, and apparently she was absorbed in her pursuit, but her mind wandered, and the page was never turned. She indulged in an unconscious reverie; her fancy was with her mother on her visit; the old abbey rose up before her: she painted the scene without an effort: the court, with the fountain; the grand room, with the tapestry hangings; that desolate garden, with the fallen statues; and that long, gloomy gallery. And in all these scenes appeared that little boy, who, somehow or other, seemed wonderfully blended with her imaginings. It was a very long day this; Venetia dined along with Mistress Pauncefort; the time hung very heavy; at length she fell asleep in Mistress Pauncefort's lap. A sound roused her: the carriage had returned; she ran to greet her mother, but there was no news; Mrs. Cadurcis had been absent; she had gone to a distant town to buy some furniture; and, after all, Lady Annabel had not seen the little boy.

CHAPTER VI.

A few days after the visit to Cadurcis, when Lady Annabel was sitting alone, a postchaise drove up to the hall, whence issued a short and stout woman with a rubicund countenance, and dressed in a style which remarkably blended the shabby with the tawdry. She was accompanied by a boy between eleven and twelve years of age, whose appearance, however, much contrasted with that of his mother, for he was pale and slender, with long curling black hair and large black eyes, which occasionally, by their transient flashes, agreeably relieved a face the general expression of which might be esteemed somewhat shy and sullen. The lady, of course, was Mrs. Cadurcis, who was received by Lady Annabel with the greatest courtesy.

'A terrible journey,' exclaimed Mrs. Cadurcis, fanning herself as she took her seat, 'and so very hot! Plantagenet, my love, make your bow! Have not I always told you to make a bow when you enter a room, especially where there are strangers? This is Lady Annabel Herbert, who was so kind as to call upon us. Make your bow to Lady Annabel.'

The boy gave a sort of sulky nod, but Lady Annabel received it so graciously and expressed herself so kindly to him that his features relaxed a little, though he was quite silent and sat on the edge of his chair, the picture of dogged indifference.

'Charming country, Lady Annabel,' said Mrs. Cadurcis, 'but worse roads, if possible, than we had in Northumberland, where, indeed, there were no roads at all. Cherbury a delightful place, very unlike the abbey; dreadfully lonesome I assure you I find it, Lady Annabel. Great change for us from a little town and all our kind neighbours. Very different from Morpeth; is it not, Plantagenet?'

'I hate Morpeth,' said the boy.

'Hate Morpeth!' exclaimed Mrs. Cadurcis; 'well, I am sure, that is very ungrateful, with so many kind friends as we always found. Besides, Plantagenet, have I not always told you that you are to hate nothing? It is very wicked. The trouble it costs me, Lady Annabel, to educate this dear child!' continued Mrs. Cadurcis, turning to Lady Annabel, and speaking in a semi-tone. 'I have done it all myself, I assure you; and, when he likes, he can be as good as any one. Can't you, Plantagenet?'

Lord Cadurcis gave a grim smile; seated himself at the very back of the deep chair and swung his feet, which no longer reached the ground, to and fro.

'I am sure that Lord Cadurcis always behaves well,' said Lady Annabel.

'There, Plantagenet,' exclaimed Mrs. Cadurcis, 'only listen to that. Hear what Lady Annabel Herbert says; she is sure you always behave well. Now mind, never give her ladyship cause to change her opinion.'

Plantagenet curled his lip, and half turned his back on his companions.

'I regretted so much that I was not at home when you did me the honour to call,' resumed Mrs. Cadurcis; 'but I had gone over for the day to Southport, buying furniture. What a business it is to buy furniture, Lady Annabel!' added Mrs. Cadurcis, with a piteous expression.

'It is indeed very troublesome,' said Lady Annabel.

'Ah! you have none of these cares,' continued Mrs. Cadurcis, surveying the pretty apartment. 'What a difference between Cherbury and the abbey! I suppose you have never been there?'

'Indeed, it is one of my favourite walks,' answered Lady Annabel; 'and, some two years ago, I even took the liberty of walking through the house.'

'Was there ever such a place!' exclaimed Mrs. Cadurcis. 'I assure you my poor head turns whenever I try to find my way about it. But the trustees offered it us, and I thought it my duty to my son to reside there. Besides, it was a great offer to a widow; if poor Mr. Cadurcis had been alive it would have been different. I hardly know what I shall do there, particularly in winter. My spirits are always dreadfully low. I only hope Plantagenet will behave well. If he goes into his tantrums at the abbey, and particularly in winter, I hardly know what will become of me!'

'I am sure Lord Cadurcis will do everything to make the abbey comfortable to you. Besides, it is but a short walk from Cherbury, and you must come often and see us.'

'Oh! Plantagenet can be good if he likes, I can assure you, Lady Annabel; and behaves as properly as any little boy I know. Plantagenet, my dear, speak. Have not I always told you, when you pay a visit, that you should open your mouth now and then. I don't like chattering children,' added Mrs. Cadurcis, 'but I like them to answer when they are spoken to.'

'Nobody has spoken to me,' said Lord Cadurcis, in a sullen tone.

'Plantagenet, my love!' said his mother in a solemn voice.

'Well, mother, what do you want?'

'Plantagenet, my love, you know you promised me to be good!'

'Well! what have I done?'

'Lord Cadurcis,' said Lady Annabel, interfering, 'do you like to look at pictures?'

'Thank you,' replied the little lord, in a more courteous tone; 'I like to be left alone.'

'Did you ever know such an odd child!' said Mrs. Cadurcis; 'and yet, Lady Annabel, you must not judge him by what you see. I do assure you he can behave, when he likes, as pretty as possible.'

'Pretty!' muttered the little lord between his teeth.

'If you had only seen him at Morpeth sometimes at a little tea party,' said Mrs. Cadurcis, 'he really was quite the ornament of the company.'

'No, I wasn't,' said Lord Cadurcis.

'Plantagenet!' said his mother again in a solemn tone, 'have I not always told you that you are never to contradict any one?'

The little lord indulged in a suppressed growl.

'There was a little play last Christmas,' continued Mrs. Cadurcis, 'and he acted quite delightfully. Now you would not think that, from the way he sits upon that chair. Plantagenet, my dear, I do insist upon your behaving yourself. Sit like a man.'

'I am not a man,' said Lord Cadurcis, very quietly; 'I wish I were.'

'Plantagenet!' said the mother, 'have not I always told you that you are never to answer me? It is not proper for children to answer! O Lady Annabel, if you knew what it cost me to educate my son. He never does anything I wish, and it is so provoking, because I know that he can behave as properly as possible if he likes. He does it to provoke me. You know you do it to provoke me, you little brat; now, sit properly, sir; I do desire you to sit properly. How vexatious that you should call at Cherbury for the first time, and behave in this manner! Plantagenet, do you hear me?' exclaimed Mrs. Cadurcis, with a face reddening to scarlet, and almost menacing a move from her seat.

'Yes, everybody hears you, Mrs. Cadurcis,' said the little lord.

'Don't call me Mrs. Cadurcis,' exclaimed the mother, in a dreadful rage. 'That is not the way to speak to your mother; I will not be called Mrs. Cadurcis by you. Don't answer me, sir; I desire you not to answer me. I have half a mind to get up and give you a good shake, that I have. O Lady Annabel,' sighed Mrs. Cadurcis, while a tear trickled down her cheek, 'if you only knew the life I lead, and what trouble it costs me to educate that child!'

'My dear madam,' said Lady Annabel, 'I am sure that Lord Cadurcis has no other wish but to please you. Indeed you have misunderstood him.'

'Yes! she always misunderstands me,' said Lord Cadurcis, in a softer tone, but with pouting lips and suffused eyes.

'Now he is going on,' said his mother, beginning herself to cry dreadfully. 'He knows my weak heart; he knows nobody in the world loves him like his mother; and this is the way he treats me.'

'My dear Mrs. Cadurcis,' said Lady Annabel, 'pray take luncheon after your long drive; and Lord Cadurcis, I am sure you must be fatigued.'

'Thank you, I never eat, my dear lady,' said Mrs. Cadurcis, 'except at my meals. But one glass of Mountain, if you please, I would just take the liberty of tasting, for the weather is so dreadfully hot, and Plantagenet has so aggravated me, I really do not feel myself.'

Lady Annabel sounded her silver hand-bell, and the butler brought some cakes and the Mountain. Mrs. Cadurcis revived by virtue of her single glass, and the providential co-operation of a subsequent one or two. Even the cakes and the Mountain, however, would not tempt her son to open his mouth; and this, in spite of her returning composure, drove her to desperation. A conviction that the Mountain and the cakes were delicious, an amiable desire that the palate of her spoiled child should be gratified, some reasonable maternal anxiety that after so long and fatiguing a drive he in fact needed some refreshment, and the agonising consciousness that all her own physical pleasure at the moment was destroyed by the mental sufferings she endured at having quarrelled with her son, and that he was depriving himself of what was so agreeable only to pique her, quite overwhelmed the ill-regulated mind of this fond mother. Between each sip and each mouthful, she appealed to him to follow her example, now with cajolery, now with menace, till at length, worked up by the united stimulus of the Mountain and her own ungovernable rage, she dashed down the glass and unfinished slice of cake, and, before the astonished Lady Annabel, rushed forward to give him what she had long threatened, and what she in general ultimately had recourse to, a good shake.

Her agile son, experienced in these storms, escaped in time, and pushed his chair before his infuriated mother; Mrs. Cadurcis, however, rallied, and chased him round the room; once more she flattered herself she had captured him, once more he evaded her; in her despair she took up Venetia's 'Seven Champions,' and threw the volume at his head; he laughed a fiendish laugh, as, ducking his head, the book flew on, and dashed through a pane of glass; Mrs. Cadurcis made a desperate charge, and her son, a little frightened at her almost maniacal passion, saved himself by suddenly seizing Lady Annabel's work-table, and whirling it before her; Mrs. Cadurcis fell over the leg of the table, and went into hysterics; while the bloodhound, who had long started from his repose, looked at his mistress for instructions, and in the meantime continued barking. The astonished and agitated Lady Annabel assisted Mrs.

Cadurcis to rise, and led her to a couch. Lord Cadurcis, pale and dogged, stood in a corner, and after all this uproar there was a comparative calm, only broken by the sobs of the mother, each instant growing fainter and fainter.

At this moment the door opened, and Mistress Pauncefort ushered in the little Venetia. She really looked like an angel of peace sent from heaven on a mission of concord, with her long golden hair, her bright face, and smile of ineffable loveliness.

'Mamma!' said Venetia, in the sweetest tone.

'Hush! darling,' said Lady Annabel, 'this lady is not very well.'

Mrs. Cadurcis opened her eyes and sighed. She beheld Venetia, and stared at her with a feeling of wonder. 'O Lady Annabel,' she faintly exclaimed, 'what must you think of me? But was there ever such an unfortunate mother? and I have not a thought in the world but for that boy. I have devoted my life to him, and never would have buried myself in this abbey but for his sake. And this is the way he treats me, and his father before him treated me even worse. Am I not the most unfortunate woman you ever knew?'

'My dear madam,' said the kind Lady Annabel, in a soothing tone, 'you will be very happy yet; all will be quite right and quite happy.'

'Is this angel your child?' inquired Mrs. Cadurcis, in a low voice.

'This is my little girl, Venetia. Come hither, Venetia, and speak to Mrs. Cadurcis.'

'How do you do, Mrs. Cadurcis?' said Venetia. 'I am so glad you have come to live at the abbey.'

'The angel!' exclaimed Mrs. Cadurcis. 'The sweet seraph! Oh! why did not my Plantagenet speak to you, Lady Annabel, in the same tone? And he can, if he likes; he can, indeed. It was his silence that so mortified me; it was his silence that led to all. I am so proud of him! and then he comes here, and never speaks a word. O Plantagenet, I am sure you will break my heart.'

Venetia went up to the little lord in the corner, and gently stroked his dark cheek. 'Are you the little boy?' she said.

Cadurcis looked at her; at first the glance was rather fierce, but it instantly relaxed. 'What is your name?' he said in a low, but not unkind, tone.

'Venetia!'

'I like you, Venetia,' said the boy. 'Do you live here?'

'Yes, with my mamma.'

'I like your mamma, too; but not so much as you. I like your gold hair.'

'Oh, how funny! to like my gold hair!'

'If you had come in sooner,' said Cadurcis, 'we should not have had this row.'

'What is a row, little boy?' said Venetia.

'Do not call me little boy,' he said, but not in an unkind tone; 'call me by my name.'

'What is your name?'

'Lord Cadurcis; but you may call me by my Christian name, because I like you.'

'What is your Christian name?'

'Plantagenet.'

'Plantagenet! What a long name!' said Venetia. 'Tell me then, Plantagenet, what is a row?'

'What often takes place between me and my mother, but which I am sorry now has happened here, for I like this place, and should like to come often. A row is a quarrel.'

'A quarrel! What! do you quarrel with your mamma?'

'Often.'

'Why, then, you are not a good boy.'

'Ah! my mamma is not like yours,' said the little lord, with a sigh. 'It is not my fault. But now I want to make it up; how shall I do it?'

'Go and give her a kiss.'

'Poh! that is not the way.'

'Shall I go and ask my mamma what is best to do?' said Venetia; and she stole away on tiptoe, and whispered to Lady Annabel that Plantagenet wanted her. Her mother came forward and invited Lord Cadurcis to walk on the terrace with her, leaving Venetia to amuse her other guest.

Lady Annabel, though kind, was frank and firm in her unexpected confidential interview with her new friend. She placed before him clearly the enormity of his conduct, which no provocation could justify; it was a violation of divine law, as well as human propriety. She found the little lord attentive, tractable, and repentant, and, what might not have been expected, exceedingly ingenious and intelligent. His observations, indeed, were distinguished by remarkable acuteness; and though he could not, and indeed did not even attempt to vindicate his conduct, he incidentally introduced much that might be urged in its extenuation. There was indeed in this, his milder moment, something very winning in his demeanour, and Lady Annabel deeply regretted that a nature of so much promise and capacity should, by the injudicious treatment of a parent, at once fond and violent, afford such slight hopes of future happiness. It was arranged between Lord Cadurcis and Lady Annabel that she should lead him to his mother, and that he should lament the past, and ask her forgiveness; so they re-entered the room. Venetia was listening to a long story from Mrs. Cadurcis, who appeared to have entirely recovered herself; but her countenance assumed a befitting expression of grief and gravity when she observed her son.

'My dear madam,' said Lady Annabel, 'your son is unhappy that he should have offended you, and he has asked my kind offices to effect a perfect reconciliation between a child who wishes to be dutiful to a parent who, he feels, has always been so affectionate.'

Mrs. Cadurcis began crying.

'Mother,' said her son, 'I am sorry for what has occurred; mine was the fault. I shall not be happy till you pardon me.'

'No, yours was not the fault,' said poor Mrs. Cadurcis, crying bitterly. 'Oh! no, it was not! I was in fault, only I. There, Lady Annabel, did I not tell you he was the sweetest, dearest, most generous-hearted creature that ever lived? Oh! if he would only always speak so, I am sure I should be the happiest woman that ever breathed! He puts me in mind quite of his poor dear father, who was an angel upon earth; he was indeed, when he was not vexed. O my dear Plantagenet! my only hope and joy! you are the treasure and consolation of my life, and always will be. God bless you, my darling child! You shall have that pony you wanted; I am sure I can manage it: I did not think I could.'

As Lady Annabel thought it was as well that the mother and the son should not be immediately thrown together after this storm, she kindly proposed that they should remain, and pass the day at Cherbury; and, as Plantagenet's eyes brightened at the proposal, it did not require much trouble to persuade his mother to accede to it. The day, that had commenced so inauspiciously, turned out one of the most agreeable, both to Mrs. Cadurcis and her child. The two mothers conversed together, and, as Mrs. Cadurcis was a great workwoman, there was at least one bond of sympathy between her and the tapestry of her hostess. Then they all took a stroll in the park; and as Mrs. Cadurcis was not able to walk for any length of time, the children were permitted to stroll about together, attended by Mistress Pauncefort, while Mrs. Cadurcis, chatting without ceasing, detailed to Lady Annabel all the history of her life, all the details of her various complaints and her economical arrangements, and all the secrets of her husband's treatment of her, that favourite subject on which she ever waxed most eloquent. Plantagenet, equally indulging in confidence, which with him, however, was unusual, poured all his soul into the charmed ear of Venetia. He told her how he and his mother had lived at Morpeth, and how he hated it; how poor they had been, and how rich he should be; how he loved the abbey, and especially the old gallery, and the drums and armour; how he had been a day-scholar at a little school which he abhorred, and how he was to go some day to Eton, of which he was very proud.

At length they were obliged to return, and when dinner was over the postchaise was announced. Mrs. Cadurcis parted from Lady Annabel with all the warm expressions of a heart naturally kind and generous; and Plantagenet embraced Venetia, and promised that the next day he would find his way alone from Cadurcis, through the wood, and come and take another walk with her.

CHAPTER VII.

This settlement of Mrs. Cadurcis and her son in the neighbourhood was an event of no slight importance in the life of the family at Cherbury. Venetia at length found a companion of her own age, itself an incident which, in its influence upon her character and pursuits, was not to be disregarded. There grew up between the little lord and the daughter of Lady Annabel that fond intimacy which not rarely occurs in childhood. Plantagenet and Venetia quickly imbibed for each other a singular affection, not displeasing to Lady Annabel, who observed, without dissatisfaction, the increased happiness of her child, and encouraged by her kindness the frequent visits of the boy, who soon learnt the shortest road from the abbey, and almost daily scaled the hill, and traced his way through the woods to the hall. There was much, indeed, in the character and the situation of Lord Cadurcis which interested Lady Annabel Herbert. His mild, engaging, and affectionate manners, when he was removed from the injudicious influence of his mother, won upon her feelings; she felt for this lone child, whom nature had gifted with so soft a heart and with a thoughtful mind whose outbreaks not unfrequently attracted her notice; with none to guide him, and with only one heart to look up to for fondness; and that, too, one that had already contrived to forfeit the respect even of so young a child.

Yet Lady Annabel was too sensible of the paramount claims of a mother; herself, indeed, too jealous of any encroachment on the full privileges of maternal love, to sanction in the slightest degree, by her behaviour, any neglect of Mrs. Cadurcis by her son. For his sake, therefore, she courted the society of her new neighbour; and although Mrs. Cadurcis offered little to engage Lady Annabel's attention as a companion, though she was violent in her temper, far from well informed, and, from the society in which, in spite of her original good birth, her later years had passed, very far from being refined, she was not without her good qualities. She was generous, kind-hearted, and grateful; not insensible of her own deficiencies, and respectable from her misfortunes. Lady Annabel was one of those who always judged individuals rather by their good qualities than their bad. With the exception of her violent temper, which, under the control of Lady Annabel's presence, and by the aid of all that kind person's skilful management, Mrs. Cadurcis generally contrived to bridle, her principal faults were those of manner, which, from the force of habit, every day became less painful. Mrs. Cadurcis, who, indeed, was only a child of a larger growth, became scarcely less attached to the Herbert family than her son; she felt that her life, under their influence, was happier and serener than of yore; that there were less domestic broils than in old days; that her son was more dutiful; and, as she could not help suspecting, though she found it difficult to analyse the cause, herself more amiable. The truth was, Lady Annabel always treated Mrs. Cadurcis with studied respect; and the children, and especially Venetia, followed her example. Mrs. Cadurcis' self-complacency was not only less shocked, but more gratified, than before; and this was the secret of her happiness. For no one was more mortified by her rages, when they were past, than Mrs. Cadurcis herself; she felt they compromised her dignity, and had lost her all moral command over a child whom she loved at the bottom of her heart with a kind of wild passion, though she would menace and strike him, and who often precipitated these paroxysms by denying his mother that duty and affection which were, after all, the great charm and pride of her existence.

As Mrs. Cadurcis was unable to walk to Cherbury, and as Plantagenet soon fell into the habit of passing every morning at the hall, Lady Annabel was frequent in her visits to the mother, and soon she persuaded Mrs. Cadurcis to order the old postchaise regularly on Saturday, and remain at Cherbury until the following Monday; by these means both families united together in the chapel at divine service, while the presence of Dr. Masham, at their now increased Sunday dinner, was an incident in the monotonous life of Mrs. Cadurcis far from displeasing to her. The Doctor gave her a little news of the neighbourhood, and of the country in general; amused her with an occasional anecdote of the Queen and the young Princesses, and always lent her the last number of 'Sylvanus Urban.'

This weekly visit to Cherbury, the great personal attention which she always received there, and the frequent morning walks of Lady Annabel to the abbey, effectually repressed on the whole the jealousy which was a characteristic of Mrs. Cadurcis' nature, and which the constant absence of her son from her in the mornings might otherwise have fatally developed. But Mrs. Cadurcis could not resist the conviction that the Herberts were as much her friends as her child's; her jealousy was balanced by her gratitude; she was daily, almost hourly, sensible of some kindness of Lady Annabel, for there were a thousand services in the power of the opulent and ample establishment of Cherbury to afford the limited and desolate household at the abbey. Living in seclusion, it is difficult to refrain from imbibing even a strong regard for our almost solitary companion, however incompatible may be our pursuits, and however our tastes may vary, especially when that companion is grateful, and duly sensible of the condescension of our intimacy. And so it happened that, before a year had elapsed, that very Mrs. Cadurcis, whose first introduction at Cherbury had been so unfavourable to her, and from whose temper and manners the elegant demeanour and the disciplined mind of Lady Annabel Herbert might have been excused for a moment recoiling, had succeeded in establishing a strong hold upon the affections of her refined neighbour, who sought, on every occasion, her society, and omitted few opportunities of contributing to her comfort and welfare.

In the meantime her son was the companion of Venetia, both in her pastimes and studies. The education of Lord Cadurcis had received no further assistance than was afforded by the little grammar-school at Morpeth, where he had passed three or four years as a day-scholar, and where his mother had invariably taken his part on every occasion that he had incurred the displeasure of his master. There he had obtained some imperfect knowledge of Latin; yet the boy was fond of reading, and had picked up, in an odd way, more knowledge than might have been supposed. He had read 'Baker's Chronicle,' and 'The Old Universal History,' and 'Plutarch;' and had turned over, in the book room of an old gentleman at Morpeth, who had been attracted by his intelligence, not a few curious old folios, from which he had gleaned no contemptible store of curious instances of human nature. His guardian, whom he had never seen, and who was a great nobleman and lived in London, had signified to Mrs. Cadurcis his intention of sending his ward to Eton; but that time had not yet arrived, and Mrs. Cadurcis, who dreaded parting with her son, determined to postpone it by every maternal artifice in her power. At present it would have seemed that her son's intellect was to be left utterly uncultivated, for there was no school in the neighbourhood which he could attend, and no occasional assistance which could be obtained; and to the constant presence of a tutor in the house Mrs. Cadurcis was not less opposed than his lordship could have been himself.

It was by degrees that Lord Cadurcis became the partner of Venetia in her studies. Lady Annabel had consulted Dr. Masham about the poor little boy, whose neglected state she deplored; and the good Doctor had offered to ride over to Cherbury at least once a week, besides Sunday, provided Lady Annabel would undertake that his directions, in his absence, should be attended to. This her ladyship promised cheerfully; nor had she any difficulty in persuading Cadurcis to consent to the arrangement. He listened with docility and patience to her representation of the fatal effects, in his after-life, of his neglected education; of the generous and advantageous offer of Dr. Masham; and how cheerfully she would exert herself to assist his endeavours, if Plantagenet would willingly submit to her supervision. The little lord expressed to her his determination to do all that she desired, and voluntarily promised her that she should never repent her goodness. And he kept his word. So every morning, with the full concurrence of Mrs. Cadurcis, whose advice and opinion on the affair were most formally solicited by Lady Annabel, Plantagenet arrived early at the hall, and took his writing and French lessons with Venetia, and then they alternately read aloud to Lady Annabel from the histories of Hooke and Echard. When Venetia repaired to her drawing, Cadurcis sat down to his Latin exercise, and, in encouraging and assisting him, Lady Annabel, a proficient in Italian, began herself to learn the ancient language of the Romans. With such a charming mistress even these Latin exercises were achieved. In vain Cadurcis, after turning leaf over leaf, would look round with a piteous air to his fair assistant, 'O Lady Annabel, I am sure the word is not in the dictionary;' Lady Annabel was in a moment at his side, and, by some magic of her fair fingers, the word would somehow or other make its appearance. After a little exposure of this kind, Plantagenet would labour with double energy, until, heaving a deep sigh of exhaustion and vexation, he would burst forth, 'O Lady Annabel, indeed there is not a nominative case in this sentence.' And then Lady Annabel would quit her easel, with her pencil in her hand, and give all her intellect to the puzzling construction; at length, she would say, 'I think, Plantagenet, this must be our nominative case;' and so it always was.

Thus, when Wednesday came, the longest and most laborious morning of all Lord Cadurcis' studies, and when he neither wrote, nor read, nor learnt French with Venetia, but gave up all his soul to Dr. Masham, he usually acquitted himself to that good person's satisfaction, who left him, in general, with commendations that were not lost on the pupil, and plenty of fresh exercises to occupy him and Lady Annabel until the next week. When a year had thus passed away, the happiest year yet in Lord Cadurcis' life, in spite of all his disadvantages, he had contrived to make no inconsiderable progress. Almost deprived of a tutor, he had advanced in classical acquirement more than during the whole of his preceding years of scholarship, while his handwriting began to become intelligible, he could read French with comparative facility, and had turned over many a volume in the well-stored library at Cherbury.

CHAPTER VIII.

When the hours of study were past, the children, with that zest for play which occupation can alone secure, would go forth together, and wander in the park. Here they had made a little world for themselves, of which no one dreamed; for Venetia had poured forth all her Arcadian lore into the ear of Plantagenet; and they acted together many of the adventures of the romance, under the fond names of Musidorus and Philoclea. Cherbury was Arcadia, and Cadurcis Macedon; while the intervening woods figured as the forests of Thessaly, and the breezy downs were the heights of Pindus. Unwearied was the innocent sport of their virgin imaginations; and it was a great treat if Venetia, attended by Mistress Pauncefort, were permitted to accompany Plantagenet some way on his return. Then they parted with an embrace in the woods of Thessaly, and Musidorus strolled home with a heavy heart to his Macedonian realm.

Parted from Venetia, the magic suddenly seemed to cease, and Musidorus was instantly transformed into the little Lord Cadurcis, exhausted by the unconscious efforts of his fancy, depressed by the separation from his sweet companion, and shrinking from the unpoetical reception which at the best awaited him in his ungenial home. Often, when thus alone, would he loiter on his way and seat himself on the ridge, and watch the setting sun, as its dying glory illumined the turrets of his ancient house, and burnished the waters of the lake, until the tears stole down his cheek; and yet he knew not why. No thoughts of sorrow had flitted through his mind, nor indeed had ideas of any description occurred to him. It was a trance of unmeaning abstraction; all that he felt was a mystical pleasure in watching the sunset, and a conviction that, if he were not with Venetia, that which he loved next best, was to be alone.

The little Cadurcis in general returned home moody and silent, and his mother too often, irritated by his demeanour, indulged in all the expressions of a quick and offended temper; but since his intimacy with the Herberts, Plantagenet had learnt to control his emotions, and often successfully laboured to prevent those scenes of domestic recrimination once so painfully frequent. There often, too, was a note from Lady Annabel to Mrs. Cadurcis, or some other slight memorial, borne by her son, which enlisted all the kind feelings of that lady in favour of her Cherbury friends, and then the evening was sure to pass over in peace; and, when Plantagenet was not thus armed, he exerted himself to be cordial; and so, on the whole, with some skill in management, and some trials of temper, the mother and child contrived to live together with far greater comfort than they had of old.

Bedtime was always a great relief to Plantagenet, for it secured him solitude. He would lie awake for hours, indulging in sweet and unconscious reveries, and brooding over the future morn, that always brought happiness. All that he used to sigh for, was to be Lady Annabel's son; were he Venetia's brother, then he was sure he never should be for a moment unhappy; that parting from Cherbury, and the gloomy evenings at Cadurcis, would then be avoided. In such a mood, and lying awake upon his pillow, he sought refuge from the painful reality that surrounded him in the creative solace of his imagination. Alone, in his little bed, Cadurcis was Venetia's brother, and he conjured up a thousand scenes in which they were never separated, and wherein he always played an amiable and graceful part. Yet he loved the abbey; his painful infancy was not associated with that scene; it was not connected with any of those grovelling common-places of his life, from which he had shrunk back with instinctive disgust, even at a very tender age. Cadurcis was the spot to which, in his most miserable moments at Morpeth, he had always looked forward, as the only chance of emancipation from the distressing scene that surrounded him. He had been brought up with a due sense of his future position, and although he had ever affected a haughty indifference on the subject, from his disrelish for the coarse acquaintances who were perpetually reminding him, with chuckling self-complacency, of his future greatness, in secret he had ever brooded over his destiny as his only consolation. He had imbibed from his own reflections, at a very early period of life, a due sense of the importance of his lot; he was proud of his hereditary honours, blended, as they were, with some glorious passages in the history of his country, and prouder of his still more ancient line. The eccentric exploits and the violent passions, by which his race had been ever characterised, were to him a source of secret exultation. Even the late lord, who certainly had no claims to his gratitude, for he had robbed the inheritance to the utmost of his power, commanded, from the wild decision of his life, the savage respect of his successor. In vain Mrs. Cadurcis would pour forth upon this, the favourite theme for her wrath and her lamentations, all the bitter expressions of her rage and woe. Plantagenet had never imbibed her prejudices against the departed, and had often irritated his mother by maintaining that the late lord was perfectly justified in his conduct.

But in these almost daily separations between Plantagenet and Venetia, how different was her lot to that of her companion! She was the confidante of all his domestic sorrows, and often he had requested her to exert her influence to obtain some pacifying missive from Lady Annabel, which might secure him a quiet evening at Cadurcis; and whenever this had not been obtained, the last words of Venetia were ever not to loiter, and to remember to speak to his mother as much as he possibly could. Venetia returned to a happy home, welcomed by the smile of a soft and beautiful parent, and with words of affection sweeter than music. She found an engaging companion, who had no thought but for her welfare, her amusement, and her instruction: and often, when the curtains were drawn, the candles lit, and Venetia, holding her mother's hand, opened her book, she thought of poor Plantagenet, so differently situated, with no one to be kind to him, with no one to sympathise with his thoughts, and perhaps at the very moment goaded into some unhappy quarrel with his mother.

CHAPTER IX.

The appearance of the Cadurcis family on the limited stage of her life, and the engrossing society of her companion, had entirely distracted the thoughts of Venetia from a subject to which in old days they were constantly recurring, and that was her father. By a process which had often perplexed her, and which she could never succeed in analysing, there had arisen in her mind, without any ostensible agency on the part of her mother which she could distinctly recall, a conviction that this was a topic on which she was never to speak. This idea had once haunted her, and she had seldom found herself alone without almost unconsciously musing over it. Notwithstanding the unvarying kindness of Lady Annabel, she exercised over her child a complete and unquestioned control. Venetia was brought up with strictness, which was only not felt to be severe, because the system was founded on the most entire affection, but, fervent as her love was for her mother, it was equalled by her profound respect, which every word and action of Lady Annabel tended to maintain.

In all the confidential effusions with Plantagenet, Venetia had never dwelt upon this mysterious subject; indeed, in these conversations, when they treated of their real and not ideal life, Venetia was a mere recipient: all that she could communicate, Plantagenet could observe; he it was who avenged himself at these moments for his habitual silence before third persons; it was to Venetia that he poured forth all his soul, and she was never weary of hearing his stories about Morpeth, and all his sorrows, disgusts, and afflictions. There was scarcely an individual in that little town with whom, from his lively narratives, she was not familiar; and it was to her sympathising heart that he confided all his future hopes and prospects, and confessed the strong pride he experienced in being a Cadurcis, which from all others was studiously concealed.

It had happened that the first Christmas Day after the settlement of the Cadurcis family at the abbey occurred in the middle of the week; and as the weather was severe, in order to prevent two journeys at such an inclement season, Lady Annabel persuaded Mrs. Cadurcis to pass the whole week at the hall. This arrangement gave such pleasure to Plantagenet that the walls of the abbey, as the old postchaise was preparing for their journey, quite resounded with his merriment. In vain his mother, harassed with all the mysteries of packing, indulged in a thousand irritable expressions, which at any other time might have produced a broil or even a fray; Cadurcis did nothing but laugh. There was at the bottom of this boy's heart, with all his habitual gravity and reserve, a fund of humour which would occasionally break out, and which nothing could withstand. When he was alone with Venetia, he would imitate the old maids of Morpeth, and all the ceremonies of a provincial tea party, with so much life and genuine fun, that Venetia was often obliged to stop in their rambles to indulge her overwhelming mirth. When they were alone, and he was gloomy, she was often accustomed to say, 'Now, dear Plantagenet, tell me how the old ladies at Morpeth drink tea.'

This morning at the abbey, Cadurcis was irresistible, and the more excited his mother became with the difficulties which beset her, the more gay and fluent were his quips and cranks. Puffing, panting, and perspiring, now directing her waiting-woman, now scolding her man-servant, and now ineffectually attempting to box her son's ears, Mrs. Cadurcis indeed offered a most ridiculous spectacle.

'John!' screamed Mrs. Cadurcis, in a voice of bewildered passion, and stamping with rage, 'is that the place for my cap-box? You do it on purpose, that you do!'

'John,' mimicked Lord Cadurcis, 'how dare you do it on purpose?'

'Take that, you brat,' shrieked the mother, and she struck her own hand against the doorway. 'Oh! I'll give it you, I'll give it you,' she bellowed under the united influence of rage and pain, and she pursued her agile child, who dodged her on the other side of the postchaise, which he persisted in calling the family carriage.

'Oh! ma'am, my lady,' exclaimed the waiting-woman, sallying forth from the abbey, 'what is to be done with the parrot when we are away? Mrs. Brown says she won't see to it, that she won't; 'taynt her place.'

This rebellion of Mrs. Brown was a diversion in favour of Plantagenet. Mrs. Cadurcis waddled down the cloisters with precipitation, rushed into the kitchen, seized the surprised Mrs. Brown by the shoulder, and gave her a good shake; and darting at the cage, which held the parrot, she bore it in triumph to the carriage. 'I will take the bird with me,' said Mrs. Cadurcis.

'We cannot take the bird inside, madam,' said Plantagenet, 'for it will overhear all our conversation, and repeat it. We shall not be able to abuse our friends.'

Mrs. Cadurcis threw the cage at her son's head, who, for the sake of the bird, dexterously caught it, but declared at the same time he would immediately throw it into the lake. Then Mrs. Cadurcis began to cry with rage, and, seating herself on the open steps of the chaise, sobbed hysterically. Plantagenet stole round on tip-toe, and peeped in her face: 'A merry Christmas and a happy new year, Mrs. Cadurcis,' said her son.

'How can I be merry and happy, treated as I am?' sobbed the mother. 'You do not treat Lady Annabel so. Oh! no; it is only your mother whom you use in this manner! Go to Cherbury. Go by all means, but go by yourself; I shall not go: go to your friends, Lord Cadurcis; they are your friends, not mine, and I hope they are satisfied, now that they have robbed me of the affections of my child. I have seen what they have been after all this time. I am not so blind as some people think. No! I see how it is. I am nobody. Your poor mother, who brought you up, and educated you, is nobody. This is the end of all your Latin and French, and your fine lessons. Honour your father and your mother, Lord Cadurcis; that's a finer lesson than all. Oh! oh! oh!'

This allusion to the Herberts suddenly calmed Plantagenet. He felt in an instant the injudiciousness of fostering by his conduct the latent jealousy which always lurked at the bottom of his mother's heart, and which nothing but the united talent and goodness of Lady Annabel could have hitherto baffled. So he rejoined in a kind yet playful tone, 'If you will be good, I will give you a kiss for a Christmas-box, mother; and the parrot shall go inside if you like.'

'The parrot may stay at home, I do not care about it: but I cannot bear quarrelling; it is not my temper, you naughty, very naughty boy.'

'My dear mother,' continued his lordship, in a soothing tone, 'these scenes always happen when people are going to travel. I assure you it is quite a part of packing up.'

'You will be the death of me, that you will,' said the mother, 'with all your violence. You are worse than your father, that you are.'

'Come, mother,' said her son, drawing nearer, and just touching her shoulder with his hand, 'will you not have my Christmas-box?'

The mother extended her cheek, which the son slightly touched with his lip, and then Mrs. Cadurcis jumped up as lively as ever, called for a glass of Mountain, and began rating the footboy.

At length the postchaise was packed; they had a long journey before them, because Cadurcis would go round by Southport, to call upon a tradesman whom a month before he had commissioned to get a trinket made for him in London, according to the newest fashion, as a present for Venetia. The commission was executed; Mrs. Cadurcis, who had been consulted in confidence by her son on the subject, was charmed with the result of their united taste. She had good-naturedly contributed one of her own few, but fine, emeralds to the gift; upon the back of the brooch was engraved:—

TO VENETIA, FROM HER AFFECTIONATE BROTHER, PLANTAGENET.

'I hope she will be a sister, and more than a sister, to you,' said Mrs. Cadurcis.

'Why?' inquired her son, rather confused.

'You may look farther, and fare worse,' said Mrs. Cadurcis. Plantagenet blushed; and yet he wondered why he blushed: he understood his mother, but he could not pursue the conversation; his heart fluttered.

A most cordial greeting awaited them at Cherbury; Dr. Masham was there, and was to remain until Monday. Mrs. Cadurcis would have opened about the present immediately, but her son warned her on the threshold that if she said a word about it, or seemed to be aware of its previous existence, even when it was shown, he would fling it instantly away into the snow; and her horror of this catastrophe bridled her tongue. Mrs. Cadurcis, however, was happy, and Lady Annabel was glad to see her so; the Doctor, too, paid her some charming compliments; the good lady was in the highest spirits, for she was always in extremes, and at this moment she would willingly have laid down her life if she had thought the sacrifice could have contributed to the welfare of the Herberts.

Cadurcis himself drew Venetia aside, and then, holding the brooch reversed, he said, with rather a confused air, 'Read that, Venetia.'

'Oh! Plantagenet!' she said, very much astonished.

'You see, Venetia,' he added, leaving it in her hand, 'it is yours.'

Venetia turned the jewel; her eye was dazzled with its brilliancy.

'It is too grand for a little girl, Plantagenet,' she exclaimed, a little pale.

'No, it is not,' said Plantagenet, firmly; 'besides, you will not always be a little girl; and then, if ever we do not live together as we do now, you will always remember you have a brother.'

'I must show it mamma; I must ask her permission to take it, Plantagenet.'

Venetia went up to her mother, who was talking to Mrs. Cadurcis. She had not courage to speak before that lady and Dr. Masham, so she called her mother aside.

'Mamma,' she said, 'something has happened.'

'What, my dear?' said Lady Annabel, somewhat surprised at the seriousness of her tone.

'Look at this, mamma!' said Venetia, giving her the brooch.

Lady Annabel looked at the jewel, and read the inscription. It was a more precious offering than the mother would willingly have sanctioned, but she was too highly bred, and too thoughtful of the feelings of others, to hesitate for a moment to admire it herself, and authorise its acceptance by her daughter. So she walked up to Cadurcis and gave him a mother's embrace for his magnificent present to his sister, placed the brooch itself near Venetia's heart, and then led her daughter to Mrs. Cadurcis, that the gratified mother might admire the testimony of her son's taste and affection. It was a most successful present, and Cadurcis felt grateful to his mother for her share in its production, and the very proper manner in which she received the announcement of its offering.

CHAPTER X.

This was Christmas Eve; the snow was falling briskly. After dinner they were glad to cluster round the large fire in the green drawing-room. Dr. Masham had promised to read the evening service in the chapel, which was now lit up, and the bell was sounding, that the cottagers might have the opportunity of attending.

Plantagenet and Venetia followed the elders to the chapel; they walked hand-in-hand down the long galleries.

'I should like to go all over this house,' said Plantagenet to his companion. 'Have you ever been?'

'Never,' said Venetia; 'half of it is shut up. Nobody ever goes into it, except mamma.'

In the night there was a violent snowstorm; not only was the fall extremely heavy, but the wind was so high, that it carried the snow off the hills, and all the roads were blocked up, in many places ten or twelve feet deep. All communication was stopped. This was an adventure that amused the children, though the rest looked rather grave. Plantagenet expressed to Venetia his wish that the snow would never melt, and that they might remain at Cherbury for ever.

The children were to have a holiday this week, and they had planned some excursions in the park and neighbourhood, but now they were all prisoners to the house. They wandered about, turning the staircase into mountains, the great hall into an ocean, and the different rooms into so many various regions. They amused themselves with their adventures, and went on endless voyages of discovery. Every moment Plantagenet longed still more for the opportunity of exploring the uninhabited chambers; but Venetia shook her head, because she was sure Lady Annabel would not grant them permission.

'Did you ever live at any place before you came to Cherbury?' inquired Lord Cadurcis of Venetia.

'I know I was not born here,' said Venetia; 'but I was so young that I have no recollection of any other place.'

'And did any one live here before you came?' said Plantagenet.

'I do not know,' said Venetia; 'I never heard if anybody did. I, I,' she continued, a little constrained, 'I know nothing.'

'Do you remember your papa?' said Plantagenet.

'No,' said Venetia.

'Then he must have died almost as soon as you were born, said Lord Cadurcis.

'I suppose he must,' said Venetia, and her heart trembled.

'I wonder if he ever lived here!' said Plantagenet.

'Mamma does not like me to ask questions about my papa,' said Venetia, 'and I cannot tell you anything.'

'Ah! your papa was different from mine, Venetia,' said Cadurcis; 'my mother talks of him often enough. They did not agree very well; and, when we quarrel, she always says I remind her of him. I dare say Lady Annabel loved your papa very much.'

'I am sure mamma did,' replied Venetia.

The children returned to the drawing-room, and joined their friends: Mrs. Cadurcis was sitting on the sofa, occasionally dozing over a sermon; Dr. Masham was standing with Lady Annabel in the recess of a distant window. Her ladyship's countenance was averted; she was reading a newspaper, which the Doctor had given her. As the door opened, Lady Annabel glanced round; her countenance was agitated; she folded up the newspaper rather hastily, and gave it to the Doctor.

'And what have you been doing, little folks?' inquired the Doctor of the new comers.

'We have been playing at the history of Rome,' said Venetia, 'and now that we have conquered every place, we do not know what to do.'

'The usual result of conquest,' said the Doctor, smiling.

'This snowstorm is a great trial for you; I begin to believe that, after all, you would be more pleased to take your holidays at another opportunity.'

'We could amuse ourselves very well,' said Plantagenet, 'if Lady Annabel would be so kind as to permit us to explore the part of the house that is shut up.'

'That would be a strange mode of diversion,' said Lady Annabel, quietly, 'and I do not think by any means a suitable one. There cannot be much amusement in roaming over a number of dusty unfurnished rooms.'

'And so nicely dressed as you are too!' said Mrs. Cadurcis, rousing herself: 'I wonder how such an idea could enter your head!'

'It snows harder than ever,' said Venetia; 'I think, after all, I shall learn my French vocabulary.'

'If it snows to-morrow,' said Plantagenet, 'we will do our lessons as usual. Holidays, I find, are not so amusing as I supposed.'

The snow did continue, and the next day the children voluntarily suggested that they should resume their usual course of life. With their mornings occupied, they found their sources of relaxation ample; and in the evening they acted plays, and Lady Annabel dressed them up in her shawls, and Dr. Masham read Shakspeare to them.

It was about the fourth day of the visit that Plantagenet, loitering in the hall with Venetia, said to her, 'I saw your mamma go into the locked-up rooms last night. I do so wish that she would let us go there.'

'Last night!' said Venetia; 'when could you have seen her last night?'

'Very late: the fact is, I could not sleep, and I took it into my head to walk up and down the gallery. I often do so at the abbey. I like to walk up and down an old gallery alone at night. I do not know why; but I like it very much. Everything is so still, and then you hear the owls. I cannot make out why it is; but nothing gives me more pleasure than to get up when everybody is asleep. It seems as if one were the only living person in the world. I sometimes think, when I am a man, I will always get up in the night, and go to bed in the daytime. Is not that odd?'

'But mamma!' said Venetia, 'how came you to see mamma?'

'Oh! I am certain of it,' said the boy; 'for, to tell you the truth, I was rather frightened at first; only I thought it would not do for a Cadurcis to be afraid, so I stood against the wall, in the shade, and I was determined, whatever happened, not to cry out.'

'Oh! you frighten me so, Plantagenet!' said Venetia.

'Ah! you might well have been frightened if you had been there; past midnight, a tall white figure, and a light! However, there is nothing to be alarmed about; it was Lady Annabel, nobody else. I saw her as clearly as I see you now. She walked along the gallery, and went to the very door you showed me the other morning. I marked the door; I could not mistake it. She unlocked it, and she went in.'

'And then?' inquired Venetia, eagerly.

'Why, then, like a fool, I went back to bed,' said Plantagenet. 'I thought it would seem so silly if I were caught, and I might not have had the good fortune to escape twice. I know no more.'

Venetia could not reply. She heard a laugh, and then her mother's voice. They were called with a gay summons to see a colossal snow-ball, that some of the younger servants had made and rolled to the window of the terrace-room. It was ornamented with a crown of holly and mistletoe, and the parti-coloured berries looked bright in a straggling sunbeam which had fought its way through the still-loaded sky, and fell upon the terrace.

In the evening, as they sat round the fire, Mrs. Cadurcis began telling Venetia a long rambling ghost story, which she declared was a real ghost story, and had happened in her own family. Such communications were not very pleasing to Lady Annabel, but she was too well bred to interrupt her guest. When, however, the narrative was finished, and Venetia, by her observations, evidently indicated the effect that it had produced upon her mind, her mother took the occasion of impressing upon her the little credibility which should be attached to such legends, and the rational process by which many unquestionable apparitions might be accounted for. Dr. Masham, following this train, recounted a story of a ghost which had been generally received in a neighbouring village for a considerable period, and attested by the most veracious witnesses, but which was explained afterwards by turning out to be an instance of somnambulism. Venetia appeared to be extremely interested in the subject; she inquired much about sleep-walkers and sleepwalking; and a great many examples of the habit were cited. At length she said, 'Mamma, did you ever walk in your sleep?'

'Not to my knowledge,' said Lady Annabel, smiling; 'I should hope not.'

'Well, do you know,' said Plantagenet, who had hitherto listened in silence, 'it is very curious, but I once dreamt that you did, Lady Annabel.'

'Indeed!' said the lady.

'Yes! and I dreamt it last night, too,' continued Cadurcis. 'I thought I was sleeping in the uninhabited rooms here, and the door opened, and you walked in with a light.'

'No! Plantagenet,' said Venetia, who was seated by him, and who spoke in a whisper, 'it was not—'

'Hush!' said Cadurcis, in a low voice.

'Well, that was a strange dream,' said Mrs. Cadurcis; 'was it not, Doctor?'

'Now, children, I will tell you a very curious story,' said the Doctor; 'and it is quite a true one, for it happened to myself.'

The Doctor was soon embarked in his tale, and his audience speedily became interested in the narrative; but Lady Annabel for some time maintained complete silence.

CHAPTER XI.

The spring returned; the intimate relations between the two families were each day more confirmed. Lady Annabel had presented her daughter and Plantagenet each with a beautiful pony, but their rides were at first to be confined to the park, and to be ever attended by a groom. In time, however, duly accompanied, they were permitted to extend their progress so far as Cadurcis. Mrs. Cadurcis had consented to the wishes of her son to restore the old garden, and Venetia was his principal adviser and assistant in the enterprise. Plantagenet was fond of the abbey, and nothing but the agreeable society of Cherbury on the one hand, and the relief of escaping from his mother on the other, could have induced him to pass so little of his time at home; but, with Venetia for his companion, his mornings at the abbey passed charmingly, and, as the days were now at their full length again, there was abundance of time, after their studies at Cherbury, to ride together through the woods to Cadurcis, spend several hours there, and for Venetia to return to the hall before sunset. Plantagenet always accompanied her to the limits of the Cherbury grounds, and then returned by himself, solitary and full of fancies.

Lady Annabel had promised the children that they should some day ride together to Marringhurst, the rectory of Dr. Masham, to eat strawberries and cream. This was to be a great festival, and was looked forward to with corresponding interest. Her ladyship had kindly offered to accompany Mrs. Cadurcis in the carriage, but that lady was an invalid and declined the journey; so Lady Annabel, who was herself a good horsewoman, mounted her jennet with Venetia and Plantagenet.

Marringhurst was only five miles from Cherbury by a cross-road, which was scarcely passable for carriages. The rectory house was a substantial, square-built, red brick mansion, shaded by gigantic elms, but the southern front covered with a famous vine, trained over it with elaborate care, and of which, and his espaliers, the Doctor was very proud. The garden was thickly stocked with choice fruit-trees; there was not the slightest pretence to pleasure grounds; but there was a capital bowling-green, and, above all, a grotto, where the Doctor smoked his evening pipe, and moralised in the midst of his cucumbers and cabbages. On each side extended the meadows of his glebe, where his kine ruminated at will. It was altogether a scene as devoid of the picturesque as any that could be well imagined; flat, but not low, and rich, and green, and still.

His expected guests met as warm a reception as such a hearty friend might be expected to afford. Dr. Masham was scarcely less delighted at the excursion than the children themselves, and rejoiced in the sunny day that made everything more glad and bright. The garden, the grotto, the bowling-green, and all the novelty of the spot, greatly diverted his young companions; they visited his farmyard, were introduced to his poultry, rambled over his meadows, and admired his cows, which he had collected with equal care and knowledge. Nor was the interior of this bachelor's residence devoid of amusement. Every nook and corner was filled with objects of interest; and everything was in admirable order. The goddess of neatness and precision reigned supreme, especially in his hall, which, though barely ten feet square, was a cabinet of rural curiosities. His guns, his fishing-tackle, a cabinet of birds stuffed by himself, a fox in a glass-case that seemed absolutely running, and an otter with a real fish in its mouth, in turn delighted them; but chiefly, perhaps, his chimney-corner of Dutch tiles, all Scriptural subjects, which Venetia and Plantagenet emulated each other in discovering.

Then his library, which was rare and splendid, for the Doctor was one of the most renowned scholars in the kingdom, and his pictures, his prints, and his gold fish, and his canary birds; it seemed they never could exhaust such sources of endless amusement; to say nothing of every other room in the house, for, from the garret to the dairy, his guests encouraged him in introducing them to every thing, every person, and every place.

'And this is the way we old bachelors contrive to pass our lives,' said the good Doctor; 'and now, my dear lady, Goody Blount will give us some dinner.'

The Doctor's repast was a substantial one; he seemed resolved, at one ample swoop, to repay Lady Annabel for all her hospitality; and he really took such delight in their participation of it, that his principal guest was constrained to check herself in more than one warning intimation that moderation was desirable, were it only for the sake of the strawberries and cream. All this time his housekeeper, Goody Blount, as he called her, in her lace cap and ruffles, as precise and starch as an old picture, stood behind his chair with pleased solemnity, directing, with unruffled composure, the movements of the liveried bumpkin who this day was promoted to the honour of 'waiting at table.'

'Come,' said the Doctor, as the cloth was cleared, 'I must bargain for one toast, Lady Annabel: "Church and State."'

'What is Church and State?' said Venetia.

'As good things. Miss Venetia, as strawberries and cream,' said the Doctor, laughing; 'and, like them, always best united.'

After their repast, the children went into the garden to amuse themselves. They strolled about some time, until Plantagenet at length took it into his head that he should like to learn to play at bowls; and he said, if Venetia would wait in the grotto, where they then were talking, he would run back and ask the Doctor if the servant might teach him. He was not long absent; but appeared, on his return, a little agitated. Venetia inquired if he had been successful, but he shook his head, and said he had not asked.

'Why did you not?' said Venetia.

'I did not like,' he replied, looking very serious; 'something happened.'

'What could have happened?' said Venetia.

'Something strange,' was his answer.

'Oh, do tell me, Plantagenet!'

'Why,' said he, in a low voice, 'your mamma is crying.'

'Crying!' exclaimed Venetia; 'my dear mamma crying! I must go to her directly.'

'Hush!' said Plantagenet, shaking his head, 'you must not go.'

'I must.'

'No, you must not go, Venetia,' was his reply; 'I am sure she does not want us to know she is crying.'

'What did she say to you?'

'She did not see me; the Doctor did, and he gave me a nod to go away.'

'I never saw mamma cry,' said Venetia.

'Don't you say anything about it, Venetia,' said Plantagenet, with a manly air; 'listen to what I say.'

'I do, Plantagenet, always; but still I should like to know what mamma can be crying about. Do tell me all about it.'

'Why, I came to the room by the open windows, and your mamma was standing up, with her back to me, and leaning on the mantel-piece, with her face in her handkerchief; and the Doctor was standing up too, only his back was to the fireplace; and when he saw me, he made me a sign to go away, and I went directly.'

'Are you sure mamma was crying?'

'I heard her sob.'

'I think I shall cry,' said Venetia.

'You must not; you must know nothing about it. If you let your mamma know that I saw her crying, I shall never tell you anything again.'

'What do you think she was crying about, Plantagenet?'

'I cannot say; perhaps she had been talking about your papa. I do not want to play at bowls now,' added Plantagenet; 'let us go and see the cows.'

In the course of half an hour the servant summoned the children to the house. The horses were ready, and they were now to return. Lady Annabel received them with her usual cheerfulness.

'Well, dear children,' said she, 'have you been very much amused?'

Venetia ran forward, and embraced her mother with even unusual fondness. She was mindful of Plantagenet's injunctions, and was resolved not to revive her mother's grief by any allusion that could recall the past; but her heart was, nevertheless, full of sympathy, and she could not have rode home, had she not thus expressed her love for her mother.

With the exception of this strange incident, over which, afterwards, Venetia often pondered, and which made her rather serious the whole of the ride home, this expedition to Marringhurst was a very happy day.

CHAPTER XII.

This happy summer was succeeded by a singularly wet autumn. Weeks of continuous rain rendered it difficult even for the little Cadurcis, who defied the elements, to be so constant as heretofore in his daily visits to Cherbury. His mother, too, grew daily a greater invalid, and, with increasing sufferings and infirmities, the natural captiousness of her temper proportionally exhibited itself. She insisted upon the companionship of her son, and that he should not leave the house in such unseasonable weather. If he resisted, she fell into one of her jealous rages, and taunted him with loving strangers better than his own mother. Cadurcis, on the whole, behaved very well; he thought of Lady Annabel's injunctions, and restrained his passion. Yet he was not repaid for the sacrifice; his mother made no effort to render their joint society agreeable, or even endurable. She was rarely in an amiable mood, and generally either irritable or sullen. If the weather held up a little, and he ventured to pay a visit to Cherbury, he was sure to be welcomed back with a fit of passion; either Mrs. Cadurcis was angered for being left alone, or had fermented herself into fury by the certainty of his catching a fever. If Plantagenet remained at the abbey, she was generally sullen; and, as he himself was naturally silent under any circumstances, his mother would indulge in that charming monologue, so conducive to domestic serenity, termed 'talking at a person,' and was continually insinuating that she supposed he found it very dull to pass his day with her, and that she dared say that somebody could be lively enough if he were somewhere else.

Cadurcis would turn pale, and bite his lip, and then leave the room; and whole days would sometimes pass with barely a monosyllable being exchanged between this parent and child. Cadurcis had found some opportunities of pouring forth his griefs and mortification into the ear of Venetia, and they had reached her mother; but Lady Annabel, though she sympathised with this interesting boy, invariably counselled duty. The morning studies were abandoned, but a quantity of books were sent over from Cherbury for Plantagenet, and Lady Annabel seized every opportunity of conciliating Mrs. Cadurcis' temper in favour of her child, by the attention which she paid the mother. The weather, however, prevented either herself or Venetia from visiting the abbey; and, on the whole, the communications between the two establishments and their inmates had become rare.

Though now a continual inmate of the abbey, Cadurcis was seldom the companion of his mother. They met at their meals, and that was all. He entered the room every day with an intention of conciliating; but the mutual tempers of the mother and the son were so quick and sensitive, that he always failed in his purpose, and could only avoid a storm by dogged silence. This enraged Mrs. Cadurcis more even than his impertinence; she had no conduct;

she lost all command over herself, and did not hesitate to address to her child terms of reproach and abuse, which a vulgar mind could only conceive, and a coarse tongue alone express. What a contrast to Cherbury, to the mild maternal elegance and provident kindness of Lady Annabel, and the sweet tones of Venetia's ever-sympathising voice. Cadurcis, though so young, was gifted with an innate fastidiousness, that made him shrink from a rude woman. His feelings were different in regard to men; he sympathised at a very early age with the bold and the energetic; his favourites among the peasantry were ever those who excelled in athletic sports; and, though he never expressed the opinion, he did not look upon the poacher with the evil eye of his class. But a coarse and violent woman jarred even his young nerves; and this woman was his mother, his only parent, almost his only relation; for he had no near relative except a cousin whom he had never even seen, the penniless orphan of a penniless brother of his father, and who had been sent to sea; so that, after all, his mother was the only natural friend he had. This poor little boy would fly from that mother with a sullen brow, or, perhaps, even with a harsh and cutting repartee; and then he would lock himself up in his room, and weep. But he allowed no witnesses of this weakness. The lad was very proud. If any of the household passed by as he quitted the saloon, and stared for a moment at his pale and agitated face, he would coin a smile for the instant, and say even a kind word, for he was very courteous to his inferiors, and all the servants loved him, and then take refuge in his solitary woe.

Relieved by this indulgence of his mortified heart, Cadurcis looked about him for resources. The rain was pouring in torrents, and the plash of the troubled and swollen lake might be heard even at the abbey. At night the rising gusts of wind, for the nights were always clear and stormy, echoed down the cloisters with a wild moan to which he loved to listen. In the morning he beheld with interest the savage spoils of the tempest; mighty branches of trees strewn about, and sometimes a vast trunk uprooted from its ancient settlement. Irresistibly the conviction impressed itself upon his mind that, if he were alone in this old abbey, with no mother to break that strange fountain of fancies that seemed always to bubble up in his solitude, he might be happy. He wanted no companions; he loved to be alone, to listen to the winds, and gaze upon the trees and waters, and wander in those dim cloisters and that gloomy gallery.

From the first hour of his arrival he had loved the venerable hall of his fathers. Its appearance harmonised with all the associations of his race. Power and pomp, ancestral fame, the legendary respect of ages, all that was great, exciting, and heroic, all that was marked out from the commonplace current of human events, hovered round him. In the halls of Cadurcis he was the Cadurcis; though a child, he was keenly sensible of his high race; his whole being sympathised with their glory; he was capable of dying sooner than of disgracing them; and then came the memory of his mother's sharp voice and harsh vulgar words, and he shivered with disgust.

Forced into solitude, forced to feed upon his own mind, Cadurcis found in that solitude each day a dearer charm, and in that mind a richer treasure of interest and curiosity. He loved to wander about, dream of the past, and conjure up a future as glorious. What was he to be? What should be his career? Whither should he wend his course? Even at this early age, dreams of far lands flitted over his mind; and schemes of fantastic and adventurous life. But now he was a boy, a wretched boy, controlled by a vulgar and narrow-minded woman! And this servitude must last for years; yes! years must elapse before he was his own master. Oh! if he could only pass them alone, without a human voice to disturb his musings, a single form to distract his vision!

Under the influence of such feelings, even Cherbury figured to his fancy in somewhat faded colours. There, indeed, he was loved and cherished; there, indeed, no sound was ever heard, no sight ever seen, that could annoy or mortify the high pitch of his unconscious ideal; but still, even at Cherbury, he was a child. Under the influence of daily intercourse, his tender heart had balanced, perhaps even outweighed, his fiery imagination. That constant yet delicate affection had softened all his soul: he had no time but to be grateful and to love. He returned home only to muse over their sweet society, and contrast their refined and gentle life with the harsh rude hearth that awaited him. Whatever might be his reception at home, he was thrown, back for solace on their memory, not upon his own heart; and he felt the delightful conviction that to-morrow would renew the spell whose enchantment had enabled him to endure the present vexation. But now the magic of that intercourse had ceased; after a few days of restlessness and repining, he discovered that he must find in his desolation sterner sources of support than the memory of Venetia, and the recollections of the domestic joys of Cherbury. It astonishing with what rapidity the character of Cadurcis developed itself in solitude; and strange was the contrast between the gentle child who, a few weeks before, had looked forward with so much interest to accompanying Venetia to a childish festival, and the stern and moody being who paced the solitary cloisters of Cadurcis, and then would withdraw to his lonely chamber and the amusement of a book. He was at this time deeply interested in Purchas's Pilgrimage, one of the few books of which the late lord had not despoiled him. Narratives of travels and voyages always particularly pleased him; he had an idea that he was laying up information which might be useful to him hereafter; the Cherbury collection was rich in this class of volumes, and Lady Annabel encouraged their perusal.

In this way many weeks elapsed at the abbey, during which the visits of Plantagenet to Cherbury were very few. Sometimes, if the weather cleared for an hour during the morning, he would mount his pony, and gallop, without stopping, to the hall. The rapidity of the motion excited his mind; he fancied himself, as he embraced Venetia, some chieftain who had escaped for a moment from his castle to visit his mistress; his imagination conjured up a war between the opposing towers of Cadurcis and Cherbury; and when his mother fell into a passion on his return, it passed with him only, according to its length and spirit, as a brisk skirmish or a general engagement.

CHAPTER XIII.

One afternoon, on his return from Cherbury, Plantagenet found the fire extinguished in the little room which he had appropriated to himself, and where he kept his books. As he had expressed his wish to the servant that the fire should be kept up, he complained to him of the neglect, but was informed, in reply, that the fire had been allowed to go out by his mother's orders, and that she desired in future that he would always read in the saloon. Plantagenet had sufficient self-control to make no observation before the servant, and soon after joined his mother, who looked very sullen, as if she were conscious that she had laid a train for an explosion.

Dinner was now served, a short and silent meal. Lord Cadurcis did not choose to speak because he felt aggrieved, and his mother because she was husbanding her energies for the contest which she believed impending. At length, when the table was cleared, and the servant departed, Cadurcis said in a quiet tone, 'I think I shall write to my guardian to-morrow about my going to Eton.'

'You shall do no such thing,' said Mrs. Cadurcis, bristling up; 'I never heard such a ridiculous idea in my life as a boy like you writing letters on such subjects to a person you have never yet seen. When I think it proper that you should go to Eton, I shall write.'

'I wish you would think it proper now then, ma'am.'

'I won't be dictated to,' said Mrs. Cadurcis, fiercely.

'I was not dictating,' replied her son, calmly.

'You would if you could,' said his mother.

'Time enough to find fault with me when I do, ma'am.'

'There is enough to find fault about at all times, sir.'

'On which side, Mrs. Cadurcis?' inquired Plantagenet, with a sneer.

'Don't aggravate me, Lord Cadurcis,' said his mother.

'How am I aggravating you, ma'am?'

'I won't be answered,' said the mother.

'I prefer silence myself,' said the son.

'I won't be insulted in my own room, sir,' said Mrs. Cadurcis.

'I am not insulting you, Mrs. Cadurcis,' said Plantagenet, rather fiercely; 'and, as for your own room, I never wish to enter it. Indeed I should not be here at this moment, had you not ordered my fire to be put out, and particularly requested that I should sit in the saloon.'

'Oh! you are a vastly obedient person, I dare say,' replied Mrs. Cadurcis, very pettishly. 'How long, I should like to know, have my requests received such particular attention? Pooh!'

'Well, then, I will order my fire to be lighted again,' said Plantagenet.

'You shall do no such thing,' said the mother; 'I am mistress in this house. No one shall give orders here but me, and you may write to your guardian and tell him that, if you like.'

'I shall certainly not write to my guardian for the first time,' said Lord Cadurcis, 'about any such nonsense.'

'Nonsense, sir! Nonsense you said, did you? Your mother nonsense! This is the way to treat a parent, is it? I am nonsense, am I? I will teach you what nonsense is. Nonsense shall be very good sense; you shall find that, sir, that you shall. Nonsense, indeed! I'll write to your guardian, that I will! You call your mother nonsense, do you? And where did you learn that, I should like to know? Nonsense, indeed! This comes of your going to Cherbury! So your mother is nonsense; a pretty lesson for Lady Annabel to teach you. Oh! I'll speak my mind to her, that I will.'

'What has Lady Annabel to do with it?' inquired Cadurcis, in a loud tone.

'Don't threaten me, sir,' said Mrs. Cadurcis, with violent gesture. 'I won't be menaced; I won't be menaced by my son. Pretty goings on, indeed! But I will put a stop to them; will I not? that is all. Nonsense, indeed; your mother nonsense!'

'Well, you do talk nonsense, and the greatest,' said Plantagenet, doggedly; 'you are talking nonsense now, you are always talking nonsense, and you never open your mouth about Lady Annabel without talking nonsense.'

'If I was not very ill I would give it you,' said his mother, grinding her teeth. 'O you brat! You wicked brat, you! Is this the way to address me? I have half a mind to shake your viciousness out of you, that I have!

You are worse than your father, that you are!' and here she wept with rage.

'I dare say my father was not so bad, after all!' said Cadurcis.

'What should you know about your father, sir?' said Mrs. Cadurcis. 'How dare you speak about your father!'

'Who should speak about a father but a son?'

'Hold your impudence, sir!'

'I am not impudent, ma'am.'

'You aggravating brat!' exclaimed the enraged woman, 'I wish I had something to throw at you!'

'Did you throw things at my father?' asked his lordship.

Mrs. Cadurcis went into an hysterical rage; then, suddenly jumping up, she rushed at her son. Lord Cadurcis took up a position behind the table, but the sportive and mocking air which he generally instinctively assumed on these occasions, and which, while it irritated his mother more, was in reality affected by the boy from a sort of nervous desire of preventing these dreadful exposures from assuming a too tragic tone, did not characterise his countenance on the present occasion; on the contrary, it was pale, but composed and very serious. Mrs. Cadurcis, after one or two ineffectual attempts to catch him, paused and panted for breath. He took advantage of this momentary cessation, and spoke thus, 'Mother, I am in no humour for frolics. I moved out of your way that you might not strike me, because I have made up my mind that, if you ever strike me again, I will live with you no longer. Now, I have given you warning; do what you please; I shall sit down in this chair, and not move. If you strike me, you know the consequences.' So saying, his lordship resumed his chair.

Mrs. Cadurcis simultaneously sprang forward and boxed his ears; and then her son rose without the slightest expression of any kind, and slowly quitted the chamber.

Mrs. Cadurcis remained alone in a savage sulk; hours passed away, and her son never made his appearance. Then she rang the bell, and ordered the servant to tell Lord Cadurcis that tea was ready; but the servant returned, and reported that his lordship had locked himself up in his room, and would not reply to his inquiries. Determined not to give in, Mrs. Cadurcis, at length, retired for the night, rather regretting her violence, but still sullen. Having well scolded her waiting-woman, she at length fell asleep.

The morning brought breakfast, but no Lord Cadurcis; in vain were all the messages of his mother, her son would make no reply to them. Mrs. Cadurcis, at length, personally repaired to his room and knocked at the door, but she was as unsuccessful as the servants; she began to think he would starve, and desired the servant to offer from himself to bring his meal. Still silence. Indignant at his treatment of these overtures of conciliation, Mrs. Cadurcis returned to the saloon, confident that hunger, if no other impulse, would bring her wild cub out of his lair; but, just before dinner, her waiting-woman came running into the room.

'Oh, ma'am, ma'am, I don't know where Lord Cadurcis has gone; but I have just seen John, and he says there was no pony in the stable this morning.'

'Mrs. Cadurcis sprang up, rushed to her son's chamber, found the door still locked, ordered it to be burst open, and then it turned out that his lordship had never been there at all, for the bed was unused. Mrs. Cadurcis was frightened out of her life; the servants, to console her, assured her that Plantagenet must be at Cherbury; and while she believed their representations, which were probable, she became not only more composed, but resumed her jealousy and sullenness. 'Gone to Cherbury, indeed! No doubt of it! Let him remain at Cherbury.' Execrating Lady Annabel, she flung herself into an easy chair, and dined alone, preparing herself to speak her mind on her son's return.

The night, however, did not bring him, and Mrs. Cadurcis began to recur to her alarm. Much as she now disliked Lady Annabel, she could not resist the conviction that her ladyship would not permit Plantagenet to remain at Cherbury. Nevertheless, jealous, passionate, and obstinate, she stifled her fears, vented her spleen on her unhappy domestics, and, finally, exhausting herself by a storm of passion about some very unimportant subject, again sought refuge in sleep.

She awoke early in a fright, and inquired immediately for her son. He had not been seen. She ordered the abbey bell to be sounded, sent messengers throughout the demesne, and directed all the offices to be searched. At first she thought he must have returned, and slept, perhaps in a barn; then she adopted the more probable conclusion, that he had drowned himself in the lake. Then she went into hysterics; called Plantagenet her lost darling; declared he was the best and most dutiful of sons, and the image of his poor father, then abused all the servants, and then abused herself.

About noon she grew quite distracted, and rushed about the house with her hair dishevelled, and in a dressing-gown, looked in all the closets, behind the screens, under the chairs, into her work-box, but, strange to say, with no success. Then she went off into a swoon, and her servants, alike frightened about master and mistress, mother and son, dispatched a messenger immediately to Cherbury for intelligence, advice, and assistance. In less than an hour's time the messenger returned, and informed them that Lord Cadurcis had not been at Cherbury since two days back, but that Lady Annabel was very sorry to hear that their mistress was so ill, and would come on to see her immediately. In the meantime, Lady Annabel added that she had sent to Dr. Masham, and had great hopes that Lord Cadurcis was at Marringhurst. Mrs. Cadurcis, who had now come to, as her waiting-woman described the returning consciousness of her mistress, eagerly embraced the hope held out of Plantagenet being at Marringhurst, poured forth a thousand expressions of gratitude, admiration, and affection for Lady Annabel, who, she declared, was her best, her only friend, and the being in the world whom she loved most, next to her unhappy and injured child.

After another hour of suspense Lady Annabel arrived, and her entrance was the signal for a renewed burst of hysterics from Mrs. Cadurcis, so wild and terrible that they must have been contagious to any female of less disciplined emotions than her guest.

CHAPTER XIV.

Towards evening Dr. Masham arrived at Cadurcis. He could give no intelligence of Plantagenet, who had not called at Marringhurst; but he offered, and was prepared, to undertake his pursuit. The good Doctor had his saddle-bags well stocked, and was now on his way to Southport, that being the nearest town, and where he doubted not to gain some tidings of the fugitive. Mrs. Cadurcis he found so indisposed, that he anticipated the charitable intentions of Lady Annabel not to quit her; and after having bid them place their confidence in Providence and his humble exertions, he at once departed on his researches.

In the meantime let us return to the little lord himself. Having secured the advantage of a long start, by the device of turning the key of his chamber, he repaired to the stables, and finding no one to observe him, saddled his pony and galloped away without plan or purpose. An instinctive love of novelty and adventure induced him to direct his course by a road which he had never before pursued; and, after two or three miles progress through a wild open country of brushwood, he found that he had entered that considerable forest which formed the boundary of many of the views from Cadurcis. The afternoon was clear and still, the sun shining in the light blue sky, and the wind altogether hushed. On each side of the winding road spread the bright green turf, occasionally shaded by picturesque groups of doddered oaks. The calm beauty of the sylvan scene wonderfully touched the fancy of the youthful fugitive; it soothed and gratified him. He pulled up his pony; patted its lively neck, as if in gratitude for its good service, and, confident that he could not be successfully pursued, indulged in a thousand dreams of Robin Hood and his merry men. As for his own position and prospects, he gave himself no anxiety about them: satisfied with his escape from a revolting thraldom, his mind seemed to take a bound from the difficulty of his situation and the wildness of the scene, and he felt himself a man, and one, too, whom nothing could daunt or appal.

Soon the road itself quite disappeared and vanished in a complete turfy track; but the continuing marks of cartwheels assured him that it was a thoroughfare, although he was now indeed journeying in the heart of a forest of oaks and he doubted not it would lead to some town or village, or at any rate to some farmhouse. Towards sunset, he determined to make use of the remaining light, and pushed on apace; but it soon grew so dark, that he found it necessary to resume his walking pace, from fear of the overhanging branches and the trunks of felled trees which occasionally crossed his way.

Notwithstanding the probable prospect of passing his night in the forest, our little adventurer did not lose heart. Cadurcis was an intrepid child, and when in the company of those with whom he was not familiar, and free from those puerile associations to which those who had known and lived with him long were necessarily subject, he would assume a staid and firm demeanour unusual with one of such tender years. A light in the distance was now not only a signal that the shelter he desired was at hand, but reminded him that it was necessary, by his assured port, to prove that he was not unused to travel alone, and that he was perfectly competent and qualified to be his own master.

As he drew nearer, the lights multiplied, and the moon, which now rose over the forest, showed to him that the trees, retiring on both sides to some little distance, left a circular plot of ground, on which were not only the lights which had at first attracted his attention, but the red flames of a watch-fire, round which some dark figures had hitherto been clustered. The sound of horses' feet had disturbed them, and the fire was now more and more visible. As Cadurcis approached, he observed some low tents, and in a few minutes he was in the centre of an encampment of gipsies. He was for a moment somewhat dismayed, for he had been brought up with the usual terror of these wild people; nevertheless, he was not unequal to the occasion. He was surrounded in an instant, but only with women and children; for the gipsy-men never immediately appear. They smiled with their bright eyes, and the flames of the watch-fire threw a lurid glow over their dark and flashing countenances; they held out their practised hands; they uttered unintelligible, but not unfriendly sounds. The heart of Cadurcis faltered, but his voice did not betray him.

'I am cold, good people,' said the undaunted boy; 'will you let me warm myself by your fire?'

A beautiful girl, with significant gestures, pressed her hand to her heart, then pointed in the direction of the tents, and then rushed away, soon reappearing with a short thin man, inclining to middle age, but of a compact and apparently powerful frame, lithe, supple, and sinewy. His complexion was dark, but clear; his eye large, liquid, and black; but his other features small, though precisely moulded. He wore a green jacket and a pair of black velvet breeches, his legs and feet being bare, with the exception of slippers. Round his head was twisted a red handkerchief, which, perhaps, might not have looked like a turban on a countenance less oriental.

'What would the young master?' inquired the gipsy-man, in a voice far from disagreeable, and with a gesture of courtesy; but, at the same time, he shot a scrutinising glance first at Plantagenet, and then at his pony.

'I would remain with you,' said Cadurcis; 'that is, if you will let me.'

The gipsy-man made a sign to the women, and Plantagenet was lifted by them off his pony, before he could be aware of their purpose; the children led the pony away, and the gipsy-man conducted Plantagenet to the fire, where an old woman sat, presiding over the mysteries of an enormous flesh-pot. Immediately his fellows, who had originally been clustered around it, re-appeared; fresh blocks and branches were thrown on, the flames crackled and rose, the men seated themselves around, and Plantagenet, excited by the adventure, rubbed his hands before the fire, and determined to fear nothing.

A savoury steam exuded from the flesh-pot.

'That smells well,' said Plantagenet.

'Tis a dimber cove,'[A] whispered one of the younger men to a companion.

[Footnote A: 'Tis a lively lad.]

'Our supper has but rough seasoning for such as you,' said the man who had first saluted him, and who was apparently the leader; 'but the welcome is hearty.'

The woman and girls now came with wooden bowls and platters, and, after serving the men, seated themselves in an exterior circle, the children playing round them.

'Come, old mort,' said the leader, in a very different tone to the one in which he addressed his young guest, 'tout the cobble-colter; are we to have darkmans upon us? And, Beruna, flick the panam.'[A]

[Footnote A: Come, old woman, took after the turkey. Are we to wait till night! And, Beruna, cut the bread.]

Upon this, that beautiful girl, who had at first attracted the notice of Cadurcis, called out in a sweet lively voice, 'Ay! ay! Morgana!' and in a moment handed over the heads of the women a pannier of bread, which the leader took, and offered its contents to our fugitive. Cadurcis helped himself, with a bold but gracious air. The pannier was then passed round, and the old woman, opening the pot, drew out, with a huge iron fork, a fine turkey, which she tossed into a large wooden platter, and cut up with great quickness. First she helped Morgana, but only gained a reproof for her pains, who immediately yielded his portion to Plantagenet. Each man was provided with his knife, but the guest had none. Morgana immediately gave up his own.

'Beruna!' he shouted, 'gibel a chiv for the gentry cove.'[A]

[Footnote A: Bring a knife for the gentleman.]

'Ay! ay! Morgana!' said the girl; and she brought the knife to Plantagenet himself, saying at the same time, with sparkling eyes, 'Yam, yam, gentry cove.'[A]

[Footnote A: Eat, eat, gentleman.]

Cadurcis really thought it was the most delightful meal he had ever made in his life. The flesh-pot held something besides turkeys. Rough as was the fare, it was good and plentiful. As for beverage, they drank humpty-dumpty, which is ale boiled with brandy, and which is not one of the slightest charms of a gipsy's life. When the men were satisfied, their platters were filled, and given to the women and children; and Beruna, with her portion, came and seated herself by Plantagenet, looking at him with a blended glance of delight and astonishment, like a beautiful young savage, and then turning to her female companions to stifle a laugh. The flesh-pot was carried away, the men lit their pipes, the fire was replenished, its red shadow mingled with the silver beams of the moon; around were the glittering tents and the silent woods; on all sides flashing eyes and picturesque forms. Cadurcis glanced at his companions, and gazed upon the scene with feelings of ravishing excitement; and then, almost unconscious of what he was saying, exclaimed, 'At length I have found the life that suits me!'

'Indeed, squire!' said Morgana. 'Would you be one of us?'

'From this moment,' said Cadurcis, 'if you will admit me to your band. But what can I do? And I have nothing to give you. You must teach me to earn my right to our supper.'

'We'll make a Turkey merchant[A] of you yet,' said an old gipsy, 'never fear that.'

[Footnote A: *i.e.* We will teach you to steal a turkey]

'Bah, Peter!' said Morgana, with an angry look, 'your red rag will never be still. And what was the purpose of your present travel?' he continued to Plantagenet.

'None; I was sick of silly home.'

'The gentry cove will be romboyled by his dam,' said a third gipsy. 'Queer Cuffin will be the word yet, if we don't tout.'[A]

[Footnote A: His mother will make a hue and cry after the gentleman yet; justice of the peace will be the word, if we don't look sharp.]

'Well, you shall see a little more of us before you decide,' said Morgana, thoughtfully, and turning the conversation. 'Beruna.'

'Ay! ay! Morgana!'

'Tip me the clank, like a dimber mort as you are; trim a ken for the gentry cove; he is no lanspresado, or I am a kinchin.'[A]

[Footnote A: Give me the tankard, like a pretty girl. Get a bed ready for the gentleman. He is no informer, or I am an infant.]

'Ay! ay! Morgana' gaily exclaimed the girl, and she ran off to prepare a bed for the Lord of Cadurcis.

CHAPTER XV.

Dr. Masham could gain no tidings of the object of his pursuit at Southport: here, however, he ascertained that Plantagenet could not have fled to London, for in those days public conveyances were rare. There was only one coach that ran, or rather jogged, along this road, and it went but once a week, it being expected that very night; while the innkeeper was confident that so far as Southport was concerned, his little lordship had not sought refuge in the waggon, which was more frequent, though somewhat slower, in its progress to the metropolis. Unwilling to return home, although the evening was now drawing in, the Doctor resolved to proceed to a considerable town about twelve miles further, which Cadurcis might have reached by a cross road; so drawing his cloak around him, looking to his pistols, and desiring his servant to follow his example, the stout-hearted Rector of Marringhurst pursued his way.

It was dark when the Doctor entered the town, and he proceeded immediately to the inn where the coach was expected, with some faint hope that the fugitive might be discovered abiding within its walls; but, to all his inquiries about young gentlemen and ponies, he received very unsatisfactory answers; so, reconciling himself as well as he could to the disagreeable posture of affairs, he settled himself in the parlour of the inn, with a good fire, and, lighting his pipe, desired his servant to keep a sharp look-out.

In due time a great uproar in the inn-yard announced the arrival of the stage, an unwieldy machine, carrying six inside, and dragged by as many horses. The Doctor, opening the door of his apartment, which led on to a gallery that ran round the inn-yard, leaned over the balustrade with his pipe in his mouth, and watched proceedings. It so happened that the stage was to discharge one of its passengers at this town, who had come from the north, and the Doctor recognised in him a neighbour and brother magistrate, one Squire Mountmeadow, an important personage in his way, the terror of poachers, and somewhat of an oracle on the bench, as it was said that he could take a deposition without the assistance of his clerk. Although, in spite of the ostler's lanterns, it was very dark, it was impossible ever to be unaware of the arrival of Squire Mountmeadow; for he was one of those great men who take care to remind the world of their dignity by the attention which they require on every occasion.

'Coachman!' said the authoritative voice of the Squire. 'Where is the coachman? Oh! you are there, sir, are you? Postilion! Where is the postilion? Oh! you are there, sir, are you? Host! Where is the host? Oh! you are there, sir, are you? Waiter! Where is the waiter? I say where is the waiter?'

'Coming, please your worship!'

'How long am I to wait? Oh! you are there, sir, are you? Coachman!'

'Your worship!'

'Postilion!'

'Yes, your worship!'

'Host!'

'Your worship's servant!'

'Waiter!'

'Your worship's honour's humble servant!'

'I am going to alight!'

All four attendants immediately bowed, and extended their arms to assist this very great man; but Squire Mountmeadow, scarcely deigning to avail himself of their proffered assistance, and pausing on each step, looking around him with his long, lean, solemn visage, finally reached terra firma in safety, and slowly stretched his tall, ungainly figure. It was at this moment that Dr. Masham's servant approached him, and informed his worship that his master was at the inn, and would be happy to see him. The countenance of the great Mountmeadow relaxed at the mention of the name of a brother magistrate, and in an audible voice he bade the groom 'tell my worthy friend, his worship, your worthy master, that I shall be rejoiced to pay my respects to an esteemed neighbour and a brother magistrate.'

With slow and solemn steps, preceded by the host, and followed by the waiter, Squire Mountmeadow ascended the staircase of the external gallery, pausing occasionally, and looking around him with thoughtful importance, and making an occasional inquiry as to the state of the town and neighbourhood during his absence, in this fashion: 'Stop! where are you, host? Oh! you are there, sir, are you? Well, Mr. Host, and how have we been? orderly, eh?'

'Quite orderly, your worship.'

'Hoh! Orderly! Hem! Well, very well! Never easy, if absent only four-and-twenty hours. The law must be obeyed.'

'Yes, your worship.'

'Lead on, sir. And, waiter; where are you, waiter? Oh, you are there, sir, are you? And so my brother magistrate is here?'

'Yes, your honour's worship.'

'Hem! What can he want? something in the wind; wants my advice, I dare say; shall have it. Soldiers ruly; king's servants; must be obeyed.'

'Yes, your worship; quite ruly, your worship,' said the host.

'As obliging and obstreperous as can be,' said the waiter.

'Well, very well;' and here the Squire had gained the gallery, where the Doctor was ready to receive him.

'It always gives me pleasure to meet a brother magistrate,' said Squire Mountmeadow, bowing with cordial condescension; 'and a gentleman of your cloth, too. The clergy must be respected; I stand or fall by the Church. After you, Doctor, after you.' So saying, the two magistrates entered the room.

'An unexpected pleasure, Doctor,' said the Squire; 'and what brings your worship to town?'

'A somewhat strange business,' said the Doctor; 'and indeed I am not a little glad to have the advantage of your advice and assistance.'

'Hem! I thought so,' said the Squire; 'your worship is very complimentary. What is the case? Larceny?'

'Nay, my good sir, 'tis a singular affair; and, if you please, we will order supper first, and discuss it afterwards. 'Tis for your private ear.'

'Oh! ho!' said the Squire, looking very mysterious and important. 'With your worship's permission,' he added, filling a pipe.

The host was no laggard in waiting on two such important guests. The brother magistrates despatched their rump-steak; the foaming tankard was replenished; the fire renovated. At length, the table and the room being alike clear, Squire Mountmeadow drew a long puff, and said, 'Now for business, Doctor.'

His companion then informed him of the exact object of his visit, and narrated to him so much of the preceding incidents as was necessary. The Squire listened in solemn silence, elevating his eyebrows, nodding his head, trimming his pipe, with profound interjections; and finally, being appealed to for his opinion by the Doctor, delivered himself of a most portentous 'Hem!'

'I question, Doctor,' said the Squire, 'whether we should not communicate with the Secretary of State. 'Tis no ordinary business. 'Tis a spiriting away of a Peer of the realm. It smacks of treason.'

'Egad!' said the Doctor, suppressing a smile, 'I think we can hardly make a truant boy a Cabinet question.'

The Squire glanced a look of pity at his companion. 'Prove the truancy, Doctor; prove it. 'Tis a case of disappearance; and how do we know that there is not a Jesuit at the bottom of it?'

'There is something in that,' said the Doctor.

'There is everything in it,' said the Squire, triumphantly. 'We must offer rewards; we must raise the posse comitatus.'

'For the sake of the family, I would make as little stir as necessary,' said Dr. Masham.

'For the sake of the family!' said the Squire. 'Think of the nation, sir! For the sake of the nation we must make as much stir as possible. 'Tis a Secretary of State's business; 'tis a case for a general warrant.'

'He is a well-meaning lad enough,' said the Doctor.

'Ay, and therefore more easily played upon,' said the Squire. 'Rome is at the bottom of it, brother Masham, and I am surprised that a good Protestant like yourself, one of the King's Justices of the Peace, and a Doctor of Divinity to boot, should doubt the fact for an instant.'

'We have not heard much of the Jesuits of late years,' said the Doctor.

'The very reason that they are more active,' said the Squire.

'An only child!' said Dr. Masham.

'A Peer of the realm!' said Squire Mountmeadow.

'I should think he must be in the neighbourhood.'

'More likely at St. Omer's.'

'They would scarely take him to the plantations with this war?'

'Let us drink "Confusion to the rebels!"' said the Squire. 'Any news?'

'Howe sails this week,' said the Doctor.

'May he burn Boston!' said the Squire.

'I would rather he would reduce it, without such extremities,' said Dr. Masham.

'Nothing is to be done without extremities,' said Squire Mountmeadow.

'But this poor child?' said the Doctor, leading back the conversation. 'What can we do?'

'The law of the case is clear,' said the Squire; 'we must move a habeas corpus.'

'But shall we be nearer getting him for that?' inquired the Doctor.

'Perhaps not, sir; but 'tis the regular way. We must proceed by rule.'

'I am sadly distressed,' said Dr. Masham. 'The worst is, he has gained such a start upon us; and yet he can hardly have gone to London; he would have been recognised here or at Southport.'

'With his hair cropped, and in a Jesuit's cap?' inquired the Squire, with a slight sneer. 'Ah! Doctor, Doctor, you know not the gentry you have to deal with!'

'We must hope,' said Dr. Masham. 'To-morrow we must organise some general search.'

'I fear it will be of no use,' said the Squire, replenishing his pipe. 'These Jesuits are deep fellows.'

'But we are not sure about the Jesuits, Squire.'

'I am,' said the Squire; 'the case is clear, and the sooner you break it to his mother the better. You asked me for my advice, and I give it you.'

CHAPTER XVI.

It was on the following morning, as the Doctor was under the operation of the barber, that his groom ran into the room with a pale face and agitated air, and exclaimed,

'Oh! master, master, what do you think? Here is a man in the yard with my lord's pony.'

'Stop him, Peter,' exclaimed the Doctor. 'No! watch him, watch him; send for a constable. Are you certain 'tis the pony?'

'I could swear to it out of a thousand,' said Peter.

'There, never mind my beard, my good man,' said the Doctor. 'There is no time for appearances. Here is a robbery, at least; God grant no worse. Peter, my boots!' So saying, the Doctor, half equipped, and followed by Peter and the barber, went forth on the gallery. 'Where is he?' said the Doctor.

'He is down below, talking to the ostler, and trying to sell the pony,' said Peter.

'There is no time to lose,' said the Doctor; 'follow me, like true men:' and the Doctor ran downstairs in his silk nightcap, for his wig was not yet prepared.

'There he is,' said Peter; and true enough there was a man in a smock-frock and mounted on the very pony which Lady Annabel had presented to Plantagenet.

'Seize this man in the King's name,' said the Doctor, hastily advancing to him. 'Ostler, do your duty; Peter, be firm. I charge you all; I am a justice of the peace. I charge you arrest this man.'

The man seemed very much astonished; but he was composed, and offered no resistance. He was dressed like a small farmer, in top-boots and a smock-frock. His hat was rather jauntily placed on his curly red hair.

'Why am I seized?' at length said the man.

'Where did you get that pony?' said the Doctor.

'I bought it,' was the reply.

'Of whom?'

'A stranger at market.'

'You are accused of robbery, and suspected of murder,' said Dr. Masham. 'Mr. Constable,' said the Doctor, turning to that functionary, who had now arrived, 'handcuff this man, and keep him in strict custody until further orders.'

The report that a man was arrested for robbery, and suspected of murder, at the Red Dragon, spread like wildfire through the town; and the inn-yard was soon crowded with the curious and excited inhabitants.

Peter and the barber, to whom he had communicated everything, were well qualified to do justice to the important information of which they were the sole depositaries; the tale lost nothing by their telling; and a circumstantial narrative of the robbery and murder of no less a personage than Lord Cadurcis, of Cadurcis Abbey, was soon generally prevalent.

The stranger was secured in a stable, before which the constable kept guard; mine host, and the waiter, and the ostlers acted as a sort of supernumerary police, to repress the multitude; while Peter held the real pony by the bridle, whose identity, which he frequently attested, was considered by all present as an incontrovertible evidence of the commission of the crime.

In the meantime Dr. Masham, really agitated, roused his brother magistrate, and communicated to his worship the important discovery. The Squire fell into a solemn flutter. 'We must be regular, brother Masham; we must proceed by rule; we are a bench in ourselves. Would that my clerk were here! We must send for Signsealer forthwith. I will not decide without the statutes. The law must be consulted, and it must be obeyed. The fellow hath not brought my wig. 'Tis a case of murder no doubt. A Peer of the realm murdered! You must break the intelligence to his surviving parent, and I will communicate to the Secretary of State. Can the body be found? That will prove the murder. Unless the body be found, the murder will not be proved, save the villain confess, which he will not do unless he hath sudden compunctions. I have known sudden compunctions go a great way. We had a case before our bench last month; there was no evidence. It was not a case of murder; it was of woodcutting; there was no evidence; but the defendant had compunctions. Oh! here is my wig. We must send for Signsealer. He is clerk to our bench, and he must bring the statutes. 'Tis not simple murder this; it involves petty treason.'

By this time his worship had completed his toilet, and he and his colleague took their way to the parlour they had inhabited the preceding evening. Mr. Signsealer was in attendance, much to the real, though concealed, satisfaction of Squire Mountmeadow. Their worships were seated like two consuls before the table, which Mr. Signsealer had duly arranged with writing materials and various piles of calf-bound volumes. Squire Mountmeadow then, arranging his countenance, announced that the bench was prepared, and mine host was instructed forthwith to summon the constable and his charge, together with Peter and the ostler as witnesses. There was a rush among some of the crowd who were nighest the scene to follow the prisoner into the room; and, sooth to say, the great Mountmeadow was much too enamoured of his own self-importance to be by any means a patron of close courts and private hearings; but then, though he loved his power to be witnessed, he was equally desirous that his person should be reverenced. It was his boast that he could keep a court of quarter sessions as quiet as a church; and now, when the crowd rushed in with all those sounds of tumult incidental to such a movement, it required only Mountmeadow slowly to rise, and drawing himself up to the full height of his gaunt figure, to knit his severe brow, and throw one of his peculiar looks around the chamber, to insure a most awful stillness. Instantly everything was so hushed, that you might have heard Signsealer nib his pen.

The witnesses were sworn; Peter proved that the pony belonged to Lord Cadurcis, and that his lordship had been missing from home for several days, and was believed to have quitted the abbey on this identical pony. Dr. Masham was ready, if necessary, to confirm this evidence. The accused adhered to his first account, that he had purchased the animal the day before at a neighbouring fair, and doggedly declined to answer any cross-examination. Squire Mountmeadow looked alike pompous and puzzled; whispered to the Doctor; and then shook his head at Mr. Signsealer.

'I doubt whether there be satisfactory evidence of the murder, brother Masham,' said the Squire; 'what shall be our next step?'

'There is enough evidence to keep this fellow in custody,' said the Doctor. 'We must remand him, and make inquiries at the market town. I shall proceed there immediately, He is a strange-looking fellow,' added the Doctor: 'were it not for his carroty locks, I should scarcely take him for a native.'

'Hem!' said the Squire, 'I have my suspicions. Fellow,' continued his worship, in an awful tone, 'you say that you are a stranger, and that your name is Morgan; very suspicious all this: you have no one to speak to your character or station, and you are found in possession of stolen goods. The bench will remand you for the present, and will at any rate commit you for trial for the robbery. But here is a Peer of the realm missing, fellow, and you are most grievously suspected of being concerned in his spiriting away, or even murder. You are upon tender ground, prisoner; 'tis a case verging on petty treason, if not petty treason itself. Eh! Mr. Signsealer? Thus runs the law, as I take it? Prisoner, it would be well for you to consider your situation. Have you no compunctions? Compunctions might save you, if not a principal offender. It is your duty to assist the bench in executing justice. The Crown is merciful; you may be king's evidence.'

Mr. Signsealer whispered the bench; he proposed that the prisoner's hat should be examined, as the name of its maker might afford a clue to his residence.

'True, true, Mr. Clerk,' said Squire Mountmeadow, 'I am coming to that. 'Tis a sound practice; I have known such a circumstance lead to great disclosures. But we must proceed in order. Order is everything. Constable, take the prisoner's hat off.'

The constable took the hat off somewhat rudely; so rudely, indeed, that the carroty locks came off in company with it, and revealed a profusion of long plaited hair, which had been adroitly twisted under the wig, more in character with the countenance than its previous covering.

'A Jesuit, after all!' exclaimed the Squire.

'A gipsy, as it seems to me,' whispered the Doctor.

'Still worse,' said the Squire.

'Silence in the Court!' exclaimed the awful voice of Squire Mountmeadow, for the excitement of the audience was considerable. The disguise was generally esteemed as incontestable evidence of the murder. 'Silence, or I will order the Court to be cleared. Constable, proclaim silence. This is an awful business,' added the Squire, with a very long face. 'Brother Masham, we must do our duty; but this is an awful business. At any rate we must try to discover the body. A Peer of the realm must not be suffered to lie murdered in a ditch. He must have Christian burial, if possible, in the vaults of his ancestors.'

When Morgana, for it was indeed he, observed the course affairs were taking, and ascertained that his detention under present circumstances was inevitable, he relaxed from his doggedness, and expressed a willingness to make a communication to the bench. Squire Mountmeadow lifted up his eyes to Heaven, as if entreating the interposition of Providence to guide him in his course; then turned to his brother magistrate, and then nodded to the clerk.

'He has compunctions, brother Masham,' said his worship: 'I told you so; he has compunctions. Trust me to deal with these fellows. He knew not his perilous situation; the hint of petty treason staggered him. Mr. Clerk, take down the prisoner's confession; the Court must be cleared; constable, clear the Court. Let a stout man stand on each side of the prisoner, to protect the bench. The magistracy of England will never shrink from doing their duty, but they must be protected. Now, prisoner, the bench is ready to hear your confession. Conceal nothing, and if you were not a principal in the murder, or an accessory before the fact; eh, Mr. Clerk, thus runs the law, as I take it? there may be mercy; at any rate, if you be hanged, you will have the satisfaction of having cheerfully made the only atonement to society in your power.'

'Hanging be damned!' said Morgana.

Squire Mountmeadow started from his seat, his cheeks distended with rage, his dull eyes for once flashing fire. 'Did you ever witness such atrocity, brother Masham?' exclaimed his worship. 'Did you hear the villain? I'll teach him to respect the bench. I'll fine him before he is executed, that I will!'

'The young gentleman to whom this pony belongs,' continued the gipsy, 'may or may not be a lord. I never asked him his name, and he never told it me; but he sought hospitality of me and my people, and we gave it him, and he lives with us, of his own free choice. The pony is of no use to him now, and so I came to sell it for our common good.'

'A Peer of the realm turned gipsy!' exclaimed the Squire. 'A very likely tale! I'll teach you to come here and tell your cock-and-bull stories to two of his majesty's justices of the peace. 'Tis a flat case of robbery and murder, and I venture to say something else. You shall go to gaol directly, and the Lord have mercy on your soul!'

'Nay,' said the gipsy, appealing to Dr. Marsham; 'you, sir, appear to be a friend of this youth. You will not regain him by sending me to gaol. Load me, if you will, with irons; surround me with armed men, but at least give me the opportunity of proving the truth of what I say. I offer in two hours to produce to you the youth, and you shall find he is living with my people in content and peace.'

'Content and fiddlestick!' said the Squire, in a rage.

'Brother Mountmeadow,' said the Doctor, in a low tone, to his colleague, 'I have private duties to perform to this family. Pardon me if, with all deference to your sounder judgment and greater experience, I myself accept the prisoner's offer.'

'Brother Masham, you are one of his majesty's justices of the peace, you are a brother magistrate, and you are a Doctor of Divinity; you owe a duty to your country, and you owe a duty to yourself. Is it wise, is it decorous, that one of the Quorum should go a-gipsying? Is it possible that you can credit this preposterous tale? Brother Masham, there will be a rescue, or my name is not Mountmeadow.'

In spite, however, of all these solemn warnings, the good Doctor, who was not altogether unaware of the character of his pupil, and could comprehend that it was very possible the statement of the gipsy might be genuine, continued without very much offending his colleague, who looked upon, his conduct indeed rather with pity than resentment, to accept the offer of Morgana; and consequently, well-secured and guarded, and preceding the Doctor, who rode behind the cart with his servant, the gipsy soon sallied forth from the inn-yard, and requested the driver to guide his course in the direction of the forest.

CHAPTER XVII.

It was the afternoon of the third day after the arrival of Cadurcis at the gipsy encampment, and nothing had yet occurred to make him repent his flight from the abbey, and the choice of life he had made. He had experienced nothing but kindness and hospitality, while the beautiful Beruna seemed quite content to pass her life in studying his amusement. The weather, too, had been extremely favourable to his new mode of existence; and stretched at his length upon the rich turf, with his head on Beruna's lap, and his eyes fixed upon the rich forest foliage glowing in the autumnal sunset, Plantagenet only wondered that he could have endured for so many years the shackles of his common-place home.

His companions were awaiting the return of their leader, Morgana, who had been absent since the preceding day, and who had departed on Plantagenet's pony. Most of them were lounging or strolling in the vicinity of their tents; the children were playing; the old woman was cooking at the fire; and altogether, save that the hour was not so late, the scene presented much the same aspect as when Cadurcis had first beheld it. As for his present occupation, Beruna was giving him a lesson in the gipsy language, which he was acquiring with a rapid facility, which quite exceeded all his previous efforts in such acquisitions.

Suddenly a scout sang out that a party was in sight. The men instantly disappeared; the women were on the alert; and one ran forward as a spy, on pretence of telling fortunes. This bright-eyed professor of palmistry soon, however, returned running, and out of breath, yet chatting all the time with inconceivable rapidity, and accompanying the startling communication she was evidently making with the most animated gestures. Beruna started up, and, leaving the astonished Cadurcis, joined them. She seemed alarmed. Cadurcis was soon convinced there was consternation in the camp.

Suddenly a horseman galloped up, and was immediately followed by a companion. They called out, as if encouraging followers, and one of them immediately galloped away again, as if to detail the results of their reconnaissance. Before Cadurcis could well rise and make inquiries as to what was going on, a light cart, containing several men, drove up, and in it, a prisoner, he detected Morgana. The branches of the trees concealed for a moment two other horsemen who followed the cart; but Cadurcis, to his infinite alarm and mortification, soon recognised Dr. Masham and Peter.

When the gipsies found their leader was captive, they no longer attempted to conceal themselves; they all came forward, and would have clustered round the cart, had not the riders, as well as those who more immediately guarded the prisoner, prevented them. Morgana spoke some words in a loud voice to the gipsies, and they immediately appeared less agitated; then turning to Dr. Masham, he said in English, 'Behold your child!'

Instantly two gipsy men seized Cadurcis, and led him to the Doctor.

'How now, my lord!' said the worthy Rector, in a stern voice, 'is this your duty to your mother and your friends?'

Cadurcis looked down, but rather dogged than ashamed.

'You have brought an innocent man into great peril,' continued the Doctor. 'This person, no longer a prisoner, has been arrested on suspicion of robbery, and even murder, through your freak. Morgana, or whatever your name may be, here is some reward for your treatment of this child, and some compensation for your detention. Mount your pony, Lord Cadurcis, and return to your home with me.'

'This is my home, sir,' said Plantagenet.

'Lord Cadurcis, this childish nonsense must cease; it has already endangered the life of your mother, nor can I answer for her safety, if you lose a moment in returning.'

'Child, you must return,' said Morgana.

'Child!' said Plantagenet, and he walked some steps away, and leant against a tree. 'You promised that I should remain,' said he, addressing himself reproachfully to Morgana.

'You are not your own master,' said the gipsy; 'your remaining here will only endanger and disturb us. Fortunately we have nothing to fear from laws we have never outraged; but had there been a judge less wise and gentle than the master here, our peaceful family might have been all harassed and hunted to the very death.'

He waved his hand, and addressed some words to his tribe, whereupon two brawny fellows seized Cadurcis, and placed him again, in spite of his struggling, upon his pony, with the same irresistible facility with which they had a few nights before dismounted him. The little lord looked very sulky, but his position was beginning to get ludicrous. Morgana, pocketing his five guineas, leaped over the side of the cart, and offered to guide the Doctor and his attendants through the forest. They moved on accordingly. It was the work of an instant, and Cadurcis suddenly found himself returning home between the Rector and Peter. Not a word, however, escaped his lips; once only he moved; the light branch of a tree, aimed with delicate precision, touched his back; he looked round; it was Beruna. She kissed her hand to him, and a tear stole down his pale, sullen cheek, as, taking from his breast his handkerchief, he threw it behind him, unperceived, that she might pick it up, and keep it for his sake.

After proceeding two or three miles under the guidance of Morgana, the equestrians gained the road, though it still ran through the forest. Here the Doctor dismissed the gipsy-man, with whom he had occasionally conversed during their progress; but not a sound ever escaped from the mouth of Cadurcis, or rather, the captive, who was now substituted in Morgana's stead. The Doctor, now addressing himself to Plantagenet, informed him that it was of importance that they should make the best of their way, and so he put spurs to his mare, and Cadurcis sullenly complied with the intimation. At this rate, in the course of little more than another hour, they arrived in sight of the demesne of Cadurcis, where they pulled up their steeds.

They entered the park, they approached the portal of the abbey; at length they dismounted. Their coming was announced by a servant, who had recognised his lord at a distance, and had ran on before with the tidings. When they entered the abbey, they were met by Lady Annabel in the cloisters; her countenance was very serious. She shook hands with Dr. Masham, but did not speak, and immediately led him aside. Cadurcis remained standing in the very spot where Doctor Masham left him, as if he were quite a stranger in the place, and was no longer master of his own conduct. Suddenly Doctor Masham, who was at the end of the cloister, while Lady Annabel was mounting the staircase, looked round with a pale face, and said in an agitated voice, 'Lord Cadurcis, Lady Annabel wishes to speak to you in the saloon.'

Cadurcis immediately, but slowly, repaired to the saloon. Lady Annabel was walking up and down in it. She seemed greatly disturbed. When she saw him, she put her arm round his neck affectionately, and said in a low voice, 'My dearest Plantagenet, it has devolved upon me to communicate to you some distressing intelligence.' Her voice faltered, and the tears stole down her cheek.

'My mother, then, is dangerously ill?' he inquired in a calm but softened tone.

'It is even sadder news than that, dear child.'

Cadurcis looked about him wildly, and then with an inquiring glance at Lady Annabel:

'There can be but one thing worse than that,' he at length said.

'What if it have happened?' said Lady Annabel.

He threw himself into a chair, and covered his face with his hands. After a few minutes he looked up and said, in a low but distinct voice, 'It is too terrible to think of; it is too terrible to mention; but, if it have happened, let me be alone.'

Lady Annabel approached him with a light step; she embraced him, and, whispering that she should be found in the next room, she quitted the apartment.

Cadurcis remained seated for more than half an hour without changing in the slightest degree his position. The twilight died away; it grew quite dark; he looked up with a slight shiver, and then quitted the apartment.

In the adjoining room, Lady Annabel was seated with Doctor Masham, and giving him the details of the fatal event. It had occurred that morning. Mrs. Cadurcis, who had never slept a wink since her knowledge of her son's undoubted departure, and scarcely for an hour been free from violent epileptic fits, had fallen early in the morning into a doze, which lasted about half an hour, and from which her medical attendant, who with Pauncefort had sat up with her during the night, augured the most favourable consequences. About half-past six o'clock she woke, and inquired whether Plantagenet had returned. They answered her that Doctor Masham had not yet arrived, but would probably be at the abbey in the course of the morning. She said it would be too late. They endeavoured to encourage her, but she asked to see Lady Annabel, who was immediately called, and lost no time in repairing to her. When Mrs. Cadurcis recognised her, she held out her hand, and said in a dying tone, 'It was my fault; it was ever my fault; it is too late now; let him find a mother in you.' She never spoke again, and in the course of an hour expired.

While Lady Annabel and the Doctor were dwelling on these sad circumstances, and debating whether he should venture to approach Plantagenet, and attempt to console him, for the evening was now far advanced, and nearly three hours had elapsed since the fatal communication had been made to him, it happened that Mistress Pauncefort chanced to pass Mrs. Cadurcis' room, and as she did so she heard some one violently sobbing. She listened, and hearing the sounds frequently repeated, she entered the room, which, but for her candle, would have been quite dark, and there she found Lord Cadurcis kneeling and weeping by his mother's bedside. He seemed annoyed at being seen and disturbed, but his spirit was too broken to murmur. 'La! my lord,' said Mistress Pauncefort, 'you must not take on so; you must not indeed. I am sure this dark room is enough to put any one in low spirits. Now do go downstairs, and sit with my lady and the Doctor, and try to be cheerful; that is a dear good young gentleman. I wish Miss Venetia were here, and then she would amuse you. But you must not take on, because there is no use in it. You must exert yourself, for what is done cannot be undone; and, as the Doctor told us last Sunday, we must all die; and well for those who die with a good conscience; and I am sure the poor dear lady that is gone must have had a good conscience, because she had a good heart, and I never heard any one say the contrary. Now do exert yourself, my dear lord, and try to be cheerful, do; for there is nothing like a little exertion in these cases, for God's will must be done, and it is not for us to say yea or nay, and taking on is a murmuring against God's providence.' And so Mistress Pauncefort would have continued urging the usual topics of coarse and common-place consolation; but Cadurcis only answered with a sigh that came from the bottom of his heart, and said with streaming eyes, 'Ah! Mrs. Pauncefort, God had only given me one friend in this world, and there she lies.'

CHAPTER XVIII.

The first conviction that there is death in the house is perhaps the most awful moment of youth. When we are young, we think that not only ourselves, but that all about us, are immortal. Until the arrow has struck a victim round our own hearth, death is merely an unmeaning word; until then, its casual mention has stamped no idea upon our brain. There are few, even among those least susceptible of thought and emotion, in whose hearts and minds the first death in the family does not act as a powerful revelation of the mysteries of life, and of their own being; there are few who, after such a catastrophe, do not look upon the world and the world's ways, at least for a time, with changed and tempered feelings. It recalls the past; it makes us ponder over the future; and youth, gay and light-hearted youth, is taught, for the first time, to regret and to fear.

On Cadurcis, a child of pensive temperament, and in whose strange and yet undeveloped character there was, amid lighter elements, a constitutional principle of melancholy, the sudden decease of his mother produced a profound effect. All was forgotten of his parent, except the intimate and natural tie, and her warm and genuine affection. He was now alone in the world; for reflection impressed upon him at this moment what the course of existence too generally teaches to us all, that mournful truth, that, after all, we have no friends that we can depend upon in this life but our parents. All other intimacies, however ardent, are liable to cool; all other confidence, however unlimited, to be violated. In the phantasmagoria of life, the friend with whom we have cultivated mutual trust for years is often suddenly or gradually estranged from us, or becomes, from, painful, yet irresistible circumstances, even our deadliest foe. As for women, as for the mistresses of our hearts, who has not learnt that the links of passion are fragile as they are glittering; and that the bosom on which we have reposed with idolatry all our secret sorrows and sanguine hopes, eventually becomes the very heart that exults in our misery and baffles our welfare? Where is the enamoured face that smiled upon our early love, and was to shed tears over our grave? Where are the choice companions of our youth, with whom we were to breast the difficulties and share the triumphs of existence? Even in this inconstant world, what changes like the heart? Love is a dream, and friendship a delusion. No wonder we grow callous; for how few have the opportunity of returning to the hearth which they quitted in levity or thoughtless weariness, yet which alone is faithful to them; whose sweet affections require not the stimulus of prosperity or fame, the lure of accomplishments, or the tribute of flattery; but which are constant to us in distress, and console us even in disgrace!

Before she retired for the night, Lady Annabel was anxious to see Plantagenet. Mistress Pauncefort had informed her of his visit to his mother's room. Lady Annabel found Cadurcis in the gallery, now partially lighted by the moon which had recently risen. She entered with her light, as if she were on her way to her own room, and not seeking him.

'Dear Plantagenet,' she said, 'will you not go to bed?'

'I do not intend to go to bed to-night,' he replied.

She approached him and took him by the hand, which he did not withdraw from her, and they walked together once or twice up and down the gallery.

'I think, dear child,' said Lady Annabel, 'you had better come and sit with us.'

'I like to be alone,' was his answer; but not in a sullen voice, low and faltering.

'But in sorrow we should be with our friends,' said Lady Annabel.

'I have no friends,' he answered. 'I only had one.'

'I am your friend, dear child; I am your mother now, and you shall find me one if you like. And Venetia, have you forgotten your sister? Is she not your friend? And Dr. Masham, surely you cannot doubt his friendship?'

Cadurcis tried to stifle a sob. 'Ay, Lady Annabel,' he said, 'you are my friend now, and so are you all; and you know I love you much. But you were not my friends two years ago; and things will change again; they will, indeed. A mother is your friend as long as she lives; she cannot help being your friend.'

'You shall come to Cherbury and live with us,' said Lady Annabel.' You know you love Cherbury, and you shall find it a home, a real home.'

He pressed her hand to his lips; the hand was covered with his tears.

'We will go to Cherbury to-morrow, dear Plantagenet; remaining here will only make you sad.'

'I will never leave Cadurcis again while my mother is in this house,' he said, in a firm and serious voice. And then, after a moment's pause, he added, 'I wish to know when the burial is to take place.'

'We will ask Dr. Masham,' replied Lady Annabel. 'Come, let us go to him; come, my own child.'

He permitted himself to be led away. They descended to the small apartment where Lady Annabel had been previously sitting. They found the Doctor there; he rose and pressed Plantagenet's hand with great emotion. They made room for him at the fire between them; he sat in silence, with his gaze intently fixed upon the decaying embers, yet did not quit his hold of Lady Annabel's hand. He found it a consolation to him; it linked him to a being who seemed to love him. As long as he held her hand he did not seem quite alone in the world.

Now nobody spoke; for Lady Annabel felt that Cadurcis was in some degree solaced; and she thought it unwise to interrupt the more composed train of his thoughts. It was, indeed, Plantagenet himself who first broke silence.

'I do not think I can go to bed, Lady Annabel,' he said. 'The thought of this night is terrible to me. I do not think it ever can end. I would much sooner sit up in this room.'

'Nay! my child, sleep is a great consoler; try to go to bed, love.'

'I should like to sleep in my mother's room,' was his strange reply. 'It seems to me that I could sleep there. And if I woke in the night, I should like to see her.'

Lady Annabel and the Doctor exchanged looks.

'I think,' said the Doctor, 'you had better sleep in my room, and then, if you wake in the night, you will have some one to speak to. You will find that a comfort.'

'Yes, that you will,' said Lady Annabel. 'I will go and have the sofa bed made up in the Doctor's room for you. Indeed that will be the very best plan.'

So at last, but not without a struggle, they persuaded Cadurcis to retire. Lady Annabel embraced him tenderly when she bade him good night; and, indeed, he felt consoled by her affection.

As nothing could persuade Plantagenet to leave the abbey until his mother was buried, Lady Annabel resolved to take up her abode there, and she sent the next morning for Venetia. There were a great many arrangements to make about the burial and the mourning; and Lady Annabel and Dr. Masham were obliged, in consequence, to go the next morning to Southport; but they delayed their departure until the arrival of Venetia, that Cadurcis might not be left alone.

The meeting between himself and Venetia was a very sad one, and yet her companionship was a great solace. Venetia urged every topic that she fancied could reassure his spirits, and upon the happy home he would find at Cherbury.

'Ah!' said Cadurcis, 'they will not leave me here; I am sure of that. I think our happy days are over, Venetia.'

What mourner has not felt the magic of time? Before the funeral could take place, Cadurcis had recovered somewhat of his usual cheerfulness, and would indulge with Venetia in plans of their future life. And living, as they all were, under the same roof, sharing the same sorrows, participating in the same cares, and all about to wear the same mournful emblems of their domestic calamity, it was difficult for him to believe that he was indeed that desolate being he had at first correctly estimated himself. Here were true friends, if such could exist; here were fine sympathies, pure affections, innocent and disinterested hearts! Every domestic tie yet remained perfect, except the spell-bound tie of blood. That wanting, all was a bright and happy vision, that might vanish in an instant, and for ever; that perfect, even the least graceful, the most repulsive home, had its irresistible charms; and its loss, when once experienced, might be mourned for ever, and could never be restored.

CHAPTER XIX.

After the funeral of Mrs. Cadurcis, the family returned to Cherbury with Plantagenet, who was hereafter to consider it his home. All that the most tender solicitude could devise to reconcile him to the change in his life was fulfilled by Lady Annabel and her daughter, and, under their benignant influence, he soon regained his usual demeanour. His days were now spent as in the earlier period of their acquaintance, with the exception of those painful returns to home, which had once been a source to him of so much gloom and unhappiness. He pursued his studies as of old, and shared the amusements of Venetia. His allotted room was ornamented by her drawings, and in the evenings they read aloud by turns to Lady Annabel the volume which she selected. The abbey he never visited again after his mother's funeral.

Some weeks had passed in this quiet and contented manner, when one day Doctor Masham, who, since the death of his mother, had been in correspondence with his guardian, received a letter from that nobleman, to announce that he had made arrangements for sending his ward to Eton, and to request that he would accordingly instantly proceed to the metropolis. This announcement occasioned both Cadurcis and Venetia poignant affliction. The idea of separation was to both of them most painful; and although Lady Annabel herself was in some degree prepared for an arrangement, which sooner or later she considered inevitable, she was herself scarcely less distressed. The good Doctor, in some degree to break the bitterness of parting, proposed accompanying Plantagenet to London, and himself personally delivering the charge, in whose welfare they were so much interested, to his guardian. Nevertheless, it was a very sad affair, and the week which was to intervene before his departure found both himself and Venetia often in tears. They no longer took any delight in their mutual studies but passed the day walking about and visiting old haunts, and endeavouring to console each other for what they both deemed a great calamity, and which was indeed, the only serious misfortune Venetia had herself experienced in the whole course of her serene career.

'But if I were really your brother,' said Plantagenet, 'I must have quitted you the same, Venetia. Boys always go to school; and then we shall be so happy when I return.'

'Oh! but we are so happy now, Plantagenet. I cannot believe that we are going to part. And are you sure that you will return? Perhaps your guardian will not let you, and will wish you to spend your holidays at his house. His house will be your home now.'

It was impossible for a moment to forget the sorrow that was impending over them. There were so many preparations to be made for his departure, that every instant something occurred to remind them of their sorrow. Venetia sat with tears in her eyes marking his new pocket-handkerchiefs which they had all gone to Southport to purchase, for Plantagenet asked, as a particular favour, that no one should mark them but Venetia. Then Lady Annabel gave Plantagenet a writing-case, and Venetia filled it with pens and paper, that he might never want means to communicate with them; and her evenings were passed in working him a purse, which Lady Annabel took care should be well stocked. All day long there seemed something going on to remind them of what was about to happen; and as for Pauncefort, she flounced in and out the room fifty times a day, with 'What is to be done about my lord's shirts, my lady? I think his lordship had better have another dozen, your la'ship. Better too much than too little, I always say;' or, 'O! my lady, your la'ship cannot form an idea of what a state my lord's stockings are in, my lady. I think I had better go over to Southport with John, my lady, and buy him some;' or, 'Please, my lady, did I understand your la'ship spoke to the tailor on Thursday about my lord's things? I suppose your la'ship knows my lord has got no great-coat?'

Every one of these inquiries made Venetia's heart tremble. Then there was the sad habit of dating every coming day by its distance from the fatal one. There was the last day but four, and the last day but three, and the last day but two. The last day but one at length arrived; and at length, too, though it seemed incredible, the last day itself.

Plantagenet and Venetia both rose very early, that they might make it as long as possible. They sighed involuntarily when they met, and then they went about to pay last visits to every creature and object of which they had been so long fond. Plantagenet went to bid farewell to the horses and adieu to the cows, and then walked down to the woodman's cottage, and then to shake hands with the keeper. He would not say 'Good-bye' to the household until the very last moment; and as for Marmion, the bloodhound, he accompanied both of them so faithfully in this melancholy ramble, and kept so close to both, that it was useless to break the sad intelligence to him yet.

'I think now, Venetia, we have been to see everything,' said Plantagenet, 'I shall see the peacocks at breakfast time. I wish Eton was near Cherbury, and then I could come home on Sunday. I cannot bear going to Cadurcis again, but I should like you to go once a week, and try to keep up our garden, and look after everything, though there is not much that will not take care of itself, except the garden. We made that together, and I could not bear its being neglected.'

Venetia could not assure him that no wish of his should be neglected, because she was weeping.

'I am glad the Doctor,' he continued, 'is going to take me to town. I should be very wretched by myself. But he will put me in mind of Cherbury, and we can talk together of Lady Annabel and you. Hark! the bell rings; we must go to breakfast, the last breakfast but one.'

Lady Annabel endeavoured, by unusual good spirits, to cheer up her little friends. She spoke of Plantagenet's speedy return so much as a matter of course, and the pleasant things they were to do when he came back, that she really succeeded in exciting a smile in Venetia's April face, for she was smiling amid tears.

Although it was the last day, time hung heavily on their hands. After breakfast they went over the house together; and Cadurcis, half with genuine feeling, and half in a spirit of mockery of their sorrow, made a speech to the inanimate walls, as if they were aware of his intended departure. At length, in their progress, they passed the door of the closed apartments, and here, holding Venetia's hand, he stopped, and, with an expression of irresistible humour, making a low bow to them, he said, very gravely, 'And good-bye rooms that I have never entered; perhaps, before I come back, Venetia will find out what is locked up in you!'

Dr. Masham arrived for dinner, and in a postchaise. The unusual conveyance reminded them of the morrow very keenly. Venetia could not bear to see the Doctor's portmanteau taken out and carried into the hall. She had hopes, until then, that something would happen and prevent all this misery. Cadurcis whispered her, 'I say, Venetia, do not you wish this was winter?'

'Why, Plantagenet?'

'Because then we might have a good snowstorm, and be blocked up again for a week.'

Venetia looked at the sky, but not a cloud was to be seen.

The Doctor was glad to warm himself at the hall-fire, for it was a fresh autumnal afternoon.

'Are you cold, sir?' said Venetia, approaching him.

'I am, my little maiden,' said the Doctor.

'Do you think there is any chance of its snowing, Doctor Masham?'

'Snowing! my little maiden; what can you be thinking of?'

The dinner was rather gayer than might have been expected. The Doctor was jocular, Lady Annabel lively, and Plantagenet excited by an extraordinary glass of wine. Venetia alone remained dispirited. The Doctor made mock speeches and proposed toasts, and told Plantagenet that he must learn to make speeches too, or what would he do when he was in the House of Lords? And then Plantagenet tried to make a speech, and proposed Venetia's health; and then Venetia, who could not bear to hear herself praised by him on such a day, the last day, burst into tears. Her mother called her to her side and consoled her, and Plantagenet jumped up and wiped her eyes with one of those very pocket-handkerchiefs on which she had embroidered his cipher and coronet with her own beautiful hair. Towards evening Plantagenet began to experience the reaction of his artificial spirits. The Doctor had fallen into a gentle slumber, Lady Annabel had quitted the room, Venetia sat with her hand in Plantagenet's on a stool by the fireside. Both were sad and silent. At last Venetia said, 'O Plantagenet, I wish I were your real sister! Perhaps, when I see you again, you will forget this,' and she turned the jewel that was suspended round her neck, and showed him the inscription.

'I am sure when I see you-again, Venetia,' he replied, 'the only difference will be, that I shall love you more than ever.'

'I hope so,' said Venetia.

'I am sure of it. Now remember what we are talking about. When we meet again, we shall see which of us two will love each other the most.'

'O Plantagenet, I hope they will be kind to you at Eton.'

'I will make them.'

'And, whenever you are the least unhappy, you will write to us?'

'I shall never be unhappy about anything but being away from you. As for the rest, I will make people respect me; I know what I am.'

'Because if they do not behave well to you, mamma could ask Dr. Masham to go and see you, and they will attend to him; and I would ask him too. I wonder,' she continued after a moment's pause, 'if you have everything you want. I am quite sure the instant you are gone, we shall remember something you ought to have; and then I shall be quite brokenhearted.'

'I have got everything.'

'You said you wanted a large knife.'

'Yes! but I am going to buy one in London. Dr. Masham says he will take me to a place where the finest knives in the world are to be bought. It is a great thing to go to London with Dr. Masham.'

'I have never written your name in your Bible and Prayer-book. I will do it this evening.'

'Lady Annabel is to write it in the Bible, and you are to write it in the Prayer-book.'

'You are to write to us from London by Dr. Masham, if only a line.'

'I shall not fail.'

'Never mind about your handwriting; but mind you write.'

At this moment Lady Annabel's step was heard, and Plantagenet said, 'Give me a kiss, Venetia, for I do not mean to bid good-bye to-night.'

'But you will not go to-morrow before we are up?'

'Yes, we shall.'

'Now, Plantagenet, I shall be up to bid you good-bye, mind that'

Lady Annabel entered, the Doctor woke, lights followed, the servant made up the fire, and the room looked cheerful again. After tea, the names were duly written in the Bible and Prayer-book; the last arrangements were made, all the baggage was brought down into the hall, all ransacked their memory and fancy, to see if it were possible that anything that Plantagenet could require was either forgotten or had been omitted. The clock struck ten; Lady Annabel rose. The travellers were to part at an early hour: she shook hands with Dr. Masham, but Cadurcis was to bid her farewell in her dressing-room, and then, with heavy hearts and glistening eyes, they all separated. And thus ended the last day!

CHAPTER XX.

Venetia passed a restless night. She was so resolved to be awake in time for Plantagenet's departure, that she could not sleep; and at length, towards morning, fell, from exhaustion, into a light slumber, from which she sprang up convulsively, roused by the sound of the wheels of the postchaise. She looked out of her window, and saw the servant strapping on the portmanteaus. Shortly after this she heard Plantagenet's step in the vestibule; he passed her room, and proceeded to her mother's dressing-room, at the door of which she heard him knock, and then there was silence.

'You are in good time,' said Lady Annabel, who was seated in an easy chair when Plantagenet entered her room. 'Is the Doctor up?'

'He is breakfasting.'

'And have you breakfasted?'

'I have no appetite.'

'You should take something, my child, before you go. Now, come hither, my dear Plantagenet,' she said, extending her hand; 'listen to me, one word. When you arrive in London, you will go to your guardian's. He is a great man, and I believe a very good one, and the law and your father's will have placed him in the position of a parent to you. You must therefore love, honour, and obey him; and I doubt not he will deserve all your affection, respect, and duty. Whatever he desires or counsels you will perform, and follow. So long as you act according to his wishes, you cannot be wrong. But, my dear Plantagenet, if by any chance it ever happens, for strange things sometimes happen in this world, that you are in trouble and require a friend, remember that Cherbury is also your home; the home of your heart, if not of the law; and that not merely from my own love for you, but because I promised your poor mother on her death-bed, I esteem myself morally, although not legally, in the light of a parent to you. You will find Eton a great change; you will experience many trials and temptations; but you will triumph over and withstand them all, if you will attend to these few directions. Fear God; morning and night let nothing induce you ever to omit your prayers to Him; you will find that praying will make you happy. Obey your superiors; always treat your masters with respect. Ever speak the truth. So long as you adhere to this rule, you never can be involved in any serious misfortune. A deviation from truth is, in general, the foundation of all misery. Be kind to your companions, but be firm. Do not be laughed into doing that which you know to be wrong. Be modest and humble, but ever respect yourself. Remember who you are, and also that it is your duty to excel. Providence has given you a great lot. Think ever that you are born to perform great duties.

'God bless you, Plantagenet!' she continued, after a slight pause, with a faltering voice, 'God bless you, my sweet child. And God will bless you if you remember Him. Try also to remember us,' she added, as she embraced him, and placed in his hand Venetia's well-lined purse. 'Do not forget Cherbury and all it contains; hearts that love you dearly, and will pray ever for your welfare.'

Plantagenet leant upon her bosom. He had entered the room resolved to be composed, with an air even of cheerfulness, but his tender heart yielded to the first appeal to his affections. He could only murmur out some broken syllables of devotion, and almost unconsciously found that he had quitted the chamber.

With streaming eyes and hesitating steps he was proceeding along the vestibule, when he heard his name called by a low sweet voice. He looked around; it was Venetia. Never had he beheld such a beautiful vision. She was muffled up in her dressing-gown, her small white feet only guarded from the cold by her slippers. Her golden hair seemed to reach her waist, her cheek was flushed, her large blue eyes glittered with tears.

'Plantagenet,' she said—

Neither of them could speak. They embraced, they mingled their tears together, and every instant they wept more plenteously. At length a footstep was heard; Venetia murmured a blessing, and vanished.

Cadurcis lingered on the stairs a moment to compose himself. He wiped his eyes; he tried to look undisturbed. All the servants were in the hall; from Mistress Pauncefort to the scullion there was not a dry eye. All loved the little lord, he was so gracious and so gentle. Every one asked leave to touch his hand before he went. He tried to smile and say something kind to all. He recognised the gamekeeper, and told him to do what he liked at Cadurcis; said something to the coachman about his pony; and begged Mistress Pauncefort, quite aloud, to take great care of her young mistress. As he was speaking, he felt something rubbing against his hand: it was Marmion, the old bloodhound. He also came to bid his adieus. Cadurcis patted him with affection, and said, 'Ah! my old fellow, we shall yet meet again.'

The Doctor appeared, smiling as usual, made his inquiries whether all were right, nodded to the weeping household, called Plantagenet his brave boy, and patted him on the back, and bade him jump into the chaise. Another moment, and Dr. Masham had also entered; the door was closed, the fatal 'All right' sung out, and Lord Cadurcis was whirled away from that Cherbury where he was so loved.

BOOK II.

CHAPTER I.

Life is not dated merely by years. Events are sometimes the best calendars. There are epochs in our existence which cannot be ascertained by a formal appeal to the registry. The arrival of the Cadurcis family at their old abbey, their consequent intimacy at Cherbury, the death of the mother, and the departure of the son: these were events which had been crowded into a space of less than two years; but those two years were not only the most eventful in the life of Venetia Herbert, but in their influence upon the development of her mind, and the formation of her character, far exceeded the effects of all her previous existence.

Venetia once more found herself with no companion but her mother, but in vain she attempted to recall the feelings she had before experienced under such circumstances, and to revert to the resources she had before commanded. No longer could she wander in imaginary kingdoms, or transform the limited world of her experience into a boundless region of enchanted amusement. Her play-pleasure hours were fled for ever. She sighed for her faithful and sympathising companion. The empire of fancy yielded without a struggle to the conquering sway of memory.

For the first few weeks Venetia was restless and dispirited, and when she was alone she often wept. A mysterious instinct prompted her, however, not to exhibit such emotion before her mother. Yet she loved to hear Lady Annabel talk of Plantagenet, and a visit to the abbey was ever her favourite walk. Sometimes, too, a letter arrived from Lord Cadurcis, and this was great joy; but such communications were rare. Nothing is more difficult than for a junior boy at a public school to maintain a correspondence; yet his letters were most affectionate, and always dwelt upon the prospect of his return. The period for this hoped-for return at length arrived, but it brought no Plantagenet. His guardian wished that the holidays should be spent under his roof. Still at intervals Cadurcis wrote to Cherbury, to which, as time flew on, it seemed destined he never was to return. Vacation followed vacation, alike passed with his guardian, either in London, or at a country seat still more remote from Cherbury, until at length it became so much a matter of course that his guardian's house should be esteemed his home, that Plantagenet ceased to allude even to the prospect of return. In time his letters became rarer and rarer, until, at length, they altogether ceased. Meanwhile Venetia had overcome the original pang of separation; if not as gay as in old days, she was serene and very studious; delighting less in her flowers and birds, but much more in her books, and pursuing her studies with an earnestness and assiduity which her mother was rather fain to check than to encourage. Venetia Herbert, indeed, promised to become a most accomplished woman. She had a fine ear for music, a ready tongue for languages; already she emulated her mother's skill in the arts; while the library of Cherbury afforded welcome and inexhaustible resources to a girl whose genius deserved the richest and most sedulous cultivation, and whose peculiar situation, independent of her studious predisposition, rendered reading a pastime to her rather than a task. Lady Annabel watched the progress of her daughter with lively interest, and spared no efforts to assist the formation of her principles and her taste. That deep religious feeling which was the characteristic of the mother had been carefully and early cherished in the heart of the child, and in time the unrivalled writings of the great divines of our Church became a principal portion of her reading. Order, method, severe study, strict religious exercise, with no amusement or relaxation but of the most simple and natural character, and with a complete seclusion from society, altogether formed a system, which, acting upon a singularly susceptible and gifted nature, secured the promise in Venetia Herbert, at fourteen years of age, of an extraordinary woman; a system, however, against which her lively and somewhat restless mind might probably have rebelled, had not that system been so thoroughly imbued with all the melting spell of maternal affection. It was the inspiration of this sacred love that hovered like a guardian angel over the life of Venetia. It roused her from her morning slumbers with an embrace, it sanctified her evening pillow with a blessing; it anticipated the difficulty of the student's page, and guided the faltering hand of the hesitating artist; it refreshed her memory, it modulated her voice; it accompanied her in the cottage, and knelt by her at the altar. Marvellous and beautiful is a mother's love. And when Venetia, with her strong feelings and enthusiastic spirit, would look around and mark that a graceful form and a bright eye were for ever watching over her wants and wishes, instructing with sweetness, and soft even with advice, her whole soul rose to her mother, all thoughts and feelings were concentrated in that sole existence, and she desired no happier destiny than to pass through life living in the light of her mother's smiles, and clinging with passionate trust to that beneficent and guardian form.

But with all her quick and profound feelings Venetia was thoughtful and even shrewd, and when she was alone her very love for her mother, and her gratitude for such an ineffable treasure as parental affection, would force her mind to a subject which at intervals had haunted her even from her earliest childhood. Why had she only one parent? What mystery was this that enveloped that great tie? For that there was a mystery Venetia felt as assured as that she was a daughter. By a process which she could not analyse, her father had become a forbidden subject. True, Lady Annabel had placed no formal prohibition upon its mention; nor at her present age was Venetia one who would be influenced in her conduct by the bygone and arbitrary intimations of a menial; nevertheless, that the mention of her father would afford pain to the being she loved best in the world, was a conviction which had grown with her years and strengthened with her strength. Pardonable, natural, even laudable as was the anxiety of the daughter upon such a subject, an instinct with which she could not struggle closed the lips of Venetia for ever upon this topic. His name was never mentioned, his past existence was never alluded to. Who was he? That he was of noble family and great position her name betokened, and the state in which they lived. He must have died very early; perhaps even before her mother gave her birth. A dreadful lot indeed; and yet was the grief that even such a dispensation might occasion, so keen, so overwhelming, that after fourteen long years his name might not be permitted, even for an instant, to pass the lips of his bereaved wife? Was his child to be deprived of the only solace for his loss, the consolation of cherishing his memory? Strange, passing strange indeed, and bitter! At Cherbury the family of Herbert were honoured only from tradition. Until the arrival of Lady Annabel, as we have before mentioned, they had not resided at the hall for more than half a century. There were no old retainers there from whom Venetia might glean, without suspicion, the information for which she panted. Slight, too, as was Venetia's experience of society, there were times when she could not resist the impression that her mother was not happy; that there was some secret sorrow that weighed upon her spirit, some grief that gnawed at her heart. Could it be still the recollection of her lost sire? Could one so religious, so resigned, so assured of meeting the lost one in a better world, brood with a repining soul over the will of her Creator? Such conduct was entirely at variance with all the tenets of Lady Annabel. It was not thus she consoled the bereaved, that she comforted the widow, and solaced the orphan. Venetia, too, observed everything and forgot nothing. Not an incident of her earliest childhood that was not as fresh in her memory as if it had occurred yesterday. Her memory was naturally keen; living in solitude, with nothing to distract it, its impressions never faded away. She had never forgotten her mother's tears the day that she and Plantagenet had visited Marringhurst. Somehow or other Dr. Masham seemed connected with this sorrow. Whenever Lady Annabel was most dispirited it was after an interview with that gentleman; yet the presence of the Doctor always gave her pleasure, and he was the most kind-hearted and cheerful of men. Perhaps, after all, it was only her illusion; perhaps, after all, it was the memory of her father to which her mother was devoted, and which occasionally overcame her; perhaps she ventured to speak of him to Dr. Masham, though not to her daughter, and this might account for that occasional agitation which Venetia had observed at his visits. And yet, and yet, and yet; in vain she reasoned. There is a strange sympathy which whispers convictions that no evidence can authorise, and no arguments dispel. Venetia Herbert, particularly as she grew older, could not refrain at times from yielding to the irresistible belief that her existence was enveloped in some mystery. Mystery too often presupposes the idea of guilt. Guilt! Who was guilty? Venetia shuddered at the current of her own thoughts. She started from the garden seat in which she had fallen into this dangerous and painful reverie; flew to her mother, who received her with smiles; and buried her face in the bosom of Lady Annabel.

CHAPTER II.

We have indicated in a few pages the progress of three years. How differently passed to the two preceding ones, when the Cadurcis family were settled at the abbey! For during this latter period it seemed that not a single incident had occurred. They had glided away in one unbroken course of study, religion, and domestic love, the enjoyment of nature, and the pursuits of charity; like a long summer sabbath-day, sweet and serene and still, undisturbed by a single passion, hallowed and hallowing.

If the Cadurcis family were now not absolutely forgotten at Cherbury, they were at least only occasionally remembered. These last three years so completely harmonised with the life of Venetia before their arrival, that, taking a general view of her existence, their residence at the abbey figured only as an episode in her career; active indeed and stirring, and one that had left some impressions not easily discarded; but, on the whole, mellowed by the magic of time, Venetia looked back to her youthful friendship as an event that was only an exception in her lot, and she viewed herself as a being born and bred up in a seclusion which she was never to quit, with no aspirations beyond the little world in which she moved, and where she was to die in peace, as she had lived in purity.

One Sunday, the conversation after dinner fell upon Lord Cadurcis. Doctor Masham had recently met a young Etonian, and had made some inquiries about their friend of old days. The information he had obtained was not very satisfactory. It seemed that Cadurcis was a more popular boy with his companions than his tutors; he had been rather unruly, and had only escaped expulsion by the influence of his guardian, who was not only a great noble, but a powerful minister.

This conversation recalled old times. They talked over the arrival of Mrs. Cadurcis at the abbey, her strange character, her untimely end. Lady Annabel expressed her conviction of the natural excellence of Plantagenet's disposition, and her regret of the many disadvantages under which he laboured; it gratified Venetia to listen to his praise.

'He has quite forgotten us, mamma,' said Venetia.

'My love, he was very young when he quitted us,' replied Lady Annabel; 'and you must remember the influence of a change of life at so tender an age. He lives now in a busy world.'

'I wish that he had not forgotten to write to us sometimes,' said Venetia.

'Writing a letter is a great achievement for a schoolboy,' said the Doctor; 'it is a duty which even grown-up persons too often forget to fulfil, and, when postponed, it is generally deferred for ever. However, I agree with Lady Annabel, Cadurcis was a fine fellow, and had he been properly brought up, I cannot help thinking, might have turned out something.'

'Poor Plantagenet!' said Venetia, 'how I pity him. His was a terrible lot, to lose both his parents! Whatever were the errors of Mrs. Cadurcis, she was his mother, and, in spite of every mortification, he clung to her. Ah! I shall never forget when Pauncefort met him coming out of her room the night before the burial, when he said, with streaming eyes, "I only had one friend in the world, and now she is gone." I could not love Mrs. Cadurcis, and yet, when I heard of these words, I cried as much as he.'

'Poor fellow!' said the Doctor, filling his glass.

'If there be any person in the world whom I pity,' said Venetia, "tis an orphan. Oh! what should I be without mamma? And Plantagenet, poor Plantagenet! he has no mother, no father.' Venetia added, with a faltering voice: 'I can sympathise with him in some degree; I, I, I know, I feel the misfortune, the misery;' her face became crimson, yet she could not restrain the irresistible words, 'the misery of never having known a father,' she added.

There was a dead pause, a most solemn silence. In vain Venetia struggled to look calm and unconcerned; every instant she felt the blood mantling in her cheek with a more lively and spreading agitation. She dared not look up; it was not possible to utter a word to turn the conversation. She felt utterly confounded and absolutely mute. At length, Lady Annabel spoke. Her tone was severe and choking, very different to her usual silvery voice.

'I am sorry that my daughter should feel so keenly the want of a parent's love,' said her ladyship.

What would not Venetia have given for the power or speech! but it seemed to have deserted her for ever. There she sat mute and motionless, with her eyes fixed on the table, and with a burning cheek, as if she were conscious of having committed some act of shame, as if she had been detected in some base and degrading deed. Yet, what had she done? A daughter had delicately alluded to her grief at the loss of a parent, and expressed her keen sense of the deprivation.

It was an autumnal afternoon: Doctor Masham looked at the sky, and, after a long pause, made an observation about the weather, and then requested permission to order his horses, as the evening came on apace, and he had some distance to ride. Lady Annabel rose; the Doctor, with a countenance unusually serious, offered her his arm; and Venetia followed them like a criminal. In a few minutes the horses appeared; Lady Annabel bid adieu to her friend in her usual kind tone, and with her usual sweet smile; and then, without noticing Venetia, instantly retired to her own chamber.

And this was her mother; her mother who never before quitted her for an instant without some sign and symbol of affection, some playful word of love, a winning smile, a passing embrace, that seemed to acknowledge that the pang of even momentary separation could only be alleviated by this graceful homage to the heart. What had she done? Venetia was about to follow Lady Annabel, but she checked herself. Agony at having offended her mother, and, for the first time, was blended with a strange curiosity as to the cause, and some hesitating indignation at her treatment. Venetia remained anxiously awaiting the return of Lady Annabel; but her ladyship did not reappear. Every instant, the astonishment and the grief of Venetia increased. It was the first domestic difference that had occurred between them. It shocked her much. She thought of Plantagenet and Mrs. Cadurcis. There was a mortifying resemblance, however slight, between the respective situations of the two families. Venetia, too, had quarrelled with her mother; that mother who, for fourteen years, had only looked upon her with fondness and joy; who had been ever kind, without being ever weak, and had rendered her child happy by making her good; that mother whose beneficent wisdom had transformed duty into delight; that superior, yet gentle being, so indulgent yet so just, so gifted yet so condescending, who dedicated all her knowledge, and time, and care, and intellect to her daughter.

Venetia threw herself upon a couch and wept. They were the first tears of unmixed pain that she had ever shed. It was said by the household of Venetia when a child, that she had never cried; not a single tear had ever sullied that sunny face. Surrounded by scenes of innocence, and images of happiness and content, Venetia smiled on a world that smiled on her, the radiant heroine of a golden age. She had, indeed, wept over the sorrows and the departure of Cadurcis; but those were soft showers of sympathy and affection sent from a warm heart, like drops from a summer sky. But now this grief was agony: her brow throbbed, her hand was clenched, her heart beat with tumultuous palpitation; the streaming torrent came scalding down her cheek like fire rather than tears, and instead of assuaging her emotion, seemed, on the contrary, to increase its fierce and fervid power.

The sun had set, the red autumnal twilight had died away, the shadows of night were brooding over the halls of Cherbury. The moan of the rising wind might be distinctly heard, and ever and anon the branches of neighbouring trees swung with a sudden yet melancholy sound against the windows of the apartment, of which the curtains had remained undrawn. Venetia looked up; the room would have been in perfect darkness but for a glimmer which just indicated the site of the expiring fire, and an uncertain light, or rather modified darkness, that seemed the sky. Alone and desolate! Alone and desolate and unhappy! Alone and desolate and unhappy, and for the first time! Was it a sigh, or a groan, that issued from the stifling heart of Venetia

Herbert? That child of innocence, that bright emanation of love and beauty, that airy creature of grace and gentleness, who had never said an unkind word or done an unkind thing in her whole career, but had glanced and glided through existence, scattering happiness and joy, and receiving the pleasure which she herself imparted, how overwhelming was her first struggle with that dark stranger, Sorrow!

Some one entered the room; it was Mistress Pauncefort. She held a taper in her hand, and came tripping gingerly in, with a new cap streaming with ribands, and scarcely, as it were, condescending to execute the mission with which she was intrusted, which was no greater than fetching her lady's reticule. She glanced at the table, but it was not there; she turned up her nose at a chair or two, which she even condescended to propel a little with a saucy foot, as if the reticule might be hid under the hanging drapery, and then, unable to find the object of her search, Mistress Pauncefort settled herself before the glass, elevating the taper above her head, that she might observe what indeed she had been examining the whole day, the effect of her new cap. With a complacent simper, Mistress Pauncefort then turned from pleasure to business, and, approaching the couch, gave a faint shriek, half genuine, half affected, as she recognised the recumbent form of her young mistress. 'Well to be sure,' exclaimed Mistress Pauncefort, 'was the like ever seen! Miss Venetia, as I live! La! Miss Venetia, what can be the matter? I declare I am all of a palpitation.'

Venetia, affecting composure, said she was rather unwell; that she had a headache, and, rising, murmured that she would go to bed. 'A headache!' exclaimed Mistress Pauncefort, 'I hope no worse, for there is my lady, and she is as out of sorts as possible. She has a headache too; and when I shut the door just now, I am sure as quiet as a lamb, she told me not to make so much noise when I left the room. "Noise!" says I; "why really, my lady, I don't pretend to be a spirit; but if it comes to noise—" "Never answer me, Pauncefort," says my lady. "No, my lady," says I, "I never do, and, I am sure, when I have a headache myself, I don't like to be answered." But, to be sure, if you have a headache, and my lady has a headache too, I only hope we have not got the epidemy. I vow, Miss Venetia, that your eyes are as red as if you had been running against the wind. Well, to be sure, if you have not been crying! I must go and tell my lady immediately.'

'Light me to my room,' said Venetia; 'I will not disturb my mother, as she is unwell.'

Venetia rose, and Mistress Pauncefort followed her to her chamber, and lit her candles. Venetia desired her not to remain; and when she had quitted the chamber, Venetia threw herself in her chair and sighed.

To sleep, it was impossible; it seemed to Venetia that she could never rest again. She wept no more, but her distress was very great. She felt it impossible to exist through the night without being reconciled to her mother; but she refrained from going to her room, from the fear of again meeting her troublesome attendant. She resolved, therefore, to wait until she heard Mistress Pauncefort retire for the night, and she listened with restless anxiety for the sign of her departure in the sound of her footsteps along the vestibule on which the doors of Lady Annabel's and her daughter's apartments opened.

An hour elapsed, and at length the sound was heard. Convinced that Pauncefort had now quitted her mother for the night, Venetia ventured forth, and stopping before the door of her mother's room, she knocked gently. There was no reply, and in a few minutes Venetia knocked again, and rather louder. Still no answer. 'Mamma,' said Venetia, in a faltering tone, but no sound replied. Venetia then tried the door, and found it fastened. Then she gave up the effort in despair, and retreating to her own chamber, she threw herself on her bed, and wept bitterly.

Some time elapsed before she looked up again; the candles were flaring in their sockets. It was a wild windy night; Venetia rose, and withdrew the curtain of her window. The black clouds were scudding along the sky, revealing, in their occasional but transient rifts, some glimpses of the moon, that seemed unusually bright, or of a star that trembled with supernatural brilliancy. She stood a while gazing on the outward scene that harmonised with her own internal agitation: her grief was like the storm, her love like the light of that bright moon and star. There came over her a desire to see her mother, which she felt irresistible; she was resolved that no difficulty, no impediment, should prevent her instantly from throwing herself on her bosom. It seemed to her that her brain would burn, that this awful night could never end without such an interview. She opened her door, went forth again into the vestibule, and approached with a nervous but desperate step her mother's chamber. To her astonishment the door was ajar, but there was a light within. With trembling step and downcast eyes, Venetia entered the chamber, scarcely daring to advance, or to look up.

'Mother,' she said, but no one answered; she heard the tick of the clock; it was the only sound. 'Mother,' she repeated, and she dared to look up, but the bed was empty. There was no mother. Lady Annabel was not in the room. Following an irresistible impulse, Venetia knelt by the side of her mother's bed and prayed. She addressed, in audible and agitated tones, that Almighty and Beneficent Being of whom she was so faithful and pure a follower. With sanctified simplicity, she communicated to her Creator and her Saviour all her distress, all her sorrow, all the agony of her perplexed and wounded spirit. If she had sinned, she prayed for forgiveness, and declared in solitude, to One whom she could not deceive, how unintentional was the trespass; if she were only misapprehended, she supplicated for comfort and consolation, for support under the heaviest visitation she had yet experienced, the displeasure of that earthly parent whom she revered only second to her heavenly Father.

'For thou art my Father,' said Venetia, 'I have no other father but thee, O God! Forgive me, then, my heavenly parent, if in my wilfulness, if in my thoughtless and sinful blindness, I have sighed for a father on earth, as well as in heaven! Great have thy mercies been to me, O God! in a mother's love. Turn, then, again to me the heart of that mother whom I have offended! Let her look upon her child as before; let her continue to me a double parent, and let me pay to her the duty and the devotion that might otherwise have been divided!'

'Amen!' said a sweet and solemn voice; and Venetia was clasped in her mother's arms.

CHAPTER III.

If the love of Lady Annabel for her child were capable of increase, it might have been believed that it absolutely became more profound and ardent after that short-lived but painful estrangement which we have related in the last chapter. With all Lady Annabel's fascinating qualities and noble virtues, a fine observer of human nature enjoying opportunities of intimately studying her character, might have suspected that an occasion only was wanted to display or develop in that lady's conduct no trifling evidence of a haughty, proud, and even inexorable spirit. Circumstanced as she was at Cherbury, with no one capable or desirous of disputing her will, the more gracious and exalted qualities of her nature were alone apparent. Entertaining a severe, even a sublime sense of the paramount claims of duty in all conditions and circumstances of life, her own conduct afforded an invariable and consistent example of her tenet; from those around her she required little, and that was cheerfully granted; while, on the other hand, her more eminent situation alike multiplied her own obligations and enabled her to fulfil them; she appeared, therefore, to pass her life in conferring happiness and in receiving gratitude. Strictly religious, of immaculate reputation, rigidly just, systematically charitable, dignified in her manners, yet more than courteous to her inferiors, and gifted at the same time with great self-control and great decision, she was looked up to by all within her sphere with a sentiment of affectionate veneration. Perhaps there was only one person within her little world who, both by disposition and relative situation, was qualified in any way to question her undoubted sway, or to cross by independence of opinion the tenour of the discipline she had established, and this was her child. Venetia, with one of the most affectionate and benevolent natures in the world, was gifted with a shrewd, inquiring mind, and a restless imagination. She was capable of forming her own opinions, and had both reason and feeling at command to gauge their worth. But to gain an influence over this child had been the sole object of Lady Annabel's life, and she had hitherto met that success which usually awaits in this world the strong purpose of a determined spirit. Lady Annabel herself was far too acute a person not to have detected early in life the talents of her child, and she was proud of them. She had cultivated them with exemplary devotion and with admirable profit. But Lady Annabel had not less discovered that, in the ardent and susceptible temperament of Venetia, means were offered by which the heart might be trained not only to cope with but overpower the intellect. With great powers of pleasing, beauty, accomplishments, a sweet voice, a soft manner, a sympathetic heart, Lady Annabel was qualified to charm the world; she had contrived to fascinate her daughter. She had inspired Venetia with the most romantic attachment for her: such as rather subsists between two female friends of the same age and hearts, than between individuals in the relative situations which they bore to each other. Yet while Venetia thus loved her mother, she could not but also respect and revere the superior being whose knowledge was her guide on all subjects, and whose various accomplishments deprived her secluded education of all its disadvantages; and when she felt that one so gifted had devoted her life to the benefit of her child, and that this beautiful and peerless lady had no other ambition but to be her guardian and attendant spirit; gratitude, fervent and profound, mingled with admiring reverence and passionate affection, and together formed a spell that encircled the mind of Venetia with talismanic sway.

Under the despotic influence of these enchanted feelings, Venetia was fast growing into womanhood, without a single cloud having ever disturbed or sullied the pure and splendid heaven of her domestic life. Suddenly the horizon had become clouded, a storm had gathered and burst, and an eclipse could scarcely have occasioned more terror to the untutored roamer of the wilderness, than this unexpected catastrophe to one so inexperienced in the power of the passions as our heroine. Her heaven was again serene; but such was the effect of this ebullition on her character, so keen was her dread of again encountering the agony of another misunderstanding with her mother, that she recoiled with trembling from that subject which had so often and so deeply engaged her secret thoughts; and the idea of her father, associated as it now was with pain, mortification, and misery, never rose to her imagination but instantly to be shunned as some unhallowed image, of which the bitter contemplation was fraught with not less disastrous consequences than the denounced idolatry of the holy people.

Whatever, therefore, might be the secret reasons which impelled Lady Annabel to shroud the memory of the lost parent of her child in such inviolate gloom, it is certain that the hitherto restless though concealed curiosity of Venetia upon the subject, the rash demonstration to which it led, and the consequence of her boldness, instead of threatening to destroy in an instant the deep and matured system of her mother, had, on the whole, greatly contributed to the fulfilment of the very purpose for which Lady Annabel had so long laboured. That lady spared no pains in following up the advantage which her acuteness and knowledge of her daughter's character assured her that she had secured. She hovered round her child more like an enamoured lover than a fond mother; she hung upon her looks, she read her thoughts, she anticipated every want and wish; her dulcet tones seemed even sweeter than before; her soft and elegant manners even more tender and refined. Though even in her childhood Lady Annabel had rather guided than commanded Venetia; now she rather consulted than guided her. She seized advantage of the advanced character and mature appearance of Venetia to treat her as a woman rather than a child, and as a friend rather than a daughter. Venetia yielded herself up to this flattering and fascinating condescension. Her love for her mother amounted to passion; she had no other earthly object or desire but to pass her entire life in her sole and sweet society; she could conceive no sympathy deeper or more delightful; the only unhappiness she had ever known had been occasioned by a moment trenching upon its exclusive privilege; Venetia could not picture to herself that such a pure and entrancing existence could ever experience a change.

And this mother, this devoted yet mysterious mother, jealous of her child's regret for a father that she had lost, and whom she had never known! shall we ever penetrate the secret of her heart?

CHAPTER IV.

It was in the enjoyment of these exquisite feelings that a year, and more than another year, elapsed at our lone hall of Cherbury. Happiness and content seemed at least the blessed destiny of the Herberts. Venetia grew in years, and grace, and loveliness; each day apparently more her mother's joy, and each day bound to that mother by, if possible, more ardent love. She had never again experienced those uneasy thoughts which at times had haunted her from her infancy; separated from her mother, indeed, scarcely for an hour together, she had no time to muse. Her studies each day becoming more various and interesting, and pursued with so gifted and charming a companion, entirely engrossed her; even the exercise that was her relaxation was participated by Lady Annabel; and the mother and daughter, bounding together on their steeds, were fanned by the same breeze, and freshened by the same graceful and healthy exertion.

One day the post, that seldom arrived at Cherbury, brought a letter to Lady Annabel, the perusal of which evidently greatly agitated her. Her countenance changed as her eye glanced over the pages; her hand trembled as she held it. But she made no remark; and succeeded in subduing her emotion so quickly that Venetia, although she watched her mother with anxiety, did not feel justified in interfering with inquiring sympathy. But while Lady Annabel resumed her usual calm demeanour, she relapsed into unaccustomed silence, and, soon rising from the breakfast table, moved to the window, and continued apparently gazing on the garden, with her face averted from Venetia for some time. At length she turned to her, and said, 'I think, Venetia, of calling on the Doctor to-day; there is business on which I wish to consult him, but I will not trouble you, dearest, to accompany me. I must take the carriage, and it is a long and tiring drive.'

There was a tone of decision even in the slightest observations of Lady Annabel, which, however sweet might be the voice in which they were uttered, scarcely encouraged their propriety to be canvassed. Now Venetia was far from desirous of being separated from her mother this morning. It was not a vain and idle curiosity, prompted by the receipt of the letter and its consequent effects, both in the emotion of her mother and the visit which it had rendered necessary, that swayed her breast. The native dignity of a well-disciplined mind exempted Venetia from such feminine weakness. But some consideration might be due to the quick sympathy of an affectionate spirit that had witnessed, with corresponding feeling, the disturbance of the being to whom she was devoted. Why this occasional and painful mystery that ever and anon clouded the heaven of their love, and flung a frigid shadow over the path of a sunshiny life? Why was not Venetia to share the sorrow or the care of her only friend, as well as participate in her joy and her content? There were other claims, too, to this confidence, besides those of the heart. Lady Annabel was not merely her only friend; she was her parent, her only parent, almost, for aught she had ever heard or learnt, her only relative. For her mother's family, though she was aware of their existence by the freedom with which Lady Annabel ever mentioned them, and though Venetia was conscious that an occasional correspondence was maintained between them and Cherbury, occupied no station in Venetia's heart, scarcely in her memory. That noble family were nullities to her; far distant, apparently estranged from her hearth, except in form she had never seen them; they were associated in her recollection with none of the sweet ties of kindred. Her grandfather was dead without her ever having received his blessing; his successor, her uncle, was an ambassador, long absent from his country; her only aunt married to a soldier, and established at a foreign station. Venetia envied Dr. Masham the confidence which was extended to him; it seemed to her, even leaving out of sight the intimate feelings that subsisted between her and her mother, that the claims of blood to this confidence were at least as strong as those of friendship. But Venetia stifled these emotions; she parted from her mother with a kind, yet somewhat mournful expression. Lady Annabel might have read a slight sentiment of affectionate reproach in the demeanour of her daughter when she bade her farewell. Whatever might be the consciousness of the mother, she was successful in concealing her impression. Very kind, but calm and inscrutable, Lady Annabel, having given directions for postponing the dinner-hour, embraced her child and entered the chariot.

Venetia, from the terrace, watched her mother's progress through the park. After gazing for some minutes, a tear stole down her cheek. She started, as if surprised at her own emotion. And now the carriage was out of sight, and Venetia would have recurred to some of those resources which were ever at hand for the employment or amusement of her secluded life. But the favourite volume ceased to interest this morning, and almost fell from her hand. She tried her spinet, but her ear seemed to have lost its music; she looked at her easel, but the cunning had fled from her touch.

Restless and disquieted, she knew not why, Venetia went forth again into the garden. All nature smiled around her; the flitting birds were throwing their soft shadows over the sunny lawns, and rustling amid the blossoms of the variegated groves. The golden wreaths of the laburnum and the silver knots of the chestnut streamed and glittered around; the bees were as busy as the birds, and the whole scene was suffused and penetrated with brilliancy and odour. It still was spring, and yet the gorgeous approach of summer, like the advancing procession of some triumphant king, might almost be detected amid the lingering freshness of the year; a lively and yet magnificent period, blending, as it were, Attic grace with Roman splendour; a time when hope and fruition for once meet, when existence is most full of delight, alike delicate and voluptuous, and when the human frame is most sensible to the gaiety and grandeur of nature.

And why was not the spirit of the beautiful and innocent Venetia as bright as the surrounding scene? There are moods of mind that baffle analysis, that arise from a mysterious sympathy we cannot penetrate. At this moment the idea of her father irresistibly recurred to the imagination of Venetia. She could not withstand the conviction that the receipt of the mysterious letter and her mother's agitation were by some inexplicable connexion linked with that forbidden subject. Strange incidents of her life flitted across her memory: her mother weeping on the day they visited Marringhurst; the mysterious chambers; the nocturnal visit of Lady Annabel that Cadurcis had witnessed; her unexpected absence from her apartment when Venetia, in her despair, had visited her some months ago. What was the secret that enveloped her existence? Alone, which was unusual; dispirited, she knew not why; and brooding over thoughts which haunted her like evil spirits, Venetia at length yielded to a degree of nervous excitement which amazed her. She looked up to the uninhabited wing of the mansion with an almost fierce desire to penetrate its mysteries. It seemed to her that a strange voice came whispering on the breeze, urging her to the fulfilment of a mystical mission. With a vague, yet wild, purpose she entered the house, and took her way to her mother's chamber. Mistress Pauncefort was there. Venetia endeavoured to assume her accustomed serenity. The waiting-woman bustled about, arranging the toilet-table, which had been for a moment discomposed, putting away a cap, folding up a shawl, and indulging in a multitude of inane observations which little harmonised with the high-strung tension of Venetia's mind. Mistress Pauncefort opened a casket with a spring lock, in which she placed some trinkets of her mistress. Venetia stood by her in silence; her eye, vacant and wandering, beheld the interior of the casket. There must have been something in it, the sight of which greatly agitated her, for Venetia turned pale, and in a moment left the chamber and retired to her own room.

She locked her door, threw herself in a chair; almost gasping for breath, she covered her face with her hands. It was some minutes before she recovered comparative composure; she rose and looked in the mirror; her face was quite white, but her eyes glittering with excitement. She walked up and down her room with a troubled step, and a scarlet flush alternately returned to and retired from her changing cheek. Then she leaned against a cabinet in thought. She was disturbed from her musings by the sound of Pauncefort's step along the vestibule, as she quitted her mother's chamber. In a few minutes Venetia herself stepped forth into the vestibule and listened. All was silent. The golden morning had summoned the whole household to its enjoyment. Not a voice, not a domestic sound, broke the complete stillness.

Venetia again repaired to the apartment of Lady Annabel. Her step was light, but agitated; it seemed that she scarcely dared to breathe. She opened the door, rushed to the cabinet, pressed the spring lock, caught at something that it contained, and hurried again to her own chamber.

And what is this prize that the trembling Venetia holds almost convulsively in her grasp, apparently without daring even to examine it? Is this the serene and light-hearted girl, whose face was like the cloudless splendour of a sunny day? Why is she so pallid and perturbed? What strong impulse fills her frame? She clutches in her hand a key!

On that tempestuous night of passionate sorrow which succeeded the first misunderstanding between Venetia and her mother, when the voice of Lady Annabel had suddenly blended with that of her kneeling child, and had ratified with her devotional concurrence her wailing supplications; even at the moment when Venetia, in a rapture of love and duty, felt herself pressed to her mother's reconciled heart, it had not escaped her that Lady Annabel held in her hand a key; and though the feelings which that night had so forcibly developed, and which the subsequent conduct of Lady Annabel had so carefully and skilfully cherished, had impelled Venetia to banish and erase from her thought and memory all the associations which that spectacle, however slight, was calculated to awaken, still, in her present mood, the unexpected vision of the same instrument, identical she could not doubt, had triumphed in an instant over all the long discipline of her mind and conduct, in an instant had baffled and dispersed her self-control, and been hailed as the providential means by which she might at length penetrate that mystery which she now felt no longer supportable.

The clock of the belfry of Cherbury at this moment struck, and Venetia instantly sprang from her seat. It reminded her of the preciousness of the present morning. Her mother was indeed absent, but her mother would return. Before that event a great fulfilment was to occur. Venetia, still grasping the key, as if it were the talisman of her existence, looked up to Heaven as if she required for her allotted task an immediate and special protection; her lips seemed to move, and then she again quitted her apartment. As she passed through an oriel in her way towards the gallery, she observed Pauncefort in the avenue of the park, moving in the direction of the keeper's lodge. This emboldened her. With a hurried step she advanced along the gallery, and at length stood before the long-sealed door that had so often excited her strange curiosity. Once she looked around; but no one was near, not a sound was heard. With a faltering hand she touched the lock; but her powers deserted her: for a minute she believed that the key, after all, would not solve the mystery. And yet the difficulty arose only from her own agitation. She rallied her courage; once more she made the trial; the key fitted with completeness, and the lock opened with ease, and Venetia found herself in a small and scantily-furnished ante-chamber. Closing the door with noiseless care, Venetia stood trembling in the mysterious chamber, where apparently there was nothing to excite wonder. The chamber into which the ante-room opened was still closed, and it was some minutes before the adventurous daughter of Lady Annabel could summon courage for the enterprise which awaited her.

The door yielded without an effort. Venetia stepped into a spacious and lofty chamber. For a moment she paused almost upon the threshold, and looked around her with a vague and misty vision. Anon she distinguished something of the character of the apartment. In the recess of a large oriel window that looked upon the park, and of which the blinds were nearly drawn, was an old-fashioned yet sumptuous toilet-table of considerable size, arranged as if for use. Opposite this window, in a corresponding recess, was what might be deemed a bridal bed, its furniture being of white satin richly embroidered; the curtains half closed; and suspended from the canopy was a wreath of roses that had once emulated, or rather excelled, the lustrous purity of the hangings, but now were wan and withered. The centre of the inlaid and polished floor of the apartment was covered with a Tournay carpet of brilliant yet tasteful decoration. An old cabinet of fanciful workmanship, some chairs of ebony, and some girandoles of silver completed the furniture of the room, save that at its extreme end, exactly opposite to the door by which Venetia entered, covered with a curtain of green velvet, was what she concluded must be a picture.

An awful stillness pervaded the apartment: Venetia herself, with a face paler even than the hangings of the mysterious bed, stood motionless with suppressed breath, gazing on the distant curtain with a painful glance of agitated fascination. At length, summoning her energies as if for the achievement of some terrible yet inevitable enterprise, she crossed the room, and averting her face, and closing her eyes in a paroxysm of nervous excitement, she stretched forth her arm, and with a rapid motion withdrew the curtain. The harsh sound of the brass rings drawn quickly over the rod, the only noise that had yet met her ear in this mystical chamber, made her start and tremble. She looked up, she beheld, in a broad and massy frame, the full-length portrait of a man.

A man in the very spring of sunny youth, and of radiant beauty. Above the middle height, yet with a form that displayed exquisite grace, he was habited in a green tunic that enveloped his figure to advantage, and became the scene in which he was placed: a park, with a castle in the distance; while a groom at hand held a noble steed, that seemed impatient for the chase. The countenance of its intended rider met fully the gaze of the spectator. It was a countenance of singular loveliness and power. The lips and the moulding of the chin resembled the eager and impassioned tenderness of the shape of

Antinous; but instead of the effeminate sullenness of the eye, and the narrow smoothness of the forehead, shone an expression of profound and piercing thought. On each side of the clear and open brow descended, even to the shoulders, the clustering locks of golden hair; while the eyes, large and yet deep, beamed with a spiritual energy, and shone like two wells of crystalline water that reflect the all-beholding heavens.

Now when Venetia Herbert beheld this countenance a change came over her. It seemed that when her eyes met the eyes of the portrait, some mutual interchange of sympathy occurred between them. She freed herself in an instant from the apprehension and timidity that before oppressed her. Whatever might ensue, a vague conviction of having achieved a great object pervaded, as it were, her being. Some great end, vast though indefinite, had been fulfilled. Abstract and fearless, she gazed upon the dazzling visage with a prophetic heart. Her soul was in a tumult, oppressed with thick-coming fancies too big for words, panting for expression. There was a word which must be spoken: it trembled on her convulsive lip, and would not sound. She looked around her with an eye glittering with unnatural fire, as if to supplicate some invisible and hovering spirit to her rescue, or that some floating and angelic chorus might warble the thrilling word whose expression seemed absolutely necessary to her existence. Her cheek is flushed, her eye wild and tremulous, the broad blue veins of her immaculate brow quivering and distended; her waving hair falls back over her forehead, and rustles like a wood before the storm. She seems a priestess in the convulsive throes of inspiration, and about to breathe the oracle. The picture, as we have mentioned, was hung in a broad and massy frame. In the centre of its base was worked an escutcheon, and beneath the shield this inscription:

MARMION HERBERT, AET. XX.

Yet there needed not these letters to guide the agitated spirit of Venetia, for, before her eye had reached them, the word was spoken; and falling on her knees before the portrait, the daughter of Lady Annabel had exclaimed, 'My father!'

CHAPTER V.

The daughter still kneels before the form of the father, of whom she had heard for the first time in her life. He is at length discovered. It was, then, an irresistible destiny that, after the wild musings and baffled aspirations of so many years, had guided her to this chamber. She is the child of Marmion Herbert; she beholds her lost parent. That being of supernatural beauty, on whom she gazes with a look of blended reverence and love, is her father. What a revelation! Its reality exceeded the wildest dreams of her romance; her brightest visions of grace and loveliness and genius seemed personified in this form; the form of one to whom she was bound by the strongest of all earthly ties, of one on whose heart she had a claim second only to that of the being by whose lips his name was never mentioned. Was he, then, no more? Ah! could she doubt that bitterest calamity? Ah! was it, was it any longer a marvel, that one who had lived in the light of those seraphic eyes, and had watched them until their terrestrial splendour had been for ever extinguished, should shrink from the converse that could remind her of the catastrophe of all her earthly hopes! This chamber, then, was the temple of her mother's woe, the tomb of her baffled affections and bleeding heart. No wonder that Lady Annabel, the desolate Lady Annabel, that almost the same spring must have witnessed the most favoured and the most disconsolate of women, should have fled from the world that had awarded her at the same time a lot so dazzling and so full of despair. Venetia felt that the existence of her mother's child, her own fragile being, could have been that mother's sole link to life. The heart of the young widow of Marmion Herbert must have broken but for Venetia; and the consciousness of that remaining tie, and the duties that it involved, could alone have sustained the victim under a lot of such unparalleled bitterness. The tears streamed down her cheek as she thought of her mother's misery, and her mother's gentle love; the misery that she had been so cautious her child should never share; the vigilant affection that, with all her own hopes blighted, had still laboured to compensate to her child for a deprivation the fulness of which Venetia could only now comprehend.

When, where, why did he die? Oh that she might talk of him to her mother for ever! It seemed that life might pass away in listening to his praises. Marmion Herbert! and who was Marmion Herbert? Young as he was, command and genius, the pride of noble passions, all the glory of a creative mind, seemed stamped upon his brow. With all his marvellous beauty, he seemed a being born for greatness. Dead! in the very burst of his spring, a spring so sweet and splendid; could he be dead? Why, then, was he ever born? It seemed to her that he could not be dead; there was an animated look about the form, that seemed as if it could not die without leaving mankind a prodigal legacy of fame.

Venetia turned and looked upon her parents' bridal bed. Now that she had discovered her father's portrait, every article in the room interested her, for her imagination connected everything with him. She touched the wreath of withered roses, and one instantly broke away from the circle, and fell; she knelt down, and gathered up the scattered leaves, and placed them in her bosom. She approached the table in the oriel: in its centre was a volume, on which reposed a dagger of curious workmanship; the volume bound in velvet, and the word 'ANNABEL' embroidered upon it in gold. Venetia unclasped it. The volume was his; in a fly-leaf were written these words:

'TO THE LADY OF MY LOVE, FROM HER MARMION HERBERT.'

With a fluttering heart, yet sparkling eye, Venetia sank into a chair, which was placed before the table, with all her soul concentred in the contents of this volume. Leaning on her right hand, which shaded her agitated brow, she turned a page of the volume with a trembling hand. It contained a sonnet, delineating the feelings of a lover at the first sight of his beloved, a being to him yet unknown. Venetia perused with breathless interest the graceful and passionate picture of her mother's beauty. A series of similar compositions detailed the history of the poet's heart, and all the thrilling adventures of his enchanted life. Not an incident, not a word, not a glance, in that spell-bound prime of existence, that was not commemorated by his lyre in strains as sweet and as witching! Now he poured forth his passion; now his doubts; now his hopes; now came the glowing hour when he was first assured of his felicity; the next page celebrated her visit to the castle of his fathers; and another led her to the altar.

With a flushed cheek and an excited eye, Venetia had rapidly pored over these ardent annals of the heart from whose blood she had sprung. She turns the page; she starts; the colour deserts her countenance; a mist glides over her vision; she clasps her hands with convulsive energy; she sinks back in her chair. In a few moments she extends one hand, as if fearful again to touch the book that had excited so much emotion, raises herself in her seat, looks around her with a vacant and perplexed gaze, apparently succeeds in collecting herself, and then seizes, with an eager grasp, the volume, and throwing herself on her, knees before the chair, her long locks hanging on each side over a cheek crimson as the sunset, loses her whole soul in the lines which the next page reveals.

ON THE NIGHT OUR DAUGHTER WAS BORN.

I.

> Within our heaven of love, the new-born star
> We long devoutly watched, like shepherd kings,

Steals into light, and, floating from afar,
Methinks some bright transcendent seraph sings,
Waving with flashing light her radiant wings,
Immortal welcome to the stranger fair:
To us a child is born. With transport clings
The mother to the babe she sighed to bear;
Of all our treasured loves the long-expected heir!

II.

My daughter! can it be a daughter now
Shall greet my being with her infant smile?
And shall I press that fair and taintless brow
With my fond lips, and tempt, with many a wile
Of playful love, those features to beguile
A parent with their mirth? In the wild sea
Of this dark life, behold a little isle
Rises amid the waters, bright and free,
A haven for my hopes of fond security!

III.

And thou shalt bear a name my line has loved,
And their fair daughters owned for many an age,
Since first our fiery blood a wanderer roved,
And made in sunnier lands his pilgrimage,
Where proud defiance with the waters wage
The sea-born city's walls; the graceful towers
Loved by the bard and honoured by the sage!
My own VENETIA now shall gild our bowers,
And with her spell enchain our life's enchanted hours!

IV.

Oh! if the blessing of a father's heart
Hath aught of sacred in its deep-breath'd prayer,
Skilled to thy gentle being to impart,
As thy bright form itself, a fate as fair;
On thee I breathe that blessing! Let me share,
O God! her joys; and if the dark behest
Of woe resistless, and avoidless care,
Hath, not gone forth, oh! spare this gentle guest.
And wreak thy needful wrath on my resigned breast!

An hour elapsed, and Venetia did not move. Over and over again she conned the only address from the lips of her father that had ever reached her ear. A strange inspiration seconded the exertion of an exercised memory. The duty was fulfilled, the task completed. Then a sound was heard without. The thought that her mother had returned occurred to her; she looked up, the big tears streaming down her face; she listened, like a young hind just roused by the still-distant huntsman, quivering and wild: she listened, and she sprang up, replaced the volume, arranged the chair, cast one long, lingering, feverish glance at the portrait, skimmed through the room, hesitated one moment in the ante-chamber; opened, as all was silent, the no longer mysterious door, turned the noiseless lock, tripped lightly along the vestibule; glided into her mother's empty apartment, reposited the key that had opened so many wonders in the casket; and, then, having hurried to her own chamber, threw herself on her bed in a paroxysm of contending emotions, that left her no power of pondering over the strange discovery that had already given a new colour to her existence.

CHAPTER VI.

Her mother had not returned; it was a false alarm; but Venetia could not quit her bed. There she remained, repeating to herself her father's verses. Then one thought alone filled her being. Was he dead? Was this fond father, who had breathed this fervent blessing over her birth, and invoked on his own head all the woe and misfortunes of her destiny, was he, indeed, no more? How swiftly must the arrow have sped after he received the announcement that a child was given to him,

Of all his treasured loves the long-expected heir!

He could scarcely have embraced her ere the great Being, to whom he had offered his prayer, summoned him to his presence! Of that father she had not the slightest recollection; she had ascertained that she had reached Cherbury a child, even in arms, and she knew that her father had never lived under the roof. What an awful bereavement! Was it wonderful that her mother was inconsolable? Was it wonderful that she could not endure even his name to be mentioned in her presence; that not the slightest allusion to his existence could be tolerated by a wife who had been united to such a peerless being, only to behold him torn away from her embraces? Oh! could he, indeed, be dead? That inspired countenance that seemed immortal, had it in a moment been dimmed? and all the symmetry of that matchless form, had it indeed been long mouldering in the dust? Why should she doubt it? Ah! why, indeed? How could she doubt it? Why, ever and anon, amid the tumult of her excited mind, came there an unearthly whisper to her ear, mocking her with the belief that he still lived? But he was dead; he must be dead; and why did she live? Could she survive what she had seen and learnt this day? Did she wish to survive it? But her mother, her mother with all her sealed-up sorrows, had survived him. Why? For her sake; for her child; for 'his own Venetia!' His own!

She clenched her feverish hand, her temples beat with violent palpitations, her brow was burning hot. Time flew on, and every minute Venetia was more sensible of the impossibility of rising to welcome her mother. That mother at length returned; Venetia could not again mistake the wheels of the returning carriage. Some minutes passed, and there was a knock at her door. With a choking voice Venetia bade them enter. It was Pauncefort.

'Well, Miss,' she exclaimed, 'if you ayn't here, after all! I told my lady, "My lady," says I, "I am sure Miss Venetia must be in the park, for I saw her go out myself, and I have never seen her come home." And, after all, you are here. My lady has come home, you know, Miss, and has been inquiring for you several times.'

'Tell mamma that I am not very well,' said Venetia, in a low voice, 'and that I have been obliged to lie down.'

'Not well, Miss,' exclaimed Pauncefort; 'and what can be the matter with you? I am afraid you have walked too much; overdone it, I dare say; or, mayhap, you have caught cold; it is an easterly wind: for I was saying to John this morning, "John," says I, "if Miss Venetia will walk about with only a handkerchief tied round her head, why, what can be expected?"'

'I have only a headache, a very bad headache, Pauncefort; I wish to be quiet,' said Venetia.

Pauncefort left the room accordingly, and straightway proceeded to Lady Annabel, when she communicated the information that Miss Venetia was in the house, after all, though she had never seen her return, and that she was lying down because she had a very bad headache. Lady Annabel, of course, did not lose a moment in visiting her darling. She entered the room softly, so softly that she was not heard; Venetia was lying on her bed, with her back to the door. Lady Annabel stood by her bedside for some moments unnoticed. At length Venetia heaved a deep sigh. Her mother then said in a soft voice, 'Are you in pain, darling?'

'Is that mamma?' said Venetia, turning with quickness.

'You are ill, dear,' said Lady Annabel, taking her hand. 'Your hand is hot; you are feverish. How long has my Venetia felt ill?'

Venetia could not answer; she did nothing but sigh. Her strange manner excited her mother's wonder. Lady Annabel sat by the bedside, still holding her daughter's hand in hers, watching her with a glance of great anxiety.

'Answer me, my love,' she repeated in a voice of tenderness. 'What do you feel?'

'My head, my head,' murmured Venetia.

Her mother pressed her own hand to her daughter's brow; it was very hot. 'Does that pain you?' inquired Lady Annabel; but Venetia did not reply; her look was wild and abstracted. Her mother gently withdrew her hand, and then summoned Pauncefort, with whom she communicated without permitting her to enter the room.

'Miss Herbert is very ill,' said Lady Annabel, pale, but in a firm tone. 'I am alarmed about her. She appears to me to have fever; send instantly to Southport for Mr. Hawkins; and let the messenger use and urge all possible expedition. Be in attendance in the vestibule, Pauncefort; I shall not quit her room, but she must be kept perfectly quiet.'

Lady Annabel then drew her chair to the bedside of her daughter, and bathed her temples at intervals with rose-water; but none of these attentions apparently attracted the notice of the sufferer. She was, it would seem, utterly unconscious of all that was occurring. She now lay with her face turned towards her mother, but did not exchange even looks with her. She was restless, and occasionally she sighed deeply.

Once, by way of experiment, Lady Annabel again addressed her, but Venetia gave no answer. Then the mother concluded what, indeed, had before attracted her suspicion, that Venetia's head was affected. But then, what was this strange, this sudden attack, which appeared to have prostrated her daughter's faculties in an instant? A few hours back, and Lady Annabel had parted from Venetia in all the glow of health and beauty. The season was most genial; her exercise had doubtless been moderate; as for her general health, so complete was her constitution, and so calm the tenour of her life, that Venetia had scarcely experienced in her whole career a single hour of indisposition. It was an anxious period of suspense until the medical attendant arrived from Southport. Fortunately he was one in whom, from reputation, Lady Annabel was disposed to place great trust; and his matured years, his thoughtful manner, and acute inquiries, confirmed her favourable opinion of him. All that Mr. Hawkins could say, however, was, that Miss Herbert had a great deal of fever, but the cause was concealed, and the suddenness of the attack perplexed him. He administered one of the usual remedies; and after an hour had elapsed, and no favourable change occurring, he blooded her. He quitted Cherbury, with the promise of returning late in the evening, having several patients whom he was obliged to visit.

The night drew on; the chamber was now quite closed, but Lady Annabel never quitted it. She sat reading, removed from her daughter, that her presence might not disturb her, for Venetia seemed inclined to sleep. Suddenly Venetia spoke; but she said only one word, 'Father!'

Lady Annabel started; her book nearly fell from her hand; she grew very pale. Quite breathless, she listened, and again Venetia spoke, and again called upon her father. Now, with a great effort, Lady Annabel stole on tiptoe to the bedside of her daughter. Venetia was lying on her back, her eyes were closed, her lips still as it were quivering with the strange word they had dared to pronounce. Again her voice sounded; she chanted, in an unearthly voice, verses. The perspiration stood in large drops on the pallid forehead of the mother as she listened. Still Venetia proceeded; and Lady Annabel, throwing herself on her knees, held up her hands to Heaven in an agony of astonishment, terror, and devotion.

Now there was again silence; but her mother remained apparently buried in prayer. Again Venetia spoke; again she repeated the mysterious stanzas. With convulsive agony her mother listened to every fatal line that she unconsciously pronounced.

The secret was then discovered. Yes! Venetia must have penetrated the long-closed chamber; all the labours of years had in a moment been subverted; Venetia had discovered her parent, and the effects of the discovery might, perhaps, be her death. Then it was that Lady Annabel, in the torture of her mind, poured forth her supplications that the life or the heart of her child might never be lost to her, 'Grant, O merciful God!' she exclaimed, 'that this sole hope of my being may be spared to me. Grant, if she be spared, that she may never desert her mother! And for him, of whom she has heard this day for the first time, let him be to her as if he were no more! May she never learn that he lives! May she never comprehend the secret agony of her mother's life! Save her, O God! save her from his fatal, his irresistible influence! May she remain pure and virtuous as she has yet lived! May she remain true to thee, and true to thy servant, who now bows before thee! Look down upon me at this moment with gracious mercy; turn to me my daughter's heart; and, if it be my dark doom to be in this world a widow, though a wife, add not to this bitterness that I shall prove a mother without a child!'

At this moment the surgeon returned. It was absolutely necessary that Lady Annabel should compose herself. She exerted all that strength of character for which she was remarkable. From this moment she resolved, if her life were the forfeit, not to quit for an instant the bedside of Venetia until she was declared out of danger; and feeling conscious that if she once indulged her own feelings, she might herself soon be in a situation scarcely less hazardous than her daughter's, she controlled herself with a mighty effort. Calm as a statue, she received the medical attendant, who took the hand of the unconscious Venetia with apprehension too visibly impressed upon his grave countenance. As he took her hand, Venetia opened her eyes, stared at her mother and her attendant, and then immediately closed them.

'She has slept?' inquired Lady Annabel.

'No,' said the surgeon, 'no: this is not sleep; it is a feverish trance that brings her no refreshment.' He took out his watch, and marked her pulse with great attention; then he placed his hand on her brow, and shook his head. 'These beautiful curls must come off,' he said. Lady Annabel glided to the table, and instantly brought the scissors, as if the delay of an instant might be fatal. The surgeon cut off those long golden locks. Venetia raised her hand to her head, and said, in a low voice, 'They are for my father.' Lady Annabel leant upon the surgeon's arm and shook.

Now he led the mother to the window, and spoke in a hushed tone.

'Is it possible that there is anything on your daughter's mind, Lady Annabel?' he inquired.

The agitated mother looked at the inquirer, and then at her daughter; and then for a moment she raised her hand to her eyes; then she replied, in a low but firm voice, 'Yes.'

'Your ladyship must judge whether you wish me to be acquainted with it,' said Mr. Hawkins, calmly.

'My daughter has suddenly become acquainted, sir, with some family incidents of a painful nature, and the knowledge of which I have hitherto spared her. They are events long past, and their consequences are now beyond all control.'

'She knows, then, the worst?'

'Without her mind, I cannot answer that question,' said Lady Annabel.

'It is my duty to tell you that Miss Herbert is in imminent danger; she has every appearance of a fever of a malignant character. I cannot answer for her life.'

'O God!' exclaimed Lady Annabel.

'Yet you must compose yourself, my dear lady. Her chance of recovery greatly depends upon the vigilance of her attendants. I shall bleed her again, and place leeches on her temples. There is inflammation on the brain. There are other remedies also not less powerful. We must not despair; we have no cause to despair until we find these fail. I shall not leave her again; and, for your satisfaction, not for my own, I shall call in additional advice, the aid of a physician.'

A messenger accordingly was instantly despatched for the physician, who resided at a town more distant than Southport; the very town, by-the-bye, where Morgana, the gipsy, was arrested. They contrived, with the aid of Pauncefort, to undress Venetia, and place her in her bed, for hitherto they had refrained from this exertion. At this moment the withered leaves of a white rose fell from Venetia's dress. A sofa-bed was then made for Lady Annabel, of which, however, she did not avail herself. The whole night she sat by her daughter's side, watching every movement of Venetia, refreshing her hot brow and parched lips, or arranging, at every opportunity, her disordered pillows. About an hour past midnight the surgeon retired to rest, for a few hours, in the apartment prepared for him, and Pauncefort, by the desire of her mistress, also withdrew: Lady Annabel was alone with her child, and with those agitated thoughts which the strange occurrences of the day were well calculated to excite.

CHAPTER VII.

Early in the morning the physician arrived at Cherbury. It remained for him only to approve of the remedies which had been pursued. No material change, however, had occurred in the state of Venetia: she had not slept, and still she seemed unconscious of what was occurring. The gracious interposition of Nature seemed the only hope. When the medical men had withdrawn to consult in the terrace-room, Lady Annabel beckoned to Pauncefort, and led her to the window of Venetia's apartment, which she would not quit.

'Pauncefort,' said Lady Annabel, 'Venetia has been in her father's room.'

'Oh! impossible, my lady,' burst forth Mistress Pauncefort; but Lady Annabel placed her finger on her lip, and checked her. 'There is no doubt of it, there can be no doubt of it, Pauncefort; she entered it yesterday; she must have passed the morning there, when you believed she was in the park.'

'But, my lady,' said Pauncefort, 'how could it be? For I scarcely left your la'ship's room a second, and Miss Venetia, I am sure, never was near it. And the key, my lady, the key is in the casket. I saw it half an hour ago with my own eyes.'

'There is no use arguing about it, Pauncefort,' said Lady Annabel, with decision. 'It is as I say. I fear great misfortunes are about to commence at Cherbury.'

'Oh! my lady, don't think of such things,' said Pauncefort, herself not a little alarmed. 'What can happen?'

'I fear more than I know,' said Lady Annabel; 'but I do fear much. At present I can only think of her.'

'Well! my lady,' said poor Mistress Pauncefort, looking bewildered, 'only to think of such a thing! and after all the pains I have taken! I am sure I have not opened my lips on the subject these fifteen years; and the many questions I have been asked too! I am sure there is not a servant in the house—'

'Hush! hush!' said Lady Annabel, 'I do not blame you, and therefore you need not defend yourself. Go, Pauncefort, I must be alone.' Pauncefort withdrew, and Lady Annabel resumed her seat by her daughter's side.

On the fourth day of her attack the medical attendants observed a favourable change in their patient, and were not, of course, slow in communicating this joyful intelligence to her mother. The crisis had occurred and was past: Venetia had at length sunk into slumber. How different was her countenance from the still yet settled features they had before watched with such anxiety! She breathed lightly, the tension of the eyelids had disappeared, her mouth was slightly open. The physician and his colleague declared that immediate danger was past, and they counselled Lady Annabel to take repose. On condition that one of them should remain by the side of her daughter, the devoted yet miserable mother quitted, for the first time her child's apartment. Pauncefort followed her to her room.

'Oh! my lady,' said Pauncefort, 'I am so glad your la'ship is going to lie down a bit.'

'I am not going to lie down, Pauncefort. Give me the key.'

And Lady Annabel proceeded alone to the forbidden chamber, that chamber which, after what has occurred, we may now enter with her, and where, with so much labour, she had created a room exactly imitative of their bridal apartment at her husband's castle. With a slow but resolved step she entered the apartment, and proceeding immediately to the table, took up the book; it opened at the stanzas to Venetia. The pages had recently been bedewed with tears. Lady Annabel then looked at the bridal bed, and marked the missing rose in the garland: it was as she expected. She seated herself then in the chair opposite the portrait, on which she gazed with a glance rather stern than fond.

'Marmion,' she exclaimed, 'for fifteen years, a solitary votary, I have mourned over, in this temple of baffled affections, the inevitable past. The daughter of our love has found her way, perhaps by an irresistible destiny, to a spot sacred to my long-concealed sorrows. At length she knows her father. May she never know more! May she never learn that the being, whose pictured form has commanded her adoration, is unworthy of those glorious gifts that a gracious Creator has bestowed upon him! Marmion, you seem to smile upon me; you seem to exult in your triumph over the heart of your child. But there is a power in a mother's love that yet shall baffle you. Hitherto I have come here to deplore the past; hitherto I have come here to dwell upon the form that, in spite of all that has happened, I still was, perhaps, weak enough, to love. Those feelings are past for ever. Yes! you would rob me of my child, you would tear from my heart the only consolation you have left me. But Venetia shall still be mine; and I, I am no longer yours. Our love, our still lingering love, has vanished. You have been my enemy, now I am yours. I gaze upon your portrait for the last time; and thus I prevent the magical fascination of that face again appealing to the sympathies of my child. Thus and thus!' She seized the ancient dagger that we have mentioned as lying on the volume, and, springing on the chair, she plunged it into the canvas; then, tearing with unflinching resolution the severed parts, she scattered the fragments over the chamber, shook into a thousand leaves the melancholy garland, tore up the volume of his enamoured Muse, and then quitting the chamber, and locking and double locking the door, she descended the staircase, and proceeding to the great well of Cherbury, hurled into it the fatal key.

'Oh! my lady,' said Mistress Pauncefort, as she met Lady Annabel returning in the vestibule, 'Doctor Masham is here.'

'Is he?' said Lady Annabel, as calm as usual. 'I will see him before I lie down. Do not go into Venetia's room. She sleeps, and Mr. Hawkins has promised me to let me know when she wakes.'

CHAPTER VIII.

As Lady Annabel entered the terrace-room, Doctor Masham came forward and grasped her hand.

'You have heard of our sorrow!' said her ladyship in a faint voice.

'But this instant,' replied the Doctor, in a tone of great anxiety.' Immediate danger—'

'Is past. She sleeps,' replied Lady Annabel.

'A most sudden and unaccountable attack,' said the Doctor.

It is difficult to describe the contending emotions of the mother as her companion made this observation. At length she replied, 'Sudden, certainly sudden; but not unaccountable. Oh! my friend,' she added, after a moment's pause, 'they will not be content until they have torn my daughter from me.'

'They tear your daughter from you!' exclaimed Doctor Masham. 'Who?'

'He, he,' muttered Lady Annabel; her speech was incoherent, her manner very disturbed.

'My dear lady,' said the Doctor, gazing on her with extreme anxiety, 'you are yourself unwell.'

Lady Annabel heaved a deep sigh; the Doctor bore her to a seat. 'Shall I send for any one, anything?'

'No one, no one,' quickly answered Lady Annabel. 'With you, at least, there is no concealment necessary.'

She leant back in her chair, the Doctor holding her hand, and standing by her side.

Still Lady Annabel continued sighing deeply: at length she looked up and said, 'Does she love me? Do you think, after all, she loves me?'

'Venetia?' inquired the Doctor, in a low and doubtful voice, for he was greatly perplexed.

'She has seen him; she loves him; she has forgotten her mother.'

'My dear lady, you require rest,' said Doctor Masham. 'You are overcome with strange fancies. Whom has your daughter seen?'

'Marmion.'

'Impossible! you forget he is—'

'Here also. He has spoken to her: she loves him: she will recover: she will fly to him; sooner let us both die!'

'Dear lady!'

'She knows everything. Fate has baffled me; we cannot struggle with fate. She is his child; she is like him; she is not like her mother. Oh! she hates me; I know she hates me.'

'Hush! hush! hush!' said the Doctor, himself very agitated. 'Venetia loves you, only you. Why should she love any one else?'

'Who can help it? I loved him. I saw him. I loved him. His voice was music. He has spoken to her, and she yielded: she yielded in a moment. I stood by her bedside. She would not speak to me; she would not know me; she shrank from me. Her heart is with her father: only with him.'

'Where did she see him? How?'

'His room: his picture. She knows all. I was away with you, and she entered his chamber.'

'Ah!'

'Oh! Doctor, you have influence with her. Speak to her. Make her love me! Tell her she has no father; tell her he is dead.'

'We will do that which is well and wise,' replied Doctor Masham: 'at present let us be calm; if you give way, her life may be the forfeit. Now is the moment for a mother's love.'

'You are right. I should not have left her for an instant. I would not have her wake and find her mother not watching over her. But I was tempted. She slept; I left her for a moment; I went to destroy the spell. She cannot see him again. No one shall see him again. It was my weakness, the weakness of long years; and now I am its victim.'

'Nay, nay, my sweet lady, all will be quite well. Be but calm; Venetia will recover.'

'But will she love me? Oh! no, no, no! She will think only of him. She will not love her mother. She will yearn for her father now. She has seen him, and she will not rest until she is in his arms. She will desert me, I know it.'

'And I know the contrary,' said the Doctor, attempting to reassure her; 'I will answer for Venetia's devotion to you. Indeed she has no thought but your happiness, and can love only you. When there is a fitting time, I will speak to her; but now, now is the time for repose. And you must rest, you must indeed.'

'Rest! I cannot. I slumbered in the chair last night by her bedside, and a voice roused me. It was her own. She was speaking to her father. She told him how she loved him; how long, how much she thought of him; that she would join him when she was well, for she knew he was not dead; and, if he were dead, she would die also. She never mentioned me.'

'Nay! the light meaning of a delirious brain.' 'Truth, truth, bitter, inevitable truth. Oh! Doctor, I could bear all but this; but my child, my beautiful fond child, that made up for all my sorrows. My joy, my hope, my life! I knew it would be so; I knew he would have her heart. He said she never could be alienated from him; he said she never could be taught to hate him. I did not teach her to hate him. I said nothing. I deemed, fond, foolish mother, that the devotion of my life might bind her to me. But what is a mother's love? I cannot contend with him. He gained the mother; he will gain the daughter too.'

'God will guard over you,' said Masham, with streaming eyes; 'God will not desert a pious and virtuous woman.'

'I must go,' said Lady Annabel, attempting to rise, but the Doctor gently controlled her; 'perhaps she is awake, and I am not at her side. She will not ask for me, she will ask for him; but I will be there; she will desert me, but she shall not say I ever deserted her.'

'She will never desert you,' said the Doctor; 'my life on her pure heart. She has been a child of unbroken love and duty; still she will remain so. Her mind is for a moment overpowered by a marvellous discovery. She will recover, and be to you as she was before.'

'We'll tell her he is dead,' said Lady Annabel, eagerly. 'You must tell her. She will believe you. I cannot speak to her of him; no, not to secure her heart; never, never, never can I speak to Venetia of her father.'

'I will speak,' replied the Doctor, 'at the just time. Now let us think of her recovery. She is no longer in danger. We should be grateful, we should be glad.'

'Let us pray to God! Let us humble ourselves,' said Lady Annabel. 'Let us beseech him not to desert this house. We have been faithful to him, we have struggled to be faithful to him. Let us supplicate him to favour and support us!'

'He will favour and support you,' said the Doctor, in a solemn tone. 'He has upheld you in many trials; he will uphold you still.'

'Ah! why did I love him! Why did I continue to love him! How weak, how foolish, how mad I have been! I have alone been the cause of all this misery. Yes, I have destroyed my child.'

'She lives, she will live. Nay, nay! you must reassure yourself. Come, let me send for your servant, and for a moment repose. Nay! take my arm. All depends upon you. We have great cares now; let us not conjure up fantastic fears.'

'I must go to my daughter's room. Perhaps by her side I might rest. Nowhere else. You will attend me to the door, my friend. Yes! it is something in this life to have a friend.'

Lady Annabel took the arm of the good Masham. They stopped at her daughter's door.

'Rest here a moment,' she said, as she entered the room without a sound. In a moment she returned. 'She still sleeps,' said the mother; 'I shall remain with her, and you—?'

'I will not leave you,' said the Doctor, 'but think not of me. Nay! I will not leave you. I will remain under this roof. I have shared its serenity and joy; let me not avoid it in this time of trouble and tribulation.'

CHAPTER IX.

Venetia still slept: her mother alone in the chamber watched by her side. Some hours had elapsed since her interview with Dr. Masham; the medical attendant had departed for a few hours.

Suddenly Venetia moved, opened her eyes, and said in a faint voice, 'Mamma!'

The blood rushed to Lady Annabel's heart. That single word afforded her the most exquisite happiness.

'I am here, dearest,' she replied.

'Mamma, what is all this?' inquired Venetia.

'You have not been well, my own, but now you are much better.'

'I thought I had been dreaming,' replied Venetia, 'and that all was not right; somebody, I thought, struck me on my head. But all is right now, because you are here, my dear mamma.'

But Lady Annabel could not speak for weeping.

'Are you sure, mamma, that nothing has been done to my head?' continued Venetia. 'Why, what is this?' and she touched a light bandage on her brow.

'My darling, you have been ill, and you have lost blood; but now you are getting quite well. I have been very unhappy about you; but now I am quite happy, my sweet, sweet child.'

'How long have I been ill?'

'You have been very ill indeed for four or five days; you have had a fever, Venetia; but now the fever is gone; and you are only a little weak, and you will soon be well.'

'A fever! and how did I get the fever?'

'Perhaps you caught cold, my child; but we must not talk too much.'

'A fever! I never had a fever before. A fever is like a dream.'

'Hush! sweet love. Indeed you must not speak.'

'Give me your hand, mamma; I will not speak if you will let me hold your hand. I thought in the fever that we were parted.'

'I have never left your side, my child, day or night,' said Lady Annabel, not without agitation.

'All this time! all these days and nights! No one would do that but you, mamma. You think only of me.'

'You repay me by your love, Venetia,' said Lady Annabel, feeling that her daughter ought not to speak, yet irresistibly impelled to lead out her thoughts.

'How can I help loving you, my dear mamma?'

'You do love me, you do love me very much; do you not, sweet child?'

'Better than all the world,' replied Venetia to her enraptured parent. 'And yet, in the fever I seemed to love some one else: but fevers are like dreams; they are not true.'

Lady Annabel pressed her lips gently to her daughter's, and whispered her that she must speak no more.

When Mr. Hawkins returned, he gave a favourable report of Venetia. He said that all danger was now past, and that all that was required for her recovery were time, care, and repose. He repeated to Lady Annabel alone that the attack was solely to be ascribed to some great mental shock which her daughter had received, and which suddenly had affected her circulation; leaving it, after this formal intimation, entirely to the mother to take those steps in reference to the cause, whatever it might be, which she should deem expedient.

In the evening, Lady Annabel stole down for a few moments to Dr. Masham, laden with joyful intelligence; assured of the safety of her child, and, what was still more precious, of her heart, and even voluntarily promising her friend that she should herself sleep this night in her daughter's chamber, on the sofa-bed. The Doctor, therefore, now bade her adieu, and said that he should ride over from Marringhurst every day, to hear how their patient was proceeding.

From this time, the recovery of Venetia, though slow, was gradual. She experienced no relapse, and in a few weeks quitted her bed. She was rather surprised at her altered appearance when it first met her glance in the mirror, but scarcely made any observation on the loss of her locks. During this interval, the mind of Venetia had been quite dormant; the rage of the fever, and the violent remedies to which it had been necessary to have recourse, had so exhausted her, that she had not energy enough to think. All that she felt was a strange indefinite conviction that some occurrence had taken place with which her memory could not grapple. But as her strength returned, and as she gradually resumed her usual health, by proportionate though almost invisible degrees her memory returned to her, and her intelligence. She clearly recollected and comprehended what had taken place. She recalled the past, compared incidents, weighed circumstances, sifted and balanced the impressions that now crowded upon her consciousness. It is difficult to describe each link in the metaphysical chain which at length connected the mind of Venetia Herbert with her actual experience and precise situation. It was, however, at length perfect, and gradually formed as she sat in an invalid chair, apparently listless, not yet venturing on any occupation, or occasionally amused for a moment by her mother reading to her. But when her mind had thus resumed its natural tone, and in time its accustomed vigour, the past demanded all her solicitude. At length the mystery of her birth was revealed to her. She was the daughter of Marmion Herbert; and who was Marmion Herbert? The portrait rose before her. How distinct was the form, how definite the countenance! No common personage was Marmion Herbert, even had he not won his wife, and celebrated his daughter in such witching strains. Genius was stamped on his lofty brow, and spoke in his brilliant eye; nobility was in all his form. This chivalric poet was her father. She had read, she had dreamed of such beings, she had never seen them. If she quitted the solitude in which she lived, would she see men like her father? No other could ever satisfy her imagination; all beneath that standard would rank but as imperfect creations in her fancy. And this father, he was dead. No doubt. Ah! was there indeed no doubt? Eager as was her curiosity on this all-absorbing subject, Venetia could never summon courage to speak upon it to her mother. Her first disobedience, or rather her first deception of her mother, in reference to this very subject, had brought, and brought so swiftly on its retributive wings, such disastrous consequences, that any allusion to Lady Annabel was restrained by a species of superstitious fear, against which Venetia could not contend. Then her father was either dead or living. That was certain. If dead, it was clear that his memory, however cherished by his relict, was associated with feelings too keen to admit of any other but solitary indulgence. If living, there was a mystery connected with her parents, a mystery evidently of a painful character, and one which it was a prime object with her mother to conceal and to suppress. Could Venetia, then, in defiance of that mother, that fond devoted mother, that mother who had watched through long days and long nights over her sick bed, and who now, without a murmur, was a prisoner to this very room, only to comfort and console her child: could Venetia take any step which might occasion this matchless parent even a transient pang? No; it was impossible. To her mother she could never speak. And yet, to remain enveloped in the present mystery, she was sensible, was equally insufferable. All she asked, all she wanted to know, was he alive? If he were alive, then, although she could not see him, though she might never see him, she could exist upon his idea; she could conjure up romances of future existence with him; she could live upon the fond hope of some day calling him father, and receiving from his hands the fervid blessing he had already breathed to her in song.

In the meantime her remaining parent commanded all her affections. Even if he were no more, blessed was her lot with such a mother! Lady Annabel seemed only to exist to attend upon her daughter. No lover ever watched with such devotion the wants or even the caprices of his mistress. A thousand times every day Venetia found herself expressing her fondness and her gratitude. It seemed that the late dreadful contingency of losing her daughter had developed in Lady Annabel's heart even additional powers of maternal devotion; and Venetia, the fond and grateful Venetia, ignorant of the strange past, which she believed she so perfectly comprehended, returned thanks to Heaven that her mother was at least spared the mortification of knowing that her daughter, in her absence, had surreptitiously invaded the sanctuary of her secret sorrow.

CHAPTER X.

When Venetia had so far recovered that, leaning on her mother's arm, she could resume her walks upon the terrace, Doctor Masham persuaded his friends, as a slight and not unpleasant change of scene, to pay him a visit at Marringhurst. Since the chamber scene, indeed, Lady Annabel's tie to Cherbury was much weakened. There were certain feelings of pain, and fear, and mortification, now associated with that place which she could not bear to dwell upon, and which greatly balanced those sentiments of refuge and repose, of peace and love, with which the old hall, in her mind, was heretofore connected. Venetia ever adopted the slightest intimations of a wish on the part of her mother, and so she readily agreed to fall into the arrangement.

It was rather a long and rough journey to Marringhurst, for they were obliged to use the old chariot; but Venetia forgot her fatigues in the cordial welcome of their host, whose sparkling countenance well expressed the extreme gratification their arrival occasioned him. All that the tenderest solicitude could devise for the agreeable accommodation of the invalid had been zealously concerted; and the constant influence of Dr. Masham's cheerful mind was as beneficial to Lady Annabel as to her daughter. The season was gay, the place was pleasant; and although they were only a few miles from home, in a house with which they were familiar, and their companion one whom they had known intimately all their lives, and of late almost daily seen; yet such is the magic of a change in our habits, however slight, and of the usual theatre of their custom, that this visit to Marringhurst assumed quite the air of an adventure, and seemed at first almost invested with the charm and novelty of travel.

The surrounding country, which, though verdant, was flat, was well adapted to the limited exertions and still feeble footsteps of an invalid, and Venetia began to study botany with the Doctor, who indeed was not very profound in his attainments in this respect, but knew quite enough to amuse his scholar. By degrees also, as her strength daily increased, they extended their walks; and at length she even mounted her pony, and was fast recovering her elasticity both of body and mind. There were also many pleasant books with which she was unacquainted; a cabinet of classic coins, prints, and pictures. She became, too, interested in the Doctor's rural pursuits; would watch him with his angle, and already meditated a revolution in his garden. So time, on the whole, flew cheerfully on, certainly without any weariness; and the day seldom passed that they did not all congratulate themselves on the pleasant and profitable change.

In the meantime Venetia, when alone, still recurred to that idea that was now so firmly rooted in her mind, that it was quite out of the power of any social discipline to divert her attention from it. She was often the sole companion of the Doctor, and she had long resolved to seize a favourable opportunity to appeal to him on the subject of her father. It so happened that she was walking alone with him one morning in the neighbourhood of Marringhurst, having gone to visit the remains of a Roman encampment in the immediate vicinity. When they had arrived at the spot, and the Doctor had delivered his usual lecture on the locality, they sat down together on a mound, that Venetia might rest herself.

'Were you ever in Italy, Doctor Masham?' said Venetia.

'I never was out of my native country,' said the Doctor. 'I once, indeed, was about making the grand tour with a pupil of mine at Oxford, but circumstances interfered which changed his plans, and so I remain a regular John Bull.'

'Was my father at Oxford?' said Venetia, quietly.

'He was,' replied the Doctor, looking confused.

'I should like to see Oxford much,' said Venetia.

'It is a most interesting seat of learning,' said the Doctor, quite delighted to change the subject. 'Whether we consider its antiquity, its learning, the influence it has exercised upon the history of the country, its magnificent endowments, its splendid buildings, its great colleges, libraries, and museums, or that it is one of the principal head-quarters of all the hope of England, our youth, it is not too much to affirm that there is scarcely a spot on the face of the globe of equal interest and importance.'

'It is not for its colleges, or libraries, or museums, or all its splendid buildings,' observed Venetia, 'that I should wish to see it. I wish to see it because my father was once there. I should like to see a place where I was quite certain my father had been.'

'Still harping of her father,' thought the Doctor to himself, and growing uneasy; yet, from his very anxiety to turn the subject, quite incapable of saying an appropriate word.

'Do you remember my father at Oxford, Doctor Masham?' said Venetia.

'Yes! no, yes!' said the Doctor, rather colouring; 'that he must have been there in my time, I rather think.'

'But you do not recollect him?' said Venetia, pressing question.

'Why,' rejoined the Doctor, a little more collected, 'when you remember that there are between two and three thousand young men at the university, you must not consider it very surprising that I might not recollect your father.'

'No,' said Venetia, 'perhaps not: and yet I cannot help thinking that he must always have been a person who, if once seen, would not easily have been forgotten.'

'Here is an Erica vagans,' said the Doctor, picking a flower; 'it is rather uncommon about here;' and handing it at the same time to Venetia.

'My father must have been very young when he died?' said Venetia, scarcely looking at the flower.

'Yes, your father was very young,' he replied.

'Where did he die?'

'I cannot answer that question.'

'Where was he buried?'

'You know, my dear young lady, that the subject is too tender for any one to converse with your poor mother upon it. It is not in my power to give you the information you desire. Be satisfied, my dear Miss Herbert, that a gracious Providence has spared to you one parent, and one so inestimable.'

'I trust I know how to appreciate so great a blessing,' replied Venetia; 'but I should be sorry if the natural interest which all children must take in those who have given them birth, should be looked upon as idle and unjustifiable curiosity.'

'My dear young lady, you misapprehend me.'

'No, Doctor Masham, indeed I do not,' replied Venetia, with firmness. 'I can easily conceive that the mention of my father may for various reasons be insupportable to my mother; it is enough for me that I am convinced such is the case: my lips are sealed to her for ever upon the subject; but I cannot recognise the necessity of this constraint to others. For a long time I was kept in ignorance whether I had a father or not. I have discovered, no matter how, who he was. I believe, pardon me, my dearest friend, I cannot help believing, that you were acquainted, or, at least, that you know something of him; and I entreat you! yes,' repeated Venetia with great emphasis, laying her hand upon his arm, and looking with earnestness in his face, 'I entreat you, by all your kind feelings to my mother and myself, by all that friendship we so prize, by the urgent solicitation of a daughter who is influenced in her curiosity by no light or unworthy feeling; yes! by all the claims of a child to information which ought not to be withheld from her, tell me, tell me all, tell me something! Speak, Dr. Masham, do speak!'

'My dear young lady,' said the Doctor, with a glistening eye, 'it is better that we should both be silent.'

'No, indeed,' replied Venetia, 'it is not better; it is not well that we should be silent. Candour is a great virtue. There is a charm, a healthy charm, in frankness. Why this mystery? Why these secrets? Have they worked good? Have they benefited us? O! my friend, I would not say so to my mother, I would not be tempted by any sufferings to pain for an instant her pure and affectionate heart; but indeed, Doctor Masham, indeed, indeed, what I tell you is true, all my late illness, my present state, all, all are attributable but to one cause, this mystery about my father!'

'What can I tell you?' said the unhappy Masham.

'Tell me only one fact. I ask no more. Yes! I promise you, solemnly I promise you, I will ask no more. Tell me, does he live?'

'He does!' said the Doctor. Venetia sank upon his shoulder.

'My dear young lady, my darling young lady!' said the Doctor; 'she has fainted. What can I do?' The unfortunate Doctor placed Venetia in a reclining posture, and hurried to a brook that was nigh, and brought water in his hand to sprinkle on her. She revived; she made a struggle to restore herself.

'It is nothing,' she said, 'I am resolved to be well. I am well. I am myself again. He lives; my father lives! I was confident of it! I will ask no more. I am true to my word. O! Doctor Masham, you have always been my kind friend, but you have never yet conferred on me a favour like the one you have just bestowed.'

'But it is well,' said the Doctor, 'as you know so much, that you should know more.'

'Yes! yes!'

'As we walk along,' he continued, 'we will converse, or at another time; there is no lack of opportunity.'

'No, now, now!' eagerly exclaimed Venetia, 'I am quite well. It was not pain or illness that overcame me. Now let us walk, now let us talk of these things. He lives?'

'I have little to add,' said Dr. Masham, after a moment's thought; 'but this, however painful, it is necessary for you to know, that your father is unworthy of your mother, utterly; they are separated; they never can be reunited.'

'Never?' said Venetia.

'Never,' replied Dr. Masham; 'and I now warn you; if, indeed, as I cannot doubt, you love your mother; if her peace of mind and happiness are, as I hesitate not to believe, the principal objects of your life, upon this subject with her be for ever silent. Seek to penetrate no mysteries, spare all allusions, banish, if possible, the idea of your father from your memory. Enough, you know he lives. We know no more. Your mother labours to forget him; her only consolation for sorrows such as few women ever experienced, is her child, yourself, your love. Now be no niggard with it. Cling to this unrivalled parent, who has dedicated her life to you. Soothe her sufferings, endeavour to make her share your happiness; but, of this be certain, that if you raise up the name and memory of your father between your mother and yourself, her life will be the forfeit!'

'His name shall never pass my lips,' said Venetia; 'solemnly I vow it. That his image shall be banished from my heart is too much to ask, and more than it is in my power to grant. But I am my mother's child. I will exist only for her; and if my love can console her, she shall never be without solace. I thank you, Doctor, for all your kindness. We will never talk again upon the subject; yet, believe me, you have acted wisely, you have done good.'

CHAPTER XI.

Venetia observed her promise to Doctor Masham with strictness. She never alluded to her father, and his name never escaped her mother's lips. Whether Doctor Masham apprised Lady Annabel of the conversation that had taken place between himself and her daughter, it is not in our power to mention. The visit to Marringhurst was not a short one. It was a relief both to Lady Annabel and Venetia, after all that had occurred, to enjoy the constant society of their friend; and this change of life, though apparently so slight, proved highly beneficial to Venetia. She daily recovered her health, and a degree of mental composure which she had not for some time enjoyed. On the whole she was greatly satisfied with the discoveries which she had made. She had ascertained the name and the existence of her father: his very form and appearance were now no longer matter for conjecture; and in a degree she had even communicated with him. Time, she still believed, would develop even further wonders. She clung to an irresistible conviction that she should yet see him; that he might even again be united to her mother. She indulged in dreams as to his present pursuits and position; she repeated to herself his verses, and remembered his genius with pride and consolation.

They returned to Cherbury, they resumed the accustomed tenour of their lives, as if nothing had occurred to disturb it. The fondness between the mother and her daughter was unbroken and undiminished. They shared again the same studies and the same amusements. Lady Annabel perhaps indulged the conviction that Venetia had imbibed the belief that her father was no more, and yet in truth that father was the sole idea on which her child ever brooded. Venetia had her secret now; and often as she looked up at the windows of the uninhabited portion of the building, she remembered with concealed, but not less keen exultation, that she had penetrated their mystery. She could muse for hours over all that chamber had revealed to her, and indulge in a thousand visions, of which her father was the centre. She was his 'own Venetia.' Thus he had hailed her at her birth, and thus he might yet again acknowledge her. If she could only ascertain where he existed! What if she could, and she were to communicate with him? He must love her. Her heart assured her he must love her. She could not believe, if they were to meet, that his breast could resist the silent appeal which the sight merely of his only child would suffice to make. Oh! why had her parents parted? What could have been his fault? He was so young! But a few, few years older than herself, when her mother must have seen him for the last time. Yes! for the last time beheld that beautiful form, and that countenance that seemed breathing only with genius and love. He might have been imprudent, rash, violent; but she would not credit for an instant that a stain could attach to the honour or the spirit of Marmion Herbert.

The summer wore away. One morning, as Lady Annabel and Venetia were sitting together, Mistress Pauncefort bustled into the room with a countenance radiant with smiles and wonderment. Her ostensible business was to place upon the table a vase of flowers, but it was evident that her presence was occasioned by affairs of far greater urgency. The vase was safely deposited; Mistress Pauncefort gave the last touch to the arrangement of the flowers; she lingered about Lady Annabel. At length she said, 'I suppose you have heard the news, my lady?'

'Indeed, Pauncefort, I have not,' replied Lady Annabel. 'What news?'

'My lord is coming to the abbey.'

'Indeed!'

'Oh! yes, my lady,' said Mistress Pauncefort; 'I am not at all surprised your ladyship should be so astonished. Never to write, too! Well, I must say he might have given us a line. But he is coming, I am certain sure of that, my lady. My lord's gentleman has been down these two days; and all his dogs and guns too, my lady. And the keeper is ordered to be quite ready, my lady, for the first. I wonder if there is going to be a party. I should not be at all surprised.'

'Plantagenet returned!' said Lady Annabel. 'Well, I shall be very glad to see him again.'

'So shall I, my lady,' said Mistress Pauncefort; 'but I dare say we shall hardly know him again, he must be so grown. Trimmer has been over to the abbey, my lady, and saw my lord's valet. Quite the fine gentleman, Trimmer says. I was thinking of walking over myself this afternoon, to see poor Mrs. Quin, my lady; I dare say we might be of use, and neighbours should be handy, as they say. She is a very respectable woman, poor Mrs. Quin, and I am sure for my part, if your ladyship has no objection, I should be very glad to be of service to her.'

'I have of course no objection, Pauncefort, to your being of service to the housekeeper, but has she required your assistance?'

'Why no, my lady, but poor Mrs. Quin would hardly like to ask for anything, my lady; but I am sure we might be of very great use, for my lord's gentleman seems very dissatisfied at his reception, Trimmer says. He has his hot breakfast every morning, my lady, and poor Mrs. Quin says—'

'Well, Pauncefort, that will do,' said Lady Annabel, and the functionary disappeared.

'We have almost forgotten Plantagenet, Venetia,' added Lady Annabel, addressing herself to her daughter.

'He has forgotten us, I think, mamma,' said Venetia.

END OF BOOK II

BOOK III.

CHAPTER I.

Five years had elapsed since Lord Cadurcis had quitted the seat of his fathers, nor did the fair inhabitants of Cherbury hear of his return without emotion. Although the intercourse between them during this interval had from the first been too slightly maintained, and of late years had entirely died off, his return was, nevertheless, an event which recalled old times and revived old associations. His visit to the hall was looked forward to with interest. He did not long keep his former friends in suspense; for although he was not uninfluenced by some degree of embarrassment from the consciousness of neglect on his side, rendered more keen now that he again found himself in the scene endeared by the remembrance of their kindness, he was, nevertheless, both too well bred and too warm-hearted to procrastinate the performance of a duty which the regulations of society and natural impulse alike assured him was indispensable. On the very morning, therefore, after his arrival, having sauntered awhile over the old abbey and strolled over the park, mused over his mother's tomb with emotion, not the less deep because there was no outward and visible sign of its influence, he ordered his horses, and directed his way through the accustomed woods to Cherbury.

Five years had not passed away without their effects at least upon the exterior being of Cadurcis. Although still a youth, his appearance was manly. A thoughtful air had become habitual to a countenance melancholy even in his childhood. Nor was its early promise of beauty unfulfilled; although its expression was peculiar, and less pleasing than impressive. His long dark locks shaded a pale and lofty brow that well became a cast of features delicately moulded, yet reserved and haughty, and perhaps even somewhat scornful. His figure had set into a form of remarkable slightness and elegance, and distinguished for its symmetry. Altogether his general mien was calculated to attract attention and to excite interest.

His vacations while at Eton had been spent by Lord Cadurcis in the family of his noble guardian, one of the king's ministers. Here he had been gradually initiated in the habits and manners of luxurious and refined society. Since he had quitted Eton he had passed a season, previous to his impending residence at Cambridge, in the same sphere. The opportunities thus offered had not been lost upon a disposition which, with all its native reserve, was singularly susceptible. Cadurcis had quickly imbibed the tone and adopted the usages of the circle in which he moved. Naturally impatient of control, he endeavoured by his precocious manhood to secure the respect and independence which would scarcely have been paid or permitted to his years. From an early period he never permitted himself to be treated as a boy; and his guardian, a man whose whole soul was concentred in the world, humoured a bent which he approved and from which he augured the most complete success. Attracted by the promising talents and the premature character of his ward, he had spared more time to assist the development of his mind and the formation of his manners than might have been expected from a minister of state. His hopes, indeed, rested with confidence on his youthful relative, and he looked forward with no common emotion to the moment when he should have the honour of introducing to public life one calculated to confer so much credit on his tutor, and shed so much lustre on his party. The reader will, therefore, not be surprised if at this then unrivalled period of political excitement, when the existence of our colonial empire was at stake, Cadurcis, with his impetuous feelings, had imbibed to their fullest extent all the plans, prejudices, and passions of his political connections. He was, indeed, what the circumstances of the times and his extreme youth might well excuse, if not justify, a most violent partisan. Bold, sanguine, resolute, and intolerant, it was difficult to persuade him that any opinions could be just which were opposed to those of the circle in which he lived; and out of that pale, it must be owned, he was as little inclined to recognise the existence of ability as of truth.

As Lord Cadurcis slowly directed his way through the woods and park of Cherbury, past years recurred to him like a faint yet pleasing dream. Among these meads and bowers had glided away the only happy years of his boyhood, the only period of his early life to which he could look back without disgust. He recalled the secret exultation with which, in company with his poor mother, he had first repaired to Cadurcis, about to take possession of what, to his inexperienced imagination, then appeared a vast and noble inheritance, and for the first time in his life to occupy a position not unworthy of his rank. For how many domestic mortifications did the first sight of that old abbey compensate! How often, in pacing its venerable galleries and solemn cloisters, and musing over the memory of an ancient and illustrious ancestry, had he forgotten those bitter passages of daily existence, so humbling to his vanity and so harassing to his heart! Ho had beheld that morn, after an integral of many years, the tomb of his mother. That simple and solitary monument had revived and impressed upon him a conviction that too easily escaped in the various life and busy scenes in which he had since moved, the conviction of his worldly desolation and utter loneliness. He had no parents, no relations; now that he was for a moment free from the artificial life in which he had of late mingled, he felt that he had no friends. The image of his mother came back to him, softened by the magical tint of years; after all she was his mother, and a deep sharer in all his joys and woes. Transported to the old haunts of his innocent and warm-hearted childhood. He sighed for a finer and a sweeter sympathy than was ever yielded by the roof which he had lately quitted; a habitation, but not a home. He conjured up the picture of his guardian, existing in a whirl of official bustle and social excitement. A dreamy reminiscence of finer impulses stole over the heart of

Cadurcis. The dazzling pageant of metropolitan splendour faded away before the bright scene of nature that surrounded him. He felt the freshness of the fragrant breeze; he gazed with admiration on the still and ancient woods, and his pure and lively blood bubbled beneath the influence of the golden sunbeams. Before him rose the halls of Cherbury, that roof where he had been so happy, that roof to which he had appeared so ungrateful. The memory of a thousand acts of kindness, of a thousand soft and soothing traits of affection, recurred to him with a freshness which startled as much as it pleased him. Not to him only, but to his mother, that mother whose loss he had lived to deplore, had the inmates of Cherbury been ministering angels of peace and joy. Oh! that indeed had been a home; there indeed had been days of happiness; there indeed he had found sympathy, and solace, and succour! And now he was returning to them a stranger, to fulfil one of the formal duties of society in paying them his cold respects; an attention which he could scarcely have avoided offering had he been to them the merest acquaintance, instead of having found within those walls a home not merely in words, but friendship the most delicate and love the most pure, a second parent, and the only being whom he had ever styled sister!

The sight of Cadurcis became dim with emotion as the associations of old scenes and his impending interview with Venetia brought back the past with a power which he had rarely experienced in the playing-fields of Eton, or the saloons of London. Five years! It was an awful chasm in their acquaintance.

He despaired of reviving the kindness which had been broken by such a dreary interval, and broken on his side so wilfully; and yet he began to feel that unless met with that kindness he should be very miserable. Sooth to say, he was not a little embarrassed, and scarcely knew which contingency he most desired, to meet, or to escape from her. He almost repented his return to Cadurcis, and yet to see Venetia again he felt must be exquisite pleasure. Influenced by these feelings he arrived at the hall steps, and so, dismounting and giving his horse to his groom, Cadurcis, with a palpitating heart and faltering hand, formally rang the bell of that hall which in old days he entered at all seasons without ceremony.

Never perhaps did a man feel more nervous; he grew pale, paler even than usual, and his whole frame trembled as the approaching footstep of the servant assured him the door was about to open. He longed now that the family might not be at home, that he might at least gain four-and-twenty hours to prepare himself. But the family were at home and he was obliged to enter. He stopped for a moment in the hall under the pretence of examining the old familiar scene, but it was merely to collect himself, for his sight was clouded; spoke to the old servant, to reassure himself by the sound of his own voice, but the husky words seemed to stick in his throat; ascended the staircase with tottering steps, and leant against the banister as he heard his name announced. The effort, however, must be made; it was too late to recede; and Lord Cadurcis, entering the terrace-room, extended his hand to Lady Annabel Herbert. She was not in the least changed, but looked as beautiful and serene as usual. Her salutation, though far from deficient in warmth, was a little more dignified than that which Plantagenet remembered; but still her presence reassured him, and while he pressed her hand with earnestness he contrived to murmur forth with pleasing emotion, his delight at again meeting her. Strange to say, in the absorbing agitation of the moment, all thought of Venetia had vanished; and it was when he had turned and beheld a maiden of the most exquisite beauty that his vision had ever lighted on, who had just risen from her seat and was at the moment saluting him, that he entirely lost his presence of mind; he turned scarlet, was quite silent, made an awkward bow, and then stood perfectly fixed.

'My daughter,' said Lady Annabel, slightly pointing to Venetia; 'will not you be seated?'

Cadurcis fell into a chair in absolute confusion. The rare and surpassing beauty of Venetia, his own stupidity, his admiration of her, his contempt for himself, the sight of the old chamber, the recollection of the past, the minutest incidents of which seemed all suddenly to crowd upon his memory, the painful consciousness of the revolution which had occurred in his position in the family, proved by his first being obliged to be introduced to Venetia, and then being addressed so formally by his title by her mother; all these impressions united overcame him; he could not speak, he sat silent and confounded; and had it not been for the imperturbable self-composure and delicate and amiable consideration of Lady Annabel, it would have been impossible for him to have remained in a room where he experienced agonising embarrassment.

Under cover, however, of a discharge of discreet inquiries as to when he arrived, how long he meant to stay, whether he found Cadurcis altered, and similar interrogations which required no extraordinary exertion of his lordship's intellect to answer, but to which he nevertheless contrived to give inconsistent and contradictory responses, Cadurcis in time recovered himself sufficiently to maintain a fair though not very brilliant conversation, and even ventured occasionally to address an observation to Venetia, who was seated at her work perfectly composed, but who replied to all his remarks with the same sweet voice and artless simplicity which had characterised her childhood, though time and thought had, by their blended influence, perhaps somewhat deprived her of that wild grace and sparkling gaiety for which she was once so eminent.

These great disenchanters of humanity, if indeed they had stolen away some of the fascinating qualities of infancy, had amply recompensed Venetia

Herbert for the loss by the additional and commanding charms which they had conferred on her. From a beautiful child she had expanded into a most beautiful woman. She had now entirely recovered from her illness, of which the only visible effect was the addition that it had made to her stature, already slightly above the middle height, but of exquisite symmetry. Like her mother, she did not wear powder, then usual in society; but her auburn hair, of the finest texture, descended in long and luxuriant tresses far over her shoulders, braided with ribands, perfectly exposing her pellucid brow, here and there tinted with an undulating vein, for she had retained, if possible with increased lustre, the dazzling complexion of her infancy. If the rose upon the cheek were less vivid than of yore, the dimples were certainly more developed; the clear grey eye was shadowed by long dark lashes, and every smile and movement of those ruby lips revealed teeth exquisitely small and regular, and fresh and brilliant as pearls just plucked by a diver.

Conversation proceeded and improved. Cadurcis became more easy and more fluent. His memory, which seemed suddenly to have returned to him with unusual vigour, wonderfully served him. There was scarcely an individual of whom he did not contrive to inquire, from Dr. Masham to Mistress Pauncefort; he was resolved to show that if he had neglected, he had at least not forgotten them. Nor did he exhibit the slightest indication of terminating his visit; so that Lady Annabel, aware that he was alone at the abbey and that he could have no engagement in the neighbourhood, could not refrain from inviting him to remain and dine with them. The invitation was accepted without hesitation. In due course of time Cadurcis attended the ladies in their walk; it was a delightful stroll in the park, though he felt some slight emotion when he found himself addressing Venetia by the title of 'Miss Herbert.' When he had exhausted all the topics of local interest, he had a great deal to say about himself in answer to the inquiries of Lady Annabel. He spoke with so much feeling and simplicity of his first days at Eton, and the misery he experienced on first quitting Cherbury, that his details could not fail of being agreeable to those whose natural self-esteem they so agreeably mattered. Then he dwelt upon his casual acquaintance with London society, and Lady Annabel was gratified to observe, from many incidental observations, that his principles were in every respect of the right tone; and that he had zealously enlisted himself in the ranks of that national party who opposed themselves to the disorganising opinions then afloat. He spoke of his impending residence at the university with the affectionate anticipations which might have been expected from a devoted child of the ancient and orthodox institutions of his country, and seemed perfectly impressed with the responsible duties for which he was destined, as an hereditary legislator of England. On the whole, his carriage and conversation afforded a delightful evidence of a pure, and earnest, and frank, and gifted mind, that had acquired at an early age much of the mature and fixed character of manhood, without losing anything of that boyish sincerity and simplicity too often the penalty of experience.

The dinner passed in pleasant conversation, and if they were no longer familiar, they were at least cordial. Cadurcis spoke of Dr. Masham with affectionate respect, and mentioned his intention of visiting Marringhurst on the following day. He ventured to hope that Lady Annabel and Miss Herbert might accompany him, and it was arranged that his wish should be gratified. The evening drew on apace, and Lady Annabel was greatly pleased when Lord Cadurcis expressed his wish to remain for their evening prayers. He was indeed sincerely religious; and as he knelt in the old chapel that had been the hallowed scene of his boyish devotions, he offered his ardent thanksgivings to his Creator who had mercifully kept his soul pure and true, and allowed him, after so long an estrangement from the sweet spot of his childhood, once more to mingle his supplications with his kind and virtuous friends.

Influenced by the solemn sounds still lingering in his ear, Cadurcis bade them farewell for the night, with an earnestness of manner and depth of feeling which he would scarcely have ventured to exhibit at their first meeting. 'Good night, dear Lady Annabel,' he said, as he pressed her hand; 'you know not how happy, how grateful I feel, to be once more at Cherbury. Good night, Venetia!'

That last word lingered on his lips; it was uttered in a tone at once mournful and sweet, and her hand was unconsciously retained for a moment in his; but for a moment; and yet in that brief instant a thousand thoughts seemed to course through his brain.

Before Venetia retired to rest she remained for a few minutes in her mother's room. 'What do you think of him, mamma?' she said; 'is he not very changed?'

'He is, my love,' replied Lady Annabel; 'what I sometimes thought he might, what I always hoped he would, be.'

'He really seemed happy to meet us again, and yet how strange that for years he should never have communicated with us.'

'Not so very strange, my love! He was but a child when we parted, and he has felt embarrassment in resuming connections which for a long interval had been inevitably severed. Remember what a change his life had to endure; few, after such an interval, would have returned with feelings so kind and so pure!'

'He was always a favourite of yours, mamma!'

'I always fancied that I observed in him the seeds of great virtues and great talents; but I was not so sanguine that they would have flourished as they appear to have done.'

In the meantime the subject of their observations strolled home on foot, for he had dismissed his horses, to the abbey. It was a brilliant night, and the white beams of the moon fell full upon the old monastic pile, of which massy portions were in dark shade while the light gracefully rested on the projecting ornaments of the building, and played, as it were, with the fretted and fantastic pinnacles. Behind were the savage hills, softened by the hour; and on the right extended the still and luminous lake. Cadurcis rested for a moment and gazed upon the fair, yet solemn scene. The dreams of ambition that occasionally distracted him were dead. The surrounding scene harmonised with the thoughts of purity, repose, and beauty that filled his soul. Why should he ever leave this spot, sacred to him by the finest emotions of his nature? Why should he not at once quit that world which he had just entered, while he could quit it without remorse? If ever there existed a being who was his own master, who might mould his destiny at his will, it seemed to be Cadurcis. His lone yet independent situation, his impetuous yet firm volition, alike qualified him to achieve the career most grateful to his disposition. Let him, then, achieve it here; here let him find that solitude he had ever loved, softened by that affection for which he had ever sighed, and which here only he had ever found. It seemed to him that there was only one being in the world whom he had ever loved, and that was Venetia Herbert: it seemed to him that there was only one thing in this world worth living for, and that was the enjoyment of her sweet heart. The pure-minded, the rare, the gracious creature! Why should she ever quit these immaculate bowers wherein she had been so mystically and delicately bred? Why should she ever quit the fond roof of Cherbury, but to shed grace and love amid the cloisters of Cadurcis? Her life hitherto had been an enchanted tale; why should the spell ever break? Why should she enter that world where care, disappointment, mortification, misery, must await her? He for a season had left the magic circle of her life, and perhaps it was well. He was a man, and so he should know all. But he had returned, thank Heaven! he had returned, and never again would he quit her. Fool that he had been ever to have neglected her! And for a reason that ought to have made him doubly her friend, her solace, her protector. Oh! to think of the sneers or the taunts of the world calling for a moment the colour from that bright cheek, or dusking for an instant the radiance of that brilliant eye! His heart ached at the thought of her unhappiness, and he longed to press her to it, and cherish her like some innocent dove that had flown from the terrors of a pursuing hawk.

CHAPTER II.

'Well, Pauncefort,' said Lord Cadurcis, smiling, as he renewed his acquaintance with his old friend, 'I hope you have not forgotten my last words, and have taken care of your young lady.'

'Oh! dear, my lord,' said Mistress Pauncefort, blushing and simpering. 'Well to be sure, how your lordship has surprised us all! I thought we were never going to see you again!'

'You know I told you I should return; and now I mean never to leave you again.'

'Never is a long word, my lord,' said Mistress Pauncefort, looking very archly.

'Ah! but I mean to settle, regularly to settle here,' said Lord Cadurcis.

'Marry and settle, my lord,' said Mistress Pauncefort, still more arch.

'And why not?' inquired Lord Cadurcis, laughing.

'That is just what I said last night,' exclaimed Mistress Pauncefort, eagerly. 'And why not? for I said, says I, his lordship must marry sooner or later, and the sooner the better, say I: and to be sure he is very young, but what of that? for, says I, no one can say he does not look quite a man. And really, my lord, saving your presence, you are grown indeed.'

'Pish!' said Lord Cadurcis, turning away and laughing, 'I have left off growing, Pauncefort, and all those sort of things.'

'You have not forgotten our last visit to Marringhurst?' said Lord Cadurcis to Venetia, as the comfortable mansion of the worthy Doctor appeared in sight.

'I have forgotten nothing,' replied Venetia with a faint smile; 'I do not know what it is to forget. My life has been so uneventful that every past incident, however slight, is as fresh in my memory as if it occurred yesterday.'

'Then you remember the strawberries and cream?' said Lord Cadurcis.

'And other circumstances less agreeable,' he fancied Venetia observed, but her voice was low.

'Do you know, Lady Annabel,' said Lord Cadurcis, 'that I was very nearly riding my pony to-day? I wish to bring back old times with the utmost possible completeness; I wish for a moment to believe that I have never quitted Cherbury.'

'Let us think only of the present now,' said Lady Annabel in a cheerful voice, 'for it is very agreeable. I see the good Doctor; he has discovered us.'

'I wonder whom he fancies Lord Cadurcis to be?' said Venetia.

'Have you no occasional cavalier for whom at a distance I may be mistaken?' inquired his lordship in a tone of affected carelessness, though in truth it was an inquiry that he made not without anxiety.

'Everything remains here exactly as you left it,' replied Lady Annabel, with some quickness, yet in a lively tone.

'Happy Cherbury!' exclaimed Lord Cadurcis. 'May it indeed never change!'

They rode briskly on; the Doctor was standing at his gate. He saluted Lady Annabel and Venetia with his accustomed cordiality, and then stared at their companion as if waiting for an introduction.

'You forget an old friend, my dear Doctor,' said Cadurcis.

'Lord Cadurcis!' exclaimed Dr. Masham. His lordship had by this time dismounted and eagerly extended his hand to his old tutor.

Having quitted their horses they all entered the house, nor was there naturally any want of conversation. Cadurcis had much information to give and many questions to answer. He was in the highest spirits and the most amiable mood; gay, amusing, and overflowing with kind-heartedness. The Doctor seldom required any inspiration, to be joyous, and Lady Annabel was unusually animated. Venetia alone, though cheerful, was calmer than pleased Cadurcis. Time, he sorrowfully observed, had occasioned a greater change in her manner than he could have expected. Youthful as she still was, indeed but on the threshold of womanhood, and exempted, as it seemed she had been, from anything to disturb the clearness of her mind, that enchanting play of fancy which had once characterised her, and which he recalled with a sigh, appeared in a great degree to have deserted her. He watched her countenance with emotion, and, supremely beautiful as it undeniably was, there was a cast of thoughtfulness or suffering impressed upon the features which rendered him mournful he knew not why, and caused him to feel as if a cloud had stolen unexpectedly over the sun and made him shiver.

But there was no time or opportunity for sad reflections; he had to renew his acquaintance with all the sights and curiosities of the rectory, to sing to the canaries, and visit the gold fish, admire the stuffed fox, and wonder that in the space of five years the voracious otter had not yet contrived to devour its prey. Then they refreshed themselves after their ride with a stroll in the Doctor's garden; Cadurcis persisted in attaching himself to Venetia, as in old days, and nothing would prevent him from leading her to the grotto. Lady

Annabel walked behind, leaning on the Doctor's arm, narrating, with no fear of being heard, all the history of their friend's return.

'I never was so surprised in my life,' said the Doctor; 'he is vastly improved; he is quite a man; his carriage is very finished.'

'And his principles,' said Lady Annabel. 'You have no idea, my dear Doctor, how right his opinions seem to be on every subject. He has been brought up in a good school; he does his guardian great credit. He is quite loyal and orthodox in all his opinions; ready to risk his life for our blessed constitution in Church and State. He requested, as a favour, that he might remain at our prayers last night. It is delightful for me to see him turn out so well!'

In the meantime Cadurcis and Venetia entered the grotto.

'The dear Doctor!' said Cadurcis: 'five years have brought no visible change even to him; perhaps he may be a degree less agile, but I will not believe it. And Lady Annabel; it seems to me your mother is more youthful and beautiful than ever. There is a spell in our air,' continued his lordship, with a laughing eye; 'for if we have changed, Venetia, ours is, at least, an alteration that bears no sign of decay. We are advancing, but they have not declined; we are all enchanted.'

'I feel changed,' said Venetia gravely.

'I left you a child and I find you a woman,' said Lord Cadurcis, 'a change which who can regret?'

'I would I were a child again,' said Venetia.

'We were happy,' said Lord Cadurcis, in a thoughtful tone; and then in an inquiring voice he added, 'and so we are now?'

Venetia shook her head.

'Can you be unhappy?'

'To be unhappy would be wicked,' said Venetia; 'but my mind has lost its spring.'

'Ah! say not so, Venetia, or you will make even me gloomy. I am happy, positively happy. There must not be a cloud upon your brow.'

'You are joyous,' said Venetia, 'because you are excited. It is the novelty of return that animates you. It will wear off; you will grow weary, and when you go to the university you will think yourself happy again.'

'I do not intend to go to the university,' said Cadurcis.

'I understood from you that you were going there immediately.'

'My plans are changed,' said Cadurcis; 'I do not intend ever to leave home again.'

'When you go to Cambridge,' said Dr. Masham, who just then reached them, 'I shall trouble you with a letter to an old friend of mine whose acquaintance you may find valuable.'

Venetia smiled; Cadurcis bowed, expressed his thanks, and muttered something about talking over the subject with the Doctor.

After this the conversation became general, and at length they all returned to the house to partake of the Doctor's hospitality, who promised to dine at the hall on the morrow. The ride home was agreeable and animated, but the conversation on the part of the ladies was principally maintained by Lady Annabel, who seemed every moment more delighted with the society of Lord Cadurcis, and to sympathise every instant more completely with his frank exposition of his opinions on all subjects. When they returned to Cherbury, Cadurcis remained with them as a matter of course. An invitation was neither expected nor given. Not an allusion was made to the sports of the field, to enjoy which was the original purpose of his visit to the abbey; and he spoke of to-morrow as of a period which, as usual, was to be spent entirely in their society. He remained with them, as on the previous night, to the latest possible moment. Although reserved in society, no one could be more fluent with those with whom he was perfectly unembarrassed. He was indeed exceedingly entertaining, and Lady Annabel relaxed into conversation beyond her custom. As for Venetia, she did not speak often, but she listened with interest, and was evidently amused. When Cadurcis bade them goodnight Lady Annabel begged him to breakfast with them; while Venetia, serene, though kind, neither seconded the invitation, nor seemed interested one way or the other in its result.

CHAPTER III.

Except returning to sleep at the abbey, Lord Cadurcis was now as much an habitual inmate of Cherbury Hall as in the days of his childhood. He was there almost with the lark, and never quitted its roof until its inmates were about to retire for the night. His guns and dogs, which had been sent down from London with so much pomp of preparation, were unused and unnoticed; and he passed his days in reading Richardson's novels, which he had brought with him from town, to the ladies, and then in riding with them about the country, for he loved to visit all his old haunts, and trace even the very green sward where he first met the gipsies, and fancied that he had achieved his emancipation from all the coming cares and annoyances of the world. In this pleasant life several weeks had glided away: Cadurcis had entirely resumed his old footing in the family, nor did he attempt to conceal the homage he was paying to the charms of Venetia. She indeed seemed utterly unconscious that such projects had entered, or indeed could enter, the brain of her old playfellow, with whom, now that she was habituated to his presence, and revived by his inspiriting society, she had resumed all her old familiar intimacy, addressing him by his Christian name, as if he had never ceased to be her brother. But Lady Annabel was not so blind as her daughter, and had indeed her vision been as clouded, her faithful minister, Mistress Pauncefort, would have taken care quickly to couch it; for a very short time had elapsed before that vigilant gentlewoman, resolved to convince her mistress that nothing could escape her sleepless scrutiny, and that it was equally in vain for her mistress to hope to possess any secrets without her participation, seized a convenient opportunity before she bid her lady good night, just to inquire 'when it might be expected to take place?' and in reply to the very evident astonishment which Lady Annabel testified at this question, and the expression of her extreme displeasure at any conversation on a circumstance for which there was not the slightest foundation, Mistress Pauncefort, after duly flouncing about with every possible symbol of pettish agitation and mortified curiosity, her cheek pale with hesitating impertinence, and her nose quivering with inquisitiveness, condescended to admit with a sceptical sneer, that, of course, no doubt her ladyship knew more of such a subject than she could; it was not her place to know anything of such business; for her part she said nothing; it was not her place, but if it were, she certainly must say that she could not help believing that my lord was looking remarkably sweet on Miss Venetia, and what was more, everybody in the house thought the same, though for her part, whenever they mentioned the circumstance to her, she said nothing, or bid them hold their tongues, for what was it to them; it was not their business, and they could know nothing; and that nothing would displease her ladyship more than chattering on such subjects, and many's the match as good as finished, that's gone off by no worse means than the chitter-chatter of those who should hold their tongues. Therefore she should say no more; but if her ladyship wished her to contradict it, why she could, and the sooner, perhaps, the better.

Lady Annabel observed to her that she wished no such thing, but she desired that Pauncefort would make no more observations on the subject, either to her or to any one else. And then Pauncefort bade her ladyship good night in a huff, catching up her candle with a rather impertinent jerk, and gently slamming the door, as if she had meant to close it quietly, only it had escaped out of her fingers.

Whatever might be the tone, whether of surprise or displeasure, which Lady Annabel thought fit to assume to her attendant on her noticing Lord Cadurcis' attentions to her daughter, there is no doubt that his conduct had early and long engaged her ladyship's remark, her consideration, and her approval. Without meditating indeed an immediate union between Cadurcis and Venetia, Lady Annabel pleased herself with the prospect of her daughter's eventual marriage with one whom she had known so early and so intimately; who was by nature of a gentle, sincere, and affectionate disposition, and in whom education had carefully instilled the most sound and laudable principles and opinions; one apparently with simple tastes, moderate desires, fair talents, a mind intelligent, if not brilliant, and passions which at the worst had been rather ill-regulated than violent; attached also to Venetia from her childhood, and always visibly affected by her influence. All these moral considerations seemed to offer a fair security for happiness; and the material ones were neither less promising, nor altogether disregarded by the mother. It was an union which would join broad lands and fair estates; which would place on the brow of her daughter one of the most ancient coronets in England; and, which indeed was the chief of these considerations, would, without exposing Venetia to that contaminating contact with the world from which Lady Annabel recoiled, establish her, without this initiatory and sorrowful experience, in a position superior to which even the blood of the Herberts, though it might flow in so fair and gifted a form as that of Venetia, need not aspire.

Lord Cadurcis had not returned to Cherbury a week before this scheme entered into the head of Lady Annabel. She had always liked him; had always given him credit for good qualities; had always believed that his early defects were the consequence of his mother's injudicious treatment; and that at heart he was an amiable, generous, and trustworthy being, one who might be depended on, with a naturally good judgment, and substantial and sufficient talents, which only required cultivation. When she met him again after so long an interval, and found her early prognostics so fairly, so completely fulfilled, and watched his conduct and conversation, exhibiting alike a well-informed mind, an obliging temper, and, what Lady Annabel valued even above all gifts and blessings, a profound conviction of the truth of all her own opinions, moral, political, and religious, she was quite charmed; she was moved to unusual animation; she grew excited in his praise; his presence delighted her; she entertained for him the warmest affection, and reposed in him unbounded confidence. All her hopes became concentred in the wish of seeing him her son-in-law; and she detected with lively satisfaction the immediate impression which Venetia had made upon his heart; for indeed it should not be forgotten, that although Lady Annabel was still young, and although her frame and temperament were alike promising of a long life, it was natural, when she reflected upon the otherwise lone condition of her daughter, that she should tremble at the thought of quitting this world without leaving her child a protector. To Doctor Masham, from whom Lady Annabel had no secrets, she confided in time these happy but covert hopes, and he was not less anxious than herself for their fulfilment. Since the return of Cadurcis the Doctor contrived to be a more frequent visitor at the hall than usual, and he lost no opportunity of silently advancing the object of his friend.

As for Cadurcis himself, it was impossible for him not quickly to discover that no obstacle to his heart's dearest wish would arise on the part of the parent. The demeanour of the daughter somewhat more perplexed him. Venetia indeed had entirely fallen into her old habits of intimacy and frankness with Plantagenet; she was as affectionate and as unembarrassed as in former days, and almost as gay; for his presence and companionship had in a great degree insensibly removed that stillness and gravity which had gradually influenced her mind and conduct. But in that conduct there was, and he observed it with some degree of mortification, a total absence of the consciousness of being the object of the passionate admiration of another. She treated Lord Cadurcis as a brother she much loved, who had returned to his home after a long absence. She liked to listen to his conversation, to hear of his adventures, to consult over his plans. His arrival called a smile to her face, and his departure for the night was always alleviated by some allusion to their meeting on the morrow. But many an ardent gaze on the part of Cadurcis, and many a phrase of emotion, passed unnoticed and unappreciated. His gallantry was entirely thrown away, or, if observed, only occasioned a pretty stare at the unnecessary trouble he gave himself, or the strange ceremony which she supposed an acquaintance with society had taught him. Cadurcis attributed this reception of his veiled and delicate overtures to her ignorance of the world; and though he sighed for as passionate a return to his strong feelings as the sentiments which animated himself, he was on the whole not displeased, but rather interested, by these indications of a pure and unsophisticated spirit.

CHAPTER IV.

Cadurcis had proposed, and Lady Annabel had seconded the proposition with eager satisfaction, that they should seek some day at the abbey whatever hospitality it might offer; Dr. Masham was to be of the party, which was, indeed, one of those fanciful expeditions where the same companions, though they meet at all times without restraint and with every convenience of life, seek increased amusement in the novelty of a slight change of habits. With the aid of the neighbouring town of Southport, Cadurcis had made preparations for his friends not entirely unworthy of them, though he affected to the last all the air of a conductor of a wild expedition of discovery, and laughingly impressed upon them the necessity of steeling their minds and bodies to the experience and endurance of the roughest treatment and the most severe hardships.

The morning of this eventful day broke as beautifully as the preceding ones. Autumn had seldom been more gorgeous than this year. Although he was to play the host, Cadurcis would not deprive himself of his usual visit to the hall; and he appeared there at an early hour to accompany his guests, who were to ride over to the abbey, to husband all their energies for their long rambles through the demesne.

Cadurcis was in high spirits, and Lady Annabel scarcely less joyous. Venetia smiled with her usual sweetness and serenity. They congratulated each other on the charming season; and Mistress Pauncefort received a formal invitation to join the party and go a-nutting with one of her fellow-servants and his lordship's valet. The good Doctor was rather late, but he arrived at last on his stout steed, in his accustomed cheerful mood. Here was a party of pleasure which all agreed must be pleasant; no strangers to amuse, or to be amusing, but formed merely of four human beings who spent every day of their lives in each other's society, between whom there was the most complete sympathy and the most cordial good-will.

By noon they were all mounted on their steeds, and though the air was warmed by a meridian sun shining in a clear sky, there was a gentle breeze abroad, sweet and grateful; and moreover they soon entered the wood and enjoyed the shelter of its verdant shade. The abbey looked most picturesque when they first burst upon it; the nearer and wooded hills, which formed its immediate background, just tinted by the golden pencil of autumn, while the meads of the valley were still emerald green; and the stream, now lost, now winding, glittered here and there in the sun, and gave a life and sprightliness to the landscape which exceeded even the effect of the more distant and expansive lake.

They were received at the abbey by Mistress Pauncefort, who had preceded them, and who welcomed them with a complacent smile. Cadurcis hastened to assist Lady Annabel to dismount, and was a little confused but very pleased when she assured him she needed no assistance but requested him to take care of Venetia. He was just in time to receive her in his arms, where she found herself without the slightest embarrassment. The coolness of the cloisters was grateful after their ride, and they lingered and looked upon the old fountain, and felt the freshness of its fall with satisfaction which all alike expressed. Lady Annabel and Venetia then retired for a while to free themselves from their riding habits, and Cadurcis affectionately taking the arm of Dr. Masham led him a few paces, and then almost involuntarily exclaimed, 'My dear Doctor, I think I am the happiest fellow that ever lived!'

'That I trust you may always be, my dear boy,' said Dr. Masham; 'but what has called forth this particular exclamation?'

'To feel that I am once more at Cadurcis; to feel that I am here once more with you all; to feel that I never shall leave you again.'

'Not again?'

'Never!' said Cadurcis. 'The experience of these last few weeks, which yet have seemed an age in my existence, has made me resolve never to quit a society where I am persuaded I may obtain a degree of happiness which what is called the world can never afford me.'

'What will your guardian say?'

'What care I?'

'A dutiful ward!'

'Poh! the relations between us were formed only to secure my welfare. It is secured; it will be secured by my own resolution.'

'And what is that?' inquired Dr. Masham.

'To marry Venetia, if she will accept me.'

'And that you do not doubt.'

'We doubt everything when everything is at stake,' replied Lord Cadurcis. 'I know that her consent would ensure my happiness; and when I reflect, I cannot help being equally persuaded that it would secure hers. Her mother, I think, would not be adverse to our union. And you, my dear sir, what do you think?'

'I think,' said Dr. Masham, 'that whoever marries Venetia will marry the most beautiful and the most gifted of God's creatures; I hope you may marry her;

I wish you to marry her; I believe you will marry her, but not yet; you are too young, Lord Cadurcis.'

'Oh, no! my dear Doctor, not too young to marry Venetia. Remember I have known her all my life, at least so long as I have been able to form an opinion. How few are the men, my dear Doctor, who are so fortunate as to unite themselves with women whom they have known, as I have known Venetia, for more than seven long years!'

'During five of which you have never seen or heard of her.'

'Mine was the fault! And yet I cannot help thinking, as it may probably turn out, as you yourself believe it will turn out, that it is as well that we have been separated for this interval. It has afforded me opportunities for observation which I should never have enjoyed at Cadurcis; and although my lot either way could not have altered the nature of things, I might have been discontented, I might have sighed for a world which now I do not value. It is true I have not seen Venetia for five years, but I find her the same, or changed only by nature, and fulfilling all the rich promise which her childhood intimated. No, my dear Doctor, I respect your opinion more than that of any man living; but nobody, nothing, can persuade me that I am not as intimately acquainted with Venetia's character, with all her rare virtues, as if we had never separated.'

'I do not doubt it,' said the Doctor; 'high as you may pitch your estimate you cannot overvalue her.'

'Then why should we not marry?'

'Because, my dear friend, although you may be perfectly acquainted with Venetia, you cannot be perfectly acquainted with yourself.'

'How so?' exclaimed Lord Cadurcis in a tone of surprise, perhaps a little indignant.

'Because it is impossible. No young man of eighteen ever possessed such precious knowledge. I esteem and admire you; I give you every credit for a good heart and a sound head; but it is impossible, at your time of life, that your character can be formed; and, until it be, you may marry Venetia and yet be a very miserable man.'

'It is formed,' said his lordship firmly; 'there is not a subject important to a human being on which my opinions are not settled.'

'You may live to change them all,' said the Doctor, 'and that very speedily.'

'Impossible!' said Lord Cadurcis. 'My dear Doctor, I cannot understand you; you say that you hope, that you wish, even that you believe that I shall marry

Venetia; and yet you permit me to infer that our union will only make us miserable. What do you wish me to do?'

'Go to college for a term or two.'

'Without Venetia! I should die.'

'Well, if you be in a dying state you can return.'

'You joke, my dear Doctor.'

'My dear boy, I am perfectly serious.'

'But she may marry somebody else?'

'I am your only rival,' said the Doctor, with a smile; 'and though even friends can scarcely be trusted under such circumstances, I promise you not to betray you.'

'Your advice is not very pleasant,' said his lordship.

'Good advice seldom is,' said the Doctor.

'My dear Doctor, I have made up my mind to marry her, and marry her at once. I know her well, you admit that yourself. I do not believe that there ever was a woman like her, that there ever will be a woman like her. Nature has marked her out from other women, and her education has not been less peculiar. Her mystic breeding pleases me. It is something to marry a wife so fair, so pure, so refined, so accomplished, who is, nevertheless, perfectly ignorant of the world. I have dreamt of such things; I have paced these old cloisters when a boy and when I was miserable at home, and I have had visions, and this was one. I have sighed to live alone with a fair spirit for my minister. Venetia has descended from heaven for me, and for me alone. I am resolved I will pluck this flower with the dew upon its leaves.'

'I did not know I was reasoning with a poet,' said the Doctor, with a smile. 'Had I been conscious of it, I would not have been so rash.'

'I have not a grain of poetry in my composition,' said his lordship; 'I never could write a verse; I was notorious at Eton for begging all their old manuscripts from boys when they left school, to crib from; but I have a heart, and I can feel. I love Venetia, I have always loved her, and, if possible, I will marry her, and marry her at once.'

CHAPTER V.

The reappearance of the ladies at the end of the cloister terminated this conversation, the result of which was rather to confirm Lord Cadurcis in his resolution of instantly urging his suit, than the reverse. He ran forward to greet his friends with a smile, and took his place by the side of Venetia, whom, a little to her surprise, he congratulated in glowing phrase on her charming costume. Indeed she looked very captivating, with a pastoral hat, then much in fashion, and a dress as simple and as sylvan, both showing to admirable advantage her long descending hair, and her agile and springy figure.

Cadurcis proposed that they should ramble over the abbey, he talked of projected alterations, as if he really had the power immediately to effect them, and was desirous of obtaining their opinions before any change was made. So they ascended the staircase which many years before Venetia had mounted for the first time with her mother, and entered that series of small and ill-furnished rooms in which Mrs. Cadurcis had principally resided, and which had undergone no change. The old pictures were examined; these, all agreed, never must move; and the new furniture, it was settled, must be in character with the building. Lady Annabel entered into all the details with an interest and animation which rather amused Dr. Masham. Venetia listened and suggested, and responded to the frequent appeals of Cadurcis to her judgment with an unconscious equanimity not less diverting.

'Now here we really can do something,' said his lordship as they entered the saloon, or rather refectory; 'here I think we may effect wonders. The tapestry must always remain. Is it not magnificent, Venetia? But what hangings shall we have? We must keep the old chairs, I think. Do you approve of the old chairs, Venetia? And what shall we cover them with? Shall it be damask? What do you think, Venetia? Do you like damask? And what colour shall it be? Shall it be crimson? Shall it be crimson damask, Lady Annabel? Do you think Venetia would like crimson damask? Now, Venetia, do give us the benefit of your opinion.'

Then they entered the old gallery; here was to be a great transformation. Marvels were to be effected in the old gallery, and many and multiplied were the appeals to the taste and fancy of Venetia.

'I think,' said Lord Cadurcis, 'I shall leave the gallery to be arranged when I am settled. The rooms and the saloon shall be done at once, I shall give orders for them to begin instantly. Whom do you recommend, Lady Annabel? Do you think there is any person at Southport who could manage to do it, superintended by our taste? Venetia, what do you think?'

Venetia was standing at the window, rather apart from her companions, looking at the old garden. Lord Cadurcis joined her. 'Ah! it has been sadly neglected since my poor mother's time. We could not do much in those days, but still she loved this garden. I must depend upon you entirely to arrange my garden, Venetia. This spot is sacred to you. You have not forgotten our labours here, have you, Venetia? Ah! those were happy days, and these shall be more happy still. This is your garden; it shall always be called Venetia's garden.'

'I would have taken care of it when you were away, but—'

'But what?' inquired Lord Cadurcis anxiously.

'We hardly felt authorised,' replied Venetia calmly. 'We came at first when you left Cadurcis, but at last it did not seem that our presence was very acceptable.'

'The brutes!' exclaimed Lord Cadurcis.

'No, no; good simple people, they were unused to orders from strange masters, and they were perplexed. Besides, we had no right to interfere.'

'No right to interfere! Venetia, my little fellow-labourer, no right to interfere! Why all is yours! Fancy your having no right to interfere at Cadurcis!'

Then they proceeded to the park and wandered to the margin of the lake. There was not a spot, not an object, which did not recall some adventure or incident of childhood. Every moment Lord Cadurcis exclaimed, 'Venetia! do you remember this?' 'Venetia! have you forgotten that?' and every time Venetia smiled, and proved how faithful was her memory by adding some little unmentioned trait to the lively reminiscences of her companion.

'Well, after all,' said Lord Cadurcis with a sigh, 'my poor mother was a strange woman, and, God bless her! used sometimes to worry me out of my senses! but still she always loved you. No one can deny that. Cherbury was a magic name with her. She loved Lady Annabel, and she loved you, Venetia. It ran in the blood, you see. She would be happy, quite happy, if she saw us all here together, and if she knew—'

'Plantagenet,' said Lady Annabel, 'you must build a lodge at this end of the park. I cannot conceive anything more effective than an entrance from the Southport road in this quarter.'

'Certainly, Lady Annabel, certainly we must build a lodge. Do not you think so, Venetia?'

'Indeed I think it would be a great improvement,' replied Venetia; 'but you must take care to have a lodge in character with the abbey.'

'You shall make a drawing for it,' said Lord Cadurcis; 'it shall be built directly, and it shall be called Venetia Lodge.'

The hours flew away, loitering in the park, roaming in the woods. They met Mistress Pauncefort and her friends loaded with plunder, and they offered to Venetia a trophy of their success; but when Venetia, merely to please their kind hearts, accepted their tribute with cordiality, and declared there was nothing she liked better, Lord Cadurcis would not be satisfied unless he immediately commenced nutting, and each moment he bore to Venetia the produce of his sport, till in time she could scarcely sustain the rich and increasing burden. At length they bent their steps towards home, sufficiently wearied to look forward with welcome to rest and their repast, yet not fatigued, and exhilarated by the atmosphere, for the sun was now in its decline, though in this favoured season there were yet hours enough remaining of enchanting light.

In the refectory they found, to the surprise of all but their host, a banquet. It was just one of those occasions when nothing is expected and everything is welcome and surprising; when, from the unpremeditated air generally assumed, all preparation startles and pleases; when even ladies are not ashamed to eat, and formality appears quite banished. Game of all kinds, teal from the lake, and piles of beautiful fruit, made the table alike tempting and picturesque. Then there were stray bottles of rare wine disinterred from venerable cellars; and, more inspiriting even than the choice wine, a host under the influence of every emotion, and swayed by every circumstance that can make a man happy and delightful. Oh! they were very gay, and it seemed difficult to believe that care or sorrow, or the dominion of dark or ungracious passions, could ever disturb sympathies so complete and countenances so radiant.

At the urgent request of Cadurcis, Venetia sang to them; and while she sang, the expression of her countenance and voice harmonising with the arch hilarity of the subject, Plantagenet for a moment believed that he beheld the little Venetia of his youth, that sunny child so full of mirth and grace, the very recollection of whose lively and bright existence might enliven the gloomiest hour and lighten the heaviest heart.

Enchanted by all that surrounded him, full of hope, and joy, and plans of future felicity, emboldened by the kindness of the daughter, Cadurcis now ventured to urge a request to Lady Annabel, and the request was granted, for all seemed to feel that it was a day on which nothing was to be refused to their friend. Happy Cadurcis! The child had a holiday, and it fancied itself a man enjoying a triumph. In compliance, therefore, with his wish, it was settled that they should all walk back to the hall; even Dr. Masham declared he was competent to the exertion, but perhaps was half entrapped into the declaration by the promise of a bed at Cherbury. This consent enchanted Cadurcis, who looked forward with exquisite pleasure to the evening walk with Venetia.

CHAPTER VI.

Although the sun had not set, it had sunk behind the hills leading to Cherbury when our friends quitted the abbey. Cadurcis, without hesitation, offered his arm to Venetia, and whether from a secret sympathy with his wishes, or merely from some fortunate accident, Lady Annabel and Dr. Masham strolled on before without busying themselves too earnestly with their companions.

'And how do you think our expedition to Cadurcis has turned out?' inquired the young lord, of Venetia, 'Has it been successful?'

'It has been one of the most agreeable days I ever passed,' was the reply.

'Then it has been successful,' rejoined his lordship; 'for my only wish was to amuse you.'

'I think we have all been equally amused,' said Venetia. 'I never knew mamma in such good spirits. I think ever since you returned she has been unusually light-hearted.'

'And you: has my return lightened only her heart, Venetia?'

'Indeed it has contributed to the happiness of every one.'

'And yet, when I first returned, I heard you utter a complaint; the first that to my knowledge ever escaped your lips.'

'Ah! we cannot be always equally gay.'

'Once you were, dear Venetia.'

'I was a child then.'

'And I, I too was a child; yet I am happy, at least now that I am with you.'

'Well, we are both happy now.'

'Oh! say that again, say that again, Venetia; for indeed you made me miserable when you told me that you had changed. I cannot bear that you, Venetia, should ever change.'

'It is the course of nature, Plantagenet; we all change, everything changes. This day that was so bright is changing fast.'

'The stars are as beautiful as the sun, Venetia.'

'And what do you infer?'

'That Venetia, a woman, is as beautiful as Venetia, a little girl; and should be as happy.'

'Is beauty happiness, Plantagenet?'

'It makes others happy, Venetia; and when we make others happy we should be happy ourselves.'

'Few depend upon my influence, and I trust all of them are happy.'

'No one depends upon your influence more than I do.'

'Well, then, be happy always.'

'Would that I might! Ah, Venetia! can I ever forget old days? You were the solace of my dark childhood; you were the charm that first taught me existence was enjoyment. Before I came to Cherbury I never was happy, and since that hour—Ah, Venetia! dear, dearest Venetia! who is like to you?'

'Dear Plantagenet, you were always too kind to me. Would we were children once more!'

'Nay, my own Venetia! you tell me everything changes, and we must not murmur at the course of nature. I would not have our childhood back again, even with all its joys, for there are others yet in store for us, not less pure, not less beautiful. We loved each other then, Venetia, and we love each other now.'

'My feelings towards you have never changed, Plantagenet; I heard of you always with interest, and I met you again with heartfelt pleasure.'

'Oh, that morning! Have you forgotten that morning? Do you know, you will smile very much, but I really believe that I expected to see my Venetia still a little girl, the very same who greeted me when I first arrived with my mother and behaved so naughtily! And when I saw you, and found what you had become, and what I ought always to have known you must become, I was so confused I entirely lost my presence of mind. You must have thought me very awkward, very stupid?'

'Indeed, I was rather gratified by observing that you could not meet us again without emotion. I thought it told well for your heart, which I always believed to be most kind, at least, I am sure, to us.'

'Kind! oh, Venetia! that word but ill describes what my heart ever was, what it now is, to you. Venetia! dearest, sweetest Venetia! can you doubt for a moment my feelings towards your home, and what influence must principally impel them? Am I so dull, or you so blind, Venetia? Can I not express, can you not discover how much, how ardently, how fondly, how devotedly, I, I, I love you?'

'I am sure we always loved each other, Plantagenet.'

'Yes! but not with this love; not as I love you now!'

Venetia stared.

'I thought we could not love each other more than we did, Plantagenet,' at length she said. 'Do you remember the jewel that you gave me? I always wore it until you seemed to forget us, and then I thought it looked so foolish! You remember what is inscribed on it: 'TO VENETIA, FROM HER AFFECTIONATE BROTHER, PLANTAGENET.' And as a brother I always loved you; had I indeed been your sister I could not have loved you more warmly and more truly.'

'I am not your brother, Venetia; I wish not to be loved as a brother: and yet I must be loved by you, or I shall die.'

'What then do you wish?' inquired Venetia, with great simplicity.

'I wish you to marry me,' replied Lord Cadurcis.

'Marry!' exclaimed Venetia, with a face of wonder. 'Marry! Marry you! Marry you, Plantagenet!'

'Ay! is that so wonderful? I love you, and if you love me, why should we not marry?'

Venetia was silent and looked upon the ground, not from agitation, for she was quite calm, but in thought; and then she said, 'I never thought of marriage in my life, Plantagenet; I have no intention, no wish to marry; I mean to live always with mamma.'

'And you shall always live with mamma, but that need not prevent you from marrying me,' he replied. 'Do not we all live together now? What will it signify if you dwell at Cadurcis and Lady Annabel at Cherbury? Is it not one home? But at any rate, this point shall not be an obstacle; for if it please you we will all live at Cherbury.'

'You say that we are happy now, Plantagenet; oh! let us remain as we are.'

'My own sweet girl, my sister, if you please, any title, so it be one of fondness, your sweet simplicity charms me; but, believe me, it cannot be as you wish; we cannot remain as we are unless we marry.'

'Why not?'

'Because I shall be wretched and must live elsewhere, if indeed I can live at all.'

'Oh, Plantagenet! indeed I thought you were my brother; when I found you after so long a separation as kind as in old days, and kinder still, I was so glad; I was so sure you loved me; I thought I had the kindest brother in the world. Let us not talk of any other love. It will, indeed it will, make mamma so miserable!'

'I am greatly mistaken,' replied Lord Cadurcis, who saw no obstacles to his hopes in their conversation hitherto, 'if, on the contrary, our union would not prove far from disagreeable to your mother, Venetia; I will say our mother, for indeed to me she has been one.'

'Plantagenet,' said Venetia, in a very earnest tone, 'I love you very much; but, if you love me, press me on this subject no more at present. You have surprised, indeed you have bewildered me. There are thoughts, there are feelings, there are considerations, that must be respected, that must influence me. Nay! do not look so sorrowful, Plantagenet. Let us be happy now. To-morrow, only to-morrow, and to-morrow we are sure to meet, we will speak further of all this; but now, now, for a moment let us forget it, if we can forget anything so strange. Nay! you shall smile!'

He did. Who could resist that mild and winning glance! And indeed Lord Cadurcis was scarcely disappointed, and not at all mortified at his reception, or, as he esteemed it, the progress of his suit. The conduct of Venetia he attributed entirely to her unsophisticated nature and the timidity of a virgin soul. It made him prize even more dearly the treasure that he believed awaited him. Silent, then, though for a time they both struggled to speak on different subjects, silent, and almost content, Cadurcis proceeded, with the arm of Venetia locked in his and ever and anon unconsciously pressing it to his heart. The rosy twilight had faded away, the stars were stealing forth, and the moon again glittered. With a soul softer than the tinted shades of eve and glowing like the heavens, Cadurcis joined his companions as they entered the gardens of Cherbury. When they had arrived at home it seemed that exhaustion had suddenly succeeded all the excitement of the day. The Doctor, who was wearied, retired immediately. Lady Annabel pressed Cadurcis to remain and take tea, or, at least to ride home; but his lordship, protesting that he was not in the slightest degree fatigued, and anticipating their speedy union on the morrow, bade her good night, and pressing with fondness the hand of Venetia, retraced his steps to the now solitary abbey.

CHAPTER VII.

Cadurcis returned to the abbey, but not to slumber. That love of loneliness which had haunted him from his boyhood, and which ever asserted its sway when under the influence of his passions, came over him now with irresistible power. A day of enjoyment had terminated, and it left him melancholy. Hour after hour he paced the moon-lit cloisters of his abbey, where not a sound disturbed him, save the monotonous fall of the fountain, that seems by some inexplicable association always to blend with and never to disturb our feelings; gay when we are joyful, and sad amid our sorrow.

Yet was he sorrowful! He was gloomy, and fell into a reverie about himself, a subject to him ever perplexing and distressing. His conversation of the morning with Doctor Masham recurred to him. What did the Doctor mean by his character not being formed, and that he might yet live to change all his opinions? Character! what was character? It must be will; and his will was violent and firm. Young as he was, he had early habituated himself to reflection, and the result of his musings had been a desire to live away from the world with those he loved. The world, as other men viewed it, had no charms for him. Its pursuits and passions seemed to him on the whole paltry and faint. He could sympathise with great deeds, but not with bustling life. That which was common did not please him. He loved things that were rare and strange; and the spell that bound him so strongly to Venetia Herbert was her unusual life, and the singular circumstances of her destiny that were not unknown to him. True he was young; but, lord of himself, youth was associated with none of those mortifications which make the juvenile pant for manhood. Cadurcis valued his youth and treasured it. He could not conceive love, and the romantic life that love should lead, without the circumambient charm of youth adding fresh lustre to all that was bright and fair, and a keener relish to every combination of enjoyment. The moonbeam fell upon his mother's monument, a tablet on the cloister wall that recorded the birth and death of KATHERINE CADURCIS. His thoughts flew to his ancestry. They had conquered in France and Palestine, and left a memorable name to the annalist of his country. Those days were past, and yet Cadurcis felt within him the desire, perhaps the power, of emulating them; but what remained? What career was open in this mechanical age to the chivalric genius of his race? Was he misplaced then in life? The applause of nations, there was something grand and exciting in such a possession. To be the marvel of mankind what would he not hazard? Dreams, dreams! If his ancestors were valiant and celebrated it remained for him to rival, to excel them, at least in one respect. Their coronet had never rested on a brow fairer than the one for which he destined it. Venetia then, independently of his passionate love, was the only apparent object worth his pursuit, the only thing in this world that had realised his dreams, dreams sacred to his own musing soul, that even she had never shared or guessed. And she, she was to be his. He could not doubt it: but to-morrow would decide; to-morrow would seal his triumph.

His sleep was short and restless; he had almost out-watched the stars, and yet he rose with the early morn. His first thought was of Venetia; he was impatient for the interview, the interview she promised and even proposed. The fresh air was grateful to him; he bounded along to Cherbury, and brushed the dew in his progress from the tall grass and shrubs. In sight of the hall, he for a moment paused. He was before his accustomed hour; and yet he was always too soon. Not to-day, though, not to-day; suddenly he rushes forward and springs down the green vista, for Venetia is on the terrace, and alone!

Always kind, this morning she greeted him with unusual affection. Never had she seemed to him so exquisitely beautiful. Perhaps her countenance to-day was more pale than wont. There seemed a softness in her eyes usually so brilliant and even dazzling; the accents of her salutation were suppressed and tender.

'I thought you would be here early,' she remarked, 'and therefore I rose to meet you.'

Was he to infer from this artless confession that his image had haunted her in her dreams, or only that she would not delay the conversation on which his happiness depended? He could scarcely doubt which version to adopt when she took his arm and led him from the terrace to walk where they could not be disturbed.

'Dear Plantagenet,' she said, 'for indeed you are very dear to me; I told you last night that I would speak to you to-day on your wishes, that are so kind to me and so much intended for my happiness. I do not love suspense; but indeed last night I was too much surprised, too much overcome by what occurred, that exhausted as I naturally was by all our pleasure, I could not tell you what I wished; indeed I could not, dear Plantagenet.'

'My own Venetia!'

'So I hope you will always deem me; for I should be very unhappy if you did not love me, Plantagenet, more unhappy than I have even been these last two years; and I have been very unhappy, very unhappy indeed, Plantagenet.'

'Unhappy, Venetia! my Venetia unhappy?'

'Listen! I will not weep. I can control my feelings. I have learnt to do this; it is very sad, and very different to what my life once was; but I can do it.'

'You amaze me!'

Venetia sighed, and then resumed, but in a tone mournful and low, and yet to a degree firm.

'You have been away five years, Plantagenet.'

'But you have pardoned that.'

'I never blamed you; I had nothing to pardon. It was well for you to be away; and I rejoice your absence has been so profitable to you.'

'But it was wicked to have been so silent.'

'Oh! no, no, no! Such ideas never entered into my head, nor even mamma's. You were very young; you did as all would, as all must do. Harbour not such thoughts. Enough, you have returned and love us yet.'

'Love! adore!'

'Five years are a long space of time, Plantagenet. Events will happen in five years, even at Cherbury. I told you I was changed.'

'Yes!' said Lord Cadurcis, in a voice of some anxiety, with a scrutinising eye.

'You left me a happy child; you find me a woman, and a miserable one.'

'Good God, Venetia! this suspense is awful. Be brief, I pray you. Has any one—'

Venetia looked at him with an air of perplexity. She could not comprehend the idea that impelled his interruption.

'Go on,' Lord Cadurcis added, after a short pause; 'I am indeed all anxiety.'

'You remember that Christmas which you passed at the hall and walking at night in the gallery, and—'

'Well! Your mother, I shall never forget it.'

'You found her weeping when you were once at Marringhurst. You told me of it.'

'Ay, ay!'

'There is a wing of our house shut up. We often talked of it.'

'Often, Venetia; it was a mystery.'

'I have penetrated it,' replied Venetia in a solemn tone; 'and never have I known what happiness is since.'

'Yes, yes!' said Lord Cadurcis, very pale, and in a whisper.

'Plantagenet, I have a father.'

Lord Cadurcis started, and for an instant his arm quitted Venetia's. At length he said in a gloomy voice, 'I know it.'

'Know it!' exclaimed Venetia with astonishment. 'Who could have told you the secret?'

'It is no secret,' replied Cadurcis; 'would that it were!'

'Would that it were! How strange you speak, how strange you look, Plantagenet! If it be no secret that I have a father, why this concealment then? I know that I am not the child of shame!' she added, after a moment's pause, with an air of pride. A tear stole down the cheek of Cadurcis.

'Plantagenet! dear, good Plantagenet! my brother! my own brother! see, I kneel to you; Venetia kneels to you! your own Venetia! Venetia that you love! Oh! if you knew the load that is on my spirit bearing me down to a grave which I would almost welcome, you would speak to me; you would tell me all. I have sighed for this; I have longed for this; I have prayed for this. To meet some one who would speak to me of my father; who had heard of him, who knew him; has been for years the only thought of my being, the only object for which I existed. And now, here comes Plantagenet, my brother! my own brother! and he knows all, and he will tell me; yes, that he will; he will tell his Venetia all, all!'

'Is there not your mother?' said Lord Cadurcis, in a broken tone.

'Forbidden, utterly forbidden. If I speak, they tell me her heart will break; and therefore mine is breaking.'

'Have you no friend?'

'Are not you my friend?'

'Doctor Masham?'

'I have applied to him; he tells me that he lives, and then he shakes his head.'

'You never saw your father; think not of him.'

'Not think of him!' exclaimed Venetia, with extraordinary energy. 'Of what else? For what do I live but to think of him? What object have I in life but to see him? I have seen him, once.'

'Ah!'

'I know his form by heart, and yet it was but a shade. Oh, what a shade! what a glorious, what an immortal shade! If gods were upon earth they would be like my father!'

'His deeds, at least, are not godlike,' observed Lord Cadurcis dryly, and with some bitterness.

'I deny it!' said Venetia, her eyes sparkling with fire, her form dilated with enthusiasm, and involuntarily withdrawing her arm from her companion. Lord Cadurcis looked exceedingly astonished.

'You deny it!' he exclaimed. 'And what should you know about it?'

'Nature whispers to me that nothing but what is grand and noble could be breathed by those lips, or fulfilled by that form.'

'I am glad you have not read his works,' said Lord Cadurcis, with increased bitterness. 'As for his conduct, your mother is a living evidence of his honour, his generosity, and his virtue.'

'My mother!' said Venetia, in a softened voice; 'and yet he loved my mother!'

'She was his victim, as a thousand others may have been.'

'She is his wife!' replied Venetia, with some anxiety.

'Yes, a deserted wife; is that preferable to being a cherished mistress? More honourable, but scarcely less humiliating.'

'She must have misunderstood him,' said Venetia. 'I have perused the secret vows of his passion. I have read his praises of her beauty. I have pored over the music of his emotions when he first became a father; yes, he has gazed on me, even though but for a moment, with love! Over me he has breathed forth the hallowed blessing of a parent! That transcendent form has pressed his lips to mine, and held me with fondness to his heart! And shall I credit aught to his dishonour? Is there a being in existence who can persuade me he is heartless or abandoned? No! I love him! I adore him! I am devoted to him with all the energies of my being! I live only on the memory that he lives, and, were he to die, I should pray to my God that I might join him without delay in a world where it cannot be justice to separate a child from a father.'

And this was Venetia! the fair, the serene Venetia! the young, the inexperienced Venetia! pausing, as it were, on the parting threshold of girlhood, whom, but a few hours since, he had fancied could scarcely have proved a passion; who appeared to him barely to comprehend the meaning of his advances; for whose calmness or whose coldness he had consoled himself by the flattering conviction of her unknowing innocence. Before him stood a beautiful and inspired Moenad, her eye flashing supernatural fire, her form elevated above her accustomed stature, defiance on her swelling brow, and passion on her quivering lip!

Gentle and sensitive as Cadurcis ever appeared to those he loved, there was in his soul a deep and unfathomed well of passions that had been never stirred, and a bitter and mocking spirit in his brain, of which he was himself unconscious. He had repaired this hopeful morn to Cherbury to receive, as he believed, the plighted faith of a simple and affectionate, perhaps grateful, girl. That her unsophisticated and untutored spirit might not receive the advances of his heart with an equal and corresponding ardour, he was prepared. It pleased him that he should watch the gradual development of this bud of sweet affections, waiting, with proud anxiety, her fragrant and her full-blown love. But now it appeared that her coldness or her indifference might be ascribed to any other cause than the one to which he had attributed it, the innocence of an inexperienced mind. This girl was no stranger to powerful passions; she could love, and love with fervency, with devotion, with enthusiasm. This child of joy was a woman of deep and thoughtful sorrows, brooding in solitude over high resolves and passionate aspirations. Why were not the emotions of such a tumultuous soul excited by himself? To him she was calm and imperturbable; she called him brother, she treated him as a child. But a picture, a fantastic shade, could raise in her a tempestuous swell of sentiment that transformed her whole mind, and changed the colour of all her hopes and thoughts. Deeply prejudiced against her father, Cadurcis now hated him, and with a fell and ferocious earnestness that few bosoms but his could prove. Pale with rage, he ground his teeth and watched her with a glance of sarcastic aversion.

'You led me here to listen to a communication which interested me,' he at length said. 'Have I heard it?'

His altered tone, the air of haughtiness which he assumed, were not lost upon Venetia. She endeavoured to collect herself, but she hesitated to reply.

'I repeat my inquiry,' said Cadurcis. 'Have you brought me here only to inform me that you have a father, and that you adore him, or his picture?'

'I led you here,' replied Venetia, in a subdued tone, and looking on the ground, 'to thank you for your love, and to confess to you that I love another.'

'Love another!' exclaimed Cadurcis, in a tone of derision. Simpleton! The best thing your mother can do is to lock you up in the chamber with the picture that has produced such marvellous effects.'

'I am no simpleton, Plantagenet,' rejoined Venetia, quietly, 'but one who is acting as she thinks right; and not only as her mind, but as her heart prompts her.'

They had stopped in the earlier part of this conversation on a little plot of turf surrounded by shrubs; Cadurcis walked up and down this area with angry steps, occasionally glancing at Venetia with a look of mortification and displeasure.

'I tell you, Venetia,' he at length said, 'that you are a little fool. What do you mean by saying that you cannot marry me because you love another? Is not that other, by your own account, your father? Love him as much as you like. Is that to prevent you from loving your husband also?'

'Plantagenet, you are rude, and unnecessarily so,' said Venetia. 'I repeat to you again, and for the last time, that all my heart is my father's. It would be wicked in me to marry you, because I cannot love you as a husband should be loved. I can never love you as I love my father. However, it is useless to talk upon this subject. I have not even the power of marrying you if I wished, for I have dedicated myself to my father in the name of God; and I have offered a vow, to be registered in heaven, that thenceforth I would exist only for the purpose of being restored to his heart.'

'I congratulate you on your parent, Miss Herbert.'

'I feel that I ought to be proud of him, though, alas I can only feel it. But, whatever your opinion may be of my father, I beg you to remember that you are speaking to his child.'

'I shall state my opinion respecting your father, madam, with the most perfect unreserve, wherever and whenever I choose; quite convinced that, however you esteem that opinion, it will not be widely different from the real sentiments of the only parent whom you ought to respect, and whom you are bound to obey.'

'And I can tell you, sir, that whatever your opinion is on any subject it will never influence mine. If, indeed, I were the mistress of my own destiny, which I am not, it would have been equally out of my power to have acted as you have so singularly proposed. I do not wish to marry, and marry I never will; but were it in my power, or in accordance with my wish, to unite my fate for ever with another's, it should at least be with one to whom I could look up with reverence, and even with admiration. He should be at least a man, and a great man; one with whose name the world rung; perhaps, like my father, a genius and a poet.'

'A genius and a poet!' exclaimed Lord Cadurcis, in a fury, stamping with passion; 'are these fit terms to use when speaking of the most abandoned profligate of his age? A man whose name is synonymous with infamy, and which no one dares to breathe in civilised life; whose very blood is pollution, as you will some day feel; who has violated every tie, and derided every principle, by which society is maintained; whose life is a living illustration of his own shameless doctrines; who is, at the same time, a traitor to his king and an apostate from his God!'

Curiosity, overpowering even indignation, had permitted Venetia to listen even to this tirade. Pale as her companion, but with a glance of withering scorn, she exclaimed, 'Passionate and ill-mannered boy! words cannot express the disgust and the contempt with which you inspire me.' She spoke and she disappeared. Cadurcis was neither able nor desirous to arrest her flight. He remained rooted to the ground, muttering to himself the word 'boy!' Suddenly raising his arm and looking up to the sky, he exclaimed, 'The illusion is vanished! Farewell, Cherbury! farewell, Cadurcis! a wider theatre awaits me! I have been too long the slave of soft affections! I root them out of my heart for ever!' and, fitting the action to the phrase, it seemed that he hurled upon the earth all the tender emotions of his soul. 'Woman! henceforth you shall be my sport! I have now no feeling but for myself. When she spoke I might have been a boy; I am a boy no longer. What I shall do I know not; but this I know, the world shall ring with my name; I will be a man, and a great man!'

CHAPTER VIII.

The agitation of Venetia on her return was not unnoticed by her mother; but Lady Annabel ascribed it to a far different cause than the real one. She was rather surprised when the breakfast passed, and Lord Cadurcis did not appear; somewhat perplexed when her daughter seized the earliest opportunity of retiring to her own chamber; but, with that self-restraint of which she was so complete a mistress, Lady Annabel uttered no remark.

Once more alone, Venetia could only repeat to herself the wild words that had burst from Plantagenet's lips in reference to her father. What could they mean? His morals might be misrepresented, his opinions might be misunderstood; stupidity might not comprehend his doctrines, malignity might torture them; the purest sages have been accused of immorality, the most pious philosophers have been denounced as blasphemous: but, 'a traitor to his king,' that was a tangible, an intelligible proposition, one with which all might grapple, which could be easily disproved if false, scarcely propounded were it not true. 'False to his God!' How false? Where? When? What mystery involved her life? Unhappy girl! in vain she struggled with the overwhelming burden of her sorrows. Now she regretted that she had quarrelled with Cadurcis; it was evident that he knew everything and would have told her all. And then she blamed him for his harsh and unfeeling demeanour, and his total want of sympathy with her cruel and perplexing situation. She had intended, she had struggled to be so kind to him; she thought she had such a plain tale to tell that he would have listened to it in considerate silence, and bowed to her necessary and inevitable decision without a murmur. Amid all these harassing emotions her mind tossed about like a ship without a rudder, until, in her despair, she almost resolved to confess everything to her mother, and to request her to soothe and enlighten her agitated and confounded mind. But what hope was there of solace or information from such a quarter? Lady Annabel's was not a mind to be diverted from her purpose. Whatever might have been the conduct of her husband, it was evident that Lady Annabel had traced out a course from which she had resolved not to depart. She remembered the earnest and repeated advice of Dr. Masham, that virtuous and intelligent man who never advised anything but for their benefit. How solemnly had he enjoined upon her never to speak to her mother upon the subject, unless she wished to produce misery and distress! And what could her mother tell her? Her father lived, he had abandoned her, he was looked upon as a criminal, and shunned by the society whose laws and prejudices he had alike outraged. Why should she revive, amid the comparative happiness and serenity in which her mother now lived, the bitter recollection of the almost intolerable misfortune of her existence? No! Venetia was resolved to be a solitary victim. In spite of her passionate and romantic devotion to her father she loved her mother with perfect affection, the mother who had dedicated her life to her child, and at least hoped she had spared her any share in their common unhappiness. And this father, whose image haunted her dreams, whose unknown voice seemed sometimes to float to her quick ear upon the wind, could he be that abandoned being that Cadurcis had described, and that all around her, and all the circumstances of her life, would seem to indicate? Alas! it might be truth; alas! it seemed like truth: and for one so lost, so utterly irredeemable, was she to murmur against that pure and benevolent parent who had cherished her with such devotion, and snatched her perhaps from disgrace, dishonour, and despair!

And Cadurcis, would he return? With all his violence, the kind Cadurcis! Never did she need a brother more than now; and now he was absent, and she had parted with him in anger, deep, almost deadly: she, too, who had never before uttered a harsh word to a human being, who had been involved in only one quarrel in her life, and that almost unconsciously, and which had nearly broken her heart. She wept, bitterly she wept, this poor Venetia!

By one of those mental efforts which her strange lot often forced her to practise, Venetia at length composed herself, and returned to the room where she believed she would meet her mother, and hoped she should see Cadurcis. He was not there: but Lady Annabel was seated as calm and busied as usual; the Doctor had departed. Even his presence would have proved a relief, however slight, to Venetia, who dreaded at this moment to be alone with her mother. She had no cause, however, for alarm; Lord Cadurcis never appeared, and was absent even from dinner; the day died away, and still he was wanting; and at length Venetia bade her usual good night to Lady Annabel, and received her usual blessing and embrace without his name having been even mentioned.

Venetia passed a disturbed night, haunted by painful dreams, in which her father and Cadurcis were both mixed up, and with images of pain, confusion, disgrace, and misery; but the morrow, at least, did not prolong her suspense, for just as she had joined her mother at breakfast, Mistress Pauncefort, who had been despatched on some domestic mission by her mistress, entered with a face of wonder, and began as usual: 'Only think, my lady; well to be sure, who have thought it? I am quite confident, for my own part, I was quite taken aback when I heard it; and I could not have believed my ears, if John had not told me himself, and he had it from his lordship's own man.'

'Well, Pauncefort, what have you to say?' inquired Lady Annabel, very calmly.

'And never to send no note, my lady; at least I have not seen one come up. That makes it so very strange.'

'Makes what, Pauncefort?'

'Why, my lady, doesn't your la'ship know his lordship left the abbey yesterday, and never said nothing to nobody; rode off without a word, by your leave or with your leave? To be sure he always was the oddest young gentleman as ever I met with; and, as I said to John: John, says I, I hope his lordship has not gone to join the gipsies again.'

Venetia looked into a teacup, and then touched an egg, and then twirled a spoon; but Lady Annabel seemed quite imperturbable, and only observed, 'Probably his guardian is ill, and he has been suddenly summoned to town. I wish you would bring my knitting-needles, Pauncefort.'

The autumn passed, and Lord Cadurcis never returned to the abbey, and never wrote to any of his late companions. Lady Annabel never mentioned his name; and although she seemed to have no other object in life but the pleasure and happiness of her child, this strange mother never once consulted Venetia on the probable occasion of his sudden departure, and his strange conduct.

BOOK IV.

CHAPTER I.

Party feeling, perhaps, never ran higher in England than during the period immediately subsequent to the expulsion of the Coalition Ministry. After the indefatigable faction of the American war, and the flagrant union with Lord North, the Whig party, and especially Charles Fox, then in the full vigour of his bold and ready mind, were stung to the quick that all their remorseless efforts to obtain and preserve the government of the country should terminate in the preferment and apparent permanent power of a mere boy.

Next to Charles Fox, perhaps the most eminent and influential member of the Whig party was Lady Monteagle. The daughter of one of the oldest and most powerful peers in the kingdom, possessing lively talents and many fascinating accomplishments, the mistress of a great establishment, very beautiful, and, although she had been married some years, still young, the celebrated wife of Lord Monteagle found herself the centre of a circle alike powerful, brilliant, and refined. She was the Muse of the Whig party, at whose shrine every man of wit and fashion was proud to offer his flattering incense; and her house became not merely the favourite scene of their social pleasures, but the sacred, temple of their political rites; here many a manoeuvre was planned, and many a scheme suggested; many a convert enrolled, and many a votary initiated.

Reclining on a couch in a boudoir, which she was assured was the exact facsimile of that of Marie Antoinette, Lady Monteagle, with an eye sparkling with excitement and a cheek flushed with emotion, appeared deeply interested in a volume, from which she raised her hand as her husband entered the room.

'Gertrude, my love,' said his lordship, 'I have asked the new bishop to dine with us to-day.'

'My dear Henry,' replied her ladyship, 'what could induce you to do anything so strange?'

'I suppose I have made a mistake, as usual,' said his lordship, shrugging his shoulders, with a smile.

'My dear Henry, you know you may ask whomever you like to your house. I never find fault with what you do. But what could induce you to ask a Tory bishop to meet a dozen of our own people?'

'I thought I had done wrong directly I had asked him,' rejoined his lordship; 'and yet he would not have come if I had not made such a point of it. I think I will put him off.'

'No, my love, that would be wrong; you cannot do that.'

'I cannot think how it came into my head. The fact is, I lost my presence of mind. You know he was my tutor at Christchurch, when poor dear Herbert and I were such friends, and very kind he was to us both; and so, the moment I saw him, I walked across the House, introduced myself, and asked him to dinner.'

'Well, never mind,' said Lady Monteagle, smiling. 'It is rather ridiculous: but I hope nothing will be said to offend him.'

'Oh! do not be alarmed about that: he is quite a man of the world, and, although he has his opinions, not at all a partisan. I assure you poor dear Herbert loved him to the last, and to this very moment has the greatest respect and affection for him.'

'How very strange that not only your tutor, but Herbert's, should be a bishop,' remarked the lady, smiling.

'It is very strange,' said his lordship, 'and it only shows that it is quite useless in this world to lay plans, or reckon on anything. You know how it happened?'

'Not I, indeed; I have never given a thought to the business; I only remember being very vexed that that stupid old Bangerford should not have died when we were in office, and then, at any rate, we should have got another vote.'

'Well, you know,' said his lordship, 'dear old Masham, that is his name, was at Weymouth this year; with whom do you think, of all people in the world?'

'How should I know? Why should I think about it, Henry?'

'Why, with Herbert's wife.'

'What, that horrid woman?'

'Yes, Lady Annabel.'

'And where was his daughter? Was she there?'

'Of course. She has grown up, and a most beautiful creature they say she is; exactly like her father.'

'Ah! I shall always regret I never saw him,' said her ladyship.

'Well, the daughter is in bad health; and so, after keeping her shut up all her life, the mother was obliged to take her to Weymouth; and Masham, who has a living in their neighbourhood, which, by-the-bye, Herbert gave him, and is their chaplain and counsellor, and friend of the family, and all that sort of thing, though I really believe he has always acted for the best, he was with them. Well, the King took the greatest fancy to these Herberts; and the Queen, too, quite singled them out; and, in short, they were always with the royal family. It ended by his Majesty making Masham his chaplain; and now he has made him a bishop.'

'Very droll indeed,' said her ladyship; 'and the drollest thing of all is, that he is now coming to dine here.'

'Have you seen Cadurcis to-day?' said Lord Monteagle.

'Of course,' said her ladyship.

'He dines here?'

'To be sure. I am reading his new poem; it will not be published till to-morrow.'

'Is it good?'

'Good! What crude questions you do always ask, Henry!' exclaimed Lady Monteagle. 'Good! Of course it is good. It is something better than good.'

'But I mean is it as good as his other things? Will it make as much noise as his last thing?'

'Thing! Now, Henry, you know very well that if there be anything I dislike in the world, it is calling a poem a thing.'

'Well, my dear, you know I am no judge of poetry. But if you are pleased, I am quite content. There is a knock. Some of your friends. I am off. I say, Gertrude, be kind to old Masham, that is a dear creature!'

Her ladyship extended her hand, to which his lordship pressed his lips, and just effected his escape as the servant announced a visitor, in the person of Mr. Horace Pole.

'Oh! my dear Mr. Pole, I am quite exhausted,' said her ladyship; 'I am reading Cadurcis' new poem; it will not he published till to-morrow, and it really has destroyed my nerves. I have got people to dinner to-day, and I am sure I shall not be able to encounter them.'

'Something outrageous, I suppose,' said Mr. Pole, with a sneer. 'I wish Cadurcis would study Pope.'

'Study Pope! My dear Mr. Pole, you have no imagination.'

'No, I have not, thank Heaven!' drawled out Mr. Pole.

'Well, do not let us have a quarrel about Cadurcis,' said Lady Monteagle. 'All you men are jealous of him.'

'And some of you women, I think, too,' said Mr. Pole.

Lady Monteagle faintly smiled.

'Poor Cadurcis!' she exclaimed; 'he has a very hard life of it. He complains bitterly that so many women are in love with him. But then he is such an interesting creature, what can he expect?'

'Interesting!' exclaimed Mr. Pole. 'Now I hold he is the most conceited, affected fellow that I ever met,' he continued with unusual energy.

'Ah! you men do not understand him,' said Lady Monteagle, shaking her head. 'You cannot,' she added, with a look of pity.

'I cannot, certainly,' said Mr. Pole, 'or his writings either. For my part I think the town has gone mad.'

'Well, you must confess,' said her ladyship, with a glance of triumph, 'that it was very lucky for us that I made him a Whig.'

'I cannot agree with you at all on that head,' said Mr. Pole. 'We certainly are not very popular at this moment, and I feel convinced that a connection with a person who attracts so much notice as Cadurcis unfortunately does, and whose opinions on morals and religion must be so offensive to the vast majority of the English public, must ultimately prove anything but advantageous to our party.'

'Oh! my dear Mr. Pole,' said her ladyship, in a tone of affected deprecation, 'think what a genius he is!'

'We have very different ideas of genius, Lady Monteagle, I suspect,' said her visitor.

'You cannot deny,' replied her ladyship, rising from her recumbent posture, with some animation, 'that he is a poet?'

'It is difficult to decide upon our contemporaries,' said Mr. Pole dryly.

'Charles Fox thinks he is the greatest poet that ever existed,' said her ladyship, as if she were determined to settle the question.

'Because he has written a lampoon on the royal family,' rejoined Mr. Pole.

'You are a very provoking person,' said Lady Monteagle; 'but you do not provoke me; do not flatter yourself you do.'

'That I feel to be an achievement alike beyond my power and my ambition,' replied Mr. Pole, slightly bowing, but with a sneer.

'Well, read this,' said Lady Monteagle, 'and then decide upon the merits of Cadurcis.'

Mr. Pole took the extended volume, but with no great willingness, and turned over a page or two and read a passage here and there.

'Much the same as his last effusion, I think' he observed, as far as I can judge from so cursory a review. Exaggerated passion, bombastic language, egotism to excess, and, which perhaps is the only portion that is genuine, mixed with common-place scepticism and impossible morals, and a sort of vague, dreamy philosophy, which, if it mean anything, means atheism, borrowed from his idol, Herbert, and which he himself evidently does not comprehend.'

'Monster!' exclaimed Lady Monteagle, with a mock assumption of indignation, 'and you are going to dine with him here to-day. You do not deserve it.'

'It is a reward which is unfortunately too often obtained by me,' replied Mr. Pole. 'One of the most annoying consequences of your friend's popularity, Lady Monteagle, is that there is not a dinner party where one can escape him. I met him yesterday at Fanshawe's. He amused himself by eating only biscuits, and calling for soda water, while we quaffed our Burgundy. How very original! What a thing it is to be a great poet!'

'Perverse, provoking mortal!' exclaimed Lady Monteagle. 'And on what should a poet live? On coarse food, like you coarse mortals? Cadurcis is all spirit, and in my opinion his diet only makes him more interesting.'

'I understand,' said Mr. Pole, 'that he cannot endure a woman to eat at all. But you are all spirit, Lady Monteagle, and therefore of course are not in the least inconvenienced. By-the-bye, do you mean to give us any of those charming little suppers this season?'

'I shall not invite you,' replied her ladyship; 'none but admirers of Lord Cadurcis enter this house.'

'Your menace effects my instant conversion,' replied Mr. Pole. 'I will admire him as much as you desire, only do not insist upon my reading his works.'

'I have not the slightest doubt you know them by heart,' rejoined her ladyship.

Mr. Pole smiled, bowed, and disappeared; and Lady Monteagle sat down to write a billet to Lord Cadurcis, to entreat him to be with her at five o'clock, which was at least half an hour before the other guests were expected. The Monteagles were considered to dine ridiculously late.

CHAPTER II.

Marmion Herbert, sprung from one of the most illustrious families in England, became at an early age the inheritor of a great estate, to which, however, he did not succeed with the prejudices or opinions usually imbibed or professed by the class to which he belonged. While yet a boy, Marmion Herbert afforded many indications of possessing a mind alike visionary and inquisitive, and both, although not in an equal degree, sceptical and creative. Nature had gifted him with precocious talents; and with a temperament essentially poetic, he was nevertheless a great student. His early reading, originally by accident and afterwards by an irresistible inclination, had fallen among the works of the English freethinkers: with all their errors, a profound and vigorous race, and much superior to the French philosophers, who were after all only their pupils and their imitators. While his juvenile studies, and in some degree the predisposition of his mind, had thus prepared him to doubt and finally to challenge the propriety of all that was established and received, the poetical and stronger bias of his mind enabled him quickly to supply the place of everything he would remove and destroy; and, far from being the victim of those frigid and indifferent feelings which must ever be the portion of the mere doubter, Herbert, on the contrary, looked forward with ardent and sanguine enthusiasm to a glorious and ameliorating future, which should amply compensate and console a misguided and unhappy race for the miserable past and the painful and dreary present. To those, therefore, who could not sympathise with his views, it will be seen that Herbert, in attempting to fulfil them, became not merely passively noxious from his example, but actively mischievous from his exertions. A mere sceptic, he would have been perhaps merely pitied; a sceptic with a peculiar faith of his own, which he was resolved to promulgate, Herbert became odious. A solitary votary of obnoxious opinions, Herbert would have been looked upon only as a madman; but the moment he attempted to make proselytes he rose into a conspirator against society.

Young, irresistibly prepossessing in his appearance, with great eloquence, crude but considerable knowledge, an ardent imagination and a subtle mind, and a generous and passionate soul, under any circumstances he must have obtained and exercised influence, even if his Creator had not also bestowed upon him a spirit of indomitable courage; but these great gifts of nature being combined with accidents of fortune scarcely less qualified to move mankind, high rank, vast wealth, and a name of traditionary glory, it will not be esteemed surprising that Marmion Herbert, at an early period, should have attracted around him many enthusiastic disciples.

At Christchurch, whither he repaired at an unusually early age, his tutor was Doctor Masham; and the profound respect and singular affection with which that able, learned, and amiable man early inspired his pupil, for a time controlled the spirit of Herbert; or rather confined its workings to so limited a sphere that the results were neither dangerous to society nor himself. Perfectly comprehending and appreciating the genius of the youth entrusted to his charge, deeply interested in his spiritual as well as worldly welfare, and strongly impressed with the importance of enlisting his pupil's energies in favour of that existing order, both moral and religious, in the truth and indispensableness of which he was a sincere believer, Doctor Masham omitted no opportunity of combating the heresies of the young inquirer; and as the tutor, equally by talent, experience, and learning, was a competent champion of the great cause to which he was devoted, his zeal and ability for a time checked the development of those opinions of which he witnessed the menacing influence over Herbert with so much fear and anxiety. The college life of Marmion Herbert, therefore, passed in ceaseless controversy with his tutor; and as he possessed, among many other noble qualities, a high and philosophic sense of justice, he did not consider himself authorised, while a doubt remained on his own mind, actively to promulgate those opinions, of the propriety and necessity of which he scarcely ever ceased to be persuaded. To this cause it must be mainly attributed that Herbert was not expelled the university; for had he pursued there the course of which his cruder career at Eton had given promise, there can be little doubt that some flagrant outrage of the opinions held sacred in that great seat of orthodoxy would have quickly removed him from the salutary sphere of their control.

Herbert quitted Oxford in his nineteenth year, yet inferior to few that he left there, even among the most eminent, in classical attainments, and with a mind naturally profound, practised in all the arts of ratiocination. His general knowledge also was considerable, and he was a proficient in those scientific pursuits which were then rare. Notwithstanding his great fortune and position, his departure from the university was not a signal with him for that abandonment to the world, and that unbounded self-enjoyment naturally so tempting to youth. On the contrary, Herbert shut himself up in his magnificent castle, devoted to solitude and study. In his splendid library he consulted the sages of antiquity, and conferred with them on the nature of existence and of the social duties; while in his laboratory or his dissecting-room he occasionally flattered himself he might discover the great secret which had perplexed generations. The consequence of a year passed in this severe discipline was unfortunately a complete recurrence to those opinions that he had early imbibed, and which now seemed fixed in his conviction beyond the hope or chance of again faltering. In politics a violent republican, and an advocate, certainly a disinterested one, of a complete equality of property and conditions, utterly objecting to the very foundation of our moral system, and especially a strenuous antagonist of marriage, which he taught himself to esteem not only as an unnatural tie, but as eminently unjust towards that softer sex, who had been so long the victims of man; discarding as a mockery the received revelation of the divine will; and, if no longer an atheist, substituting merely for such an outrageous dogma a subtle and shadowy Platonism; doctrines, however, which Herbert at least had acquired by a profound study of the works of their great founder; the pupil of Doctor Masham at length deemed himself qualified to enter that world which he was resolved to regenerate; prepared for persecution, and steeled even to martyrdom.

But while the doctrines of the philosopher had been forming, the spirit of the poet had not been inactive. Loneliness, after all, the best of Muses, had stimulated the creative faculty of his being. Wandering amid his solitary woods and glades at all hours and seasons, the wild and beautiful apparitions of nature had appealed to a sympathetic soul. The stars and winds, the pensive sunset and the sanguine break of morn, the sweet solemnity of night, the ancient trees and the light and evanescent flowers, all signs and sights and sounds of loveliness and power, fell on a ready eye and a responsive ear. Gazing on the beautiful, he longed to create it. Then it was that the two passions which seemed to share the being of Herbert appeared simultaneously to assert their sway, and he resolved to call in his Muse to the assistance of his Philosophy.

Herbert celebrated that fond world of his imagination, which he wished to teach men to love. In stanzas glittering with refined images, and resonant with subtle symphony, he called into creation that society of immaculate purity and unbounded enjoyment which he believed was the natural inheritance of unshackled man. In the hero he pictured a philosopher, young and gifted as himself; in the heroine, his idea of a perfect woman. Although all those peculiar doctrines of Herbert, which, undisguised, must have excited so much odium, were more or less developed and inculcated in this work; nevertheless they were necessarily so veiled by the highly spiritual and metaphorical language of the poet, that it required some previous acquaintance with the system enforced, to be able to detect and recognise the esoteric spirit of his Muse. The public read only the history of an ideal world and of creatures of exquisite beauty, told in language that alike dazzled their fancy and captivated their ear. They were lost in a delicious maze of metaphor and music, and were proud to acknowledge an addition to the glorious catalogue of their poets in a young and interesting member of their aristocracy.

In the meanwhile Herbert entered that great world that had long expected him, and hailed his advent with triumph. How long might have elapsed before they were roused by the conduct of Herbert to the error under which they were labouring as to his character, it is not difficult to conjecture; but before he could commence those philanthropic exertions which apparently absorbed him, he encountered an individual who most unconsciously put his philosophy not merely to the test, but partially even to the rout; and this was Lady Annabel Sidney. Almost as new to the world as himself, and not less admired, her unrivalled beauty, her unusual accomplishments, and her pure and dignified mind, combined, it must be confessed, with the flattering admiration of his genius, entirely captivated the philosophical antagonist of marriage. It is not surprising that Marmion Herbert, scarcely of age, and with a heart of extreme susceptibility, resolved, after a struggle, to be the first exception to his system, and, as he faintly flattered himself, the last victim of prejudice. He wooed and won the Lady Annabel.

The marriage ceremony was performed by Doctor Masham, who had read his pupil's poem, and had been a little frightened by its indications; but this happy union had dissipated all his fears. He would not believe in any other than a future career for him alike honourable and happy; and he trusted that if any wild thoughts still lingered in Herbert's mind, that they would clear off by the same literary process; so that the utmost ill consequences of his immature opinions might be an occasional line that the wise would have liked to blot, and yet which the unlettered might scarcely be competent to comprehend. Mr. and Lady Annabel Herbert departed after the ceremony to his castle, and Doctor Masham to Marringhurst, a valuable living in another county, to which his pupil had just presented him.

Some months after this memorable event, rumours reached the ear of the good Doctor that all was not as satisfactory as he could desire in that establishment, in the welfare of which he naturally took so lively an interest. Herbert was in the habit of corresponding with the rector of Marringhurst, and his first letters were full of details as to his happy life and his perfect consent; but gradually these details had been considerably abridged, and the correspondence assumed chiefly a literary or philosophical character. Lady Annabel, however, was always mentioned with regard, and an intimation had been duly given to the Doctor that she was in a delicate and promising situation, and that they were both alike anxious that he should christen their child. It did not seem very surprising to the good Doctor, who was a man of the world, that a husband, six months after marriage, should not speak of the memorable event with all the fulness and fondness of the honeymoon; and, being one of those happy tempers that always anticipate the best, he dismissed from his mind, as vain gossip and idle exaggerations, the ominous whispers that occasionally reached him.

Immediately after the Christmas ensuing his marriage, the Herberts returned to London, and the Doctor, who happened to be a short time in the metropolis, paid them a visit. His observations were far from unsatisfactory; it was certainly too evident that Marmion was no longer enamoured of Lady Annabel, but he treated her apparently with courtesy, and even cordiality.

The presence of Dr. Masham tended, perhaps, a little to revive old feelings, for he was as much a favourite with the wife as with the husband; but, on the whole, the Doctor quitted them with an easy heart, and sanguine that the interesting and impending event would, in all probability, revive affection on the part of Herbert, or at least afford Lady Annabel the only substitute for a husband's heart.

In due time the Doctor heard from Herbert that his wife had gone down into the country, but was sorry to observe that Herbert did not accompany her. Even this disagreeable impression was removed by a letter, shortly after received from Herbert, dated from the castle, and written in high spirits, informing him that Annabel had made him the happy father of the most beautiful little girl in the world. During the ensuing three months Mr. Herbert, though he resumed his residence in London, paid frequent visits to the castle, where Lady Annabel remained; and his occasional correspondence, though couched in a careless vein, still on the whole indicated a cheerful spirit; though ever and anon were sarcastic observations as to the felicity of the married state, which, he said, was an undoubted blessing, as it kept a man out of all scrapes, though unfortunately under the penalty of his total idleness and inutility in life. On the whole, however, the reader may judge of the astonishment of Doctor Masham when, in common with the world, very shortly after the receipt of this letter, Mr. Herbert having previously proceeded to London, and awaiting, as was said, the daily arrival of his wife and child, his former tutor learned that Lady Annabel, accompanied only by Pauncefort and Venetia, had sought her father's roof, declaring that circumstances had occurred which rendered it quite impossible that she could live with Mr. Herbert any longer, and entreating his succour and parental protection.

Never was such a hubbub in the world! In vain Herbert claimed his wife, and expressed his astonishment, declaring that he had parted from her with the expression of perfect kind feeling on both sides. No answer was given to his letter, and no explanation of any kind conceded him. The world universally declared Lady Annabel an injured woman, and trusted that she would eventually have the good sense and kindness to gratify them by revealing the mystery; while Herbert, on the contrary, was universally abused and shunned, avoided by his acquaintances, and denounced as the most depraved of men.

In this extraordinary state of affairs Herbert acted in a manner the best calculated to secure his happiness, and the very worst to preserve his character. Having ostentatiously shown himself in every public place, and courted notice and inquiry by every means in his power, to prove that he was not anxious to conceal himself or avoid any inquiry, he left the country, free at last to pursue that career to which he had always aspired, and in which he had been checked by a blunder, from the consequences of which he little expected that he should so speedily and strangely emancipate himself. It was in a beautiful villa on the lake of Geneva that he finally established himself, and there for many years he employed himself in the publication of a series of works which, whether they were poetry or prose, imaginative or investigative, all tended to the same consistent purpose, namely, the fearless and unqualified promulgation of those opinions, on the adoption of which he sincerely believed the happiness of mankind depended; and the opposite principles to which, in his own case, had been productive of so much mortification and misery. His works, which were published in England, were little read, and universally decried. The critics were always hard at work, proving that he was no poet, and demonstrating in the most logical manner that he was quite incapable of reasoning on the commonest topic. In addition to all this, his ignorance was self-evident; and though he was very fond of quoting Greek, they doubted whether he was capable of reading the original authors. The general impression of the English public, after the lapse of some years, was, that Herbert was an abandoned being, of profligate habits, opposed to all the institutions of society that kept his infamy in check, and an avowed atheist; and as scarcely any one but a sympathetic spirit ever read a line he wrote, for indeed the very sight of his works was pollution, it is not very wonderful that this opinion was so generally prevalent. A calm inquirer might, perhaps, have suspected that abandoned profligacy is not very compatible with severe study, and that an author is seldom loose in his life, even if he be licentious in his writings. A calm inquirer might, perhaps, have been of opinion that a solitary sage may be the antagonist of a priesthood without absolutely denying the existence of a God; but there never are calm inquirers. The world, on every subject, however unequally, is divided into parties; and even in the case of Herbert and his writings, those who admired his genius, and the generosity of his soul, were not content without advocating, principally out of pique to his adversaries, his extreme opinions on every subject, moral, political, and religious.

Besides, it must be confessed, there was another circumstance which was almost as fatal to Herbert's character in England as his loose and heretical opinions. The travelling English, during their visits to Geneva, found out that their countryman solaced or enlivened his solitude by unhallowed ties. It is a habit to which very young men, who are separated from or deserted by their wives, occasionally have recourse. Wrong, no doubt, as most things are, but it is to be hoped venial; at least in the case of any man who is not also an atheist. This unfortunate mistress of Herbert was magnified into a seraglio; the most extraordinary tales of the voluptuous life of one who generally at his studies out-watched the stars, were rife in English society; and

Hoary marquises and stripling dukes,

who were either protecting opera dancers, or, still worse, making love to their neighbours' wives, either looked grave when the name of Herbert was mentioned in female society, or affectedly confused, as if they could a tale unfold, were they not convinced that the sense of propriety among all present was infinitely superior to their sense of curiosity.

The only person to whom Herbert communicated in England was Doctor Masham. He wrote to him immediately on his establishment at Geneva, in a calm yet sincere and serious tone, as if it were useless to dwell too fully on the past. Yet he declared, although now that it was all over he avowed his joy at the interposition of his destiny, and the opportunity which he at length possessed of pursuing the career for which he was adapted, that he had to his knowledge given his wife no cause of offence which could authorise her conduct. As for his daughter, he said he should not be so cruel as to tear her from her mother's breast; though, if anything could induce him to such behaviour, it would be the malignant and ungenerous menace of his wife's relatives, that they would oppose his preferred claim to the guardianship of his child, on the plea of his immoral life and atheistical opinions. With reference to pecuniary arrangements, as his chief seat was entailed on male heirs, he proposed that his wife should take up her abode at Cherbury, an estate which had been settled on her and her children at her marriage, and which, therefore, would descend to Venetia. Finally, he expressed his satisfaction that the neighbourhood of Marringhurst would permit his good and still faithful friend to cultivate the society and guard over the welfare of his wife and daughter.

During the first ten years of Herbert's exile, for such indeed it might be considered, the Doctor maintained with him a rare yet regular correspondence; but after that time a public event occurred, and a revolution took place in Herbert's life which terminated all communication between them; a termination occasioned, however, by such a simultaneous conviction of its absolute necessity, that it was not attended by any of those painful communications which are too often the harrowing forerunners of a formal disruption of ancient ties.

This event was the revolt of the American colonies; and this revolution in Herbert's career, his junction with the rebels against his native country. Doubtless it was not without a struggle, perhaps a pang, that Herbert resolved upon a line of conduct to which it must assuredly have required the strongest throb of his cosmopolitan sympathy, and his amplest definition of philanthropy to have impelled him. But without any vindictive feelings towards England, for he ever professed and exercised charity towards his enemies, attributing their conduct entirely to their ignorance and prejudice, upon this step he nevertheless felt it his duty to decide. There seemed in the opening prospects of America, in a world still new, which had borrowed from the old as it were only so much civilisation as was necessary to create and to maintain order; there seemed in the circumstances of its boundless territory, and the total absence of feudal institutions and prejudices, so fair a field for the practical introduction of those regenerating principles to which Herbert had devoted all the thought and labour of his life, that he resolved, after long and perhaps painful meditation, to sacrifice every feeling and future interest to its fulfilment. All idea of ever returning to his native country, even were it only to mix his ashes with the generations of his ancestors; all hope of reconciliation with his wife, or of pressing to his heart that daughter, often present to his tender fancy, and to whose affections he had feelingly appealed in an outburst of passionate poetry; all these chances, chances which, in spite of his philosophy, had yet a lingering charm, must be discarded for ever. They were discarded. Assigning his estate to his heir upon conditions, in order to prevent its forfeiture, with such resources as he could command, and which were considerable, Marmion Herbert arrived at Boston, where his rank, his wealth, his distinguished name, his great talents, and his undoubted zeal for the cause of liberty, procured him an eminent and gratifying reception. He offered to raise a regiment for the republic, and the offer was accepted, and he was enrolled among the citizens. All this occurred about the time that the Cadurcis family first settled at the abbey, and this narrative will probably throw light upon several slight incidents which heretofore may have attracted the perplexed attention of the reader: such as the newspaper brought by Dr. Masham at the Christmas visit; the tears shed at a subsequent period at Marringhurst, when he related to her the last intelligence that had been received from America. For, indeed, it is impossible to express the misery and mortification which this last conduct of her husband occasioned Lady Annabel, brought up, as she had been, with feelings of romantic loyalty and unswerving patriotism. To be a traitor seemed the only blot that remained for his sullied scutcheon, and she had never dreamed of that. An infidel, a profligate, a deserter from his home, an apostate from his God! one infamy alone remained, and now he had attained it; a traitor to his king! Why, every peasant would despise him!

General Herbert, however, for such he speedily became, at the head of his division, soon arrested the attention, and commanded the respect, of Europe. To his exertions the successful result of the struggle was, in a great measure, attributed; and he received the thanks of Congress, of which he became a member. His military and political reputation exercised a beneficial influence upon his literary fame. His works were reprinted in America, and translated into French, and published at Geneva and Basle, whence they were surreptitiously introduced into France. The Whigs, who had become very factious, and nearly revolutionary, during the American war, suddenly became proud of their countryman, whom a new world hailed as a deliverer, and Paris declared to be a great poet and an illustrious philosopher. His writings became fashionable, especially among the young; numerous editions of them appeared, and in time it was discovered that Herbert was now not only openly read, and enthusiastically admired, but had founded a school.

The struggle with America ceased about the time of Lord Cadurcis' last visit to Cherbury, when, from his indignant lips, Venetia first learnt the enormities of her father's career. Since that period some three years had elapsed until we introduced our readers to the boudoir of Lady Monteagle. During this period, among the Whigs and their partisans the literary fame of Herbert had arisen and become established. How they have passed in regard to Lady Annabel Herbert and her daughter, on the one hand, and Lord Cadurcis himself on the other, we will endeavour to ascertain in the following chapter.

CHAPTER III.

From the last departure of Lord Cadurcis from Cherbury, the health of Venetia again declined. The truth is, she brooded in solitude over her strange lot, until her nerves became relaxed by intense reverie and suppressed feeling. The attention of a mother so wrapt up in her child as Lady Annabel, was soon attracted to the increasing languor of our heroine, whose eye each day seemed to grow less bright, and her graceful form less lithe and active. No longer, fond of the sun and breeze as a beautiful bird, was Venetia seen, as heretofore, glancing in the garden, or bounding over the lawns; too often might she be found reclining on the couch, in spite of all the temptations of the spring; while her temper, once so singularly sweet that it seemed there was not in the world a word that could ruffle it, and which required so keenly and responded so quickly to sympathy, became reserved, if not absolutely sullen, or at times even captious and fretful.

This change in the appearance and demeanour of her daughter filled Lady Annabel with anxiety and alarm. In vain she expressed to Venetia her conviction of her indisposition; but Venctia, though her altered habits confirmed the suspicion, and authorised the inquiry of her parent, persisted ever in asserting that she had no ailment. Her old medical attendant was, however, consulted, and, being perplexed with the case, he recommended change of air. Lady Annabel then consulted Dr. Masham, and he gave his opinion in favour of change of air for one reason: and that was, that it would bring with it what he had long considered Venetia to stand in need of, and that was change of life.

Dr. Masham was right; but then, to guide him in forming his judgment, he had the advantage of some psychological knowledge of the case, which, in a greet degree, was a sealed book to the poor puzzled physician. We laugh very often at the errors of medical men; but if we would only, when we consult them, have strength of mind enough to extend to them something better than a half-confidence, we might be cured the sooner. How often, when the unhappy disciple of Esculapius is perplexing himself about the state of our bodies, we might throw light upon his obscure labours by simply detailing to him the state of our minds!

The result of these consultations in the Herbert family was a final resolution, on the part of Lady Annabel, to quit Cherbury for a while. As the sea air was especially recommended to Venetia, and as Lady Annabel shrank with a morbid apprehension from society, to which nothing could persuade her she was not an object either of odium or impertinent curiosity, she finally resolved to visit Weymouth, then a small and secluded watering-place, and whither she arrived and settled herself, it not being even the season when its few customary visitors were in the habit of gathering.

This residence at Weymouth quite repaid Lady Annabel for all the trouble of her new settlement, and for the change in her life very painful to her confirmed habits, which she experienced in leaving for the first time for such a long series of years, her old hall; for the rose returned to the cheek of her daughter, and the western breezes, joined with the influence of the new objects that surrounded her, and especially of that ocean, and its strange and inexhaustible variety, on which she gazed for the first time, gradually, but surely, completed the restoration of Venetia to health, and with it to much of her old vivacity.

When Lady Annabel had resided about a year at Weymouth, in the society of which she had invariably made the indisposition of Venetia a reason for not entering, a great revolution suddenly occurred at this little quiet watering-place, for it was fixed upon as the summer residence of the English court. The celebrated name, the distinguished appearance, and the secluded habits of Lady Annabel and her daughter, had rendered them the objects of general interest. Occasionally they were met in a seaside walk by some fellow-wanderer over the sands, or toiler over the shingles; and romantic reports of the dignity of the mother and the daughter's beauty were repeated by the fortunate observers to the lounging circle of the public library or the baths.

The moment that Lady Annabel was assured that the royal family had positively fixed upon Weymouth for their residence, and were even daily expected, she resolved instantly to retire. Her stern sense of duty assured her that it was neither delicate nor loyal to obtrude before the presence of an outraged monarch the wife and daughter of a traitor; her haughty, though wounded, spirit shrank from the revival of her husband's history, which must be the consequence of such a conjunction, and from the startling and painful remarks which might reach the shrouded ear of her daughter. With her characteristic decision, and with her usual stern volition, Lady Annabel quitted Weymouth instantly, but she was in some degree consoled for the regret and apprehensiveness which she felt at thus leaving a place that had otherwise so happily fulfilled all her hopes and wishes, and that seemed to agree so entirely with Venetia, by finding unexpectedly a marine villa, some few miles further up the coast, which was untenanted, and which offered to Lady Annabel all the accommodation she could desire.

It so happened this summer that Dr. Masham paid the Herberts a visit, and it was his habit occasionally to ride into Weymouth to read the newspaper, or pass an hour in that easy lounging chat, which is, perhaps, one of the principal diversions of a watering-place. A great dignitary of the church, who was about the King, and to whom Dr. Masham was known not merely by reputation, mentioned his presence to his Majesty; and the King, who was fond of the society of eminent divines, desired that Dr. Masham should be presented to him. Now, so favourable was the impression that the rector of Marringhurst made upon his sovereign, that from that moment the King was scarcely ever content unless he was in attendance. His Majesty, who was happy in asking questions, and much too acute to be baffled when he sought information, finally elicited from the Doctor all that, in order to please Lady Annabel, he long struggled to conceal; but when the King found that the deserted wife and daughter of Herbert were really living in the neighbourhood, and that they had quitted Weymouth on his arrival, from a feeling of delicate loyalty, nothing would satisfy the kind-hearted monarch but personally assuring them of the interest he took in their welfare; and accordingly, the next day, without giving Lady Annabel even the preparation of a notice, his Majesty and his royal consort, attended only by a lord in waiting, called at the marine villa, and fairly introduced themselves.

An acquaintance, occasioned by a sentiment of generous and condescending sympathy, was established and strengthened into intimacy, by the personal qualities of those thus delicately honoured. The King and Queen were equally delighted with the wife and daughter of the terrible rebel; and although, of course, not an allusion was made to his existence, Lady Annabel felt not the less acutely the cause to which she was indebted for a notice so gratifying, but which she afterwards ensured by her own merits. How strange are the accidents of life! Venetia Herbert, who had been bred up in unbroken solitude, and whose converse had been confined to two or three beings, suddenly found herself the guest of a king, and the visitor to a court! She stepped at once from solitude into the most august circle of society; yet, though she had enjoyed none of that initiatory experience which is usually held so indispensable to the votaries of fashion, her happy nature qualified her to play her part without effort and with success. Serene and graceful, she mingled in the strange and novel scene, as if it had been for ever her lot to dazzle and to charm. Ere the royal family returned to London, they extracted from Lady Annabel a compliance with their earnest wishes, that she should fix her residence, during the ensuing season, in the metropolis, and that she should herself present Venetia at St. James's. The wishes of kings are commands; and Lady Annabel, who thus unexpectedly perceived some of the most painful anticipations of her solitude at once dissipated, and that her child, instead of being subjected on her entrance into life to all the mortifications she had imagined, would, on the contrary, find her first introduction under auspices the most flattering and advantageous, bowed a dutiful assent to the condescending injunctions.

Such were the memorable consequences of this visit to Weymouth! The return of Lady Annabel to the world, and her intended residence in the metropolis, while the good Masham preceded their arrival to receive a mitre. Strange events, and yet not improbable!

In the meantime Lord Cadurcis had repaired to the university, where his rank and his eccentric qualities quickly gathered round him a choice circle of intimates, chiefly culled from his old schoolfellows. Of these the great majority were his seniors, for whose society the maturity of his mind qualified him. It so happened that these companions were in general influenced by those liberal opinions which had become in vogue during the American war, and from which Lord Cadurcis had hitherto been preserved by the society in which he had previously mingled in the house of his guardian. With the characteristic caprice and impetuosity of youth, Cadurcis rapidly and ardently imbibed all these doctrines, captivated alike by their boldness and their novelty. Hitherto the child of prejudice, he flattered himself that he was now the creature of reason, and, determined to take nothing for granted, he soon learned to question everything that was received. A friend introduced him to the writings of Herbert, that very Herbert whom he had been taught to look upon with so much terror and odium. Their perusal operated a complete revolution of his mind; and, in little more than a year from his flight from Cherbury, he had become an enthusiastic votary of the great master, for his violent abuse of whom he had been banished from those happy bowers. The courage, the boldness, the eloquence, the imagination, the strange and romantic career of Herbert, carried the spirit of Cadurcis captive. The sympathetic companions studied his works and smiled with scorn at the prejudice of which their great model had been the victim, and of which they had been so long the dupes. As for Cadurcis, he resolved to emulate him, and he commenced his noble rivalship by a systematic neglect of all the duties and the studies of his college life. His irregular habits procured him constant reprimands in which he gloried; he revenged himself on the authorities by writing epigrams, and by keeping a bear, which he declared should stand for a fellowship. At length, having wilfully outraged the most important regulations, he was expelled; and he made his expulsion the subject of a satire equally personal and philosophic, and which obtained applause for the great talent which it displayed, even from those who lamented its want of judgment and the misconduct of its writer. Flushed with success, Cadurcis at length found, to his astonishment, that Nature had intended him for a poet. He repaired to London, where he was received with open arms by the Whigs, whose party he immediately embraced, and where he published a poem, in which he painted his own character as the hero, and of which, in spite of all the exaggeration and extravagance of youth, the genius was undeniable. Society sympathised with a young and a noble poet; his poem was read by all parties with enthusiasm; Cadurcis became the fashion. To use his own expression, 'One morning he awoke, and found himself famous.' Young, singularly handsome, with every gift of nature and fortune, and with an inordinate vanity that raged in his soul, Cadurcis soon forgot the high philosophy that had for a moment attracted him, and delivered himself up to the absorbing egotism which had ever been latent in his passionate and ambitious mind. Gifted with energies that few have ever equalled, and fooled to the bent by the excited sympathies of society, he poured forth his creative and daring spirit with a license that conquered all obstacles, from the very audacity with which he assailed them. In a word, the young, the reserved, and unknown Cadurcis, who, but three years back, was to have lived in the domestic solitude for which he alone felt himself fitted, filled every heart and glittered in every eye. The men envied, the women loved, all admired him. His life was a perpetual triumph; a brilliant and applauding stage, on which he ever played a dazzling and heroic part. So sudden and so startling had been his apparition, so vigorous and unceasing the efforts by which he had maintained his first overwhelming impression, and not merely by his writings, but by his unusual manners and eccentric life, that no one had yet found time to draw his breath, to observe, to inquire, and to criticise. He had risen, and still flamed, like a comet as wild as it was beautiful, and strange is it was brilliant.

CHAPTER IV.

We must now return to the dinner party at Lord Monteagle's. When the Bishop of —— entered the room, he found nearly all the expected guests assembled, and was immediately presented by his host to the lady of the house, who received him with all that fascinating address for which she was celebrated, expressing the extreme delight which she felt at thus becoming formally acquainted with one whom her husband had long taught her to admire and reverence. Utterly unconscious who had just joined the circle, while Lord Monteagle was introducing his newly-arrived guest to many present, and to all of whom he was unknown except by reputation, Lord Cadurcis was standing apart, apparently wrapt in his own thoughts; but the truth is, in spite of all the excitement in which he lived, he had difficulty in overcoming the natural reserve of his disposition.

'Watch Cadurcis,' said Mr. Horace Pole to a fine lady. 'Does not he look sublime?'

'Show me him,' said the lady, eagerly. 'I have never seen him yet; I am actually dying to know him. You know we have just come to town.'

'And have caught the raging epidemic, I see,' said Mr. Pole, with a sneer. 'However, there is the marvellous young gentleman! "Alone in a crowd," as he says in his last poem. Very interesting!'

'Wonderful creature!' exclaimed the dame.

'Charming!' said Mr. Pole. 'If you ask Lady Monteagle, she will introduce him to you, and then, perhaps, you will be fortunate enough to be handed to dinner by him.'

'Oh! how I should like it!'

'You must take care, however, not to eat; he cannot endure a woman who eats.'

'I never do,' said the lady, simply; 'at least at dinner.'

'Ah! then you will quite suit him; I dare say he will write a sonnet to you, and call you Thyrza.'

'I wish I could get him to write some lines in my book, said the lady; 'Charles Fox has written some; he was staying with us in the autumn, and he has written an ode to my little dog.'

'How amiable!' said Mr. Pole; 'I dare say they are as good as his elegy on Mrs. Crewe's cat. But you must not talk of cats and dogs to Cadurcis. He is too exalted to commemorate any animal less sublime than a tiger or a barb.'

'You forget his beautiful lines on his Newfoundland,' said the lady.

'Very complimentary to us all,' said Mr. Horace Pole. 'The interesting misanthrope!'

'He looks unhappy.'

'Very,' said Mr. Pole. 'Evidently something on his conscience.'

'They do whisper very odd things,' said the lady, with great curiosity. 'Do you think there is anything in them?'

'Oh! no doubt,' said Mr. Pole; 'look at him; you can detect crime in every glance.'

'Dear me, how shocking! I think he must be the most interesting person that ever lived. I should so like to know him! They say he is so very odd.'

'Very,' said Mr. Pole. 'He must be a man of genius; he is so unlike everybody; the very tie of his cravat proves it. And his hair, so savage and dishevelled; none but a man of genius would not wear powder. Watch him to-day, and you will observe that he will not condescend to perform the slightest act like an ordinary mortal. I met him at dinner yesterday at Fanshawe's, and he touched nothing but biscuits and soda-water. Fanshawe, you know, is famous for his cook. Complimentary and gratifying, was it not?'

'Dear me!' said the lady, 'I am delighted to see him; and yet I hope I shall not sit by him at dinner. I am quite afraid of him.'

'He is really awful!' said Mr. Pole.

In the meantime the subject of these observations slowly withdrew to the further end of the saloon, apart from every one, and threw himself upon a couch with a somewhat discontented air. Lady Monteagle, whose eye had never left him for a moment, although her attentions had been necessarily commanded by her guests, and who dreaded the silent rages in which Cadurcis constantly indulged, and which, when once assumed for the day, were with difficulty dissipated, seized the first opportunity to join and soothe him.

'Dear Cadurcis,' she said, 'why do you sit here? You know I am obliged to speak to all these odious people, and it is very cruel of you.'

'You seemed to me to be extremely happy,' replied his lordship, in a sarcastic tone.

'Now, Cadurcis, for Heaven's sake do not play with my feelings,' exclaimed Lady Monteagle, in a deprecating tone. 'Pray be amiable. If I think you are in one of your dark humours, it is quite impossible for me to attend to these people; and you know it is the only point on which Monteagle ever has an opinion; he insists upon my attending to his guests.'

'If you prefer his guests to me, attend to them.'

'Now, Cadurcis! I ask you as a favour, a favour to me, only for to-day. Be kind, be amiable, you can if you like; no person can be more amiable; now, do!'

'I am amiable,' said his lordship; 'I am perfectly satisfied, if you are. You made me dine here.'

'Now, Cadurcis!'

'Have I not dined here to satisfy you?'

'Yes! It was very kind.'

'But, really, that I should be wearied with all the common-places of these creatures who come to eat your husband's cutlets, is too much,' said his lordship. 'And you, Gertrude, what necessity can there be in your troubling yourself to amuse people whom you meet every day of your life, and who, from the vulgar perversity of society, value you in exact proportion as you neglect them?'

'Yes, but to-day I must be attentive; for Henry, with his usual thoughtlessness, has asked this new bishop to dine with us.'

'The Bishop of———?' inquired Lord Cadurcis, eagerly. 'Is he coming?'

'He has been in the room this quarter of an hour?'

'What, Masham! Doctor Masham!' continued Lord Cadurcis.

'Assuredly.'

Lord Cadurcis changed colour, and even sighed. He rose rather quickly, and said, 'I must go and speak to him.'

So, quitting Lady Monteagle, he crossed the room, and with all the simplicity of old days, which instantly returned on him, those melancholy eyes sparkling with animation, and that languid form quick with excitement, he caught the Doctor's glance, and shook his extended hand with a heartiness which astonished the surrounding spectators, accustomed to the elaborate listlessness of his usual manner.

'My dear Doctor! my dear Lord! I am glad to say,' said Cadurcis, 'this is the greatest and the most unexpected pleasure I ever received. Of all persons in the world, you are the one whom I was most anxious to meet.'

The good Bishop appeared not less gratified with the rencounter than Cadurcis himself; but, in the midst of their mutual congratulations, dinner was announced and served; and, in due order, Lord Cadurcis found himself attending that fine lady, whom Mr. Horace Pole had, in jest, suggested should be the object of his services; while Mr. Pole himself was seated opposite to him at table.

The lady, remembering all Mr. Pole's intimations, was really much frightened; she at first could scarcely reply to the casual observations of her neighbour, and quite resolved not to eat anything. But his lively and voluble conversation, his perfectly unaffected manner, and the nonchalance with which he helped himself to every dish that was offered him, soon reassured her. Her voice became a little firmer, her manner less embarrassed, and she even began meditating a delicate assault upon a fricassee.

'Are you going to Ranelagh to-night?' inquired Lord Cadurcis; 'I think I shall take a round. There is nothing like amusement; it is the only thing worth living for; and I thank my destiny I am easily amused. We must persuade Lady Monteagle to go with us. Let us make a party, and return and sup. I like a supper; nothing in the world more charming than a supper,

A lobster salad, and champagne and chat.

That is life, and delightful. Why, really, my dear madam, you eat nothing. You will never be able to endure the fatigues of a Ranelagh campaign on the sustenance of a pâté. Pole, my good fellow, will you take a glass of wine? We had a pleasant party yesterday at Fanshawe's, and apparently a capital dinner. I was sorry that I could not play my part; but I have led rather a raking life lately. We must go and dine with him again.'

Lord Cadurcis' neighbour and Mr. Pole exchanged looks; and the lady, emboldened by the unexpected conduct of her cavalier and the exceeding good friends which he seemed resolved to be with her and every one else, began to flatter herself that she might yet obtain the much-desired inscription in her volume. So, after making the usual approaches, of having a great favour to request, which, however, she could not flatter herself would be granted, and which she even was afraid to mention; encouraged by the ready declaration of Lord Cadurcis, that he should think it would be quite impossible for any one to deny her anything, the lady ventured to state, that Mr. Fox had written something in her book, and she should be the most honoured and happiest lady in the land if—'

'Oh! I shall be most happy,' said Lord Cadurcis; 'I really esteem your request quite an honour: you know I am only a literary amateur, and cannot pretend to vie with your real authors. If you want them, you must go to Mrs. Montagu. I would not write a line for her, and no the blues have quite excommunicated me. Never mind; I leave them to Miss Hannah More; but you, you are quite a different sort of person. What shall I write?'

'I must leave the subject to you,' said his gratified friend.

'Well, then,' said his lordship, 'I dare say you have got a lapdog or a broken fan; I don't think I could soar above them. I think that is about my tether.'

This lady, though a great person, was not a beauty, and very little of a wit, and not calculated in any respect to excite the jealousy of Lady Monteagle. In the meantime that lady was quite delighted with the unusual animation of Lord Cadurcis, who was much the most entertaining member of the party. Every one present would circulate throughout the world that it was only at the Monteagle's that Lord Cadurcis condescended to be amusing. As the Bishop was seated on her right hand, Lady Monteagle seized the opportunity of making inquiries as to their acquaintance; but she only obtained from the good Masham that he had once resided in his lordship's neighbourhood, and had known him as a child, and was greatly attached to him. Her ladyship was anxious to obtain some juvenile anecdotes of her hero; but the Bishop contrived to be amusing without degenerating into gossip. She did not glean much, except that all his early friends were more astonished at his present career than the Bishop himself, who was about to add, that he always had some misgivings, but, recollecting where he was, he converted the word into a more gracious term. But if Lady Monteagle were not so successful as she could wish in her inquiries, she contrived still to speak on the, to her, ever-interesting subject, and consoled herself by the communications which she poured into a guarded yet not unwilling ear, respecting the present life and conduct of the Bishop's former pupil. The worthy dignitary had been prepared by public fame for much that was dazzling and eccentric; but it must be confessed he was not a little astonished by a great deal to which he listened. One thing, however, was clear that whatever might be the demeanour of Cadurcis to the circle in which he now moved, time, and the strange revolutions of his life, had not affected his carriage to his old friend. It gratified the Bishop while he listened to Lady Monteagle's details of the haughty, reserved, and melancholy demeanour of Cadurcis, which impressed every one with an idea that some superior being had, as a punishment, been obliged to visit their humble globe, to recall the apparently heartfelt cordiality with which he had resumed his old acquaintance with the former rector of Marringhurst.

And indeed, to speak truth, the amiable and unpretending behaviour of Cadurcis this day was entirely attributable to the unexpected meeting with this old friend. In the hurry of society he could scarcely dwell upon the associations which it was calculated to call up; yet more than once he found himself quite absent, dwelling on sweet recollections of that Cherbury that he had so loved. And ever and anon the tones of a familiar voice caught his ear, so that they almost made him start: they were not the less striking, because, as Masham was seated on the same side of the table as Cadurcis, his eye had not become habituated to the Bishop's presence, which sometimes he almost doubted.

He seized the first opportunity after dinner of engaging his old tutor in conversation. He took him affectionately by the arm, and led him, as if unintentionally, to a sofa apart from the rest of the company, and seated himself by his side. Cadurcis was agitated, for he was about to inquire of some whom he could not mention without emotion.

'Is it long since you have seen our friends?' said his lordship, 'if indeed I may call them mine.'

'Lady Annabel Herbert?' said the Bishop.

Cadurcis bowed.

'I parted from her about two months back,' continued the Bishop.

'And Cherbury, dear Cherbury, is it unchanged?'

'They have not resided there for more than two years.'

'Indeed!'

'They have lived, of late, at Weymouth, for the benefit of the sea air.'

'I hope neither Lady Annabel nor her daughter needs it?' said Lord Cadurcis, in a tone of much feeling.

'Neither now, God be praised!' replied Masham; 'but Miss Herbert has been a great invalid.'

There was a rather awkward silence. At length Lord Cadurcis said, 'We meet rather unexpectedly, my dear sir.'

'Why, you have become a great man,' said the Bishop, with a smile; 'and one must expect to meet you.'

'Ah! my dear friend,' exclaimed Lord Cadurcis, with a sigh, 'I would willingly give a whole existence of a life like this for one year of happiness at Cherbury.'

'Nay!' said the Bishop, with a look of good-natured mockery, 'this melancholy is all very well in poetry; but I always half-suspected, and I am quite sure now, that Cherbury was not particularly adapted to you.'

'You mistake me,' said Cadurcis, mournfully shaking his head.

'Hitherto I have not been so very wrong in my judgment respecting Lord Cadurcis, that I am inclined very easily to give up my opinion,' replied the Bishop.

'I have often thought of the conversation to which you allude,' replied Lord Cadurcis; 'nevertheless, there is one opinion I never changed, one sentiment that still reigns paramount in my heart.'

'You think so,' said his companion; 'but, perhaps, were it more than a sentiment, it would cease to flourish.'

'No,' said Lord Cadurcis firmly; 'the only circumstance in the world of which I venture to feel certain is my love for Venetia.'

'It raged certainly during your last visit to Cherbury,' said the Bishop, 'after an interval of five years; it has been revived slightly to-day, after an interval of three more, by the sight of a mutual acquaintance, who has reminded you of her. But what have been your feelings in the meantime? Confess the truth, and admit you have very rarely spared a thought to the person to whom you fancy yourself at this moment so passionately devoted.'

'You do not do me justice,' said Lord Cadurcis; 'you are prejudiced against me.'

'Nay! prejudice is not my humour, my good lord. I decide only from what I myself observe; I give my opinion to you at this moment as freely as I did when you last conversed with me at the abbey, and when I a little displeased you by speaking what you will acknowledge has since turned out to be the truth.'

'You mean, then, to say,' said his lordship, with some excitement, 'that you do not believe that I love Venetia?'

'I think you do, at this moment,' replied Masham; 'and I think,' he continued, smiling, 'that you may probably continue very much in love with her, even during the rest of the week.'

'You mock me!'

'Nay! I am sincerely serious.'

'What, then, do you mean?'

'I mean that your imagination, my lord, dwelling for the moment with great power upon the idea of Venetia, becomes inflamed, and your whole mind is filled with her image.'

'A metaphysical description of being in love,' said Lord Cadurcis, rather dryly.

'Nay!' said Masham, 'I think the heart has something to do with that.'

'But the imagination acts upon the heart,' rejoined his companion.

'But it is in the nature of its influence not to endure. At this moment, I repeat, your lordship may perhaps love Miss Herbert; you may go home and muse over her memory, and even deplore in passionate verses your misery in being separated from her; but, in the course of a few days, she will be again forgotten.'

'But were she mine?' urged Lord Cadurcis, eagerly.

'Why, you would probably part from her in a year, as her father parted from Lady Annabel.'

'Impossible! for my imagination could not conceive anything more exquisite than she is.'

'Then it would conceive something less exquisite,' said the Bishop. 'It is a restless quality, and is ever creative, either of good or of evil.'

'Ah! my dear Doctor, excuse me for again calling you Doctor, it is so natural,' said Cadurcis, in a tone of affection.

'Call me what you will, my dear lord,' said the good Bishop, whose heart was moved; 'I can never forget old days.'

'Believe me, then,' continued Cadurcis, 'that you misjudge me in respect of Venetia. I feel assured that, had we married three years ago, I should have been a much happier man.'

'Why, you have everything to make you happy,' said the Bishop; 'if you are not happy, who should be? You are young, and you are famous: all that is now wanted is to be wise.'

Lord Cadurcis shrugged his shoulders. I am tired of this life,' he said; 'I am wearied of the same hollow bustle, and the same false glitter day after day. Ah! my dear friend, when I remember the happy hours when I used to roam through the woods of Cherbury with Venetia, and ramble in that delicious park, both young, both innocent, lit by the sunset and guided by the stars; and then remember that it has all ended in this, and that this is success, glory, fame, or whatever be the proper title to baptize the bubble, the burthen of existence is too great for me.'

'Hush, hush!' said his friend, rising from the sofa; 'you will be happy if you be wise.'

'But what is wisdom?' said Lord Cadurcis.

'One quality of it, in your situation, my lord, is to keep your head as calm as you can. Now, I must bid you good night.'

The Bishop disappeared, and Lord Cadurcis was immediately surrounded by several fine ladies, who were encouraged by the flattering bulletin that his neighbour at dinner, who was among them, had given of his lordship's temper. They were rather disappointed to find him sullen, sarcastic, and even morose. As for going to Ranelagh, he declared that, if he had the power of awarding the punishment of his bitterest enemy, it would be to consign him for an hour to the barbarous infliction of a promenade in that temple of ennui; and as for the owner of the album, who, anxious about her verses, ventured to express a hope that his lordship would call upon her, the contemptuous bard gave her what he was in the habit of styling 'a look,' and quitted the room, without deigning otherwise to acknowledge her hopes and her courtesy.

CHAPTER V.

We must now return to our friends the Herberts, who, having quitted Weymouth, without even revisiting Cherbury, are now on their journey to the metropolis. It was not without considerable emotion that Lady Annabel, after an absence of nearly nineteen years, contemplated her return to the scene of some of the most extraordinary and painful occurrences of her life. As for Venetia, who knew nothing of towns and cities, save from the hasty observations she had made in travelling, the idea of London, formed only from books and her imagination, was invested with even awful attributes. Mistress Pauncefort alone looked forward to their future residence simply with feelings of self-congratulation at her return, after so long an interval, to the theatre of former triumphs and pleasures, and where she conceived herself so eminently qualified to shine and to enjoy.

The travellers entered town towards nightfall, by Hyde Park Corner, and proceeded to an hotel in St. James's Street, where Lady Annabel's man of business had engaged them apartments. London, with its pallid parish lamps, scattered at long intervals, would have presented but a gloomy appearance to the modern eye, habituated to all the splendour of gas; but to Venetia it seemed difficult to conceive a scene of more brilliant bustle; and she leant back in the carriage, distracted with the lights and the confusion of the crowded streets. When they were once safely lodged in their new residence, the tumult of unpacking the carriages had subsided, and the ceaseless tongue of Pauncefort had in some degree refrained from its wearying and worrying chatter, a feeling of loneliness, after all this agitation and excitement, simultaneously came over the feelings of both mother and daughter, though they alike repressed its expression. Lady Annabel was lost in many sad thoughts, and Venetia felt mournful, though she could scarcely define the cause. Both were silent, and they soon sought refuge from fatigue and melancholy in sleep.

The next morning, it being now April, was fortunately bright and clear. It certainly was a happy fortune that the fair Venetia was not greeted with a fog. She rose refreshed and cheerful, and joined her mother, who was, however, not a little agitated by an impending visit, of which Venetia had been long apprised. This was from Lady Annabel's brother, the former ambassador, who had of late returned to his native country. The brother and sister had been warmly attached in youth, but the awful interval of time that had elapsed since they parted, filled Venetia's mother with many sad and serious reflections. The Earl and his family had been duly informed of Lady Annabel's visit to the metropolis, and had hastened to offer her the hospitality of their home; but the offer had been declined, with feelings, however, not a little gratified by the earnestness with which it had been proffered.

Venetia was now, for the first time in her life, to see a relative. The anticipated meeting excited in her mind rather curiosity than sentiment. She could not share the agitation of her mother, and yet she looked forward to the arrival of her uncle with extreme inquisitiveness. She was not long kept in suspense. Their breakfast was scarcely finished, when he was announced. Lady Annabel turned rather pale; and Venetia, who felt herself as it were a stranger to her blood, would have retired, had not her mother requested her to remain; so she only withdrew to the back of the apartment.

Her uncle was ten years the senior of his sister, but not unlike her. Tall, graceful, with those bland and sympathising manners that easily win hearts, he entered the room with a smile of affection, yet with a composure of deportment that expressed at the same time how sincerely delighted he was at the meeting, and how considerately determined, at the same time, not to indulge in a scene. He embraced his sister with tenderness, assured her that she looked as young as ever, softly chided her for not making his house her home, and hoped that they should never part again; and he then turned to his niece. A fine observer, one less interested in the scene than the only witnesses, might have detected in the Earl, notwithstanding his experienced breeding, no ordinary surprise and gratification at the sight of the individual whose relationship he was now to claim for the first time.

'I must claim an uncle's privilege,' he said, in a tone of sweetness and some emotion, as he pressed with his own the beautiful lips of Venetia. 'I ought to be proud of my niece. Why, Annabel! if only for the honour of our family, you should not have kept this jewel so long enshrined in the casket of Cherbury.'

The Earl remained with them some hours, and his visit was really prolonged by the unexpected pleasure which he found in the society of his relations. He would not leave them until they promised to dine with him that day, and mentioned that he had prevented his wife from calling with him that morning, because he thought, after so long a separation, it might be better to meet thus quietly. Then they parted with affectionate cordiality on both sides; the Earl enchanted to find delightful companions where he was half afraid he might only meet tiresome relatives; Lady Annabel proud of her brother, and gratified by his kindness; and Venetia anxious to ascertain whether all her relations were as charming as her uncle.

CHAPTER VI.

When Lady Annabel and her daughter returned from their morning drive, they found the visiting ticket of the Countess on the table, who had also left a note, with which she had provided herself in case she was not so fortunate as to meet her relations. The note was affectionate, and expressed the great delight of the writer at again meeting her dear sister, and forming an acquaintance with her charming niece.

'More relations!' said Venetia, with a somewhat droll expression of countenance.

At this moment the Bishop of———, who had already called twice upon them unsuccessfully, entered the room. The sight of this old and dear friend gave great joy. He came to engage them to dine with him the next day, having already ineffectually endeavoured to obtain them for permanent guests. They sat chatting so long with him, that they were obliged at last to bid him an abrupt adieu, and hasten and make their toilettes for their dinner.

Their hostess received her relations with a warmth which her husband's praises of her sister-in-law and niece had originally prompted, but which their appearance and manners instantly confirmed. As all the Earl's children were married, their party consisted to-day only of themselves; but it was a happy and agreeable meeting, for every one was desirous of being amiable. To be sure they had not many recollections or associations in common, and no one recurred to the past; but London, and the history of its fleeting hours, was an inexhaustible source of amusing conversation; and the Countess seemed resolved that Venetia should have a brilliant season; that she should be much amused and much admired. Lady Annabel, however, put in a plea for moderation, at least until Venetia was presented; but that the Countess declared must be at the next drawing-room, which was early in the ensuing week. Venetia listened to glittering narratives of balls and routs, operas and theatres, breakfasts and masquerades, Ranelagh and the Pantheon, with the same smiling composure as if she had been accustomed to them all her life, instead of having been shut up in a garden, with no livelier or brighter companions than birds and flowers.

After dinner, as her aunt and uncle and Lady Annabel sat round the fire, talking of her maternal grandfather, a subject which did not at all interest her, Venetia stole from her chair to a table in a distant part of the room, and turned over some books and music that were lying upon it. Among these was a literary journal, which she touched almost by accident, and which opened, with the name of Lord Cadurcis on the top of its page. This, of course, instantly attracted her attention. Her eye passed hastily over some sentences which greatly astonished her, and, extending her arm for a chair without quitting the book, she was soon deeply absorbed by the marvels which rapidly unfolded themselves to her. The article in question was an elaborate criticism as well of the career as the works of the noble poet; for, indeed, as Venetia now learnt, they were inseparably blended. She gathered from these pages a faint and hasty yet not altogether unfaithful conception of the strange revolution that had occurred in the character, pursuits, and position of her former companion. In that mighty metropolis, whose wealth and luxury and power had that morning so vividly impressed themselves upon her consciousness, and to the history of whose pleasures and brilliant and fantastic dissipation she had recently been listening with a lively and diverted ear, it seemed that, by some rapid and magical vicissitude, her little Plantagenet, the faithful and affectionate companion of her childhood, whose sorrows she had so often soothed, and who in her pure and devoted love had always found consolation and happiness, had become 'the observed of all observers;' the most remarkable where all was striking, and dazzling where all were brilliant!

His last visit to Cherbury, and its strange consequences, then occurred to her; his passionate addresses, and their bitter parting. Here was surely matter enough for a maiden's reverie, and into a reverie Venetia certainly fell, from which she was roused by the voice of her uncle, who could not conceive what book his charming niece could find so interesting, and led her to feel what an ill compliment she was paying to all present. Venetia hastily closed the volume, and rose rather confused from her seat; her radiant smile was the best apology to her uncle: and she compensated for her previous inattention, by playing to him on the harpsichord. All the time, however, the image of Cadurcis flitted across her vision, and she was glad when her mother moved to retire, that she might enjoy the opportunity of pondering in silence and unobserved over the strange history that she had read.

London is a wonderful place! Four-and-twenty hours back, with a feeling of loneliness and depression amounting to pain, Venetia had fled to sleep as her only refuge; now only a day had passed, and she had both seen and heard many things that had alike startled and pleased her; had found powerful and charming friends; and laid her head upon her pillow in a tumult of emotion that long banished slumber from her beautiful eyes.

CHAPTER VII.

Venetia soon found that she must bid adieu for ever, in London, to her old habits of solitude. She soon discovered that she was never to be alone. Her aunt called upon them early in the morning, and said that the whole day must be devoted to their court dresses; and in a few minutes they were all whirled off to a celebrated milliner's. After innumerable consultations and experiments, the dress of Venetia was decided on; her aunt and Lady Annabel were both assured that it would exceed in splendour and propriety any dress at the drawing-room. Indeed, as the great artist added, with such a model to work from it would reflect but little credit on the establishment, if any approached Miss Herbert in the effect she must inevitably produce.

While her mother was undergoing some of those attentions to which Venetia had recently submitted, and had retired for a few minutes into an adjoining apartment, our little lady of Cherbury strolled about the saloon in which she had been left, until her attention was attracted by a portrait of a young man in an oriental dress, standing very sublimely amid the ruins of some desert city; a palm tree in the distance, and by his side a crouching camel, and some recumbent followers slumbering amid the fallen columns.

'That is Lord Cadurcis, my love,' said her aunt, who at the moment joined her, 'the famous poet. All the young ladies are in love with him. I dare say you know his works by heart.'

'No, indeed, aunt,' said Venetia; 'I have never even read them; but I should like very much.'

'Not read Lord Cadurcis' poems! Oh! we must go and get them directly for you. Everybody reads them. You will be looked upon quite as a little barbarian. We will stop the carriage at Stockdale's, and get them for you.'

At this moment Lady Annabel rejoined them; and, having made all their arrangements, they re-entered the carriage.

'Stop at Stockdale's,' said her ladyship to the servant; 'I must get Cadurcis' last poem for Venetia. She will be quite back in her learning, Annabel.'

'Cadurcis' last poem!' said Lady Annabel; 'do you mean Lord Cadurcis? Is he a poet?'

'To he sure! Well, you are countrified not to know Lord Cadurcis!'

'I know him very well,' said Lady Annabel, gravely; 'but I did not know he was a poet.'

The Countess laughed, the carriage stopped, the book was brought; Lady Annabel looked uneasy, and tried to catch her daughter's countenance, but, strange to say, for the first time in her life was quite unsuccessful. The Countess took the book, and immediately gave it Venetia. 'There, my dear,' said her aunt, 'there never was anything so charming. I am so provoked that Cadurcis is a Whig.'

'A Whig!' said Lady Annabel; 'he was not a Whig when I knew him.'

'Oh! my dear, I am afraid he is worse than a Whig. He is almost a rebel! But then he is such a genius! Everything is allowed, you know, to a genius!' said the thoughtless sister-in-law.

Lady Annabel was silent; but the stillness of her emotion must not be judged from the stillness of her tongue. Her astonishment at all she had heard was only equalled by what we may justly term her horror. It was impossible that she could have listened to any communication at the same time so astounding, and to her so fearful.

'We knew Lord Cadurcis when he was very young, aunt,' said Venetia, in a quiet tone. 'He lived near mamma, in the country.'

'Oh! my dear Annabel, if you see him in town bring him to me; he is the most difficult person in the world to get to one's house, and I would give anything if he would come and dine with me.'

The Countess at last set her relations down at their hotel. When Lady Annabel was once more alone with her daughter, she said, 'Venetia, dearest, give me that book your aunt lent you.'

Venetia immediately handed it to her, but her mother did not open it; but saying, 'The Bishop dines at four, darling; I think it is time for us to dress,' Lady Annabel left the room.

To say the truth, Venetia was less surprised than disappointed by this conduct of her mother's; but she was not apt to murmur, and she tried to dismiss the subject from her thoughts.

It was with unfeigned delight that the kind-hearted Masham welcomed under his own roof his two best and dearest friends. He had asked nobody to meet them; it was settled that they were to be quite alone, and to talk of nothing but Cherbury and Marringhurst. When they were seated at table, the Bishop, who had been detained at the House of Lords, and been rather hurried to be in time to receive his guests, turned to his servant and inquired whether any one had called.

'Yes, my lord, Lord Cadurcis,' was the reply.

'Our old companion,' said the Bishop to Lady Annabel, with a smile. 'He has called upon me twice, and I have on both occasions unfortunately been absent.'

Lady Annabel merely bowed an assent to the Bishop's remark. Venetia longed to speak, but found it impossible. 'What is it that represses me?' she asked herself. 'Is there to be another forbidden subject insensibly to arise between us? I must struggle against this indefinable despotism that seems to pervade my life.'

'Have you met Lord Cadurcis, sir?' at length asked Venetia.

'Once; we resumed our acquaintance at a dinner party one day; but I shall soon see a great deal of him, for he has just taken his seat. He is of age, you know.'

'I hope he has come to years of discretion in every sense,' said Lady Annabel; 'but I fear not.'

'Oh, my dear lady!' said the Bishop, 'he has become a great man; he is our star. I assure you there is nobody in London talked of but Lord Cadurcis. He asked me a great deal after you and Cherbury. He will be delighted to see you.'

'I cannot say,' replied Lady Annabel, 'that the desire of meeting is at all mutual. From all I hear, our connections and opinions are very different, and I dare say our habits likewise.'

'My aunt lent us his new poem to-day,' said Venetia, boldly.

'Have you read it?' asked the Bishop.

'I am no admirer of modern poetry,' said Lady Annabel, somewhat tartly.

'Poetry of any kind is not much in my way,' said the Bishop, 'but if you like to read his poems, I will lend them to you, for he gave me a copy; esteemed a great honour, I assure you.'

'Thank you, my lord,' said Lady Annabel, 'both Venetia and myself are much engaged now; and I do not wish her to read while she is in London. When we return to Cherbury she will have abundance of time, if desirable.'

Both Venetia and her worthy host felt that the present subject of conversation was not agreeable to Lady Annabel, and it was changed. They fell upon more gracious topics, and in spite of this somewhat sullen commencement the meeting was quite as delightful as they anticipated. Lady Annabel particularly exerted herself to please, and, as was invariably the case under such circumstances with this lady, she was eminently successful; she apparently endeavoured, by her remarkable kindness to her daughter, to atone for any unpleasant feeling which her previous manner might for an instant have occasioned. Venetia watched her beautiful and affectionate parent, as Lady Annabel now dwelt with delight upon the remembrance of their happy home, and now recurred to the anxiety she naturally felt about her daughter's approaching presentation, with feelings of love and admiration, which made her accuse herself for the recent rebellion of her heart. She thought only of her mother's sorrows, and her devotion to her child; and, grateful for the unexpected course of circumstances which seemed to be leading every member of their former little society to honour and happiness, she resolved to persist in that career of duty and devotion to her mother, from which it seemed to her she had never deviated for a moment but to experience sorrow, misfortune, and remorse. Never did Venetia receive her mother's accustomed embrace and blessing with more responsive tenderness and gratitude than this night. She banished Cadurcis and his poems from her thoughts, confident that, so long as her mother approved neither of her continuing his acquaintance, nor perusing his writings, it was well that the one should be a forgotten tie, and the other a sealed book.

CHAPTER VIII.

Among the intimate acquaintances of Lady Annabel's brother was the nobleman who had been a minister during the American war, and who had also been the guardian of Lord Cadurcis, of whom, indeed, he was likewise a distant relative. He had called with his wife on Lady Annabel, after meeting her and her daughter at her brother's, and had cultivated her acquaintance with great kindness and assiduity, so that Lady Annabel had found it impossible to refuse his invitation to dinner.

This dinner occurred a few days after the visit of the Herberts to the Bishop, and that excellent personage, her own family, and some others equally distinguished, but all of the ministerial party, were invited to meet her. Lady Annabel found herself placed at table between a pompous courtier, who, being a gourmand, was not very prompt to disturb his enjoyment by conversation, and a young man whom she found very agreeable, and who at first, indeed, attracted her attention by his resemblance to some face with which she felt she was familiar, and yet which she was not successful in recalling. His manners were remarkably frank and ingenuous, yet soft and refined. Without having any peculiar brilliancy of expression, he was apt and fluent, and his whole demeanour characterised by a gentle modesty that was highly engaging. Apparently he had travelled a great deal, for he more than once alluded to his experience of foreign countries; but this was afterwards explained by Lady Annabel discovering, from an observation he let fall, that he was a sailor. A passing question from an opposite guest also told her that he was a member of parliament. While she was rather anxiously wishing to know who he might be, and congratulating herself that one in whose favour she was so much prepossessed should be on the right side, their host saluted him from the top of the table, and said, 'Captain Cadurcis, a glass of wine.'

The countenance was now explained. It was indeed Lord Cadurcis whom he resembled, though his eyes were dark blue, and his hair light brown. This then was that cousin who had been sent to sea to make his fortune, and whom Lady Annabel had a faint recollection of poor Mrs. Cadurcis once mentioning. George Cadurcis had not exactly made his fortune, but he had distinguished himself in his profession, and especially in Rodney's victory, and had fought his way up to the command of a frigate. The frigate had recently been paid off, and he had called to pay his respects to his noble relative with the hope of obtaining his interest for a new command. The guardian of his cousin, mortified with the conduct of his hopeful ward, was not very favourably impressed towards any one who bore the name of Cadurcis; yet George, with no pretence, had a winning honest manner that made friends; his lordship took a fancy to him, and, as he could not at the moment obtain him a ship, he did the next best thing for him in his power; a borough was vacant, and he put him into parliament.

'Do you know,' said Lady Annabel to her neighbour, 'I have been fancying all dinner time that we had met before; but I find it is that you only resemble one with whom I was once acquainted.'

'My cousin!' said the Captain; 'he will be very mortified when I go home, if I tell him your ladyship speaks of his acquaintance as one that is past.'

'It is some years since we met,' said Lady Annabel, in a more reserved tone.

'Plantagenet can never forget what he owes to you,' said Captain Cadurcis. 'How often has he spoken to me of you and Miss Herbert! It was only the other night; yes! not a week ago; that he made me sit up with him all night, while he was telling stories of Cherbury: you see I am quite familiar with the spot,' he added, smiling.

'You are very intimate with your cousin, I see,' said Lady Annabel.

'I live a great deal with him,' said George Cadurcis. 'You know we had never met or communicated; and it was not Plantagenet's fault, I am sure; for of all the generous, amiable, lovable beings, Cadurcis is the best I ever met with in this world. Ever since we knew each other he has been a brother to me; and though our politics and opinions are so opposed, and we naturally live in such a different circle, he would have insisted even upon my having apartments in his house; nor is it possible for me to give you the slightest idea of the delicate and unceasing kindness I experience from him. If we had lived together all our lives, it would be impossible to be more united.'

This eulogium rather softened Lady Annabel's heart; she even observed, 'I always thought Lord Cadurcis naturally well disposed; I always hoped he would turn out well; but I was afraid, from what I heard, he was much changed. He shows, however, his sense and good feeling in selecting you for his friend; for you are his natural one,' she added, after a momentary pause.

'And then you know,' he continued, 'it is so purely kind of him; for of course I am not fit to be a companion for Cadurcis, and perhaps, as far as that, no one is. Of course we have not a thought in common. I know nothing but what I have picked up in a rough life; and he, you know, is the cleverest person that ever lived, at least I think so.'

Lady Annabel smiled.

'Well, he is very young,' she observed, 'much your junior, Captain Cadurcis; and I hope he will yet prove a faithful steward of the great gifts that God has given him.'

'I would stake all I hold dear,' said the Captain, with great animation, 'that Cadurcis turns out well. He has such a good heart. Ah! Lady Annabel, if he be now and then a little irregular, only think of the temptations that assail him. Only one-and-twenty, his own master, and all London at his feet. It is too much for any one's head. But say or think what the world may, I know him better than they do; and I know there is not a finer creature in existence. I hope his old friends will not desert him,' added Captain Cadurcis, with a smile which, seemed to deprecate the severity of Lady Annabel; 'for in spite of all his fame and prosperity, perhaps, after all, this is the time when he most needs them.'

'Very possibly,' said her ladyship rather dryly.

While the mother was engaged in this conversation with her neighbour respecting her former interesting acquaintance, such was the fame of Lord Cadurcis then in the metropolis, that he also formed the topic of conversation at another part of the table, to which the daughter was an attentive listener. The tone in which he was spoken of, however, was of a very different character. While no one disputed his genius, his principles, temper, and habits of life were submitted to the severest scrutiny; and it was with blended feelings of interest and astonishment that Venetia listened to the detail of wild opinions, capricious conduct, and extravagant and eccentric behaviour ascribed to the companion of her childhood, who had now become the spoiled child of society. A shrewd gentleman, who had taken an extremely active part in this discussion, inquired of Venetia, next to whom he was seated, whether she had read his lordship's last poem. He was extremely surprised when Venetia answered in the negative; but he seized the opportunity of giving her an elaborate criticism on the poetical genius of Cadurcis. 'As for his style,' said the critic, 'no one can deny that is his own, and he will last by his style; as for his philosophy, and all these wild opinions of his, they will pass away, because they are not genuine, they are not his own, they are borrowed. He will outwrite them; depend upon it, he will. The fact is, as a friend of mine observed the other day, Herbert's writings have turned his head. Of course you could know nothing about them, but there are wonderful things in them, I can tell you that.'

'I believe it most sincerely,' said Venetia.

The critic stared at his neighbour. 'Hush!' said he, 'his wife and daughter are here. We must not talk of these things. You know Lady Annabel Herbert? There she is; a very fine woman too. And that is his daughter there, I believe, that dark girl with a turned-up nose. I cannot say she warrants the poetical address to her:

> My precious pearl the false and glittering world
> Has ne'er polluted with, its garish light!

She does not look much like a pearl, does she? She should keep in solitude, eh?'

The ladies rose and relieved Venetia from her embarrassment.

After dinner Lady Annabel introduced George Cadurcis to her daughter; and, seated by them both, he contrived without effort, and without the slightest consciousness of success, to confirm the pleasing impression in his favour which he had already made, and, when they parted, it was even with a mutual wish that they might meet again.

CHAPTER IX.

It was the night after the drawing-room. Lord Cadurcis was at Brookes' dining at midnight, having risen since only a few hours. Being a malcontent, he had ceased to attend the Court, where his original reception had been most gracious, which he had returned by some factious votes, and a caustic lampoon.

A party of young men entered, from the Court Ball, which in those days always terminated at midnight, whence the guests generally proceeded to Ranelagh; one or two of them seated themselves at the table at which Cadurcis was sitting. They were full of a new beauty who had been presented. Their violent and even extravagant encomiums excited his curiosity. Such a creature had never been seen, she was peerless, the most radiant of acknowledged charms had been dimmed before her. Their Majesties had accorded to her the most marked reception. A Prince of the blood had honoured her with his hand. Then they began to expatiate with fresh enthusiasm on her unparalleled loveliness.

'O Cadurcis,' said a young noble, who was one of his extreme admirers, 'she is the only creature I ever beheld worthy of being one of your heroines.'

'Whom are you talking about?' asked Cadurcis in a rather listless tone.

'The new beauty, of course.'

'And who may she be?'

'Miss Herbert, to be sure. Who speaks or thinks of any one else?'

'What, Ve———, I mean Miss Herbert?' exclaimed Cadurcis, with no little energy.

'Yes. Do you know her?'

'Do you mean to say—' and Cadurcis stopped and rose from the table, and joined the party round the fire. 'What Miss Herbert is it?' he added, after a short pause.

'Why *the* Miss Herbert; Herbert's daughter, to be sure. She was presented to-day by her mother.

'Lady Annabel?'

'The same.'

'Presented to-day!' said Cadurcis audibly, yet speaking as it were to himself. 'Presented to-day! Presented! How strange!'

'So every one thinks; one of the strangest things that ever happened,' remarked a bystander.

'And I did not even know they were in town,' continued Cadurcis, for, from his irregular hours, he had not seen his cousin since the party of yesterday. He began walking up and down the room, muttering, 'Masham, Weymouth, London, presented at Court, and I know nothing. How life changes! Venetia at Court, my Venetia!' Then turning round and addressing the young nobleman who had first spoken to him, he asked 'if the ball were over.'

'Yes; all the world are going to Ranelagh. Are you inclined to take a round?'

'I have a strange fancy,' said Cadurcis, 'and if you will go with me, I will take you in my vis-à-vis. It is here.'

This was an irresistible invitation, and in a few minutes the companions were on their way; Cadurcis, apparently with no peculiar interest in the subject, leading the conversation very artfully to the presentation of Miss Herbert. His friend was heartily inclined to gratify his curiosity. He gave him ample details of Miss Herbert's person: even of her costume, and the sensation both produced; how she was presented by her mother, who, after so long an estrangement from the world, scarcely excited less impression, and the remarkable cordiality with which both mother and daughter were greeted by the sovereign and his royal consort.

The two young noblemen found Ranelagh crowded, but the presence of Lord Cadurcis occasioned a sensation the moment he was recognised. Everywhere the whisper went round, and many parties crowded near to catch a glimpse of the hero of the day. 'Which is he? That fair, tall young man? No, the other to be sure. Is it really he? How distinguished! How melancholy! Quite the poet. Do you think he is really so unhappy as he looks? I would sooner see him than the King and Queen. He seems very young, but then he has seen so much of the world! Fine eyes, beautiful hair! I wonder who is his friend? How proud he must be! Who is that lady he bowed to? That is the Duke of —— speaking to him,' Such were the remarks that might be caught in the vicinity of Lord Cadurcis as he took his round, gazed at by the assembled crowd, of whom many knew him only by fame, for the charm of Ranelagh was that it was rather a popular than a merely fashionable assembly. Society at large blended with the Court, which maintained and renewed its influence by being witnessed under the most graceful auspices. The personal authority of the aristocracy has decreased with the disappearance of Ranelagh and similar places of amusement, where rank was not exclusive, and luxury by the gratification it occasioned others seemed robbed of half its selfism.

In his second round, Lord Cadurcis recognised the approach of the Herberts. They formed the portion of a large party. Lady Annabel was leaning on her brother, whom Cadurcis knew by sight; Venetia was at the side of her aunt, and several gentlemen were hovering about them; among them, to his surprise, his cousin, George Cadurcis, in his uniform, for he had been to Court and to the Court Ball. Venetia was talking with animation. She was in her Court dress and in powder. Her appearance was strange to him. He could scarcely recognise the friend of his childhood; but without any doubt in all that assembly, unrivalled in the whole world for beauty, grace, and splendour, she was without a parallel; a cynosure on which all eyes were fixed.

So occupied were the ladies of the Herbert party by the conversation of their numerous and brilliant attendants, that the approach of any one else but Lord Cadurcis might have been unnoticed by them, but a hundred tongues before he drew nigh had prepared Venetia for his appearance. She was indeed most anxious to behold him, and though she was aware that her heart fluttered not slightly as the moment was at hand, she commanded her gaze, and her eyes met his, although she was doubtful whether he might choose or care to recognise her. He bowed almost to the ground; and when Venetia had raised her responsive head he had passed by.

'Why, Cadurcis, you know Miss Herbert?' said his friend in a tone of some astonishment.

'Well; but it is a long time since I have seen her.'

'Is she not beautiful?'

'I never doubted on that subject; I tell you, Scrope, we must contrive to join her party. I wish we had some of our friends among them. Here comes the Monteagle; aid me to escape her.'

The most fascinating smile failed in arresting the progress of Cadurcis; fortunately, the lady was the centre of a brilliant band; all that he had to do, therefore, was boldly to proceed.

'Do you think my cousin is altered since you knew him?' inquired George Cadurcis of Venetia.

'I scarcely had time to observe him,' she replied.

'I wish you would let me bring him to you. He did not know until this moment you were in town. I have not seen him since we met yesterday.'

'Oh, no,' said Venetia. 'Do not disturb him.'

In time, however, Lord Cadurcis was again in sight; and now without any hesitation he stopped, and falling into the line by Miss Herbert, he addressed her: 'I am proud of being remembered by Miss Herbert,' he said.

'I am most happy to meet you,' replied Venetia, with unaffected sincerity.

'And Lady Annabel, I have not been able to catch her eye: is she quite well? I was ignorant that you were in London until I heard of your triumph this night.'

The Countess whispered her niece, and Venetia accordingly presented Lord Cadurcis to her aunt. This was a most gratifying circumstance to him. He was anxious, by some means or other, to effect his entrance into her circle; and he had an irresistible suspicion that Lady Annabel no longer looked upon him with eyes of favour. So he resolved to enlist the aunt as his friend. Few persons could be more winning than Cadurcis, when he willed it; and every attempt to please from one whom all emulated to gratify and honour, was sure to be successful. The Countess, who, in spite of politics, was a secret votary of his, was quite prepared to be enchanted. She congratulated herself on forming, as she had long wished, an acquaintance with one so celebrated. She longed to pass Lady Monteagle in triumph. Cadurcis improved his opportunity to the utmost. It was impossible for any one to be more engaging; lively, yet at the same time gentle, and deferential with all his originality. He spoke, indeed, more to the aunt than to Venetia, but when he addressed the latter, there was a melting, almost a mournful tenderness in his tones, that alike affected her heart and charmed her imagination. Nor could she be insensible to the gratification she experienced as she witnessed, every instant, the emotion his presence excited among the passers-by, and of which Cadurcis himself seemed so properly and so utterly unconscious. And this was Plantagenet!

Lord Cadurcis spoke of his cousin, who, on his joining the party, had assisted the arrangement by moving to the other side; and he spoke of him with a regard which pleased Venetia, though Cadurcis envied him his good fortune in having the advantage of a prior acquaintance with Miss Herbert in town; 'but then we are old acquaintances in the country,' he added, half in a playful, half in a melancholy tone, 'are we not?'

'It is a long time that we have known each other, and it is a long time since we have met,' replied Venetia.

'A delicate reproach,' said Cadurcis; 'but perhaps rather my misfortune than my fault. My thoughts have been often, I might say ever, at Cherbury.'

'And the abbey; have you forgotten the abbey?'

'I have never been near it since a morning you perhaps remember,' said his lordship in a low voice. 'Ah! Miss Herbert,' he continued, with a sigh, 'I was young then; I have lived to change many opinions, and some of which you then disapproved.'

The party stopped at a box just vacant, and in which the ladies seated themselves while their carriages were inquired for. Lord Cadurcis, with a rather faltering heart, went up to pay his respects to Venetia's mother. Lady Annabel received him with a courtesy, that however was scarcely cordial, but the Countess instantly presented him to her husband with an unction which a little astonished her sister-in-law. Then a whisper, but unobserved, passed between the Earl and his lady, and in a minute Lord Cadurcis had been invited to dine with them on the next day, and meet his old friends from the country. Cadurcis was previously engaged, but hesitated not a moment in accepting the invitation. The Monteagle party now passed by; the lady looked a little surprised at the company in which she found her favourite, and not a little mortified by his neglect. What business had Cadurcis to be speaking to that Miss Herbert? Was it not enough that the whole day not another name had scarcely crossed her ear, but the night must even witness the conquest of Lord Cadurcis by the new beauty? It was such bad ton, it was so unlike him, it was so underbred, for a person of his position immediately to bow before the new idol of the hour, and a Tory girl too! It was the last thing she could have expected from him. She should, on the contrary, have thought that the universal admiration which this Miss Herbert commanded, would have been exactly the reason why a man like Cadurcis would have seemed almost unconscious of her existence. She determined to remonstrate with him; and she was sure of a speedy opportunity, for he was to dine with her on the morrow.

CHAPTER X.

Notwithstanding Lady Annabel's reserved demeanour, Lord Cadurcis, supported by the presence of his cousin, whom he had discovered to be a favourite of that lady, ventured to call upon her the next day, but she was out. They were to meet, however, at dinner, where Cadurcis determined to omit no opportunity to propitiate her. The Countess had a great deal of tact, and she contrived to make up a party to receive him, in which there were several of his friends, among them his cousin and the Bishop of——, and no strangers who were not, like herself, his great admirers; but if she had known more, she need not have given herself this trouble, for there was a charm among her guests of which she was ignorant, and Cadurcis went determined to please and to be pleased.

At dinner he was seated next to Lady Annabel, and it was impossible for any person to be more deferential, soft, and insinuating. He spoke of old days with emotion which he did not attempt to suppress; he alluded to the present with infinite delicacy. But it was very difficult to make way. Lady Annabel was courteous, but she was reserved. His lively reminiscences elicited from her no corresponding sentiment; and no art would induce her to dwell upon the present. If she only would have condescended to compliment him, it would have given him an opportunity of expressing his distaste of the life which he now led, and a description of the only life which he wished to lead; but Lady Annabel studiously avoided affording him any opening of the kind. She treated him like a stranger. She impressed upon him without effort that she would only consider him an acquaintance. How Cadurcis, satiated with the incense of the whole world, sighed for one single congratulation from Lady Annabel! Nothing could move her.

'I was so surprised to meet you last night,' at length he again observed. 'I have made so many inquiries after you. Our dear friend the Bishop was, I fear, almost wearied with my inquiries after Cherbury. I know not how it was, I felt quite a pang when I heard that you had left it, and that all these years, when I have been conjuring up so many visions of what was passing under that dear roof, you were at Weymouth.'

'Yes. We were at Weymouth some time.'

'But do not you long to see Cherbury again? I cannot tell you how I pant for it. For my part, I have seen the world, and I have seen enough of it. After all, the end of all our exertions is to be happy at home; that is the end of everything; don't you think so?'

'A happy home is certainly a great blessing,' replied Lady Annabel; 'and a rare one.'

'But why should it be rare?' inquired Lord Cadurcis.

'It is our own fault,' said Lady Annabel; 'our vanity drives us from our hearths.'

'But we soon return again, and calm and cooled. For my part, I have no object in life but to settle down at the old abbey, and never to quit again our woods. But I shall lead a dull life without my neighbours,' he added, with a smile, and in a tone half-coaxing.

'I suppose you never see Lord —— now?' said Lady Annabel, mentioning his late guardian. There was, as Cadurcis fancied, some sarcasm in the question, though not in the tone in which it was asked.

'No, I never see him,' his lordship answered firmly; 'we differ in our opinions, and I differ from him with regret; but I differ from a sense of duty, and therefore I have no alternative.'

'The claims of duty are of course paramount,' observed Lady Annabel.

'You know my cousin?' said Cadurcis, to turn the conversation.

'Yes, and I like him much; he appears to be a sensible, amiable person, of excellent principles.'

'I am not bound to admire George's principles,' said Lord Cadurcis, gaily; 'but I respect them, because I know that they are conscientious. I love George; he is my only relation, and he is my friend.'

'I trust he will always be your friend, for I think you will then, at least, know one person on whom you can depend.'

'I believe it. The friendships of the world are wind.'

'I am surprised to hear you say so,' said Lady Annabel.

'Why, Lady Annabel?'

'You have so many friends.'

Lord Cadurcis smiled. 'I wish,' he said, after a little hesitation, 'if only for "Auld lang syne," I might include Lady Annabel Herbert among them.'

'I do not think there is any basis for friendship between us, my lord,' she said, very dryly.

'The past must ever be with me,' said Lord Cadurcis, 'and I should have thought a sure and solid one.'

'Our opinions on all subjects are so adverse, that I must believe that there could be no great sympathy in our feelings.'

'My feelings are beyond my control,' he replied; 'they are, and must ever be, totally independent of my opinions.'

Lady Annabel did not reply. His lordship felt baffled, but he was resolved to make one more effort.

'Do you know,' he said, 'I can scarcely believe myself in London to-day? To be sitting next to you, to see Miss Herbert, to hear Dr. Masham's voice. Oh! does it not recall Cherbury, or Marringhurst, or that day at Cadurcis, when you were so good as to smile over my rough repast? Ah! Lady Annabel, those days were happy! those were feelings that can never die! All the glitter and hubbub of the world can never make me forget them, can never make you, I hope, Lady Annabel, quite recall them with an effort. We were friends then: let us be friends now.'

'I am too old to cultivate new friendships,' said Lady Annabel; 'and if we are to be friends, Lord Cadurcis, I am sorry to say that, after the interval that has occurred since we last parted, we should have to begin again.'

'It is a long time,' said Cadurcis, mournfully, 'a very long time, and one, in spite of what the world may think, to which I cannot look back with any self-congratulation. I wished three years ago never to leave Cadurcis again. Indeed I did; and indeed it was not my fault that I quitted it.'

'It was no one's fault, I hope. Whatever the cause may have been, I have ever remained quite ignorant of it. I wished, and wish, to remain ignorant of it. I, for one, have ever considered it the wise dispensation of a merciful Providence.'

Cadurcis ground his teeth; a dark look came over him which, when once it rose on his brow, was with difficulty dispelled; and for the remainder of the dinner he continued silent and gloomy.

He was, however, not unobserved by Venetia. She had watched his evident attempts to conciliate her mother with lively interest; she had witnessed their failure with sincere sorrow. In spite of that stormy interview, the results of which, in his hasty departure, and the severance of their acquaintance, she had often regretted, she had always retained for him the greatest affection. During these three years he had still, in her inmost heart, remained her own Plantagenet, her adopted brother, whom she loved, and in whose welfare her feelings were deeply involved. The mysterious circumstances of her birth, and the discoveries to which they had led, had filled her mind with a fanciful picture of human nature, over which she had long brooded. A great poet had become her ideal of a man. Sometimes she had sighed, when musing over her father and Plantagenet on the solitary seashore at Weymouth, that Cadurcis, instead of being the merely amiable, and somewhat narrow-minded being that she supposed, had not been invested with those brilliant and commanding qualities which she felt could alone master her esteem. Often had she, in those abstracted hours, played with her imagination in combining the genius of her father with the soft heart of that friend to whom she was so deeply attached. She had wished, in her reveries, that Cadurcis might have been a great man; that he might have existed in an atmosphere of glory amid the plaudits and admiration of his race; and that then he might have turned from all that fame, so dear to them both, to the heart which could alone sympathise with the native simplicity of his childhood.

The ladies withdrew. The Bishop and another of the guests joined them after a short interval. The rest remained below, and drank their wine with the freedom not unusual in those days, Lord Cadurcis among them, although it was not his habit. But he was not convivial, though he never passed the bottle untouched. He was in one of those dark humours of which there was a latent spring in his nature, but which in old days had been kept in check by his simple life, his inexperienced mind, and the general kindness that greeted him, and which nothing but the caprice and perversity of his mother could occasionally develope. But since the great revolution in his position, since circumstances had made him alike acquainted with his nature, and had brought all society to acknowledge its superiority; since he had gained and felt his irresistible power, and had found all the world, and all the glory of it, at his feet, these moods had become more frequent. The slightest reaction in the self-complacency that was almost unceasingly stimulated by the applause of applauded men and the love of the loveliest women, instantly took the shape and found refuge in the immediate form of the darkest spleen, generally, indeed, brooding in silence, and, if speaking, expressing itself only in sarcasm. Cadurcis was indeed, as we have already described him, the spoiled child of society; a froward and petted darling, not always to be conciliated by kindness, but furious when neglected or controlled. He was habituated to triumph; it had been his lot to come, to see, and to conquer; even the procrastination of certain success was intolerable to him; his energetic volition could not endure a check. To Lady Annabel Herbert, indeed, he was not exactly what he was to others; there was a spell in old associations from which he unconsciously could not emancipate himself, and from which it was his opinion he honoured her in not desiring to be free. He had his reasons for wishing to regain his old, his natural influence, over her heart; he did not doubt for an instant that, if Cadurcis sued, success must follow the condescending effort. He had sued, and he had been met with coldness, almost with disdain. He had addressed her in those terms of tenderness which experience had led him to believe were irresistible, yet to which he seldom had recourse, for hitherto he had not been under the degrading necessity of courting. He had dwelt with fondness on the insignificant past, because it was connected with her; he had regretted, or affected even to despise, the glorious present, because it seemed, for some indefinite cause, to have estranged him from her hearth. Yes! he had humbled himself before her; he had thrown with disdain at her feet all that dazzling fame and expanding glory which seemed his peculiar and increasing privilege. He had delicately conveyed to her that even these would be sacrificed, not only without a sigh, but with cheerful delight, to find himself once more living, as of old, in the limited world of her social affections. Three years ago he had been rejected by the daughter, because he was an undistinguished youth. Now the mother recoiled from his fame. And who was this woman? The same cold, stern heart that had alienated the gifted Herbert; the same narrow, rigid mind that had repudiated ties that every other woman in the world would have gloried to cherish and acknowledge. And with her he had passed his prejudiced youth, and fancied, like an idiot, that he had found sympathy! Yes, so long as he was a slave, a mechanical, submissive slave, bowing his mind to all the traditionary bigotry which she adored, never daring to form an opinion for himself, worshipping her idol, custom, and labouring by habitual hypocrisy to perpetuate the delusions of all around her!

In the meantime, while Lord Cadurcis was chewing the cud of these bitter feelings, we will take the opportunity of explaining the immediate cause of Lady Annabel's frigid reception of his friendly advances. All that she had heard of Cadurcis, all the information she had within these few days so rapidly acquired of his character and conduct, were indeed not calculated to dispose her to witness the renewal of their intimacy with feelings of remarkable satisfaction. But this morning she had read his poem, the poem that all London was talking of, and she had read it with horror. She looked upon Cadurcis as a lost man. With her, indeed, since her marriage, an imaginative mind had become an object of terror; but there were some peculiarities in the tone of Cadurcis' genius, which magnified to excess her general apprehension on this head. She traced, in every line, the evidences of a raging vanity, which she was convinced must prompt its owner to sacrifice, on all occasions, every feeling of duty to its gratification. Amid all the fervour of rebellious passions, and the violence of a wayward mind, a sentiment of profound egotism appeared to her impressed on every page she perused. Great as might have been the original errors of Herbert, awful as in her estimation were the crimes to which they had led him, they might in the first instance be traced rather to a perverted view of society than of himself. But self was the idol of Cadurcis; self distorted into a phantom that seemed to Lady Annabel pregnant not only with terrible crimes, but with the basest and most humiliating vices. The certain degradation which in the instance of her husband had been the consequence of a bad system, would, in her opinion, in the case of Cadurcis, be the result of a bad nature; and when she called to mind that there had once been a probability that this individual might have become the husband of her Venetia, her child whom it had been the sole purpose of her life to save from the misery of which she herself had been the victim; that she had even dwelt on the idea with complacency, encouraged its progress, regretted its abrupt termination, but consoled herself by the flattering hope that time, with even more favourable auspices, would mature it into fulfilment; she trembled, and turned pale.

It was to the Bishop that, after dinner, Lady Annabel expressed some of the feelings which the reappearance of Cadurcis had occasioned her.

'I see nothing but misery for his future,' she exclaimed; 'I tremble for him when he addresses me. In spite of the glittering surface on which he now floats, I foresee only a career of violence, degradation, and remorse.'

'He is a problem difficult to solve,' replied Masham; 'but there are elements not only in his character, but his career, so different from those of the person of whom we were speaking, that I am not inclined at once to admit, that the result must necessarily be the same.'

'I see none,' replied Lady Annabel; 'at least none of sufficient influence to work any material change.'

'What think you of his success?' replied Masham. 'Cadurcis is evidently proud of it. With all his affected scorn of the world, he is the slave of society. He may pique the feelings of mankind, but I doubt whether he will outrage them.'

'He is on such a dizzy eminence,' replied Lady Annabel, 'that I do not believe he is capable of calculating so finely. He does not believe, I am sure, in the possibility of resistance. His vanity will tempt him onwards.'

'Not to persecution,' said Masham. 'Now, my opinion of Cadurcis is, that his egotism, or selfism, or whatever you may style it, will ultimately preserve him from any very fatal, from any irrecoverable excesses. He is of the world, worldly. All his works, all his conduct, tend only to astonish mankind. He is not prompted by any visionary ideas of ameliorating his species. The instinct of self-preservation will serve him as ballast.'

'We shall see,' said Lady Annabel; 'for myself, whatever may be his end, I feel assured that great and disgraceful vicissitudes are in store for him.'

'It is strange after what, in comparison with such extraordinary changes, must be esteemed so brief an interval,' observed Masham, with a smile, 'to witness such a revolution in his position. I often think to myself, can this indeed be our little Plantagenet?'

'It is awful!' said Lady Annabel; 'much more than strange. For myself, when I recall certain indications of his feelings when he was last at Cadurcis, and think for a moment of the results to which they might have led, I shiver; I assure you, my dear lord, I tremble from head to foot. And I encouraged him! I smiled with fondness on his feelings! I thought I was securing the peaceful happiness of my child! What can we trust to in this world! It is too dreadful to dwell upon! It must have been an interposition of Providence that Venetia escaped.'

'Dear little Venetia,' exclaimed the good Bishop; 'for I believe I shall call her little Venetia to the day of my death. How well she looks to-night! Her aunt is, I think, very fond of her! See!'

'Yes, it pleases me,' said Lady Annabel; 'but I do wish my sister was not such an admirer of Lord Cadurcis' poems. You cannot conceive how uneasy it makes me. I am quite annoyed that he was asked here to-day. Why ask him?'

'Oh! there is no harm,' said Masham; 'you must forget the past. By all accounts, Cadurcis is not a marrying man. Indeed, as I understood, marriage with him is at present quite out of the question. And as for Venetia, she rejected him before, and she will, if necessary, reject him again. He has been a brother to her, and after that he can be no more. Girls never fall in love with those with whom they are bred up.'

'I hope, I believe there is no occasion for apprehension,' replied Lady Annabel; 'indeed, it has scarcely entered my head. The very charms he once admired in Venetia can have no sway over him, as I should think, now. I should believe him as little capable of appreciating Venetia now, as he was when last at Cherbury, of anticipating the change in his own character.'

'You mean opinions, my dear lady, for characters never change. Believe me, Cadurcis is radically the same as in old days. Circumstances have only developed his latent predisposition.'

'Not changed, my dear lord! what, that innocent, sweet-tempered, docile child—'

'Hush! here he comes.'

The Earl and his guests entered the room; a circle was formed round Lady Annabel; some evening visitors arrived; there was singing. It had not been the intention of Lord Cadurcis to return to the drawing-room after his rebuff by Lady Annabel; he had meditated making his peace at Monteagle House; but when the moment of his projected departure had arrived, he could not resist the temptation of again seeing Venetia. He entered the room last, and some moments after his companions. Lady Annabel, who watched the general entrance, concluded he had gone, and her attention was now fully engaged. Lord Cadurcis remained at the end of the room alone, apparently abstracted, and looking far from amiable; but his eye, in reality, was watching Venetia. Suddenly her aunt approached her, and invited the lady who was conversing with Miss Herbert to sing; Lord Cadurcis immediately advanced, and took her seat. Venetia was surprised that for the first time in her life with Plantagenet she felt embarrassed. She had met his look when he approached her, and had welcomed, or, at least, intended to welcome him with a smile, but she was at a loss for words; she was haunted with the recollection of her mother's behaviour to him at dinner, and she looked down on the ground, far from being at ease.

'Venetia!' said Lord Cadurcis.

She started.

'We are alone,' he said; 'let me call you Venetia when we are alone.'

She did not, she could not reply; she felt confused; the blood rose to her cheek.

'How changed is everything!' continued Cadurcis. 'To think the day should ever arrive when I should have to beg your permission to call you Venetia!'

She looked up; she met his glance. It was mournful; nay, his eyes were suffused with tears. She saw at her side the gentle and melancholy Plantagenet of her childhood.

'I cannot speak; I am agitated at meeting you,' she said with her native frankness. 'It is so long since we have been alone; and, as you say, all is so changed.'

'But are you changed, Venetia?' he said in a voice of emotion; 'for all other change is nothing.'

'I meet you with pleasure,' she replied; 'I hear of your fame with pride. You cannot suppose that it is possible I should cease to be interested in your welfare.'

'Your mother does not meet me with pleasure; she hears of nothing that has occurred to me with pride; your mother has ceased to take an interest in my welfare; and why should you be unchanged?'

'You mistake my mother.'

'No, no,' replied Cadurcis, shaking his head, 'I have read her inmost soul to-day. Your mother hates me; me, whom she once styled her son. She was a mother once to me, and you were my sister. If I have lost her heart, why have I not lost yours?'

'My heart, if you care for it, is unchanged,' said Venetia.

'O Venetia, whatever you may think, I never wanted the solace of a sister's love more than I do at this moment.'

'I pledged my affection to you when we were children,' replied Venetia; 'you have done nothing to forfeit it, and it is yours still.'

'When we were children,' said Cadurcis, musingly; 'when we were innocent; when we were happy. You, at least, are innocent still; are you happy, Venetia?'

'Life has brought sorrows even to me, Plantagenet.'

The blood deserted his heart when she called him Plantagenet; he breathed with difficulty.

'When I last returned to Cherbury,' he said, 'you told me you were changed, Venetia; you revealed to me on another occasion the secret cause of your affliction. I was a boy then, a foolish ignorant boy. Instead of sympathising with your heartfelt anxiety, my silly vanity was offended by feelings I should have shared, and soothed, and honoured. Ah, Venetia! well had it been for one of us that I had conducted myself more kindly, more wisely.'

'Nay, Plantagenet, believe me, I remember that interview only to regret it. The recollection of it has always occasioned me great grief. We were both to blame; but we were both children then. We must pardon each other's faults.'

'You will hear, that is, if you care to listen, Venetia, much of my conduct and opinions,' continued Lord Cadurcis, 'that may induce you to believe me headstrong and capricious. Perhaps I am less of both in all things than the world imagines. But of this be certain, that my feelings towards you have never changed, whatever you may permit them to be; and if some of my boyish judgments have, as was but natural, undergone some transformation, be you, my sweet friend, in some degree consoled for the inconsistency, since I have at length learned duly to appreciate one of whom we then alike knew little, but whom a natural inspiration taught you, at least, justly to appreciate: I need not say I mean the illustrious father of your being.'

Venetia could not restrain her tears; she endeavoured to conceal her agitated countenance behind the fan with which she was fortunately provided.

'To me a forbidden subject,' said Venetia, 'at least with them I could alone converse upon it, but one that my mind never deserts.'

'O Venetia!' exclaimed Lord Cadurcis with a sigh, 'would we were both with him!'

'A wild thought,' she murmured, 'and one I must not dwell upon.'

'We shall meet, I hope,' said Lord Cadurcis; 'we must meet, meet often. I called upon your mother to-day, fruitlessly. You must attempt to conciliate her. Why should we be parted? We, at least, are friends, and more than friends. I cannot exist unless we meet, and meet with the frankness of old days.'

'I think you mistake mamma; I think you may, indeed. Remember how lately she has met you, and after how long an interval! A little time, and she will resume her former feelings, and believe that you have never forfeited yours. Besides, we have friends, mutual friends. My aunt admires you, and here I naturally must be a great deal. And the Bishop, he still loves you; that I am sure he does: and your cousin, mamma likes your cousin. I am sure if you can manage only to be patient, if you will only attempt to conciliate a little, all will be as before. Remember, too, how changed your position is,' Venetia added with a smile; 'you allow me to forget you are a great man, but mamma is naturally restrained by all this wonderful revolution. When she finds that you really are the Lord Cadurcis whom she knew such a very little boy, the Lord Cadurcis who, without her aid, would never have been able even to write his fine poems, oh! she must love you again. How can she help it?'

Cadurcis smiled. 'We shall see,' he said. 'In the meantime do not you desert me, Venetia.'

'That is impossible,' she replied; 'the happiest of my days have been passed with you. You remember the inscription on the jewel? I shall keep to my vows.'

'That was a very good inscription so far as it went,' said Cadurcis; and then, as if a little alarmed at his temerity, he changed the subject.

'Do you know,' said Venetia, after a pause, 'I am treating you all this time as a poet, merely in deference to public opinion. Not a line have I been permitted to read; but I am resolved to rebel, and you must arrange it all.'

'Ah!' said the enraptured Cadurcis; 'this is fame!'

At this moment the Countess approached them, and told Venetia that her mother wished to speak to her. Lady Annabel had discovered the tête-à-tête, and resolved instantly to terminate it. Lord Cadurcis, however, who was quick as lightning, read all that was necessary in Venetia's look. Instead of instantly retiring, he remained some little time longer, talked to the Countess, who was perfectly enchanted with him, even sauntered up to the singers, and complimented them, and did not make his bow until he had convinced at least the mistress of the mansion, if not her sister-in-law, that it was not Venetia Herbert who was his principal attraction in this agreeable society.

CHAPTER XI.

The moment he had quitted Venetia, Lord Cadurcis returned home. He could not endure the usual routine of gaiety after her society; and his coachman, often waiting until five o'clock in the morning at Monteagle House, could scarcely assure himself of his good fortune in this exception to his accustomed trial of patience. The vis-à-vis stopped, and Lord Cadurcis bounded out with a light step and a lighter heart. His table was covered with letters. The first one that caught his eye was a missive from Lady Monteagle. Cadurcis seized it like a wild animal darting on its prey, tore it in half without opening it, and, grasping the poker, crammed it with great energy into the fire. This exploit being achieved, Cadurcis began walking up and down the room; and indeed he paced it for nearly a couple of hours in a deep reverie, and evidently under a considerable degree of excitement, for his gestures were violent, and his voice often audible. At length, about an hour after midnight, he rang for his valet, tore off his cravat, and hurled it to one corner of the apartment, called for his robe de chambre, soda water, and more lights, seated himself, and began pouring forth, faster almost than his pen could trace the words, the poem that he had been meditating ever since he had quitted the roof where he had met Venetia. She had expressed a wish to read his poems; he had resolved instantly to compose one for her solitary perusal Thus he relieved his heart:

I.

Within a cloistered pile, whose Gothic towers
Rose by the margin of a sedgy lake,
Embosomed in a valley of green bowers,
And girt by many a grove and ferny brake
Loved by the antlered deer, a tender youth
Whom Time to childhood's gentle sway of love
Still spared; yet innocent as is the dove,
Nor mounded yet by Care's relentless tooth;
Stood musing, of that fair antique domain
The orphan lord! And yet, no childish thought
With wayward purpose holds its transient reign
In his young mind, with deeper feelings fraught;
Then mystery all to him, and yet a dream,
That Time has touched with its revealing beam.

II.

There came a maiden to that lonely boy,
And like to him as is the morn to night;
Her sunny face a very type of joy,

And with her soul's unclouded lustre bright.
Still scantier summers had her brow illumed
Than that on which she threw a witching smile,
Unconscious of the spell that could beguile
His being of the burthen it was doomed
By his ancestral blood to bear: a spirit,
Rife with desponding thoughts and fancies drear,
A moody soul that men sometimes inherit,
And worse than all the woes the world may bear.
But when he met that maiden's dazzling eye,
He bade each gloomy image baffled fly.

III.

Amid the shady woods and sunny lawns
The maiden and the youth now wander, gay
As the bright birds, and happy as the fawns,
Their sportive rivals, that around them play;
Their light hands linked in love, the golden hours
Unconscious fly, while thus they graceful roam,
And careless ever till the voice of home
Recalled them from their sunshine find their flowers;
For then they parted: to his lonely pile
The orphan-chief, for though his woe to lull,
The maiden called him brother, her fond smile
Gladdened another hearth, while his was dull
Yet as they parted, she reproved his sadness,
And for his sake she gaily whispered gladness.

IV.

She was the daughter of a noble race,
That beauteous girl, and yet she owed her name
To one who needs no herald's skill to trace
His blazoned lineage, for his lofty fame
Lives in the mouth of men, and distant climes
Re-echo his wide glory; where the brave
Are honoured, where 'tis noble deemed to save
A prostrate nation, and for future times
Work with a high devotion, that no taunt,
Or ribald lie, or zealot's eager curse,
Or the short-sighted world's neglect can daunt,
That name is worshipped! His immortal verse
Blends with his god-like deeds, a double spell
To bind the coming age he loved too well!

V.

For, from his ancient home, a scatterling,
They drove him forth, unconscious of their prize,
And branded as a vile unhallowed thing,
The man who struggled only to be wise.
And even his hearth rebelled, the duteous wife,
Whose bosom well might soothe in that dark hour,
Swelled with her gentle force the world's harsh power,
And aimed her dart at his devoted life.
That struck; the rest his mighty soul might scorn,
But when his household gods averted stood,
'Twas the last pang that cannot well be borne
When tortured e'en to torpor: his heart's blood
Flowed to the unseen blow: then forth he went,
And gloried in his ruthless banishment.

VI.

A new-born pledge of love within his home,
His alien home, the exiled father left;
And when, like Cain, he wandered forth to roam,
A Cain without his solace, all bereft,
Stole down his pallid cheek the scalding tear,
To think a stranger to his tender love
His child must grow, untroubled where might rove
His restless life, or taught perchance to fear
Her father's name, and bred in sullen hate,
Shrink from his image. Thus the gentle maid,
Who with her smiles had soothed an orphan's fate,
Had felt an orphan's pang; yet undismayed,
Though taught to deem her sire the child of shame,
She clung with instinct to that reverent name!

VII.

Time flew; the boy became a man; no more
His shadow falls upon his cloistered hall,
But to a stirring world he learn'd to pour
The passion of his being, skilled to call
From the deep caverns of his musing thought
Shadows to which they bowed, and on their mind
To stamp the image of his own; the wind,
Though all unseen, with force or odour fraught,
Can sway mankind, and thus a poet's voice,
Now touched with sweetness, now inflamed with rage,

Though breath, can make us grieve and then rejoice:
Such is the spell of his creative page,
That blends with all our moods; and thoughts can yield
That all have felt, and yet till then were sealed.

VIII.

The lute is sounding in a chamber bright
With a high festival; on every side,
Soft in the gleamy blaze of mellowed light,
Fair women smile, and dancers graceful glide;
And words still sweeter than a serenade
Are breathed with guarded voice and speaking eyes,
By joyous hearts in spite of all their sighs;
But byegone fantasies that ne'er can fade
Retain the pensive spirit of the youth;
Reclined against a column he surveys
His laughing compeers with a glance, in sooth,
Careless of all their mirth: for other days
Enchain him with their vision, the bright hours
Passed with the maiden in their sunny bowers.

IX.

Why turns his brow so pale, why starts to life
That languid eye? What form before unseen,
With all the spells of hallowed memory rife,
Now rises on his vision? As the Queen
Of Beauty from her bed of sparkling foam
Sprang to the azure light, and felt the air,
Soft as her cheek, the wavy dancers bear
To his rapt sight a mien that calls his home,
His cloistered home, before him, with his dreams
Prophetic strangely blending. The bright muse
Of his dark childhood still divinely beams
Upon his being; glowing with the hues
That painters love, when raptured pencils soar
To trace a form that nations may adore!

X.

One word alone, within her thrilling ear,
Breathed with hushed voice the brother of her heart,
And that for aye is hidden. With a tear
Smiling she strove to conquer, see her start,
The bright blood rising to her quivering cheek,

And meet the glance she hastened once to greet,
When not a thought had he, save in her sweet
And solacing society; to seek
Her smiles his only life! Ah! happy prime
Of cloudless purity, no stormy fame
His unknown sprite then stirred, a golden time
Worth all the restless splendour of a name;
And one soft accent from those gentle lips
Might all the plaudits of a world eclipse.

XI.

My tale is done; and if some deem it strange
My fancy thus should droop, deign then to learn
My tale is truth: imagination's range
Its bounds exact may touch not: to discern
Far stranger things than poets ever feign,
In life's perplexing annals, is the fate
Of those who act, and musing, penetrate
The mystery of Fortune: to whose reign
The haughtiest brow must bend; 'twas passing strange
The youth of these fond children; strange the flush
Of his high fortunes and his spirit's change;
Strange was the maiden's tear, the maiden's blush;
Strange were his musing thoughts and trembling heart,
'Tis strange they met, and stranger if they part!

CHAPTER XII.

When Lady Monteagle discovered, which she did a very few hours after the mortifying event, where Lord Cadurcis had dined the day on which he had promised to be her guest, she was very indignant, but her vanity was more offended than her self-complacency. She was annoyed that Cadurcis should have compromised his exalted reputation by so publicly dangling in the train of the new beauty: still more that he should have signified in so marked a manner the impression which the fair stranger had made upon him, by instantly accepting an invitation to a house so totally unconnected with his circle, and where, had it not been to meet this Miss Herbert, it would of course never have entered his head to be a visitor. But, on the whole, Lady Monteagle was rather irritated than jealous; and far from suspecting that there was the slightest chance of her losing her influence, such as it might be, over Lord Cadurcis, all that she felt was, that less lustre must redound to her from its possession and exercise, if it were obvious to the world that his attentions could be so easily attracted and commanded.

When Lord Cadurcis, therefore, having dispatched his poem to Venetia, paid his usual visit on the next day to Monteagle House, he was received rather with sneers than reproaches, as Lady Monteagle, with no superficial knowledge of society or his lordship's character, was clearly of opinion that this new fancy of her admirer was to be treated rather with ridicule than indignation; and, in short, as she had discovered that Cadurcis was far from being insensible to mockery, that it was clearly a fit occasion, to use a phrase then very much in vogue, for *quizzing*.

'How d'ye do?' said her ladyship, with an arch smile, 'I really could not expect to see you!'

Cadurcis looked a little confused; he detested scenes, and now he dreaded one.

'You seem quite distrait,' continued Lady Monteagle, after a moment's pause, which his lordship ought to have broken. 'But no wonder, if the world be right.'

'The world cannot be wrong,' said Cadurcis sarcastically.

'Had you a pleasant party yesterday?'

'Very.'

'Lady —— must have been quite charmed to have you at last,' said Lady Monteagle. 'I suppose she exhibited you to all her friends, as if you were one of the savages that went to Court the other day.'

'She was courteous.'

'Oh! I can fancy her flutter! For my part, if there be one character in the world more odious than another, I think it is a fussy woman. Lady ——, with Lord Cadurcis dining with her, and the new beauty for a niece, must have been in a most delectable state of bustle.'

'I thought she was rather quiet,' said her companion with provoking indifference. 'She seemed to me an agreeable person.'

'I suppose you mean Miss Herbert?' said Lady Monteagle.

'Oh! these are moderate expressions to use in reference to a person like Miss Herbert.'

'You know what they said of you two at Ranelagh?' said her ladyship.

'No,' said Lord Cadurcis, somewhat changing colour, and speaking through his teeth; 'something devilish pleasant, I dare say.'

'They call you Sedition and Treason,' said Lady Monteagle.

'Then we are well suited,' said Lord Cadurcis.

'She certainly is a beautiful creature,' said her ladyship.

'I think so,' said Lord Cadurcis.

'Rather too tall, I think.'

'Do you?'

'Beautiful complexion certainly; wants delicacy, I think.'

'Do you?'

'Fine eyes! Grey, I believe. Cannot say I admire grey eyes. Certain sign of bad temper, I believe, grey eyes?'

'Are they?'

'I did not observe her hand. I dare say a little coarse. Fair people who are tall generally fail in the hand and arm. What sort of a hand and arm has she?'

'I did not observe anything coarse about Miss Herbert.'

'Ah! you admire her. And you have cause. No one can deny she is a fine girl, and every one must regret, that with her decidedly provincial air and want of style altogether, which might naturally be expected, considering the rustic way I understand she has been brought up (an old house in the country, with a methodistical mother), that she should have fallen into such hands as her aunt. Lady —— is enough to spoil any girl's fortune in London.'

'I thought that the —— were people of high consideration,' said Lord Cadurcis.

'Consideration!' exclaimed Lady Monteagle. 'If you mean that they are people of rank, and good blood, and good property, they are certainly people of consideration; but they are Goths, Vandals, Huns, Calmucks, Canadian savages! They have no fashion, no style, no ton, no influence in the world. It is impossible that a greater misfortune could have befallen your beauty than having such an aunt. Why, no man who has the slightest regard for his reputation would be seen in her company. She is a regular quiz, and you cannot imagine how everybody was laughing at you the other night.'

'I am very much obliged to them,' said Lord Cadurcis.

'And, upon my honour,' continued Lady Monteagle, 'speaking merely as your friend, and not being the least jealous (Cadurcis do not suppose that), not a twinge has crossed my mind on that score; but still I must tell you that it was most ridiculous for a man like you, to whom everybody looks up, and from whom the slightest attention is an honour, to go and fasten yourself the whole night upon a rustic simpleton, something between a wax doll and a dairymaid, whom every fool in London was staring at; the very reason why you should not have appeared to have been even aware of her existence.'

'We have all our moments of weakness, Gertrude,' said Lord Cadurcis, charmed that the lady was so thoroughly unaware and unsuspicious of his long and intimate connection with the Herberts. 'I suppose it was my cursed vanity. I saw, as you say, every fool staring at her, and so I determined to show that in an instant I could engross her attention.'

'Of course, I know it was only that; but you should not have gone and dined there, Cadurcis,' added the lady, very seriously, 'That compromised you; but, by cutting them in future in the most marked manner, you may get over it.'

'You really think I may?' inquired Lord Cadurcis, with some anxiety.

'Oh! I have no doubt of it,' said Lady Monteagle.

'What it is to have a friend like you, Gertrude,' said Cadurcis, 'a friend who is neither a Goth, nor a Vandal, nor a Hun, nor a Calmuck, nor a Canadian savage; but a woman of fashion, style, ton, influence in the world! It is impossible that a greater piece of good fortune could have befallen me than having you for a friend.'

'Ah, méchant! you may mock,' said the lady, triumphantly, for she was quite satisfied with the turn the conversation had taken; 'but I am glad for your sake that you take such a sensible view of the case.'

Notwithstanding, however, this sensible view of the case, after lounging an hour at Monteagle House, Lord Cadurcis' carriage stopped at the door of Venetia's Gothic aunt. He was not so fortunate as to meet his heroine; but, nevertheless, he did not esteem his time entirely thrown away, and consoled himself for the disappointment by confirming the favourable impression he had already made in this establishment, and cultivating an intimacy which he was assured must contribute many opportunities of finding himself in the society of Venetia. From this day, indeed, he was a frequent guest at her uncle's, and generally contrived also to meet her several times in the week at some great assembly; but here, both from the occasional presence of Lady Monteagle, although party spirit deterred her from attending many circles where Cadurcis was now an habitual visitant, and from the crowd of admirers who surrounded the Herberts, he rarely found an opportunity for any private conversation with Venetia. His friend the Bishop also, notwithstanding the prejudices of Lady Annabel, received him always with cordiality, and he met the Herberts more than once at his mansion. At the opera and in the park also he hovered about them, in spite of the sarcasms or reproaches of Lady Monteagle; for the reader is not to suppose that that lady continued to take the same self-complacent view of Lord Cadurcis' acquaintance with the Herberts which she originally adopted, and at first flattered herself was the just one. His admiration of Miss Herbert had become the topic of general conversation; it could no longer be concealed or disguised. But Lady Monteagle was convinced that Cadurcis was not a marrying man, and persuaded herself that this was a fancy which must evaporate. Moreover, Monteagle House still continued his spot of most constant resort; for his opportunities of being with Venetia were, with all his exertions, limited, and he had no other resource which pleased him so much as the conversation and circle of the bright goddess of his party. After some fiery scenes therefore with the divinity, which only led to his prolonged absence, for the profound and fervent genius of Cadurcis revolted from the base sentiment and mock emotions of society, the lady reconciled herself to her lot, still believing herself the most envied woman in London, and often ashamed of being jealous of a country girl.

The general result of the fortnight which elapsed since Cadurcis renewed his acquaintance with his Cherbury friends was, that he had become convinced of his inability of propitiating Lady Annabel, was devotedly attached to Venetia, though he had seldom an opportunity of intimating feelings, which the cordial manner in which she ever conducted herself to him gave him no reason to conclude desperate; at the same time that he had contrived that a day should seldom elapse, which did not under some circumstances, however unfavourable, bring them together, while her intimate friends and the circles in which she passed most of her life always witnessed his presence with favour.

CHAPTER XIII.

We must, however, endeavour to be more intimately acquainted with the heart and mind of Venetia in her present situation, so strongly contrasting with the serene simplicity of her former life, than the limited and constrained opportunities of conversing with the companion of his childhood enjoyed by Lord Cadurcis could possibly enable him to become. Let us recur to her on the night when she returned home, after having met with Plantagenet at her uncle's, and having pursued a conversation with him, so unexpected, so strange, and so affecting! She had been silent in the carriage, and retired to her room immediately. She retired to ponder. The voice of Cadurcis lingered in her ear; his tearful eye still caught her vision. She leant her head upon her hand, and sighed! Why did she sigh? What at this instant was her uppermost thought? Her mother's dislike of Cadurcis. 'Your mother hates me.' These had been his words; these were the words she repeated to herself, and on whose fearful sounds she dwelt. 'Your mother hates me.' If by some means she had learnt a month ago at Weymouth, that her mother hated Cadurcis, that his general conduct had been such as to excite Lady Annabel's odium, Venetia might have for a moment been shocked that her old companion in whom she had once been so interested, had by his irregular behaviour incurred the dislike of her mother, by whom he had once been so loved. But it would have been a transient emotion. She might have mused over past feelings and past hopes in a solitary ramble on the seashore; she might even have shed a tear over the misfortunes or infelicity of one who had once been to her a brother; but, perhaps, nay probably, on the morrow the remembrance of Plantagenet would scarcely have occurred to her. Long years had elapsed since their ancient fondness; a considerable interval since even his name had met her ear. She had heard nothing of him that could for a moment arrest her notice or command her attention.

But now the irresistible impression that her mother disliked this very individual filled, her with intolerable grief. What occasioned this change in her feelings, this extraordinary difference in her emotions? There was, apparently, but one cause. She had met Cadurcis. Could then a glance, could even the tender intonations of that unrivalled voice, and the dark passion of that speaking eye, work in an instant such marvels? Could they revive the past so vividly, that Plantagenet in a moment resumed his ancient place in her affections? No, it was not that: it was less the tenderness of the past that made Venetia mourn her mother's sternness to Cadurcis, than the feelings of the future. For now she felt that her mother's heart was not more changed towards this personage than was her own.

It seemed to Venetia that even before they met, from the very moment that his name had so strangely caught her eye in the volume on the first evening she had visited her relations, that her spirit suddenly turned to him. She had never heard that name mentioned since without a fluttering of the heart which she could not repress, and an emotion she could ill conceal. She loved to hear others talk of him, and yet scarcely dared speak of him herself. She recalled her emotion at unexpectedly seeing his portrait when with her aunt, and her mortification when her mother deprived her of the poem which she sighed to read. Day after day something seemed to have occurred to fix her brooding thoughts with fonder earnestness on his image. At length they met. Her emotion when she first recognised him at Ranelagh and felt him approaching her, was one of those tumults of the heart that form almost a crisis in our sensations. With what difficulty had she maintained herself! Doubtful whether he would even formally acknowledge her presence, her vision as if by fascination had nevertheless met his, and grew dizzy as he passed. In the interval that had elapsed between his first passing and then joining her, what a chaos was her mind! What a wild blending of all the scenes and incidents of her life! What random answers had she made to those with whom she had been before conversing with ease and animation! And then, when she unexpectedly found Cadurcis at her side, and listened to the sound of that familiar voice, familiar and yet changed, expressing so much tenderness in its tones, and in its words such deference and delicate respect, existence felt to her that moment affluent with a blissful excitement of which she had never dreamed!

Her life was a reverie until they met again, in which she only mused over his fame, and the strange relations of their careers. She had watched the conduct of her mother to him at dinner with poignant sorrow; she scarcely believed that she should have an opportunity of expressing to him her sympathy. And then what had followed? A conversation, every word of which had touched her heart; a conversation that would have entirely controlled her feelings even if he had not already subjected them. The tone in which he so suddenly had pronounced 'Venetia,' was the sweetest music to which she had ever listened. His allusion to her father had drawn tears, which could not be restrained even in a crowded saloon. Now she wept plenteously. It was so generous, so noble, so kind, so affectionate! Dear, dear Cadurcis, is it wonderful that you should be loved?

Then falling into a reverie of sweet and unbroken stillness, with her eyes fixed in abstraction on the fire, Venetia reviewed her life from the moment she had known Plantagenet. Not an incident that had ever occurred to them that did not rise obedient to her magical bidding. She loved to dwell upon the time when she was the consolation of his sorrows, and when Cherbury was to him a pleasant refuge! Oh! she felt sure her mother must remember those fond days, and love him as she once did! She pictured to herself the little Plantagenet of her childhood, so serious and so pensive when alone or with others, yet with her at times so gay and wild, and sarcastic; forebodings all of that deep and brilliant spirit, which had since stirred up the heart of a great nation, and dazzled the fancy of an admiring world. The change too in their mutual lots was also, to a degree, not free from that sympathy that had ever bound them together. A train of strange accidents had brought Venetia from her spell-bound seclusion, placed her suddenly in the most brilliant circle of civilisation, and classed her among not the least admired of its favoured members. And whom had she come to meet? Whom did she find in this new and splendid life the most courted and considered of its community, crowned as it were with garlands, and perfumed with the incense of a thousand altars? Her own Plantagenet. It was passing strange.

The morrow brought the verses from Cadurcis. They greatly affected her. The picture of their childhood, and of the singular sympathy of their mutual situations, and the description of her father, called forth her tears; she murmured, however, at the allusion to her other parent. It was not just, it could not be true. These verses were not, of course, shown to Lady Annabel. Would they have been shown, even if they had not contained the allusion? The question is not perplexing. Venetia had her secret, and a far deeper one than the mere reception of a poem; all confidence between her and her mother had expired. Love had stept in, and, before his magic touch, the discipline of a life expired in an instant.

From all this an idea may be formed of the mood in which, during the fortnight before alluded to, Venetia was in the habit of meeting Lord Cadurcis. During this period not the slightest conversation respecting him had occurred between her mother and herself. Lady Annabel never mentioned him, and her brow clouded when his name, as was often the case, was introduced. At the end of this fortnight, it happened that her aunt and mother were out together in the carriage, and had left her in the course of the morning at her uncle's house. During this interval, Lord Cadurcis called, and having ascertained, through a garrulous servant, that though his mistress was out, Miss Herbert was in the drawing-room, he immediately took the opportunity of being introduced. Venetia was not a little surprised at his appearance, and, conscious of her mother's feelings upon the subject, for a moment a little agitated, yet, it must be confessed, as much pleased. She seized this occasion of speaking to him about his verses, for hitherto she had only been able to acknowledge the receipt of them by a word. While she expressed without affectation the emotions they had occasioned her, she complained of his injustice to her mother: this was the cause of an interesting conversation of which her father was the subject, and for which she had long sighed. With what deep, unbroken attention she listened to her companion's enthusiastic delineation of his character and career! What multiplied questions did she not ask him, and how eagerly, how amply, how affectionately he satisfied her just and natural curiosity! Hours flew away while they indulged in this rare communion.

'Oh, that I could see him!' sighed Venetia.

'You will,' replied Plantagenet; 'your destiny requires it. You will see him as surely as you beheld that portrait that it was the labour of a life to prevent you beholding.'

Venetia shook her head; 'And yet,' she added musingly, 'my mother loves him.'

'Her life proves it,' said Cadurcis bitterly.

'I think it does,' replied Venetia, sincerely.

'I pretend not to understand her heart,' he answered; 'it is an enigma that I cannot solve. I ought not to believe that she is without one; but, at any rate, her pride is deeper than her love.'

'They were ill suited,' said Venetia, mournfully; 'and yet it is one of my dreams that they may yet meet.'

'Ah, Venetia!' he exclaimed, in a voice of great softness, 'they had not known each other from their childhood, like us. They met, and they parted, alike in haste.'

Venetia made no reply; her eyes were fixed in abstraction on a handscreen, which she was unconscious that she held.

'Tell me,' said Cadurcis, drawing his chair close to hers; 'tell me, Venetia, if—'

At this moment a thundering knock at the door announced the return of the Countess and her sister-in-law. Cadurcis rose from his seat, but his chair, which still remained close to that on which Venetia was sitting, did not escape the quick glance of her mortified mother. The Countess welcomed Cadurcis with extreme cordiality; Lady Annabel only returned his very courteous bow.

'Stop and dine with us, my dear lord,' said the Countess. 'We are only ourselves, and Lady Annabel and Venetia.'

'I thank you, Clara,' said Lady Annabel, 'but we cannot stop to-day.'

'Oh!' exclaimed her sister. 'It will be such a disappointment to Philip. Indeed you must stay,' she added, in a coaxing tone; 'we shall be such an agreeable little party, with Lord Cadurcis.'

'I cannot indeed, my dear Clara,' replied Lady Annabel; 'not to-day, indeed not to-day. Come Venetia!'

CHAPTER XIV.

Lady Annabel was particularly kind to Venetia on their return to their hotel, otherwise her daughter might have fancied that she had offended her, for she was silent. Venetia did not doubt that the presence of Lord Cadurcis was the reason that her mother would not remain and dine at her uncle's. This conviction grieved Venetia, but she did not repine; she indulged the fond hope that time would remove the strong prejudice which Lady Annabel now so singularly entertained against one in whose welfare she was originally so deeply interested. During their simple and short repast Venetia was occupied in a reverie, in which, it must be owned, Cadurcis greatly figured, and answered the occasional though kind remarks of her mother with an absent air.

After dinner, Lady Annabel drew her chair towards the fire, for, although May, the weather was chill, and said, 'A quiet evening at home, Venetia, will be a relief after all this gaiety.' Venetia assented to her mother's observation, and nearly a quarter of an hour elapsed without another word being spoken. Venetia had taken up a book, and Lady Annabel was apparently lost in her reflections. At length she said, somewhat abruptly, 'It is more than three years, I think, since Lord Cadurcis left Cherbury?'

'Yes; it is more than three years,' replied Venetia.

'He quitted us suddenly.'

'Very suddenly,' agreed Venetia.

'I never asked you whether you knew the cause, Venetia,' continued her mother, 'but I always concluded that you did. I suppose I was not in error?'

This was not a very agreeable inquiry. Venetia did not reply to it with her previous readiness and indifference. That indeed was impossible; but, with her accustomed frankness, after a moment's hesitation, she answered, 'Lord Cadurcis never specifically stated the cause to me, mamma; indeed I was myself surprised at his departure, but some conversation had occurred between us on the very morning he quitted Cadurcis, which, on reflection, I could not doubt occasioned that departure.'

'Lord Cadurcis preferred his suit to you, Venetia, and you rejected him?' said Lady Annabel.

'It is as you believe,' replied Venetia, not a little agitated.

'You did wisely, my child, and I was weak ever to have regretted your conduct.'

'Why should you think so, dearest mamma?'

'Whatever may have been the cause that impelled your conduct then,' said Lady Annabel, 'I shall ever esteem your decision as a signal interposition of Providence in your favour. Except his extreme youth, there was apparently no reason which should not have induced you to adopt a different decision. I tremble when I think what might have been the consequences.'

'Tremble, dearest mother?'

'Tremble, Venetia. My only thought in this life is the happiness of my child. It was in peril.

'Nay, I trust not that, mamma: you are prejudiced against Plantagenet. It makes me very unhappy, and him also.'

'He is again your suitor?' said Lady Annabel, with a scrutinising glance.

'Indeed he is not.'

'He will be,' said Lady Annabel. 'Prepare yourself. Tell me, then, are your feelings the same towards him as when he last quitted us?'

'Feelings, mamma!' said Venetia, echoing her mother's words; for indeed the question was one very difficult to answer; 'I ever loved Plantagenet; I love him still.'

'But do you love him now as then? Then you looked upon him as a brother. He has no soul now for sisterly affections. I beseech you tell me, my child, me, your mother, your friend, your best, your only friend, tell me, have you for a moment repented that you ever refused to extend to him any other affection?'

'I have not thought of the subject, mamma; I have not wished to think of the subject; I have had no occasion to think of it. Lord Cadurcis is not my suitor now.'

'Venetia!' said Lady Annabel, 'I cannot doubt you love me.'

'Dearest mother!' exclaimed Venetia, in a tone of mingled fondness and reproach, and she rose from her seat and embraced Lady Annabel.

'My happiness is an object to you, Venetia?' continued Lady Annabel.

'Mother, mother,' said Venetia, in a deprecatory tone. 'Do not ask such cruel questions? Whom should I love but you, the best, the dearest mother that ever existed? And what object can I have in life that for a moment can be placed in competition with your happiness?'

'Then, Venetia, I tell you,' said Lady Annabel, in a solemn yet excited voice, 'that that happiness is gone for ever, nay, my very life will be the forfeit, if I ever live to see you the bride of Lord Cadurcis.'

'I have no thought of being the bride of any one,' said Venetia. 'I am happy with you. I wish never to leave you.'

'My child, the fulfilment of such a wish is not in the nature of things,' replied Lady Annabel. 'The day will come when we must part; I am prepared for the event; nay, I look forward to it not only with resignation, but delight, when I think it may increase your happiness; but were that step to destroy it, oh! then, then I could live no more. I can endure my own sorrows, I can struggle with my own bitter lot, I have some sources of consolation which enable me to endure my own misery without repining; but yours, yours, Venetia, I could not bear. No! if once I were to behold you lingering in life as your mother, with blighted hopes and with a heart broken, if hearts can break, I should not survive the spectacle; I know myself, Venetia, I could not survive it.'

'But why anticipate such misery? Why indulge in such gloomy forebodings? Am I not happy now? Do you not love me?'

Venetia had drawn her chair close to that of her mother; she sat by her side and held her hand.

'Venetia,' said Lady Annabel, after a pause of some minutes, and in a low voice, 'I must speak to you on a subject on which we have never conversed. I must speak to you;' and here Lady Annabel's voice dropped lower and lower, but still its tones were distinct, although she expressed herself with evident effort: 'I must speak to you about—your father.'

Venetia uttered a faint cry, she clenched her mother's hand with a convulsive grasp, and sank upon her bosom. She struggled to maintain herself, but the first sound of that name from her mother's lips, and all the long-suppressed emotions that it conjured up, overpowered her. The blood seemed to desert her heart; still she did not faint; she clung to Lady Annabel, pallid and shivering.

Her mother tenderly embraced her, she whispered to her words of great affection, she attempted to comfort and console her. Venetia murmured, 'This is very foolish of me, mother; but speak, oh! speak of what I have so long desired to hear.'

'Not now, Venetia.'

'Now, mother! yes, now! I am quite composed. I could not bear the postponement of what you were about to say. I could not sleep, dear mother, if you did not speak to me. It was only for a moment I was overcome. See! I am quite composed.' And indeed she spoke in a calm and steady voice, but her pale and suffering countenance expressed the painful struggle which it cost her to command herself.

'Venetia,' said Lady Annabel, 'it has been one of the objects of my life, that you should not share my sorrows.'

Venetia pressed her mother's hand, but made no other reply.

'I concealed from you for years,' continued Lady Annabel, 'a circumstance in which, indeed, you were deeply interested, but the knowledge of which could only bring you unhappiness. Yet it was destined that my solicitude should eventually be baffled. I know that it is not from my lips that you learn for the first time that you have a father, a father living.'

'Mother, let me tell you all!' said Venetia, eagerly.

'I know all,' said Lady Annabel.

'But, mother, there is something that you do not know; and now I would confess it.'

'There is nothing that you can confess with which I am not acquainted, Venetia; and I feel assured, I have ever felt assured, that your only reason for concealment was a desire to save me pain.'

'That, indeed, has ever been my only motive,' replied Venetia, 'for having a secret from my mother.'

'In my absence from Cherbury you entered the chamber,' said Lady Annabel, calmly. 'In the delirium of your fever I became acquainted with a circumstance which so nearly proved fatal to you.'

Venetia's cheek turned scarlet.

'In that chamber you beheld the portrait of your father,' continued Lady Annabel. 'From our friend you learnt that father was still living. That is all?' said Lady Annabel, inquiringly.

'No, not all, dear mother; not all. Lord Cadurcis reproached me at Cherbury with, with, with having such a father,' she added, in a hesitating voice. 'It was then I learnt his misfortunes, mother; his misery.'

'I thought that misfortunes, that misery, were the lot of your other parent,' replied Lady Annabel, somewhat coldly.

'Not with my love,' said Venetia, eagerly; 'not with my love, mother. You have forgotten your misery in my love. Say so, say so, dearest mother.' And Venetia threw herself on her knees before Lady Annabel, and looked up with earnestness in her face.

The expression of that countenance had been for a moment stern, but it relaxed into fondness, as Lady Annabel gently bowed her head, and pressed her lips to her daughter's forehead. 'Ah, Venetia!' she said, 'all depends upon you. I can endure, nay, I can forget the past, if my child be faithful to me. There are no misfortunes, there is no misery, if the being to whom I have consecrated the devotion of my life will only be dutiful, will only be guided by my advice, will only profit by my sad experience.'

'Mother, I repeat I have no thought but for you,' said Venetia. 'My own dearest mother, if my duty, if my devotion can content you, you shall be happy. But wherein have I failed?'

'In nothing, love. Your life has hitherto been one unbroken course of affectionate obedience.'

'And ever shall be,' said Venetia. 'But you were speaking, mother, you were speaking of, of my, my father!'

'Of him!' said Lady Annabel, thoughtfully. 'You have seen his picture?'

Venetia kissed her mother's hand.

'Was he less beautiful than Cadurcis? Was he less gifted?' exclaimed Lady Annabel, with animation. 'He could whisper in tones as sweet, and pour out his vows as fervently. Yet what am I? O my child!' continued Lady Annabel, 'beware of such beings! They bear within them a spirit on which all the devotion of our sex is lavished in vain. A year, no! not a year, not one short year! and all my hopes were blighted! O Venetia! if your future should be like my bitter past! and it might have been, and I might have contributed to the fulfilment! can you wonder that I should look upon Cadurcis with aversion?'

'But, mother, dearest mother, we have known Plantagenet from his childhood. You ever loved him; you ever gave him credit for a heart, most tender and affectionate.'

'He has no heart.'

'Mother!'

'He cannot have a heart. Spirits like him are heartless. It is another impulse that sways their existence. It is imagination; it is vanity; it is self, disguised with glittering qualities that dazzle our weak senses, but selfishness, the most entire, the most concentrated. We knew him as a child: ah! what can women know? We are born to love, and to be deceived. We saw him young, helpless, abandoned; he moved our pity. We knew not his nature; then he was ignorant of it himself. But the young tiger, though cradled at our hearths and fed on milk, will in good time retire to its jungle and prey on blood. You cannot change its nature; and the very hand that fostered it will be its first victim.'

'How often have we parted!' said Venetia, in a deprecating tone; 'how long have we been separated! and yet we find him ever the same; he ever loves us. Yes! dear mother, he loves you now, the same as in old days. If you had seen him, as I have seen him, weep when he recalled your promise to be a parent to him, and then contrasted with such sweet hopes your present reserve, oh! you would believe he had a heart, you would, indeed!'

'Weep!' exclaimed Lady Annabel, bitterly, 'ay! they can weep. Sensibility is a luxury which they love to indulge. Their very susceptibility is our bane. They can weep; they can play upon our feelings; and our emotion, so easily excited, is an homage to their own power, in which they glory.

'Look at Cadurcis,' she suddenly resumed; 'bred with so much care; the soundest principles instilled into him with such sedulousness; imbibing them apparently with so much intelligence, ardour, and sincerity, with all that fervour, indeed, with which men of his temperament for the moment pursue every object; but a few years back, pious, dutiful, and moral, viewing perhaps with intolerance too youthful all that differed from the opinions and the conduct he had been educated to admire and follow. And what is he now? The most lawless of the wild; casting to the winds every salutary principle of restraint and social discipline, and glorying only in the abandoned energy of self. Three years ago, you yourself confessed to me, he reproached you with your father's conduct; now he emulates it. There is a career which such men must run, and from which no influence can divert them; it is in their blood. To-day Cadurcis may vow to you eternal devotion; but, if the world speak truth, Venetia, a month ago he was equally enamoured of another, and one, too, who cannot be his. But grant that his sentiments towards you are for the moment sincere; his imagination broods upon your idea, it transfigures it with a halo which exists only to his vision. Yield to him; become his bride; and you will have the mortification of finding that, before six months have elapsed, his restless spirit is already occupied with objects which may excite your mortification, your disgust, even your horror!'

'Ah, mother! it is not with Plantagenet as with my father; Plantagenet could not forget Cherbury, he could not forget our childhood,' said Venetia.

'On the contrary, while you lived together these recollections would be wearisome, common-place to him; when you had separated, indeed, mellowed by distance, and the comparative vagueness with which your absence would invest them, they would become the objects of his muse, and he would insult you by making the public the confidant of all your most delicate domestic feelings.'

Lady Annabel rose from her seat, and walked up and down the room, speaking with an excitement very unusual with her. 'To have all the soft secrets of your life revealed to the coarse wonder of the gloating multitude; to find yourself the object of the world's curiosity, still worse, their pity, their sympathy; to have the sacred conduct of your hearth canvassed in every circle, and be the grand subject of the pros and cons of every paltry journal, ah, Venetia! you know not, you cannot understand, it is impossible you can comprehend, the bitterness of such a lot.'

'My beloved mother!' said Venetia, with streaming eyes, 'you cannot have a feeling that I do not share.'

'Venetia, you know not what I had to endure!' exclaimed Lady Annabel, in a tone of extreme bitterness. 'There is no degree of wretchedness that you can conceive equal to what has been the life of your mother. And what has sustained me; what, throughout all my tumultuous troubles, has been the star on which I have ever gazed? My child! And am I to lose her now, after all my sufferings, all my hopes that she at least might be spared my miserable doom? Am I to witness her also a victim?' Lady Annabel clasped her hands in passionate grief.

'Mother! mother!' exclaimed Venetia, in agony, 'spare yourself, spare me!'

'Venetia, you know how I have doted upon you; you know how I have watched and tended you from your infancy. Have I had a thought, a wish, a hope, a plan? has there been the slightest action of my life, of which you have not been the object? All mothers feel, but none ever felt like me; you were my solitary joy.'

Venetia leant her face upon the table at which she was sitting and sobbed aloud.

'My love was baffled,' Lady Annabel continued. 'I fled, for both our sakes, from the world in which my family were honoured; I sacrificed without a sigh, in the very prime of my youth, every pursuit which interests woman; but I had my child, I had my child!'

'And you have her still!' exclaimed the miserable Venetia. 'Mother, you have her still!'

'I have schooled my mind,' continued Lady Annabel, still pacing the room with agitated steps; 'I have disciplined my emotions; I have felt at my heart the constant the undying pang, and yet I have smiled, that you might be happy. But I can struggle against my fate no longer. No longer can I suffer my unparalleled, yes, my unjust doom. What have I done to merit these afflictions? Now, then, let me struggle no more; let me die!'

Venetia tried to rise; her limbs refused their office; she tottered; she fell again into her seat with an hysteric cry.

'Alas! alas!' exclaimed Lady Annabel, 'to a mother, a child is everything; but to a child, a parent is only a link in the chain of her existence. It was weakness, it was folly, it was madness to stake everything on a resource which must fail me. I feel it now, but I feel it too late.'

Venetia held forth her arms; she could not speak; she was stifled with her emotion.

'But was it wonderful that I was so weak?' continued her mother, as it were communing only with herself. 'What child was like mine? Oh! the joy, the bliss, the hours of rapture that I have passed, in gazing upon my treasure, and dreaming of all her beauty and her rare qualities! I was so happy! I was so proud! Ah, Venetia! you know not how I have loved you!'

Venetia sprang from her seat; she rushed forward with convulsive energy; she clung to her mother, threw her arms round her neck, and buried her passionate woe in Lady Annabel's bosom.

Lady Annabel stood for some minutes supporting her speechless and agitated child; then, as her sobs became fainter, and the tumult of her grief gradually died away, she bore her to the sofa, and seated herself by her side, holding Venetia's hand in her own, and ever and anon soothing her with soft embraces, and still softer words.

At length, in a faint voice, Venetia said, 'Mother, what can I do to restore the past? How can we be to each other as we were, for this I cannot bear?'

'Love me, my Venetia, as I love you; be faithful to your mother; do not disregard her counsel; profit by her errors.'

'I will in all things obey you,' said Venetia, in a low voice; 'there is no sacrifice I am not prepared to make for your happiness.'

'Let us not talk of sacrifices, my darling child; it is not a sacrifice that I require. I wish only to prevent your everlasting misery.'

'What, then, shall I do?'

'Make me only one promise; whatever pledge you give, I feel assured that no influence, Venetia, will ever induce you to forfeit it.'

'Name it, mother.'

'Promise me never to marry Lord Cadurcis,' said Lady Annabel, in a whisper, but a whisper of which not a word was lost by the person to whom it was addressed.

'I promise never to marry, but with your approbation,' said Venetia, in a solemn voice, and uttering the words with great distinctness.

The countenance of Lady Annabel instantly brightened; she embraced her child with extreme fondness, and breathed the softest and the sweetest expressions of gratitude and love.

CHAPTER XV.

When Lady Monteagle discovered that of which her good-natured friends took care she should not long remain ignorant, that Venetia Herbert had been the companion of Lord Cadurcis' childhood, and that the most intimate relations had once subsisted between the two families, she became the prey of violent jealousy; and the bitterness of her feelings was not a little increased, when she felt that she had not only been abandoned, but duped; and that the new beauty, out of his fancy for whom she had flattered herself she had so triumphantly rallied him, was an old friend, whom he always admired. She seized the first occasion, after this discovery, of relieving her feelings, by a scene so violent, that Cadurcis had never again entered Monteagle House; and then repenting of this mortifying result, which she had herself precipitated, she overwhelmed him with letters, which, next to scenes, were the very things which Lord Cadurcis most heartily abhorred. These, now indignant, now passionate, now loading him with reproaches, now appealing to his love, and now to his pity, daily arrived at his residence, and were greeted at first only with short and sarcastic replies, and finally by silence. Then the lady solicited a final interview, and Lord Cadurcis having made an appointment to quiet her, went out of town the day before to Richmond, to a villa belonging to Venetia's uncle, and where, among other guests, he was of course to meet Lady Annabel and her daughter.

The party was a most agreeable one, and assumed an additional interest with Cadurcis, who had resolved to seize this favourable opportunity to bring his aspirations to Venetia to a crisis. The day after the last conversation with her, which we have noticed, he had indeed boldly called upon the Herberts at their hotel for that purpose, but without success, as they were again absent from home. He had been since almost daily in the society of Venetia; but London, to a lover who is not smiled upon by the domestic circle of his mistress, is a very unfavourable spot for confidential conversations. A villa life, with its easy, unembarrassed habits, its gardens and lounging walks, to say nothing of the increased opportunities resulting from being together at all hours, and living under the same roof, was more promising; and here he flattered himself he might defy even the Argus eye and ceaseless vigilance of his intended mother-in-law, his enemy, whom he could not propitiate, and whom he now fairly hated.

His cousin George, too, was a guest, and his cousin George was the confidant of his love. Upon this kind relation devolved the duty, far from a disagreeable one, of amusing the mother; and as Lady Annabel, though she relaxed not a jot of the grim courtesy which she ever extended to Lord Cadurcis, was no longer seriously uneasy as to his influence after the promise she had exacted from her daughter, it would seem that these circumstances combined to prevent Lord Cadurcis from being disappointed at least in the first object which he wished to obtain, an opportunity.

And yet several days elapsed before this offered itself, passed by Cadurcis, however, very pleasantly in the presence of the being he loved, and very judiciously too, for no one could possibly be more amiable and ingratiating than our friend. Every one present, except Lady Annabel, appeared to entertain for him as much affection as admiration: those who had only met him in throngs were quite surprised how their superficial observation and the delusive reports of the world had misled them. As for his hostess, whom it had ever been his study to please, he had long won her heart; and, as she could not be blind to his projects and pretensions, she heartily wished him success, assisted him with all her efforts, and desired nothing more sincerely than that her niece should achieve such a conquest, and she obtain so distinguished a nephew.

Notwithstanding her promise to her mother, Venetia felt justified in making no alteration in her conduct to one whom she still sincerely loved; and, under the immediate influence of his fascination, it was often, when she was alone, that she mourned with a sorrowing heart over the opinion which her mother entertained of him. Could it indeed be possible that Plantagenet, the same Plantagenet she had known so early and so long, to her invariably so tender and so devoted, could entail on her, by their union, such unspeakable and inevitable misery? Whatever might be the view adopted by her mother of her conduct, Venetia felt every hour more keenly that it was a sacrifice, and the greatest; and she still indulged in a vague yet delicious dream, that Lady Annabel might ultimately withdraw the harsh and perhaps heart-breaking interdict she had so rigidly decreed.

'Cadurcis,' said his cousin to him one morning, 'we are all going to Hampton Court. Now is your time; Lady Annabel, the Vernons, and myself, will fill one carriage; I have arranged that. Look out, and something may be done. Speak to the Countess.'

Accordingly Lord Cadurcis hastened to make a suggestion to a friend always flattered by his notice. 'My dear friend,' he said in his softest tone, 'let you and Venetia and myself manage to be together; it will be so delightful; we shall quite enjoy ourselves.'

The Countess did not require this animating compliment to effect the object which Cadurcis did not express. She had gradually fallen into the unacknowledged conspiracy against her sister-in-law, whose prejudice against her friend she had long discovered, and had now ceased to combat. Two carriages, and one filled as George had arranged, accordingly drove gaily away; and Venetia, and her aunt, and Lord Cadurcis were to follow them on horseback. They rode with delight through the splendid avenues of Bushey, and Cadurcis was never in a lighter or happier mood.

The month of May was in its decline, and the cloudless sky and the balmy air such as suited so agreeable a season. The London season was approaching its close; for the royal birthday was, at the period of our history, generally the signal of preparation for country quarters. The carriages arrived long before the riding party, for they had walked their steeds, and they found a messenger who requested them to join their friends in the apartments which they were visiting.

'For my part,' said Cadurcis, 'I love the sun that rarely shines in this land. I feel no inclination to lose the golden hours in these gloomy rooms. What say you, ladies fair, to a stroll in the gardens? It will be doubly charming after our ride.'

His companions cheerfully assented, and they walked away, congratulating themselves on their escape from the wearisome amusement of palace-hunting, straining their eyes to see pictures hung at a gigantic height, and solemnly wandering through formal apartments full of state beds and massy cabinets and modern armour.

Taking their way along the terrace, they struck at length into a less formal path. At length the Countess seated herself on a bench. 'I must rest,' she said, 'but you, young people, may roam about; only do not lose me.'

'Come, Venetia!' said Lord Cadurcis.

Venetia was hesitating; she did not like to leave her aunt alone, but the Countess encouraged her, 'If you will not go, you will only make me continue walking,' she said. And so Venetia proceeded, and for the first time since her visit was alone with Plantagenet.

'I quite love your aunt,' said Lord Cadurcis.

'It is difficult indeed not to love her,' said Venetia.

'Ah, Venetia! I wish your mother was like your aunt,' he continued. It was an observation which was not heard without some emotion by his companion, though it was imperceptible. 'Venetia,' said Cadurcis, 'when I recollect old days, how strange it seems that we now never should be alone, but by some mere accident, like this, for instance.'

'It is no use thinking of old days,' said Venetia.

'No use! said Cadurcis. 'I do not like to hear you say that, Venetia. Those are some of the least agreeable words that were ever uttered by that mouth. I cling to old days; they are my only joy and my only hope.'

'They are gone,' said Venetia.

'But may they not return?' said Cadurcis.

'Never,' said Venetia, mournfully.

They had walked on to a marble fountain of gigantic proportions and elaborate workmanship, an assemblage of divinities and genii, all spouting water in fantastic attitudes.

'Old days,' said Plantagenet, 'are like the old fountain at Cadurcis, dearer to me than all this modern splendour.'

'The old fountain at Cadurcis,' said Venetia, musingly, and gazing on the water with an abstracted air, 'I loved it well!'

'Venetia,' said her companion, in a tone of extreme tenderness, yet not untouched with melancholy, 'dear Venetia, let us return, and return together, to that old fountain and those old days!'

Venetia shook her head. 'Ah, Plantagenet!' she exclaimed in a mournful voice, 'we must not speak of these things.'

'Why not, Venetia?' exclaimed Lord Cadurcis, eagerly. 'Why should we be estranged from each other? I love you; I love only you; never have I loved another. And you, have you forgotten all our youthful affection? You cannot, Venetia. Our childhood can never be a blank.'

'I told you, when first we met, my heart was unchanged,' said Venetia.

'Remember the vows I made to you when last at Cherbury,' said Cadurcis. 'Years have flown on, Venetia; but they find me urging the same. At any rate, now I know myself; at any rate, I am not now an obscure boy; yet what is manhood, and what is fame, without the charm of my infancy and my youth! Yes, Venetia! you must, you will he mine?'

'Plantagenet,' she replied, in a solemn tone, 'yours I never can be.'

'You do not, then, love me?' said Cadurcis reproachfully, and in a voice of great feeling.

'It is impossible for you to be loved more than I love you,' said Venetia.

'My own Venetia!' said Cadurcis; 'Venetia that I dote on! what does this mean? Why, then, will you not be mine?'

'I cannot; there is an obstacle, an insuperable obstacle.'

'Tell it me,' said Cadurcis eagerly; 'I will overcome it.'

'I have promised never to marry without the approbation of my mother; her approbation you never can obtain.'

Cadurcis' countenance fell; this was an obstacle which he felt that even he could not overcome.

'I told you your mother hated me, Venetia.' And then, as she did not reply, he continued, 'You confess it, I see you confess it. Once you flattered me I was mistaken; but now, now you confess it.'

'Hatred is a word which I cannot understand,' replied Venetia. 'My mother has reasons for disapproving my union with you; not founded on the circumstances of your life, and therefore removable (for I know what the world says, Plantagenet, of you), but I have confidence in your love, and that is nothing; but founded on your character, on your nature; they may be unjust, but they are insuperable, and I must yield to them.'

'You have another parent, Venetia,' said Cadurcis, in a tone of almost irresistible softness, 'the best and greatest of men! Once you told me that his sanction was necessary to your marriage. I will obtain it. O Venetia! be mine, and we will join him; join that ill-fated and illustrious being who loves you with a passion second only to mine; him who has addressed you in language which rests on every lip, and has thrilled many a heart that you even can never know. My adored Venetia! picture to yourself, for one moment, a life with him; resting on my bosom, consecrated by his paternal love! Let us quit this mean and miserable existence, which we now pursue, which never could have suited us; let us shun for ever this dull and degrading life, that is not life, if life be what I deem it; let us fly to those beautiful solitudes where he communes with an inspiring nature; let us, let us be happy!'

He uttered these last words in a tone of melting tenderness; he leant forward his head, and his gaze caught hers, which was fixed upon the water. Her hand was pressed suddenly in his; his eye glittered, his lip seemed still speaking; he awaited his doom.

The countenance of Venetia was quite pale, but it was disturbed. You might see, as it were, the shadowy progress of thought, and mark the tumultuous passage of conflicting passions. Her mind, for a moment, was indeed a chaos. There was a terrible conflict between love and duty. At length a tear, one solitary tear, burst from her burning eye-ball, and stole slowly down her cheek; it relieved her pain. She pressed Cadurcis hand, and speaking in a hollow voice, and with a look vague and painful, she said, 'I am a victim, but I am resolved. I never will desert her who devoted herself to me.'

Cadurcis quitted her hand rather abruptly, and began walking up and down on the turf that surrounded the fountain.

'Devoted herself to you!' he exclaimed with a fiendish laugh, and speaking, as was his custom, between his teeth. 'Commend me to such devotion. Not content with depriving you of a father, now forsooth she must bereave you of a lover too! And this is a mother, a devoted mother! The cold-blooded, sullen, selfish, inexorable tyrant!'

'Plantagenet!' exclaimed Venetia with great animation.

'Nay, I will speak. Victim, indeed! You have ever been her slave. She a devoted mother! Ay! as devoted as a mother as she was dutiful as a wife! She has no heart; she never had a feeling. And she cajoles you with her love, her devotion, the stern hypocrite!'

'I must leave you,' said Venetia; 'I cannot bear this.'

'Oh! the truth, the truth is precious,' said Cadurcis, taking her hand, and preventing her from moving. 'Your mother, your devoted mother, has driven one man of genius from her bosom, and his country. Yet there is another. Deny me what I ask, and to-morrow's sun shall light me to another land; to this I will never return; I will blend my tears with your father's, and I will publish to Europe the double infamy of your mother. I swear it solemnly. Still I stand here, Venetia; prepared, if you will but smile upon me, to be her son, her dutiful son. Nay! her slave like you. She shall not murmur. I will be dutiful; she shall be devoted; we will all be happy,' he added in a softer tone. 'Now, now, Venetia, my happiness is on the stake, now, now.'

'I have spoken,' said Venetia. 'My heart may break, but my purpose shall not falter.'

'Then my curse upon your mother's head?' said Cadurcis, with terrible vehemency. 'May heaven rain all its plagues upon her, the Hecate!'

'I will listen no more,' exclaimed Venetia indignantly, and she moved away. She had proceeded some little distance when she paused and looked back; Cadurcis was still at the fountain, but he did not observe her. She remembered his sudden departure from Cherbury; she did not doubt that, in the present instance, he would leave them as abruptly, and that he would keep his word so solemnly given. Her heart was nearly breaking, but she could not bear the idea of parting in bitterness with the being whom, perhaps, she loved best in the world. She stopt, she called his name in a voice low indeed, but in that silent spot it reached him. He joined her immediately, but with a slow step. When he had reached her, he said, without any animation and in a frigid tone, 'I believe you called me?'

Venetia burst into tears. 'I cannot bear to part in anger, Plantagenet. I wished to say farewell in kindness. I shall always pray for your happiness. God bless you, Plantagenet!'

Lord Cadurcis made no reply, though for a moment he seemed about to speak; he bowed, and, as Venetia approached her aunt, he turned his steps in a different direction.

CHAPTER XVI.

Venetia stopped for a moment to collect herself before she joined her aunt, but it was impossible to conceal her agitation from the Countess. They had not, however, been long together before they observed their friends in the distance, who had now quitted the palace. Venetia made the utmost efforts to compose herself, and not unsuccessful ones. She was sufficiently calm on their arrival, to listen, if not to converse. The Countess, with all the tact of a woman, covered her niece's confusion by her animated description of their agreeable ride, and their still more pleasant promenade; and in a few minutes the whole party were walking back to their carriages. When they had arrived at the inn, they found Lord Cadurcis, to whose temporary absence the Countess had alluded with some casual observation which she flattered herself was very satisfactory. Cadurcis appeared rather sullen, and the Countess, with feminine quickness, suddenly discovered that both herself and her niece were extremely fatigued, and that they had better return in the carriages. There was one vacant place, and some of the gentlemen must ride outside. Lord Cadurcis, however, said that he should return as he came, and the grooms might lead back the ladies' horses; and so in a few minutes the carriages had driven off.

Our solitary equestrian, however, was no sooner mounted than he put his horse to its speed, and never drew in his rein until he reached Hyde Park Corner. The rapid motion accorded with his tumultuous mood. He was soon at home, gave his horse to a servant, for he had left his groom behind, rushed into his library, tore up a letter of Lady Monteagle's with a demoniac glance, and rang his bell with such force that it broke. His valet, not unused to such ebullitions, immediately appeared.

'Has anything happened, Spalding?' said his lordship.

'Nothing particular, my lord. Her ladyship sent every day, and called herself twice, but I told her your lordship was in Yorkshire.'

'That was right; I saw a letter from her. When did it come?'

'It has been here several days, my lord.'

'Mind, I am at home to nobody; I am not in town.'

The valet bowed and disappeared. Cadurcis threw himself into an easy chair, stretched his legs, sighed, and then swore; then suddenly starting up, he seized a mass of letters that were lying on the table, and hurled them to the other end of the apartment, dashed several books to the ground, kicked down several chairs that were in his way, and began pacing the room with his usual troubled step; and so he continued until the shades of twilight entered his apartment. Then he pulled down the other bell-rope, and Mr. Spalding again appeared.

'Order posthorses for to-morrow,' said his lordship.

'Where to, my lord?'

'I don't know; order the horses.'

Mr. Spalding again bowed and disappeared.

In a few minutes he heard a great stamping and confusion in his master's apartment, and presently the door opened and his master's voice was heard calling him repeatedly in a very irritable tone.

'Why are there no bells in this cursed room?' inquired Lord Cadurcis.

'The ropes are broken, my lord.'

'Why are they broken?'

'I can't say, my lord,'

'I cannot leave this house for a day but I find everything in confusion. Bring me some Burgundy.'

'Yes, my lord. There is a young lad, my lord, called a few minutes back, and asked for your lordship. He says he has something very particular to say to your lordship. I told him your lordship was out of town. He said your lordship would wish very much to see him, and that he had come from the Abbey.'

'The Abbey!' said Cadurcis, in a tone of curiosity. 'Why did you not show him in?'

'Your lordship said you were not at home to anybody.'

'Idiot! Is this anybody? Of course I would have seen him. What the devil do I keep you for, sir? You seem to me to have lost your head.'

Mr. Spalding retired.

'The Abbey! that is droll,' said Cadurcis. 'I owe some duties to the poor Abbey. I should not like to quit England, and leave anybody in trouble at the Abbey. I wish I had seen the lad. Some son of a tenant who has written to me, and I have never opened his letters. I am sorry.'

In a few minutes Mr. Spalding again entered the room. 'The young lad has called again, my lord. He says he thinks your lordship has come to town, and he wishes to see your lordship very much.'

'Bring lights and show him up. Show him up first.'

Accordingly, a country lad was ushered into the room, although it was so dusky that Cadurcis could only observe his figure standing at the door.

'Well, my good fellow,' said Cadurcis; 'what do you want? Are you in any trouble?'

The boy hesitated.

'Speak out, my good fellow; do not be alarmed. If I can serve you, or any one at the Abbey, I will do it.'

Here Mr. Spalding entered with the lights. The lad held a cotton handkerchief to his face; he appeared to be weeping; all that was seen of his head were his locks of red hair. He seemed a country lad, dressed in a long green coat with silver buttons, and he twirled in his disengaged hand a peasant's white hat.

'That will do, Spalding,' said Lord Cadurcis. 'Leave the room. Now, my good fellow, my time is precious; but speak out, and do not be afraid.'

'Cadurcis!' said the lad in a sweet and trembling voice.

'Gertrude, by G—d!' exclaimed Lord Cadurcis, starting. 'What infernal masquerade is this?'

'Is it a greater disguise than I have to bear every hour of my life?' exclaimed Lady Monteagle, advancing. 'Have I not to bear a smiling face with a breaking heart?'

'By Jove! a scene,' exclaimed Cadurcis in a piteous tone.

'A scene!' exclaimed Lady Monteagle, bursting into a flood of indignant tears. 'Is this the way the expression of my feelings is ever to be stigmatised? Barbarous man!'

Cadurcis stood with his back to the fireplace, with his lips compressed, and his hands under his coat-tails. He was resolved that nothing should induce him to utter a word. He looked the picture of dogged indifference.

'I know where you have been,' continued Lady Monteagle. 'You have been to Richmond; you have been with Miss Herbert. Yes! I know all. I am a victim, but I will not be a dupe. Yorkshire indeed! Paltry coward!'

Cadurcis hummed an air.

'And this is Lord Cadurcis!' continued the lady. 'The sublime, ethereal Lord Cadurcis, condescending to the last refuge of the meanest, most commonplace mind, a vulgar, wretched lie! What could have been expected from such a mind? You may delude the world, but I know you. Yes, sir! I know you. And I will let everybody know you. I will tear away the veil of charlatanism with which you have enveloped yourself. The world shall at length discover the nature of the idol they have worshipped. All your meanness, all your falsehood, all your selfishness, all your baseness, shall be revealed. I may be spurned, but at any rate I will be revenged!'

Lord Cadurcis yawned.

'Insulting, pitiful wretch!' continued the lady. 'And you think that I wish to hear you speak! You think the sound of that deceitful voice has any charm for me! You are mistaken, sir! I have listened to you too long. It was not to remonstrate with you that I resolved to see you. The tones of your voice can only excite my disgust. I am here to speak myself; to express to you the contempt, the detestation, the aversion, the scorn, the hatred, which I entertain for you!'

Lord Cadurcis whistled.

The lady paused; she had effected the professed purport of her visit; she ought now to have retired, and Cadurcis would most willingly have opened the door for her, and bowed her out of his apartment. But her conduct did not exactly accord with her speech. She intimated no intention of moving. Her courteous friend retained his position, and adhered to his policy of silence. There was a dead pause, and then Lady Monteagle, throwing herself into a chair, went into hysterics.

Lord Cadurcis, following her example, also seated himself, took up a book, and began to read.

The hysterics became fainter and fainter; they experienced all those gradations of convulsive noise with which Lord Cadurcis was so well acquainted; at length they subsided into sobs and sighs. Finally, there was again silence, now only disturbed by the sound of a page turned by Lord Cadurcis.

Suddenly the lady sprang from her seat, and firmly grasping the arm of Cadurcis, threw herself on her knees at his side.

'Cadurcis!' she exclaimed, in a tender tone, 'do you love me?'

'My dear Gertrude,' said Lord Cadurcis, coolly, but rather regretting he had quitted his original and less assailable posture, 'you know I like quiet women.'

'Cadurcis, forgive me!' murmured the lady. 'Pity me! Think only how miserable I am!'

'Your misery is of your own making,' said Lord Cadurcis. 'What occasion is there for any of these extraordinary proceedings? I have told you a thousand times that I cannot endure scenes. Female society is a relaxation to me; you convert it into torture. I like to sail upon a summer sea; and you always will insist upon a white squall.'

'But you have deserted me!'

'I never desert any one,' replied Cadurcis calmly, raising her from her supplicating attitude, and leading her to a seat. 'The last time we met, you banished me your presence, and told me never to speak to you again. Well, I obeyed your orders, as I always do.'

'But I did not mean what I said,' said Lady Monteagle.

'How should I know that?' said Lord Cadurcis.

'Your heart ought to have assured you,' said the lady.

'The tongue is a less deceptive organ than the heart,' replied her companion.

'Cadurcis,' said the lady, looking at her strange disguise, 'what do you advise me to do?'

'To go home; and if you like I will order my vis-à-vis for you directly,' and he rose from his seat to give the order.

'Ah!' you are sighing to get rid of me!' said the lady, in a reproachful, but still subdued tone.

'Why, the fact is, Gertrude, I prefer calling upon you, to your calling upon me. When I am fitted for your society, I seek it; and, when you are good-tempered, always with pleasure; when I am not in the mood for it, I stay away. And when I am at home, I wish to see no one. I have business now, and not very agreeable business. I am disturbed by many causes, and you could not have taken a step which could have given me greater annoyance than the strange one you have adopted this evening.'

'I am sorry for it now,' said the lady, weeping. 'When shall I see you again?'

'I will call upon you to-morrow, and pray receive me with smiles.'

'I ever will,' said the lady, weeping plenteously. 'It is all my fault; you are ever too good. There is not in the world a kinder and more gentle being than yourself. I shall never forgive myself for this exposure.

'Would you like to take anything?' said Lord Cadurcis: 'I am sure you must feel exhausted. You see I am drinking wine; it is my only dinner to-day, but I dare say there is some salvolatile in the house; I dare say, when my maids go into hysterics, they have it!'

'Ah, mocker!' said Lady Monteagle; 'but I can pardon everything, if you will only let me see you.'

'Au revoir! then,' said his lordship; 'I am sure the carriage must be ready. I hear it. Come, Mr. Gertrude, settle your wig; it is quite awry. By Jove! we might as well go to the Pantheon, as you are ready dressed. I have a domino.'

And so saying, Lord Cadurcis handed the lady to his carriage, and pressed her lightly by the hand, as he reiterated his promise of calling at Monteagle House the next day.

CHAPTER XVII.

Lord Cadurcis, unhappy at home, and wearied of the commonplace resources of society, had passed the night in every species of dissipation; his principal companion being that same young nobleman in whose company he had been when he first met Venetia at Ranelagh. The morn was breaking when Cadurcis and his friend arrived at his door. They had settled to welcome the dawn with a beaker of burnt Burgundy.

'Now, my dear Scrope,' said Cadurcis, 'now for quiet and philosophy. The laughter of those infernal women, the rattle of those cursed dice, and the oaths of those ruffians are still ringing in my ears. Let us compose ourselves, and moralise.'

Accustomed to their master's habits, who generally turned night into day, the household were all on the alert; a blazing fire greeted them, and his lordship ordered instantly a devil and the burnt Burgundy.

'Sit you down here, my Scrope; that is the seat of honour, and you shall have it. What is this, a letter? and marked "Urgent," and in a man's hand. It must be read. Some good fellow nabbed by a bailiff, or planted by his mistress. Signals of distress! We must assist our friends.'

The flame of the fire fell upon Lord Cadurcis' face as he read the letter; he was still standing, while his friend was stretched out in his easy chair, and inwardly congratulating himself on his comfortable prospects. The countenance of Cadurcis did not change, but he bit his lip, and read the letter twice, and turned it over, but with a careless air; and then he asked what o'clock it was. The servant informed him, and left the room.

'Scrope,' said Lord Cadurcis, quietly, and still standing, 'are you very drunk?'

'My dear fellow, I am as fresh as possible; you will see what justice I shall do to the Burgundy.'

'"Burgundy to-morrow," as the Greek proverb saith,' observed Lord Cadurcis. 'Read that.'

His companion had the pleasure of perusing a challenge from Lord Monteagle, couched in no gentle terms, and requesting an immediate meeting.

'Well, I never heard anything more ridiculous in my life,' said Lord Scrope. 'Does he want satisfaction because you have planted her?'

'D——n her!' said Lord Cadurcis. 'She has occasioned me a thousand annoyances, and now she has spoilt our supper. I don't know, though; he wants to fight quickly, let us fight at once. I will send him a cartel now, and then we can have our Burgundy. You will go out with me, of course? Hyde Park, six o'clock, and short swords.'

Lord Cadurcis accordingly sat down, wrote his letter, and dispatched it by Mr. Spalding to Monteagle House, with peremptory instructions to bring back an answer. The companions then turned to their devil.

'This is a bore, Cadurcis,' said Lord Scrope.

'It is. I cannot say I am very valorous in a bad cause. I do not like to fight "upon compulsion," I confess. If I had time to screw my courage up, I dare say I should do it very well. I dare say, for instance, if ever I am publicly executed, I shall die game.'

'God forbid!' said Lord Scrope. 'I say, Cadurcis, I would not drink any Burgundy if I were you. I shall take a glass of cold water.'

'Ah! you are only a second, and so you want to cool your valour,' said Cadurcis. 'You have all the fun.'

'But how came this blow-up?' inquired Lord Scrope. 'Letters discovered, eh? Because I thought you never saw her now?'

'By Jove! my dear fellow, she has been the whole evening here masquerading it like a very vixen, as she is; and now she has committed us both. I have burnt her letters, without reading them, for the last month. Now I call that honourable; because, as I had no longer any claim on her heart, I would not think of trenching on her correspondence. But honour, what is honour in these dishonourable days? This is my reward. She contrived to enter my house this evening, dressed like a farmer's boy, and you may imagine what ensued; rage, hysterics, and repentance. I am sure if Monteagle had seen me, he would not have been jealous. I never opened my mouth, but, like a fool, sent her home in my carriage; and now I am going to be run through the body for my politeness.'

In this light strain, blended, however, with more decorous feeling on the part of Lord Scrope, the young men conversed until the messenger's return with Lord Monteagle's answer. In Hyde Park, in the course of an hour, himself and Lord Cadurcis, attended by their friends, were to meet.

'Well, there is nothing like having these affairs over,' said Cadurcis; 'and to confess the truth, my dear Scrope, I should not much care if Monteagle were to despatch me to my fathers; for, in the whole course of my miserable life, and miserable, whatever the world may think, it has been, I never felt much more wretched than I have during the last four-and-twenty hours. By Jove! do you know I was going to leave England this morning, and I have ordered my horses, too.'

'Leave England!'

'Yes, leave England; and where I never intended to return.'

'Well, you are the oddest person I ever knew, Cadurcis. I should have thought you the happiest person that ever existed. Everybody admires, everybody envies you. You seem to have everything that man can desire. Your life is a perpetual triumph.'

'Ah! my dear Scrope, there is a skeleton in every house. If you knew all, you would not envy me.'

'Well, we have not much time,' said Lord Scrope; 'have you any arrangements to make?'

'None. My property goes to George, who is my only relative, without the necessity of a will, otherwise I should leave everything to him, for he is a good fellow, and my blood is in his veins. Just you remember, Scrope, that I will be buried with my mother. That is all; and now let us get ready.'

The sun had just risen when the young men went forth, and the day promised to be as brilliant as the preceding one. Not a soul was stirring in the courtly quarter in which Cadurcis resided; even the last watchman had stolen to repose. They called a hackney coach at the first stand they reached, and were soon at the destined spot. They were indeed before their time, and strolling by the side of the Serpentine, Cadurcis said, 'Yesterday morning was one of the happiest of my life, Scrope, and I was in hopes that an event would have occurred in the course of the day that might have been my salvation. If it had, by-the-bye, I should not have returned to town, and got into this cursed scrape. However, the gods were against me, and now I am reckless.'

Now Lord Monteagle and his friend, who was Mr. Horace Pole, appeared. Cadurcis advanced, and bowed; Lord Monteagle returned his bow, stiffly, but did not speak. The seconds chose their ground, the champions disembarrassed themselves of their coats, and their swords crossed. It was a brief affair. After a few passes, Cadurcis received a slight wound in his arm, while his weapon pierced his antagonist in the breast. Lord Monteagle dropped his sword and fell.

'You had better fly, Lord Cadurcis,' said Mr. Horace Pole. 'This is a bad business, I fear; we have a surgeon at hand, and he can help us to the coach that is waiting close by.'

'I thank you, sir, I never fly,' said Lord Cadurcis; 'and I shall wait here until I see your principal safely deposited in his carriage; he will have no objection to my friend, Lord Scrope, assisting him, who, by his presence to-day, has only fulfilled one of the painful duties that society imposes upon us.'

The surgeon gave an unfavourable report of the wound, which he dressed on the field. Lord Monteagle was then borne to his carriage, which was at hand, and Lord Scrope, the moment he had seen the equipage move slowly off, returned to his friend.

'Well Cadurcis,' he exclaimed in an anxious voice, 'I hope you have not killed him. What will you do now?'

'I shall go home, and await the result, my dear Scrope. I am sorry for you, for this may get you into trouble. For myself, I care nothing.'

'You bleed!' said Lord Scrope.

'A scratch. I almost wish our lots had been the reverse. Come, Scrope, help me on with my coat. Yesterday I lost my heart, last night I lost my money, and perhaps to-morrow I shall lose my arm. It seems we are not in luck.'

CHAPTER XVIII.

It has been well observed, that no spectacle is so ridiculous as the British public in one of its periodical fits of morality. In general, elopements, divorces, and family quarrels pass with little notice. We read the scandal, talk about it for a day, and forget it. But, once in six or seven years, our virtue becomes outrageous. We cannot suffer the laws of religion and decency to be violated. We must make a stand against vice. We must teach libertines that the English people appreciate the importance of domestic ties. Accordingly, some unfortunate man, in no respect more depraved than hundreds whose offences have been treated with lenity, is singled out as an expiatory sacrifice. If he has children, they are to be taken from him. If he has a profession, he is to be driven from it. He is cut by the higher orders, and hissed by the lower. He is, in truth, a sort of whipping boy, by whose vicarious agonies all the other transgressors of the same class are, it is supposed, sufficiently chastised. We reflect very complacently on our own severity, and compare, with great pride, the high standard of morals established in England, with the Parisian laxity. At length, our anger is satiated, our victim is ruined and heart-broken, and our virtue goes quietly to sleep for seven years more.

These observations of a celebrated writer apply to the instance of Lord Cadurcis; he was the periodical victim, the scapegoat of English morality, sent into the wilderness with all the crimes and curses of the multitude on his head. Lord Cadurcis had certainly committed a great crime: not his intrigue with Lady Monteagle, for that surely was not an unprecedented offence; not his duel with her husband, for after all it was a duel in self-defence; and, at all events, divorces and duels, under any circumstances, would scarcely have excited or authorised the storm which was now about to burst over the late spoiled child of society. But Lord Cadurcis had been guilty of the offence which, of all offences, is punished most severely: Lord Cadurcis had been overpraised. He had excited too warm an interest; and the public, with its usual justice, was resolved to chastise him for its own folly.

There are no fits of caprice so hasty and so violent as those of society. Society, indeed, is all passion and no heart. Cadurcis, in allusion to his sudden and singular success, had been in the habit of saying to his intimates, that he 'woke one morning and found himself famous.' He might now observe, 'I woke one morning and found myself infamous.' Before twenty-four hours had passed over his duel with Lord Monteagle, he found himself branded by every journal in London, as an unprincipled and unparalleled reprobate. The public, without waiting to think or even to inquire after the truth, instantly selected as genuine the most false and the most flagrant of the fifty libellous narratives that were circulated of the transaction. Stories, inconsistent with themselves, were all alike eagerly believed, and what evidence there might be for any one of them, the virtuous people, by whom they were repeated, neither cared nor knew. The public, in short, fell into a passion with their darling, and, ashamed of their past idolatry, nothing would satisfy them but knocking the divinity on the head.

Until Lord Monteagle, to the great regret of society, who really wished him to die in order that his antagonist might commit murder, was declared out of danger, Lord Cadurcis never quitted his house, and he was not a little surprised that scarcely a human being called upon him except his cousin, who immediately flew to his succour. George, indeed, would gladly have spared Cadurcis any knowledge of the storm that was raging against him, and which he flattered himself would blow over before Cadurcis was again abroad; but he was so much with his cousin, and Cadurcis was so extremely acute and naturally so suspicious, that this was impossible. Moreover, his absolute desertion by his friends, and the invectives and the lampoons with which the newspapers abounded, and of which he was the subject, rendered any concealment out of the question, and poor George passed his life in running about contradicting falsehoods, stating truth, fighting his cousin's battles, and then reporting to him, in the course of the day, the state of the campaign.

Cadurcis, being a man of infinite sensibility, suffered tortures. He had been so habituated to panegyric, that the slightest criticism ruffled him, and now his works had suddenly become the subject of universal and outrageous attack; having lived only in a cloud of incense, he suddenly found himself in a pillory of moral indignation; his writings, his habits, his temper, his person, were all alike ridiculed and vilified. In a word, Cadurcis, the petted, idolised, spoiled Cadurcis, was enduring that charming vicissitude in a prosperous existence, styled a reaction; and a conqueror, who deemed himself invincible, suddenly vanquished, could scarcely be more thunderstruck, or feel more impotently desperate.

The tortures of his mind, however, which this sudden change in his position and in the opinions of society, were of themselves competent to occasion to one of so impetuous and irritable a temperament, and who ever magnified both misery and delight with all the creative power of a brooding imagination, were excited in his case even to the liveliest agony, when he reminded himself of the situation in which he was now placed with Venetia. All hope of ever obtaining her hand had now certainly vanished, and he doubted whether even her love could survive the quick occurrence, after his ardent vows, of this degrading and mortifying catastrophe. He execrated Lady Monteagle with the most heartfelt rage, and when he remembered that all this time the world believed him the devoted admirer of this vixen, his brain was stimulated almost to the verge of insanity. His only hope of the truth reaching Venetia was through the medium of his cousin, and he impressed daily upon Captain Cadurcis the infinite consolation it would prove to him, if he could contrive to make her aware of the real facts of the case. According to the public voice, Lady Monteagle at his solicitation had fled to his house, and remained there, and her husband forced his entrance into the mansion in the middle of the night, while his wife escaped disguised in Lord Cadurcis' clothes. She did not, however, reach Monteagle House in time enough to escape detection by her lord, who had instantly sought and obtained satisfaction from his treacherous friend. All the monstrous inventions of the first week had now subsided into this circumstantial and undoubted narrative; at least this was the version believed by those who had been Cadurcis' friends. They circulated the authentic tale with the most considerate assiduity, and shook their heads, and said it was too bad, and that he must not be countenanced.

The moment Lord Monteagle was declared out of danger, Lord Cadurcis made his appearance in public. He walked into Brookes', and everybody seemed suddenly so deeply interested in the newspapers, that you might have supposed they had brought intelligence of a great battle, or a revolution, or a change of ministry at the least. One or two men spoke to him, who had never presumed to address him at any other time, and he received a faint bow from a distinguished nobleman, who had ever professed for him the greatest consideration and esteem.

Cadurcis mounted his horse and rode down to the House of Lords. There was a debate of some public interest, and a considerable crowd was collected round the Peers' entrance. The moment Lord Cadurcis was recognised, the multitude began hooting. He was agitated, and grinned a ghastly smile at the rabble. But he dismounted, without further annoyance, and took his seat. Not a single peer of his own party spoke to him. The leader of the Opposition, indeed, bowed to him, and, in the course of the evening, he received, from one or two more of his party, some formal evidences of frigid courtesy. The tone of his reception by his friends could not be concealed from the ministerial party. It was soon detected, and generally whispered, that Lord Cadurcis was cut. Nevertheless, he sat out the debate and voted. The house broke up. He felt lonely; his old friend, the Bishop of——, who had observed all that had occurred, and who might easily have avoided him, came forward, however, in the most marked manner, and, in a tone which everybody heard, said, 'How do you do, Lord Cadurcis? I am very glad to see you,' shaking his hand most cordially. This made a great impression. Several of the Tory Lords, among them Venetia's uncle, now advanced and sainted him. He received their advances with a haughty, but not disdainful, courtesy; but when his Whig friends, confused, now hurried to encumber him with their assistance, he treated them with the scorn which they well deserved.

'Will you take a seat in my carriage home, Lord Cadurcis?' said his leader, for it was notorious that Cadurcis had been mobbed on his arrival.

'Thank you, my lord,' said Cadurcis, speaking very audibly, 'I prefer returning as I came. We are really both of us such unpopular personages, that your kindness would scarcely be prudent.'

The house had been full; there was a great scuffle and confusion as the peers were departing; the mob, now considerable, were prepared for the appearance of Lord Cadurcis, and their demeanour was menacing. Some shouted out his name; then it was repeated with odious and vindictive epithets, followed by ferocious yells. A great many peers collected round Cadurcis, and entreated him not to return on horseback. It must be confessed that genuine and considerable feeling was now shown by all men of all parties. And indeed to witness this young, and noble, and gifted creature, but a few days back the idol of the nation, and from whom a word, a glance even, was deemed the greatest and most gratifying distinction, whom all orders, classes, and conditions of men had combined to stimulate with multiplied adulation, with all the glory and ravishing delights of the world, as it were, forced upon him, to see him thus assailed with the savage execrations of all those vile things who exult in the fall of everything that is great, and the abasement of everything that is noble, was indeed a spectacle which might have silenced malice and satisfied envy!

'My carriage is most heartily at your service, Lord Cadurcis,' said the noble leader of the government in the upper house; 'you can enter it without the slightest suspicion by these ruffians.' 'Lord Cadurcis; my dear lord; my good lord, for our sakes, if not for your own; Cadurcis, dear Cadurcis, my good Cadurcis, it is madness, folly, insanity; a mob will do anything, and an English mob is viler than all; for Heaven's sake!' Such were a few of the varied exclamations which resounded on all sides, but which produced on the person to whom they were addressed only the result of his desiring the attendant to call for his horses.

The lobby was yet full; it was a fine thing in the light of the archway to see Cadurcis spring into his saddle. Instantly there was a horrible yell. Yet in spite of all their menaces, the mob were for a time awed by his courage; they made way for him; he might even have rode quickly on for some few yards, but he would not; he reined his fiery steed into a slow but stately pace, and, with a countenance scornful and composed, he continued his progress, apparently unconscious of impediment. Meanwhile, the hooting continued without abatement, increasing indeed, after the first comparative pause, in violence and menace. At length a bolder ruffian, excited by the uproar, rushed forward and seized Cadurcis' bridle. Cadurcis struck the man over the eyes with his whip, and at the same time touched his horse with his spur, and the assailant was dashed to the ground. This seemed a signal for a general assault. It commenced with hideous yells. His friends at the house, who had watched everything with the keenest interest, immediately directed all the constables who were at hand to rush to his succour; hitherto they had restrained the police, lest their interference might stimulate rather than repress the mob. The charge of the constables was well timed; they laid about them with their staves; you might have heard the echo of many a broken crown. Nevertheless, though they dispersed the mass, they could not penetrate the immediate barrier that surrounded Lord Cadurcis, whose only defence indeed, for they had cut off his groom, was the terrors of his horse's heels, and whose managed motions he regulated with admirable skill, now rearing, now prancing, now kicking behind, and now turning round with a quick yet sweeping motion, before which the mob retreated. Off his horse, however, they seemed resolved to drag him; and it was not difficult to conceive, if they succeeded, what must be his eventual fate. They were infuriate, but his contact with his assailants fortunately prevented their co-mates from hurling stones at him from the fear of endangering their own friends.

A messenger to the Horse Guards had been sent from the House of Lords; but, before the military could arrive, and fortunately (for, with their utmost expedition, they must have been too late), a rumour of the attack got current in the House of Commons. Captain Cadurcis, Lord Scrope, and a few other young men instantly rushed out; and, ascertaining the truth, armed with good cudgels and such other effective weapons as they could instantly obtain, they mounted their horses and charged the nearly-triumphant populace, dealing such vigorous blows that their efforts soon made a visible diversion in Lord Cadurcis' favour. It is difficult, indeed, to convey an idea of the exertions and achievements of Captain Cadurcis; no Paladin of chivalry ever executed such marvels on a swarm of Paynim slaves; and many a bloody coxcomb and broken limb bore witness in Petty France that night to his achievements. Still the mob struggled and were not daunted by the delay in immolating their victim. As long as they had only to fight against men in plain clothes, they were valorous and obstinate enough; but the moment that the crests of a troop of Horse Guards were seen trotting down Parliament Street, everybody ran away, and in a few minutes all Palace-yard was as still as if the genius of the place rendered a riot impossible.

Lord Cadurcis thanked his friends, who were profuse in their compliments to his pluck. His manner, usually playful with his intimates of his own standing, was, however, rather grave at present, though very cordial. He asked them home to dine with him; but they were obliged to decline his invitation, as a division was expected; so, saying 'Good-bye, George, perhaps I shall see you to-night,' Cadurcis rode rapidly off.

With Cadurcis there was but one step from the most exquisite sensitiveness to the most violent defiance. The experience of this day had entirely cured him of his previous nervous deference to the feelings of society. Society had outraged him, and now he resolved to outrage society. He owed society nothing; his reception at the House of Lords and the riot in Palace-yard had alike cleared his accounts with all orders of men, from the highest to the lowest. He had experienced, indeed, some kindness that he could not forget, but only from his own kin, and those who with his associations were the same as kin. His memory dwelt with gratification on his cousin's courageous zeal, and still more on the demonstration which Masham had made in his favour, which, if possible, argued still greater boldness and sincere regard. That was a trial of true affection, and an instance of moral courage, which Cadurcis honoured, and which he never could forget. He was anxious about Venetia; he wished to stand as well with her as he deserved; no better; but he was grieved to think she could believe all those infamous tales at present current respecting himself. But, for the rest of the world, he delivered them all to the most absolute contempt, disgust, and execration; he resolved, from this time, nothing should ever induce him again to enter society, or admit the advances of a single civilised ruffian who affected to be social. The country, the people, their habits, laws, manners, customs, opinions, and everything connected with them, were viewed with the same jaundiced eye; and his only object now was to quit England, to which he resolved never to return.

CHAPTER XIX.

Venetia was, perhaps, not quite so surprised as the rest of her friends, when, on their return to Richmond, Lord Cadurcis was not again seen. She was very unhappy: she recalled the scene in the garden at Cherbury some years back; and, with the knowledge of the impetuosity of his temper, she believed she should never see him again. Poor Plantagenet, who loved her so much, and whose love she so fully returned! why might they not be happy? She neither doubted the constancy of his affection, nor their permanent felicity if they were united. She shared none of her mother's apprehensions or her prejudices, but she was the victim of duty and her vow. In the course of four-and-twenty hours, strange rumours were afloat respecting Lord Cadurcis; and the newspapers on the ensuing morning told the truth, and more than the truth. Venetia could not doubt as to the duel or the elopement; but, instead of feeling indignation, she attributed what had occurred to the desperation of his mortified mind; and she visited on herself all the fatal consequences that had happened. At present, however, all her emotions were quickly absorbed in the one terrible fear that Lord Monteagle would die. In that dreadful and urgent apprehension every other sentiment merged. It was impossible to conceal her misery, and she entreated her mother to return to town.

Very differently, however, was the catastrophe viewed by Lady Annabel. She, on the contrary, triumphed in her sagacity and her prudence. She hourly congratulated herself on being the saviour of her daughter; and though she refrained from indulging in any open exultation over Venetia's escape and her own profound discretion, it was, nevertheless, impossible for her to conceal from her daughter her infinite satisfaction and self-congratulation. While Venetia was half broken-hearted, her mother silently returned thanks to Providence for the merciful dispensation which had exempted her child from so much misery.

The day after their return to town, Captain Cadurcis called upon them. Lady Annabel never mentioned the name of his cousin; but George, finding no opportunity of conversing with Venetia alone, and being, indeed, too much excited to speak on any other subject, plunged at once into the full narrative; defended Lord Cadurcis, abused the Monteagles and the slanderous world, and, in spite of Lady Annabel's ill-concealed dissatisfaction, favoured her with an exact and circumstantial account of everything that had happened, how it happened, when it happened, and where it happened; concluding by a declaration that Cadurcis was the best fellow that ever lived; the most unfortunate, and the most ill-used; and that, if he were to be hunted down for an affair like this, over which he had no control, there was not a man in London who could be safe for ten minutes. All that George effected by his zeal, was to convince Lady Annabel that his cousin had entirely corrupted, him; she looked upon her former favourite as another victim; but Venetia listened in silence, and not without solace.

Two or three days after the riot at the House of Lords, Captain Cadurcis burst into his cousin's room with a triumphant countenance. 'Well, Plantagenet!' he exclaimed, 'I have done it; I have seen her alone, and I have put you as right as possible. Nothing can be better.'

'Tell me, my dear fellow,' said Lord Cadurcis, eagerly.

'Well, you know, I have called half-a-dozen times,' said George, 'but either Lady Annabel was there, or they were not at home, or something always occurred to prevent any private communication. But I met her to-day with her aunt; I joined them immediately, and kept with them the whole morning. I am sorry to say she, I mean Venetia, is devilish ill; she is, indeed. However, her aunt now is quite on your side, and very kind, I can tell you that. I put her right at first, and she has fought our battle bravely. Well, they stopped to call somewhere, and Venetia was so unwell that she would not get out, and I was left alone in the carriage with her. Time was precious, and I opened at once. I told her how wretched you were, and that the only thing that made you miserable was about her, because you were afraid she would think you so profligate, and all that. I went through it all; told her the exact truth, which, indeed, she had before heard; but now I assured her, on my honour, that it was exactly what happened; and she said she did not doubt it, and could not, from some conversation which you had together the day we were all at Hampton Court, and that she felt that nothing could have been premeditated, and fully believed that everything had occurred as I said; and, however she deplored it, she felt the same for you as ever, and prayed for your happiness. Then she told me what misery the danger of Lord Monteagle had occasioned her; that she thought his death must have been the forerunner of her own; but the moment he was declared out of danger seemed the happiest hour of her life. I told her you were going to leave England, and asked her whether she had any message for you; and she said, "Tell him he is the same to me that he has always been." So, when her aunt returned, I jumped out and ran on to you at once.'

'You are the best fellow that ever lived, George,' said Lord Cadurcis; 'and now the world may go to the devil!'

This message from Venetia acted upon Lord Cadurcis like a charm. It instantly cleared his mind. He shut himself up in his house for a week, and wrote a farewell to England, perhaps the most masterly effusion of his powerful spirit. It abounded in passages of overwhelming passion, and almost Satanic sarcasm. Its composition entirely relieved his long-brooding brain. It contained, moreover, a veiled address to Venetia, delicate, tender, and irresistibly affecting. He appended also to the publication, the verses he had previously addressed to her.

This volume, which was purchased with an avidity exceeding even the eagerness with which his former productions had been received, exercised extraordinary influence on public opinion. It enlisted the feelings of the nation on his side in a struggle with a coterie. It was suddenly discovered that Lord Cadurcis was the most injured of mortals, and far more interesting than ever. The address to the unknown object of his adoration, and the verses to Venetia, mystified everybody. Lady Monteagle was universally abused, and all sympathised with the long-treasured and baffled affection of the unhappy poet. Cadurcis, however, was not to be conciliated. He left his native shores in a blaze of glory, but with the accents of scorn still quivering on his lip.

END OF BOOK IV.

BOOK V.

CHAPTER I.

The still waters of the broad and winding lake reflected the lustre of the cloudless sky. The gentle declinations of the green hills that immediately bordered the lake, with an undulating margin that now retired into bays of the most picturesque form, now jutted forth into woody promontories, and then opened into valleys of sequestered beauty, which the eye delighted to pursue, were studded with white villas, and cottages scarcely less graceful, and occasionally with villages, and even towns; here and there rose a solitary chapel; and, scarcely less conspicuous, the black spire of some cypress strikingly contrasting with the fair buildings or the radiant foliage that in general surrounded them. A rampart of azure mountains raised their huge forms behind the nearer hills; and occasionally peering over these, like spectres on some brilliant festival, were the ghastly visages of the Alpine glaciers.

It was within an hour of sunset, and the long shadows had fallen upon the waters; a broad boat, with a variegated awning, rowed by two men, approached the steps of a marble terrace. The moment they had reached their point of destination, and had fastened the boat to its moorings, the men landed their oars, and immediately commenced singing a simple yet touching melody, wherewith it was their custom to apprise their employers of their arrival.

'Will they come forth this evening, think you, Vittorio?' said one boatman to the other.

'By our holy mother, I hope so!' replied his comrade, 'for this light air that is now rising will do the young signora more good than fifty doctors.'

'They are good people,' said Vittorio. 'It gives me more pleasure to row them than any persons who ever hired us.'

'Ay, ay!' said his comrade, 'It was a lucky day when we first put an oar in the lake for them, heretics though they be.'

'But they may be converted yet,' said his companion; 'for, as I was saying to Father Francisco last night, if the young signora dies, it is a sad thing to think what will become of her.'

'And what said the good Father?'

'He shook his head,' said Vittorio.

'When Father Francisco shakes his head, he means a great deal,' said his companion.

At this moment a servant appeared on the terrace, to say the ladies were at hand; and very shortly afterwards Lady Annabel Herbert, with her daughter leaning on her arm, descended the steps, and entered the boat. The countenances of the boatmen brightened when they saw them, and they both made their inquiries after the health of Venetia with tenderness and feeling.

'Indeed, my good friends,' said Venetia, 'I think you are right, and the lake will cure me after all.'

'The blessing of the lake be upon you, signora,' said the boatmen, crossing themselves.

Just as they were moving off, came running Mistress Pauncefort, quite breathless. 'Miss Herbert's fur cloak, my lady; you told me to remember, my lady, and I cannot think how I forgot it. But I really have been so very hot all day, that such a thing as furs never entered my head. And for my part, until I travelled, I always thought furs were only worn in Russia. But live and learn, as I say.'

They were now fairly floating on the calm, clear waters, and the rising breeze was as grateful to Venetia as the boatmen had imagined.

A return of those symptoms which had before disquieted Lady Annabel for her daughter, and which were formerly the cause of their residence at Weymouth, had induced her, in compliance with the advice of her physicians, to visit Italy; but the fatigue of travel had exhausted the energies of Venetia (for in those days the Alps were not passed in luxurious travelling carriages) on the very threshold of the promised land; and Lady Annabel had been prevailed upon to take a villa on the Lago Maggiore, where Venetia had passed two months, still suffering indeed from great debility, but not without advantage.

There are few spots more favoured by nature than the Italian lakes and their vicinity, combining, as they do, the most sublime features of mountainous scenery with all the softer beauties and the varied luxuriance of the plain. As the still, bright lake is to the rushing and troubled cataract, is Italy to Switzerland and Savoy. Emerging from the chaotic ravines and the wild gorges of the Alps, the happy land breaks upon us like a beautiful vision. We revel in the sunny light, after the unearthly glare of eternal snow. Our sight seems renovated as we throw our eager glance over those golden plains, clothed with such picturesque trees, sparkling with such graceful villages, watered by such noble rivers, and crowned with such magnificent cities; and all bathed and beaming in an atmosphere so soft and radiant! Every isolated object charms us with its beautiful novelty: for the first time we gaze on palaces; the garden, the terrace, and the statue, recall our dreams beneath a colder sky; and we turn from these to catch the hallowed form of some cupolaed convent, crowning the gentle elevation of some green hill, and flanked by the cypress or the pine.

The influence of all these delightful objects and of this benign atmosphere on the frame and mind of Venetia had been considerable. After the excitement of the last year of her life, and the harassing and agitating scenes with which it closed, she found a fine solace in this fair land and this soft sky, which the sad perhaps can alone experience. Its repose alone afforded a consolatory contrast to the turbulent pleasure of the great world. She looked back upon those glittering and noisy scenes with an aversion which was only modified by her self-congratulation at her escape from their exhausting and contaminating sphere. Here she recurred, but with all the advantages of a change of scene, and a scene so rich in novel and interesting associations, to the calm tenor of those days, when not a thought ever seemed to escape from Cherbury and its spell-bound seclusion. Her books, her drawings, her easel, and her harp, were now again her chief pursuits; pursuits, however, influenced by the genius of the land in which she lived, and therefore invested with a novel interest; for the literature and the history of the country naturally attracted her attention; and its fair aspects and sweet sounds, alike inspired her pencil and her voice. She had, in the society of her mother, indeed, the advantage of communing with a mind not less refined and cultivated than her own. Lady Annabel was a companion whose conversation, from reading and reflection, was eminently suggestive; and their hours, though they lived in solitude, never hung heavy. They were always employed, and always cheerful. But Venetia was not more than cheerful. Still very young, and gifted with an imaginative and therefore sanguine mind, the course of circumstances, however, had checked her native spirit, and shaded a brow which, at her time of life and with her temperament, should have been rather fanciful than pensive. If Venetia, supported by the disciplined energies of a strong mind, had schooled herself into not looking back to the past with grief, her future was certainly not tinged with the Iris pencil of Hope. It seemed to her that it was her fate that life should bring her no happier hours than those she now enjoyed. They did not amount to exquisite bliss. That was a conviction which, by no process of reflection, however ingenious, could she delude herself to credit. Venetia struggled to take refuge in content, a mood of mind perhaps less natural than it should be to one so young, so gifted, and so fair!

Their villa was surrounded by a garden in the ornate and artificial style of the country. A marble terrace overlooked the lake, crowned with many a statue and vase that held the aloe. The laurel and the cactus, the cypress and the pine, filled the air with their fragrance, or charmed the eye with their rarity and beauty: the walks were festooned with the vine, and they could raise their hands and pluck the glowing fruit which screened them, from the beam by which, it was ripened. In this enchanted domain Venetia might be often seen, a form even fairer than the sculptured nymphs among which she glided, catching the gentle breeze that played upon the surface of the lake, or watching the white sail that glittered in the sun as it floated over its purple bosom.

Yet this beautiful retreat Venetia was soon to quit, and she thought of her departure with a sigh. Her mother had been warned to avoid the neighbourhood of the mountains in the winter, and the autumn was approaching its close. If Venetia could endure the passage of the Apennines, it was the intention of Lady Annabel to pass the winter on the coast of the Mediterranean; otherwise to settle in one of the Lombard cities. At all events, in the course of a few weeks they were to quit their villa on the lake.

CHAPTER II.

A very few days after this excursion on the lake, Lady Annabel and her daughter were both surprised and pleased with a visit from a friend whose appearance was certainly very unexpected; this was Captain Cadurcis. On his way from Switzerland to Sicily, he had heard of their residence in the neighbourhood, and had crossed over from Arona to visit them.

The name of Cadurcis was still dear to Venetia, and George had displayed such gallantry and devotion in all his cousin's troubles, that she was personally attached to him; he had always been a favourite of her mother; his arrival, therefore, was welcomed by each of the ladies with great cordiality. He accepted the hospitality which Lady Annabel offered him, and remained with them a week, a period which they spent in visiting the most beautiful and interesting spots of the lake, with which they were already sufficiently familiar to allow them to prove guides as able as they were agreeable. These excursions, indeed, contributed to the pleasure and happiness of the whole party. There was about Captain Cadurcis a natural cheerfulness which animated every one in his society; a gay simplicity, difficult to define, but very charming, and which, without effort, often produced deeper impressions than more brilliant and subtle qualities. Left alone in the world, and without a single advantage save those that nature had conferred upon him, it had often been remarked, that in whatever circle he moved George Cadurcis always became the favourite and everywhere made friends. His sweet and engaging temper had perhaps as much contributed to his professional success as his distinguished gallantry and skill. Other officers, no doubt, were as brave and able as Captain Cadurcis, but his commanders always signalled him out for favourable notice; and, strange to say, his success, instead of exciting envy and ill-will, pleased even his less fortunate competitors. However hard another might feel his own lot, it was soothed by the reflection that George Cadurcis was at least more fortunate. His popularity, however, was not confined to his profession. His cousin's noble guardian, whom George had never seen until he ventured to call upon his lordship on his return to England, now looked upon him almost as a son, and omitted no opportunity of advancing his interests in the world. Of all the members of the House of Commons he was perhaps the only one that everybody praised, and his success in the world of fashion had been as remarkable as in his profession. These great revolutions in his life and future prospects had, however, not produced the slightest change in his mind and manners; and this was perhaps the secret spell of his prosperity. Though we are most of us the creatures of affectation, simplicity has a great charm, especially when attended, as in the present instance, with many agreeable and some noble qualities. In spite of the rough fortunes of his youth, the breeding of Captain Cadurcis was high;

the recollection of the race to which he belonged had never been forgotten by him. He was proud of his family. He had one of those light hearts, too, which enable their possessors to acquire accomplishments with facility: he had a sweet voice, a quick ear, a rapid eye. He acquired a language as some men learn an air. Then his temper was imperturbable, and although the most obliging and kindest-hearted creature that ever lived, there was a native dignity about him which prevented his goodnature from being abused. No sense of interest either could ever induce him to act contrary to the dictates of his judgment and his heart. At the risk of offending his patron, George sided with his cousin, although he had deeply offended his guardian, and although the whole world was against him. Indeed, the strong affection that Lord Cadurcis instantly entertained for George is not the least remarkable instance of the singular, though silent, influence that Captain Cadurcis everywhere acquired. Lord Cadurcis had fixed upon him for his friend from the first moment of their acquaintance; and though apparently there could not be two characters more dissimilar, there were at bottom some striking points of sympathy and some strong bonds of union, in the generosity and courage that distinguished both, and in the mutual blood that filled their veins.

There seemed to be a tacit understanding between the several members of our party that the name of Lord Cadurcis was not to be mentioned. Lady Annabel made no inquiry after him; Venetia was unwilling to hazard a question which would annoy her mother, and of which the answer could not bring her much satisfaction; and Captain Cadurcis did not think fit himself to originate any conversation on the subject. Nevertheless, Venetia could not help sometimes fancying, when her eyes met his, that their mutual thoughts were the same, and both dwelling on one who was absent, and of whom her companion would willingly have conversed. To confess the truth, indeed, George Cadurcis was on his way to join his cousin, who had crossed over from Spain to Barbary, and journeyed along the African coast from Tangiers to Tripoli. Their point of reunion was to be Sicily or Malta. Hearing of the residence of the Herberts on the lake, he thought it would be but kind to Plantagenet to visit them, and perhaps to bear to him some message from Venetia. There was nothing, indeed, on which Captain Cadurcis was more intent than to effect the union between his cousin and Miss Herbert. He was deeply impressed with the sincerity of Plantagenet's passion, and he himself entertained for the lady the greatest affection and admiration. He thought she was the only person whom he had ever known, who was really worthy to be his cousin's bride. And, independent of her personal charms and undoubted talents, she had displayed during the outcry against Lord Cadurcis so much good sense, such a fine spirit, and such modest yet sincere affection for the victim, that George Cadurcis had almost lost his own heart to her, when he was endeavouring to induce her not utterly to reject that of another; and it became one of the dreams of his life, that in a little time, when all, as he fondly anticipated, had ended as it should, and as he wished it, he should be able to find an occasional home at Cadurcis Abbey, and enjoy the charming society of one whom he had already taught himself to consider as a sister.

'And to-night you must indeed go?' said Venetia, as they were walking together on the terrace. It was the only time that they had been alone together during his visit.

'I must start from Arona at daybreak,' replied George; 'and I must travel quickly, for in less than a month I must be in Sicily.'

'Sicily! Why are you going to Sicily?'

Captain Cadurcis smiled. 'I am going to join a friend of ours,' he answered.

'Plantagenet?' she said.

Captain Cadurcis nodded assent.

'Poor Plantagenet!' said Venetia.

'His name has been on my lips several times,' said George.

'I am sure of that,' said Venetia. 'Is he well?'

'He writes to me in fair spirits,' said Captain Cadurcis. 'He has been travelling in Spain, and now he is somewhere in Africa; we are to meet in Sicily or Malta. I think travel has greatly benefited him. He seems quite delighted with his glimpse of Oriental manners, and I should scarcely be surprised if he were now to stretch on to Constantinople.'

'I wonder if he will ever return to England,' said Venetia, thoughtfully.

'There is only one event that would induce him,' said Captain Cadurcis. And then after a pause he added, 'You will not ask me what it is?'

'I wish he were in England, and were happy,' said Venetia.

'It is in your power to effect both results,' said her companion.

'It is useless to recur to that subject,' said Venetia. 'Plantagenet knows my feelings towards him, but fate has forbidden our destinies to be combined.'

'Then he will never return to England, and never be happy. Ah, Venetia! what shall I tell him when we meet? What message am I to bear him from you?'

'Those regards which he ever possessed, and has never forfeited,' said Venetia.

'Poor Cadurcis!' said his cousin, shaking his head, 'if any man ever had reason to be miserable, it is he.'

'We are none of us very happy, I think,' said Venetia, mournfully. 'I am sure when I look back to the last few years of my life it seems to me that there is some curse hanging over our families. I cannot penetrate it; it baffles me.'

'I am sure,' said Captain Cadurcis with great animation, 'nay, I would pledge my existence cheerfully on the venture, that if Lady Annabel would only relent towards Cadurcis, we should all be the happiest people in the world.'

'Heigho!' said Venetia. 'There are other cares in our house besides our unfortunate acquaintance with your cousin. We were the last people in the world with whom he should ever have become connected.'

'And yet it was an intimacy that commenced auspiciously,' said her friend. 'I am sure I have sat with Cadurcis, and listened to him by the hour, while he has told me of all the happy days at Cherbury when you were both children; the only happy days, according to him, that he ever knew.'

'Yes! they were happy days,' said Venetia.

'And what connection could have offered a more rational basis for felicity than your union?' he continued. 'Whatever the world may think, I, who know Cadurcis to the very bottom of his heart, feel assured that you never would have repented for an instant becoming the sharer of his life; your families were of equal rank, your estates joined, he felt for your mother the affection of a son. There seemed every element that could have contributed to earthly bliss. As for his late career, you who know all have already, have always indeed, viewed it with charity. Placed in his position, who could have acted otherwise? I know very well that his genius, which might recommend him to another woman, is viewed by your mother with more than apprehension. It is true that a man of his exquisite sensibility requires sympathies as refined to command his nature. It is no common mind that could maintain its hold over Cadurcis, and his spirit could not yield but to rare and transcendent qualities. He found them, Venetia, he found them in her whom he had known longest and most intimately, and loved from his boyhood. Talk of constancy, indeed! who has been so constant as my cousin? No, Venetia! you may think fit to bow to the feelings of your mother, and it would be impertinence in me to doubt for an instant the propriety of your conduct: I do not doubt it; I admire it; I admire you, and everything you have done; none can view your behaviour throughout all these painful transactions with more admiration, I might even say with more reverence, than myself; but, Venetia, you never can persuade me, you have never attempted to persuade me, that you yourself are incredulous of the strength and permanency of my cousin's love.'

'Ah, George! you are our friend!' said Venetia, a tear stealing down her cheek. 'But, indeed, we must not talk of these things. As for myself, I think not of happiness. I am certain I am not born to be happy. I wish only to live calmly;

contentedly, I would say; but that, perhaps, is too much. My feelings have been so harrowed, my mind so harassed, during these last few years, and so many causes of pain and misery seem ever hovering round my existence, that I do assure you, my dear friend, I have grown old before my time. Ah! you may smile, George, but my heart is heavy; it is indeed.'

'I wish I could lighten it,' said Captain Cadurcis. 'I fear I am somewhat selfish in wishing you to marry my cousin, for then you know I should have a permanent and authentic claim to your regard. But no one, at least I think so, can feel more deeply interested in your welfare than I do. I never knew any one like you, and I always tell Cadurcis so, and that I think makes him worse, but I cannot help it.'

Venetia could not refrain from smiling at the simplicity of this confession.

'Well,' continued her companion,' everything, after all, is for the best. You and Plantagenet are both very young; I live in hopes that I shall yet see you Lady Cadurcis.'

Venetia shook her head, but was not sorry that their somewhat melancholy conversation should end in a livelier vein. So they entered the villa.

The hour of parting was painful, and the natural gaiety of Captain Cadurcis deserted him. He had become greatly attached to the Herberts. Without any female relatives of his own, their former intimacy and probable connection with his cousin had taught him to look upon them in some degree in the light of kindred. He had originally indeed become acquainted with them in all the blaze of London society, not very calculated to bring out the softer tints and more subdued tones of our character, but even then the dignified grace of Lady Annabel and the radiant beauty of Venetia, had captivated him, and he had cultivated their society with assiduity and extreme pleasure. The grand crisis of his cousin's fortunes had enabled him to become intimate with the more secret and serious qualities of Venetia, and from that moment he had taken the deepest interest in everything connected with her. His happy and unexpected meeting in Italy had completed the spell; and now that he was about to leave them, uncertain even if they should ever meet again, his soft heart trembled, and he could scarcely refrain from tears as he pressed their hands, and bade them his sincere adieus.

The moon had risen, ere he entered his boat, and flung a rippling line of glittering light on the bosom of the lake. The sky was without a cloud, save a few thin fleecy vapours that hovered over the azure brow of a distant mountain. The shores of the lake were suffused with the serene effulgence, and every object was so distinct, that the eye was pained by the lights of the villages, that every instant became more numerous and vivid. The bell of a small chapel on the opposite shore, and the distant chant of some fishermen still working at their nets, were the only sounds that broke the silence which they did not disturb. Reclined in his boat, George Cadurcis watched the vanishing villa of the Herberts, until the light in the principal chamber was the only sign that assured him of its site. That chamber held Venetia, the unhappy Venetia! He covered his face with his hand when even the light of her chamber vanished, and, full of thoughts tender and disconsolate, he at length arrived at Arona.

CHAPTER III.

Pursuant to their plans, the Herberts left the Lago Maggiore towards the end of October, and proceeded by gentle journeys to the Apennines. Before they crossed this barrier, they were to rest awhile in one of the Lombard cities; and now they were on the point of reaching Arquâ, which Venetia had expressed a strong desire to visit.

At the latter part of the last century, the race of tourists, the offspring of a long peace, and the rapid fortunes made during the war, did not exist. Travelling was then confined to the aristocracy, and though the English, when opportunity offered, have ever been a restless people, the gentle bosom of the Euganean Hills was then rarely disturbed amid its green and sequestered valleys.

There is not perhaps in all the Italian region, fertile as it is in interesting associations and picturesque beauty, a spot that tradition and nature have so completely combined to hallow, as the last residence of Petrarch. It seems, indeed, to have been formed for the retirement of a pensive and poetic spirit. It recedes from the world by a succession of delicate acclivities clothed with vineyards and orchards, until, winding within these hills, the mountain hamlet is at length discovered, enclosed by two ridges that slope towards each other, and seem to shut out all the passions of a troubled race. The houses are scattered at intervals on the steep sides of these summits, and on a little knoll is the mansion of the poet, built by himself, and commanding a rich and extensive view, that ends only with the shores of the Adriatic sea. His tomb, a sarcophagus of red marble, supported by pillars, doubtless familiar to the reader, is at hand; and, placed on an elevated site, gives a solemn impression to a scene, of which the character would otherwise be serenely cheerful.

Our travellers were surprised to find that the house of the poet was inhabited by a very different tenant to the rustic occupier they had anticipated. They heard that a German gentleman had within the last year fixed upon it as the residence of himself and his wife. The peasants were profuse in their panegyrics of this visitor, whose arrival had proved quite an era in the history of their village. According to them, a kinder and more charitable gentleman never breathed; his whole life was spent in studying and contributing to the happiness of those around him. The sick, the sorrowful, and the needy were ever sure of finding a friend in him, and merit a generous patron. From him came portions to the portionless; no village maiden need despair of being united to her betrothed, while he could assist her; and at his own cost he had sent to the academy of Bologna, a youth whom his father would have made a cowherd, but whom nature predisposed to be a painter. The inhabitants believed this benevolent and generous person was a physician, for he attended the sick, prescribed for their complaints, and had once even performed an operation with great success. It seemed that, since Petrarch, no one had ever been so popular at Arquâ as this kind German. Lady Annabel and Venetia were interested with the animated narratives of the ever-active beneficence of this good man, and Lady Annabel especially regretted that his absence deprived her of the gratification of becoming acquainted with a character so rare and so invaluable. In the meantime they availed themselves of the offer of his servants to view the house of Petrarch, for their master had left orders, that his absence should never deprive a pilgrim from paying his homage to the shrine of genius.

The house, consisting of two floors, had recently been repaired by the present occupier. It was simply furnished. The ground-floor was allotted to the servants. The upper story contained five rooms, three of which were of good size, and two closets. In one of these were the traditionary chair and table of Petrarch, and here, according to their guides, the master of the house passed a great portion of his time in study, to which, by their account, he seemed devoted. The adjoining chamber was his library; its windows opened on a balcony looking on two lofty and conical hills, one topped with a convent, while the valley opened on the side and spread into a calm and very pleasant view. Of the other apartments, one served as a saloon, but there was nothing in it remarkable, except an admirably painted portrait of a beautiful woman, which the servant informed them was their mistress.

'But that surely is not a German physiognomy?' said Lady Annabel.

'The mistress is an Italian,' replied the servant.

'She is very handsome, of whatever nation she may be,' replied Lady Annabel.

'Oh! how I should have liked to have met these happy people, mamma,' said Venetia, 'for happy they surely must be.'

'They seem to be good people,' said Lady Annabel. 'It really lightened my heart to hear of all this gentleman's kind deeds.'

'Ah! if the signora only knew the master,' said their guide, 'she would indeed know a good man.'

They descended to the garden, which certainly was not like the garden of their villa; it had been but lately a wilderness of laurels, but there were evidences that the eye and hand of taste were commencing its restoration with effect.

'The master did this,' said their guide. 'He will allow no one to work in the garden but himself. It is a week since he went to Bologna, to see our Paulo. He gained a prize at the academy, and his father begged the master to be present when it was conferred on him; he said it would do his son so much good! So the master went, though it is the only time he has quitted Quâ since he came to reside here.'

'And how long has he resided here?' inquired Venetia.

"Tis the second autumn,' said the guide, 'and he came in the spring. If the signora would only wait, we expect the master home to-night or to-morrow, and he would be glad to see her.'

'We cannot wait, my friend,' said Lady Annabel, rewarding the guide; 'but you will thank your master in our names, for the kindness we have experienced. You are all happy in such a friend.'

'I must write my name in Petrarch's house,' said Venetia. 'Adieu, happy Arquâ! Adieu, happy dwellers in this happy valley!'

CHAPTER IV.

Just as Lady Annabel and her daughter arrived at Rovigo, one of those sudden and violent storms that occasionally occur at the termination of an Italian autumn raged with irresistible fury. The wind roared with a noise that overpowered the thunder; then came a rattling shower of hail, with stones as big as pigeons' eggs, succeeded by rain, not in showers, but literally in cataracts. The only thing to which a tempest of rain in Italy can be compared is the bursting of a waterspout. Venetia could scarcely believe that this could be the same day of which the golden morning had found her among the sunny hills of Arquâ. This unexpected vicissitude induced Lady Annabel to alter her plans, and she resolved to rest at Rovigo, where she was glad to find that they could be sheltered in a commodious inn.

The building had originally been a palace, and in its halls and galleries, and the vast octagonal vestibule on which the principal apartments opened, it retained many noble indications of the purposes to which it was formerly destined.

At present, a lazy innkeeper who did nothing; his bustling wife, who seemed equally at home in the saloon, the kitchen, and even the stable; and a solitary waiter, were the only inmates, except the Herberts, and a travelling party, who had arrived shortly after them, and who, like them, had been driven by stress of weather to seek refuge at a place where otherwise they had not intended to remain.

A blazing fire of pine wood soon gave cheerfulness to the vast and somewhat desolate apartment into which our friends had been ushered; their sleeping-room was adjoining, but separated. In spite of the lamentations of Pauncefort, who had been drenched to the skin, and who required much more waiting upon than her mistress, Lady Annabel and Venetia at length produced some degree of comfort. They drew the table near the fire; they ensconced themselves behind an old screen; and, producing their books and work notwithstanding the tempest, they contrived to domesticate themselves at Rovigo.

'I cannot help thinking of Arquâ and its happy tenants, mamma,' said Venetia.

'And yet, perhaps, they may have their secret sorrows,' said Lady Annabel. 'I know not why, I always associate seclusion with unhappiness.'

Venetia remembered Cherbury. Their life at Cherbury was like the life of the German at Arquâ. A chance visitor to Cherbury in their absence, viewing the beautiful residence and the fair domain, and listening to the tales which they well might hear of all her mother's grace and goodness, might perhaps too envy its happy occupiers. But were they happy? Had they no secret sorrows? Was their seclusion associated with unhappiness? These were reflections that made Venetia grave; but she opened her journal, and, describing the adventures and feelings of the morning, she dissipated some mournful reminiscences.

The storm still raged, Venetia had quitted the saloon in which her mother and herself had been sitting, and had repaired to the adjoining chamber to fetch a book. The door of this room opened, as all the other entrances of the different apartments, on to the octagonal vestibule. Just as she was quitting the room, and about to return to her mother, the door of the opposite chamber opened, and there came forward a gentleman in a Venetian dress of black velvet. His stature was much above the middle height, though his figure, which was remarkably slender, was bowed; not by years certainly, for his countenance, though singularly emaciated, still retained traces of youth. His hair, which he wore very long, descended over his shoulders, and must originally have been of a light golden colour, but now was severely touched with grey. His countenance was very pallid, so colourless indeed that its aspect was almost unearthly; but his large blue eyes, that were deeply set in his majestic brow, still glittered with fire, and their expression alone gave life to a visage, which, though singularly beautiful in its outline, from its faded and attenuated character seemed rather the countenance of a corpse than of a breathing being.

The glance of the stranger caught that of Venetia, and seemed to fascinate her. She suddenly became motionless; wildly she stared at the stranger, who, in his turn, seemed arrested in his progress, and stood still as a statue, with his eyes fixed with absorbing interest on the beautiful apparition before him. An expression of perplexity and pain flitted over the amazed features of Venetia; and then it seemed that, by some almost supernatural effort, confusion amounting to stupefaction suddenly brightened and expanded into keen and overwhelming intelligence. Exclaiming in a frenzied tone, 'My father!' Venetia sprang forward, and fell senseless on the stranger's breast.

Such, after so much mystery, so many aspirations, so much anxiety, and so much suffering, such was the first meeting of Venetia Herbert with her father!

Marmion Herbert, himself trembling and speechless, bore the apparently lifeless Venetia into his apartment. Not permitting her for a moment to quit his embrace, he seated himself, and gazed silently on the inanimate and unknown form he held so strangely within his arms. Those lips, now closed as if in death, had uttered however one word which thrilled to his heart, and still echoed, like a supernatural annunciation, within his ear. He examined with an eye of agitated scrutiny the fair features no longer sensible of his presence. He gazed upon that transparent brow, as if he would read some secret in its pellucid veins; and touched those long locks of golden hair with a trembling finger, that seemed to be wildly seeking for some vague and miraculous proof of inexpressible identity. The fair creature had called him 'Father.' His dreaming reveries had never pictured a being half so beautiful! She called him 'Father!' Tha word had touched his brain, as lightning cuts a tree. He looked around him with a distracted air, then gazed on the tranced form he held with a glance which would have penetrated her soul, and murmured unconsciously the wild word she had uttered. She called him 'Father!' He dared not think who she might be. His thoughts were wandering in a distant land; visions of another life, another country, rose before him, troubled and obscure. Baffled aspirations, and hopes blighted in the bud, and the cherished secrets of his lorn existence, clustered like clouds upon his perplexed, yet creative, brain. She called him, 'Father!' It was a word to make him mad. 'Father!' This beautiful being had called him 'Father,' and seemed to have expired, as it were, in the irresistible expression. His heart yearned to her; he had met her embrace with an inexplicable sympathy; her devotion had seemed, as it were, her duty and his right. Yet who was she? He was a father. It was a fact, a fact alike full of solace and mortification, the consciousness of which never deserted him. But he was the father of an unknown child; to him the child of his poetic dreams, rather than his reality. And now there came this radiant creature, and called him 'Father!' Was he awake, and in the harsh busy world; or was it the apparition of au over-excited imagination, brooding too constantly on one fond idea, on which he now gazed so fixedly? Was this some spirit? Would that she would speak again! Would that those sealed lips would part and utter but one word, would but again call him 'Father,' and he asked no more!

'Father!' to be called 'Father' by one whom he could not name, by one over whom he mused in solitude, by one to whom he had poured forth all the passion of his desolate soul; to be called 'Father' by this being was the aspiring secret of his life. He had painted her to himself in his loneliness, he had conjured up dreams of ineffable loveliness, and inexpressible love; he had led with her an imaginary life of thrilling tenderness; he had indulged in a delicious fancy of mutual interchange of the most exquisite offices of our nature; and then, when he had sometimes looked around him, and found no daughter there, no beaming countenance of purity to greet him with its constant smile, and receive the quick and ceaseless tribute of his vigilant affection, the tears had stolen down his lately-excited features, all the consoling beauty of his visions had vanished into air, he had felt the deep curse of his desolation, and had anathematised the cunning brain that made his misery a thousand-fold keener by the mockery of its transporting illusions.

And now there came this transcendent creature, with a form more glowing than all his dreams; a voice more musical than a seraphic chorus, though it had uttered but one thrilling word: there came this transcendent creature, beaming with grace, beauty, and love, and had fallen upon his heart, and called him 'Father!'

Herbert looked up to heaven as if waiting for some fresh miracle to terminate the harrowing suspense of his tortured mind; Herbert looked down upon his mysterious companion; the rose was gradually returning to her cheek, her lips seemed to tremble with reviving breath. There was only one word more strange to his ear than that which she had uttered, but an irresistible impulse sent forth the sound.

'Venetia!' he exclaimed.

The eyes of the maiden slowly opened; she stared around her with a vague glance of perplexity, not unmingled with pain; she looked up; she caught the rapt gaze of her father, bending over her with fondness yet with fear; his lips moved, for a moment they refused to articulate, yet at length they again uttered, 'Venetia!' And the only response she made was to cling to him with nervous energy, and hide her face in his bosom.

Herbert pressed her to his heart. Yet even now he hesitated to credit the incredible union. Again he called her by her name, but added with rising confidence, 'My Venetia!'

'Your child, your child,' she murmured. 'Your own Venetia.'

He pressed his lips to hers; he breathed over her a thousand blessings; she felt his tears trickling on her neck.

At length Venetia looked up and sighed; she was exhausted by the violence of her emotions: her father relaxed his grasp with infinite tenderness, watching her with delicate solicitude; she leaned her arm upon his shoulder with downcast eyes.

Herbert gently took her disengaged hand, and pressed it to his lips. 'I am as in a dream,' murmured Venetia.

'The daughter of my heart has found her sire,' said Herbert in an impassioned voice. 'The father who has long lived upon her fancied image; the father, I fear, she has been bred up to hate.'

'Oh! no, no!' said Venetia, speaking rapidly and with a slight shiver; 'not hate! it was a secret, his being was a secret, his name was never mentioned; it was unknown.'

'A secret! My existence a secret from my child, my beautiful fond child!' exclaimed Herbert in a tone even more desolate than bitter. 'Why did they not let you at least hate me!'

'My father!' said Venetia, in a firmer voice, and with returning animation, yet gazing around her with a still distracted air, 'Am I with my father? The clouds clear from my brain. I remember that we met. Where was it? Was it at Arquâ? In the garden? I am with my father!' she continued in a rapid tone and with a wild smile. 'Oh! let me look on him;' and she turned round, and gazed upon Herbert with a serious scrutiny. 'Are you my father?' she continued, in a still, small voice. 'Your hair has grown grey since last I saw you; it was golden then, like mine. I know you are my father,' she added, after a pause, and in a tone almost of gaiety. 'You cannot deceive me. I know your name. They did not tell it me; I found it out myself, but it made me very ill, very; and I do not think I have ever been quite well since. You are Marmion Herbert. My mother had a dog called Marmion, when I was a little girl, but I did not know I had a father then.'

'Venetia!' exclaimed Herbert, with streaming eyes, as he listened with anguish to these incoherent sentences. 'My Venetia loves me!'

'Oh! she always loved you,' replied Venetia; always, always. Before she knew her father she loved him. I dare say you think I do not love you, because I am not used to speak to a father. Everything must be learnt, you know,' she said, with a faint, sad smile; 'and then it was so sudden! I do not think my mother knows it yet. And after all, though I found you out in a moment, still, I know not why, I thought it was a picture. But I read your verses, and I knew them by heart at once; but now my memory has worn out, for I am ill, and everything has gone cross with me. And all because my father wrote me verses. 'Tis very strange, is not it?'

'Sweet lamb of my affections,' exclaimed Herbert to himself, 'I fear me much this sudden meeting with one from whose bosom you ought never to have been estranged, has been for the moment too great a trial for this delicate brain.'

'I will not tell my mother,' said Venetia; 'she will be angry.'

'Your mother, darling; where is your mother?' said Herbert, looking, if possible, paler than he was wont.

She was at Arquâ with me, and on the lake for months, but where we are now, I cannot say. If I could only remember where we are now,' she added with earnestness, and with a struggle to collect herself, 'I should know everything.'

'This is Rovigo, my child, the inn of Rovigo. You are travelling with your mother. Is it not so?'

'Yes! and we came this morning, and it rained. Now I know everything,' said Venetia, with an animated and even cheerful air.

'And we met in the vestibule, my sweet,' continued Herbert, in a soothing voice; 'we came out of opposite chambers, and you knew me; my Venetia knew me. Try to tell me, my darling,' he added, in a tone of coaxing fondness, 'try to remember how Venetia knew her father.'

'He was so like his picture at Cherbury,' replied Venetia.

'Cherbury!' exclaimed Herbert, with a deep-drawn sigh.

'Only your hair has grown grey, dear father; but it is long, quite as long as in your picture.'

'Her dog called Marmion!' murmured Herbert to himself, 'and my portrait, too! You saw your father's portrait, then, every day, love?'

'Oh, no! said Venetia, shaking her head, 'only once, only once. And I never told mamma. It was where no one could go, but I went there one day. It was in a room that no one ever entered except mamma, but I entered it. I stole the key, and had a fever, and in my fever I confessed all. But I never knew it. Mamma never told me I confessed it, until many, many years afterwards. It was the first, the only time she ever mentioned to me your name, my father.'

'And she told you to shun me, to hate me? She told you I was a villain, a profligate, a demon? eh? eh? Was it not so, Venetia?'

'She told me that you had broken her heart,' said Venetia; 'and she prayed to God that her child might not be so miserable.'

'Oh, my Venetia!' exclaimed Herbert, pressing her to his breast, and in a voice stifled with emotion, 'I feel now we might have been happy!'

In the meantime the prolonged absence of her daughter surprised Lady Annabel. At length she rose, and walked into their adjoining apartment, but to her surprise Venetia was not there. Returning to her saloon, she found Pauncefort and the waiter arranging the table for dinner.

'Where is Miss Herbert, Pauncefort?' inquired Lady Annabel.

'I am sure, my lady, I cannot say. I have no doubt she is in the other room.'

'She is not there, for I have just quitted it,' replied Lady Annabel. 'How very strange! You have not seen the signora?' inquired Lady Annabel of the waiter.

'The signora is in the room with the gentleman.'

'The gentleman!' exclaimed Lady Annabel. 'Tell me, good man, what do you mean? I am inquiring for my daughter.'

'I know well the signora is talking of her daughter,' replied the waiter.

'But do you know my daughter by sight? Surely you you must mean some one else.'

'Do I know the signora's daughter?' said the waiter. 'The beautiful young lady, with hair like Santa Marguerita, in the church of the Holy Trinity! I tell the signora, I saw her carried into numero 4, in the arms of the Signor Forestiere, who arrived this morning.'

'Venetia is ill,' said Lady Annabel. 'Show me to the room, my friend.'

Lady Annabel accordingly, with a hurried step, following her guide, quitted the chamber. Pauncefort remained fixed to the earth, the very picture of perplexity.

'Well, to be sure!' she exclaimed, 'was anything ever so strange! In the arms of Signor Forestiere! Forestiere. An English name. There is no person of the name of Forest that I know. And in his arms, too! I should not wonder if it was my lord after all. Well, I should be glad if he were to come to light again, for, after all, my lady may say what she likes, but if Miss Venetia don't marry Lord Cadurcis, I must say marriages were never made in heaven!'

CHAPTER V.

The waiter threw open the door of Mr. Herbert's chamber, and Lady Annabel swept in with a majesty she generally assumed when about to meet strangers. The first thing she beheld was her daughter in the arms of a man whose head was bent, and who was embracing her. Notwithstanding this astounding spectacle, Lady Annabel neither started nor screamed; she only said in an audible tone, and one rather expressing astonishment than agitation, 'Venetia!'

Immediately the stranger looked up, and Lady Annabel beheld her husband!

She was rooted to the earth. She turned deadly pale; for a moment her countenance expressed only terror, but the terror quickly changed into aversion. Suddenly she rushed forward, and exclaimed in a tone in which decision conquered dismay, 'Restore me my child!'

The moment Herbert had recognised his wife he had dexterously disengaged himself from the grasp of Venetia, whom he left on the chair, and meeting Lady Annabel with extended arms, that seemed to deprecate her wrath, he said, 'I seek not to deprive you of her; she is yours, and she is worthy of you; but respect, for a few moments, the feelings of a father who has met his only child in a manner so unforeseen.'

The presence of her mother instantaneously restored Venetia to herself. Her mind was in a moment cleared and settled. Her past and peculiar life, and all its incidents, recurred to her with their accustomed order, vividness, and truth. She thoroughly comprehended her present situation. Actuated by long-cherished feelings and the necessity of the occasion, she rose and threw herself at her mother's feet and exclaimed, 'O mother! he is my father, love him!'

Lady Annabel stood with an averted countenance, Venetia clinging to her hand, which she had caught when she rushed forward, and which now fell passive by Lady Annabel's side, giving no sign, by any pressure or motion, of the slightest sympathy with her daughter, or feeling for the strange and agonising situation in which they were both placed.

'Annabel,' said Herbert, in a voice that trembled, though the speaker struggled to appear calm, 'be charitable! I have never intruded upon your privacy; I will not now outrage it. Accident, or some diviner motive, has brought us together this day. If you will not treat me with kindness, look not upon me with aversion before our child.'

Still she was silent and motionless, her countenance hidden from her husband and her daughter, but her erect and haughty form betokening her inexorable mind. 'Annabel,' said Herbert, who had now withdrawn to some distance, and leant against a pillar, 'will not then nearly twenty years of desolation purchase one moment of intercourse? I have injured you. Be it so. This is not the moment I will defend myself. But have I not suffered? Is not this meeting a punishment deeper even than your vengeance could devise? Is it nothing to behold this beautiful child, and feel that she is only yours? Annabel, look on me, look on me only one moment! My frame is bowed, my hair is grey, my heart is withered; the principle of existence waxes faint and slack in this attenuated frame. I am no longer that Herbert on whom you once smiled, but a man stricken with many sorrows. The odious conviction of my life cannot long haunt you; yet a little while, and my memory will alone remain. Think of this, Annabel; I beseech you, think of it. Oh! believe me, when the speedy hour arrives that will consign me to the grave, where I shall at least find peace, it will not be utterly without satisfaction that you will remember that we met if even by accident, and parted at least not with harshness!'

'Mother, dearest mother!' murmured Venetia, 'speak to him, look on him!'

'Venetia,' said her mother, without turning her head, but in a calm, firm tone, 'your father has seen you, has conversed with you. Between your father and myself there can be nothing to communicate, either of fact or feeling. Now let us depart.'

'No, no, not depart!' said Venetia franticly. 'You did not say depart, dear mother! I cannot go,' she added in a low and half-hysterical voice.

'Desert me, then,' said the mother. 'A fitting consequence of your private communications with your father,' she added in a tone of bitter scorn; and Lady Annabel moved to depart, but Venetia, still kneeling, clung to her convulsively.

'Mother, mother, you shall not go; you shall not leave me; we will never part, mother,' continued Venetia, in a tone almost of violence, as she perceived her mother give no indication of yielding to her wish. 'Are my feelings then nothing?' she then exclaimed. 'Is this your sense of my fidelity? Am I for ever to be a victim?' She loosened her hold of her mother's hand, her mother moved on, Venetia fell upon her forehead and uttered a faint scream. The heart of Lady Annabel relented when she fancied her daughter suffered physical pain, however slight; she hesitated, she turned, she hastened to her child; her husband had simultaneously advanced; in the rapid movement and confusion her hand touched that of Herbert.

'I yield her to you, Annabel,' said Herbert, placing Venetia in her mother's arms. 'You mistake me, as you have often mistaken me, if you think I seek to practise on the feelings of this angelic child. She is yours; may she compensate you for the misery I have caused you, but never sought to occasion!'

'I am not hurt, dear mother,' said Venetia, as her mother tenderly examined her forehead. 'Dear, dear mother, why did you reproach me?'

'Forget it,' said Lady Annabel, in a softened tone; 'for indeed you are irreproachable.'

'O Annabel!' said Herbert, 'may not this child be some atonement, this child, of whom I solemnly declare I would not deprive you, though I would willingly forfeit my life for a year of her affection; and your, your sufferance,' he added.

'Mother! speak to him,' said Venetia, with her head on her mother's bosom, who still, however, remained rigidly standing. But Lady Annabel was silent.

'Your mother was ever stern and cold, Venetia,' said Herbert, the bitterness of his heart at length expressing itself.

'Never,' said Venetia, with great energy; 'never; you know not my mother. Was she stern and cold when she visited each night in secret your portrait?' said Venetia, looking round upon her astonished father, with her bright grey eye. 'Was she stern and cold when she wept over your poems, those poems whose characters your own hand had traced? Was she stern and cold when she hung a withered wreath on your bridal bed, the bed to which I owe my miserable being? Oh, no, my father! sad was the hour of separation for my mother and yourself. It may have dimmed the lustre of her eye, and shaded your locks with premature grey; but whatever may have been its inscrutable cause, there was one victim of that dark hour, less thought of than yourselves, and yet a greater sufferer than both, the being in whose heart you implanted affections, whose unfulfilled tenderness has made that wretched thing they call your daughter.'

'Annabel!' exclaimed Herbert, rapidly advancing, with an imploring gesture, and speaking in a tone of infinite anguish, 'Annabel, Annabel, even now we can be happy!'

The countenance of his wife was troubled, but its stern expression had disappeared. The long-concealed, yet at length irrepressible, emotion of Venetia had touched her heart. In the conflict of affection between the claims of her two parents, Lady Annabel had observed with a sentiment of sweet emotion, in spite of all the fearfulness of the meeting, that Venetia had not faltered in her devotion to her mother. The mental torture of her child touched her to the quick. In the excitement of her anguish, Venetia had expressed a profound sentiment, the irresistible truth of which Lady Annabel could no longer withstand. She had too long and too fondly schooled herself to look upon the outraged wife as the only victim. There was then, at length it appeared to this stern-minded woman, another. She had laboured in the flattering delusion that the devotion of a mother's love might compensate to

Venetia for the loss of that other parent, which in some degree Lady Annabel had occasioned her; for the worthless husband, had she chosen to tolerate the degrading connection, might nevertheless have proved a tender father. But Nature, it seemed, had shrunk from the vain effort of the isolated mother. The seeds of affection for the father of her being were mystically implanted in the bosom of his child. Lady Annabel recalled the harrowing hours that this attempt by her to curb and control the natural course and rising sympathies of filial love had cost her child, on whom she had so vigilantly practised it. She recalled her strange aspirations, her inspired curiosity, her brooding reveries, her fitful melancholy, her terrible illness, her resignation, her fidelity, her sacrifices: there came across the mind of Lady Annabel a mortifying conviction that the devotion to her child, on which she had so rated herself, might after all only prove a subtle form of profound selfishness; and that Venetia, instead of being the idol of her love, might eventually be the martyr of her pride. And, thinking of these things, she wept.

This evidence of emotion, which in such a spirit Herbert knew how to estimate, emboldened him to advance; he fell on one knee before her and her daughter; gently he stole her hand, and pressed it to his lips. It was not withdrawn, and Venetia laid her hand upon theirs, and would have bound them together had her mother been relentless. It seemed to Venetia that she was at length happy, but she would not speak, she would not disturb the still and silent bliss of the impending reconciliation. Was it then indeed at hand? In truth, the deportment of Herbert throughout the whole interview, so delicate, so subdued, so studiously avoiding the slightest rivalry with his wife in the affections of their child, and so carefully abstaining from attempting in the slightest degree to control the feelings of Venetia, had not been lost upon Lady Annabel. And when she thought of him, so changed from what he had been, grey, bent, and careworn, with all the lustre that had once so fascinated her, faded, and talking of that impending fate which his wan though spiritual countenance too clearly intimated, her heart melted.

Suddenly the door burst open, and there stalked into the room a woman of eminent but most graceful stature, and of a most sovereign and voluptuous beauty. She was habited in the Venetian dress; her dark eyes glittered with fire, her cheek was inflamed with no amiable emotion, and her long black hair was disordered by the violence of her gesture.

'And who are these?' she exclaimed in a shrill voice.

All started; Herbert sprang up from his position with a glance of withering rage. Venetia was perplexed, Lady Annabel looked round, and recognised the identical face, however distorted by passion, that she had admired in the portrait at Arquâ.

'And who are these?' exclaimed the intruder, advancing. 'Perfidious Marmion! to whom do you dare to kneel?'

Lady Annabel drew herself up to a height that seemed to look down even upon this tall stranger. The expression of majestic scorn that she cast upon the intruder made her, in spite of all her violence and excitement, tremble and be silent: she felt cowed she knew not why.

'Come, Venetia,' said Lady Annabel with all her usual composure, 'let me save my daughter at least from this profanation,'

'Annabel!' said Herbert, rushing after them, 'be charitable, be just!' He followed them to the threshold of the door; Venetia was silent, for she was alarmed.

'Adieu, Marmion!' said Lady Annabel, looking over her shoulder with a bitter smile, but placing her daughter before her, as if to guard her. 'Adieu, Marmion! adieu for ever!'

CHAPTER VI.

The moon shone brightly on the house of Petrarch, and the hamlet slept in peace. Not a sound was heard, save the shrill voice of the grasshoppers, so incessant that its monotony blended, as it were, with the stillness. Over the green hills and the far expanse of the sheeny plain, the beautiful light of heaven fell with all the magical repose of the serene hour, an hour that brought to one troubled breast, and one distracted spirit, in that still and simple village, no quietude.

Herbert came forth into the balcony of his residence, and leaning over the balustrade, revolved in his agitated mind the strange and stirring incidents of the day. His wife and his child had quitted the inn of Rovigo instantly after that mortifying rencounter that had dashed so cruelly to the ground all his sweet and quickly-rising hopes. As for his companion, she had by his peremptory desire returned to Arquâ alone; he was not in a mood to endure her society; but he had conducted himself to her mildly, though with firmness; he had promised to follow her, and, in pursuance of his pledge, he rode home alone.

He was greeted on his return by his servant, full of the the visit of the morning. With an irresistible curiosity, Herbert had made him describe every incident that had occurred, and repeat a hundred times every word that the visitors had uttered. He listened with some consolation, however mournful, to his wife's praises of the unknown stranger's life; he gazed with witching interest upon the autograph of his daughter on the wall of his library. He had not confessed to his mistress the relation which the two strangers bore to him; yet he was influenced in concealing the real circumstances, only by an indefinite sentiment, that made him reluctant to acknowledge to her ties so pure. The feelings of the parent overpowered the principles of the philosopher. This lady indeed, although at the moment she had indulged in so violent an ebullition of temper, possessed little influence over the mind of her companion. Herbert, however fond of solitude, required in his restricted world the graceful results of feminine superintendence. Time had stilled his passions, and cooled the fervour of his soul. The age of his illusions had long passed. This was a connection that had commenced in no extravagant or romantic mood, and perhaps for that reason had endured. He had become acquainted with her on his first unknown arrival in Italy, from America, now nearly two years back. It had been maintained on his side by a temper naturally sweet, and which, exhausted by years of violent emotion, now required only repose; seeking, in a female friend, a form that should not outrage an eye ever musing on the beautiful, and a disposition that should contribute to his comfort, and never ruffle his feelings. Separated from his wife by her own act, whatever might have been its impulse, and for so long an interval, it was a connection which the world in general might have looked upon with charity, which in her calmer hours one would imagine even Lady Annabel might have glanced over without much bitterness. Certainly it was one which, under all the circumstances of the case, could scarcely be esteemed by her as an outrage or an insult; but even Herbert felt, with all his philosophy and proud freedom from prejudice, that the rencounter of the morning was one which no woman could at the moment tolerate, few eventually excuse, and which of all incidents was that which would most tend to confirm his wife in her stoical obduracy. Of his offences towards her, whatever were their number or their quality, this surely was the least, and yet its results upon his life and fortunes would in all probability only be equalled by the mysterious cause of their original separation. But how much more bitter than that original separation was their present parting! Mortifying and annoying as had been the original occurrence, it was one that many causes and considerations combined to enable Herbert to support. He was then in the very prime of youth, inexperienced, sanguine, restless, and adventurous, with the whole world and its unknown results before him, and freedom for which he ever sighed to compensate for the loss of that domestic joy that he was then unable to appreciate. But now twenty years, which, in the career of such a spirit, were equal to a century of the existence of coarser clay, had elapsed; he was bowed with thought and suffering, if not by time; his conscience was light, but it was sad; his illusions had all vanished; he knew the world, and all that the world could bring, and he disregarded them; and the result of all his profound study, lofty aspirations, and great conduct was, that he sighed for rest. The original catastrophe had been merely a separation between a husband and a wife; the one that had just happened, involved other feelings; the father was also separated from his child, and a child of such surpassing qualities, that his brief acquaintance with her had alone sufficed to convert his dream of domestic repose into a vision of domestic bliss.

Beautiful Venetia! so fair, and yet so dutiful; with a bosom teeming with such exquisite sensibilities, and a mind bright with such acute and elevated intelligence! An abstract conception of the sentiments that might subsist between a father and a daughter, heightened by all the devices of a glowing imagination, had haunted indeed occasionally the solitary musing of Marmion Herbert; but what was this creation of his poetic brain compared with the reality that now had touched his human heart? Vainly had he believed that repose was the only solace that remained for his exhausted spirit. He found that a new passion now swayed his soul; a passion, too, that he had never proved; of a nature most peculiar; pure, gentle, refined, yet ravishing and irresistible, compared with which all former transports, no matter how violent, tumultuous, and exciting, seemed evanescent and superficial: they were indeed the wind, the fire, and the tempest that had gone before, but this was the still small voice that followed, excelled, and survived their might and majesty, unearthly and eternal!

His heart melted to his daughter, nor did he care to live without her love and presence. His philosophical theories all vanished. He felt how dependent we are in this world on our natural ties, and how limited, with all his arrogance, is the sphere of man. Dreaming of philanthropy, he had broken his wife's heart, and bruised, perhaps irreparably, the spirit of his child; he had rendered those miserable who depended on his love, and for whose affection his heart now yearned to that degree, that he could not contemplate existence without their active sympathy.

Was it then too late! Was it then impossible to regain that Paradise he had forfeited so weakly, and of whose amaranthine bowers, but a few hours since, he had caught such an entrancing glimpse, of which the gate for a moment seemed about to re-open! In spite of all, then, Annabel still loved him, loved him passionately, visited his picture, mused over the glowing expression of their loves, wept over the bridal bed so soon deserted! She had a dog, too, when Venetia was a child, and called it Marmion.

The recollection of this little trait, so trifling, yet so touching, made him weep even with wildness. The tears poured down his cheeks in torrents, he sobbed convulsively, his very heart seemed to burst. For some minutes he leant over the balustrade in a paroxysm of grief.

He looked up. The convent hill rose before him, bright in the moon; beneath was his garden; around him the humble roofs that he made happy. It was not without an effort that he recalled the locality, that he remembered he was at Arquâ. And who was sleeping within the house? Not his wife, Annabel was far away with their daughter. The vision of his whole life passed before him. Study and strife, and fame and love; the pride of the philosopher, the rapture of the poet, the blaze of eloquence, the clash of arms, the vows of passion, the execration and the applause of millions; both once alike welcome to his indomitable soul! And what had they borne to him? Misery. He called up the image of his wife, young, beautiful, and noble, with a mind capable of comprehending his loftiest and his finest moods, with a soul of matchless purity, and a temper whose winning tenderness had only been equalled by her elevated sense of self-respect; a woman that might have figured in the days of chivalry, soft enough to be his slave, but too proud to be his victim. He called up her image in the castle of his fathers, exercising in a domain worthy of such a mistress, all those sweet offices of life which here, in this hired roof in a strange land, and with his crippled means, he had yet found solacing. He conjured before him a bud by the side of that beauteous flower, sharing all her lustre and all her fragrance, his own Venetia! What happiness might not have been his? And for what had he forfeited it? A dream, with no dream-like beauty; a perturbed, and restless, and agitated dream, from which he had now woke shattered and exhausted.

He had sacrificed his fortune, he had forfeited his country, he had alienated his wife, and he had lost his child; the home of his heroic ancestry, the ancient land whose fame and power they had created, the beauteous and gifted woman who would have clung for ever to his bosom, and her transcendant offspring worthy of all their loves! Profound philosopher!

The clock of the convent struck the second hour after midnight. Herbert started. And all this time where were Annabel and Venetia? They still lived, they were in the same country, an hour ago they were under the same roof, in the same chamber; their hands had joined, their hearts had opened, for a moment he had dared to believe that all that he cared for might be regained. And why was it not? The cause, the cause? It recurred to him with associations of dislike, of disgust, of wrath, of hatred, of which one whose heart was so tender, and whose reason was so clear, could under the influence of no other feelings have been capable. The surrounding scene, that had so often soothed his mournful soul, and connected it with the last hours of a spirit to whom he bore much resemblance, was now looked upon with aversion. To rid himself of ties, now so dreadful, was all his ambition. He entered the house quickly, and, seating himself in his closet, he wrote these words:

'You beheld this morning my wife and child; we can meet no more. All that I can effect to console you under this sudden separation shall be done. My banker from Bologna will be here in two days; express to him all your wishes.'

It was written, sealed, directed, and left upon the table at which they had so often been seated. Herbert descended into the garden, saddled his horse, and in a few minutes, in the heart of night, had quitted Arquà.

CHAPTER VII.

The moment that the wife of Marmion Herbert re-entered her saloon, she sent for her courier and ordered horses to her carriage instantly. Until they were announced as ready, Lady Annabel walked up and down the room with an impatient step, but was as completely silent as the miserable Venetia, who remained weeping on the sofa. The confusion and curiosity of Mistress Pauncefort were extraordinary. She still had a lurking suspicion that the gentleman was Lord Cadurcis and she seized the first opportunity of leaving the room, and flouncing into that of the stranger, as if by mistake, determined to catch a glimpse of him; but all her notable skill was baffled, for she had scarcely opened the door before she was met by the Italian lady, who received Mistress Pauncefort's ready-made apology, and bowed her away. The faithful attendant then hurried downstairs to crossexamine the waiter, but, though she gained considerable information from that functionary, it was of a perplexing nature; for from him she only learnt that the stranger lived at Arquâ. 'The German gentleman!' soliloquised Mistress Pauncefort; 'and what could he have to say to Miss Venetia! and a married man, too! Well, to be sure, there is nothing like travelling for adventures! And I must say, considering all that I know, and how I have held my tongue for nearly twenty years, I think it is very strange indeed of my lady to have any secrets from me. Secrets, indeed! Poh!' and Mistress Pauncefort flounced again into Lady Annabel's room, with a face of offended pride, knocking the books about, dashing down writing cases, tossing about work, and making as much noise and disturbance as if she had a separate quarrel with every single article under her superintendence.

In the meantime the carriage was prepared, to which they were obliged almost to carry Venetia, feeble and stupefied with grief. Uncertain of her course, but anxious, in the present state of her daughter, for rest and quiet, Lady Annabel ordered the courier to proceed to Padua, at which city they arrived late at night, scarcely a word having been interchanged during the whole journey between Lady Annabel and her child, though infinite were the soft and soothing attentions which the mother lavished upon her. Night, however, brought no rest to Venetia; and the next day, her state appeared so alarming to Lady Annabel, that she would have instantly summoned medical assistance, had it not been for Venetia's strong objections. 'Indeed, dear mother,' she said, 'it is not physicians that I require. They cannot cure me. Let me be quiet.'

The same cause, indeed, which during the last five years had at intervals so seriously menaced the existence of this unhappy girl, was now at work with renovated and even irresistible influence. Her frame could no longer endure the fatal action of her over-excited nerves. Her first illness, however alarming, had been baffled by time, skill, and principally by the vigour of an extremely youthful frame, then a stranger to any serious indisposition. At a later period, the change of life induced by their residence at Weymouth had permitted her again to rally. She had quitted England with renewed symptoms of her former attack, but a still more powerful change, not only of scene, but of climate and country, and the regular and peaceful life she had led on the Lago Maggiore, had again reassured the mind of her anxious mother. This last adventure at Rovigo, however, prostrated her. The strange surprise, the violent development of feeling, the agonising doubts and hopes, the terrible suspense the profound and bitter and overwhelming disappointment, all combined to shake her mind to its very foundations. She felt for the first time, that she could no longer bear up against the torture of her singular position. Her energy was entirely exhausted; she was no longer capable of making the slightest exertion; she took refuge in that torpid resignation that results from utter hopelessness.

Lying on her sofa with her eyes fixed in listless abstraction, the scene at Rovigo flitted unceasingly before her languid vision. At length she had seen that father, that unknown and mysterious father, whose idea had haunted her infancy as if by inspiration; to gain the slightest knowledge of whom had cost her many long and acute suffering; and round whose image for so many years every thought of her intelligence, and every feeling of her heart, had clustered like spirits round some dim and mystical altar, At length she had beheld him; she had gazed on that spiritual countenance; she had listened to the tender accents of that musical voice; within his arms she had been folded with rapture, and pressed to a heart that seemed to beat only for her felicity. The blessing of her father, uttered by his long-loved lips, had descended on her brow, and been sealed with his passionate embrace.

The entrance of her mother, that terrible contest of her lacerated heart, when her two parents, as it were, appealed to her love, which they would not share; the inspiration of her despair, that so suddenly had removed the barriers of long years, before whose irresistible pathos her father had bent a penitent, and her mother's inexorable pride had melted; the ravishing bliss that for a moment had thrilled through her, being experienced too for the first time, when she felt that her parents were again united and bound by the sweet tie of her now happy existence; this was the drama acted before her with an almost ceaseless repetition of its transporting incidents; and when she looked round, and beheld her mother sitting alone, and watching her with a countenance almost of anguish, it was indeed with extreme difficulty that Venetia could persuade herself that all had not been a reverie; and she was only convinced of the contrary by that heaviness of the heart which too quickly assures us of the reality of those sorrows of which fancy for a moment may cheat us into scepticism.

And indeed her mother was scarcely less miserable. The sight of Herbert, so changed from the form that she remembered; those tones of heart-rending sincerity, in which he had mournfully appealed to the influence of time and sorrow on his life, still greatly affected her. She had indulged for a moment in a dream of domestic love, she had cast to the winds the inexorable determination of a life, and had mingled her tears with those of her husband and her child. And how had she been repaid? By a degrading catastrophe, from whose revolting associations her mind recoiled with indignation and disgust. But her lingering feeling for her husband, her own mortification, were as nothing compared with the harrowing anxiety she now entertained for her daughter. To converse with Venetia on the recent occurrence was impossible. It was a subject which admitted of no discussion. They had passed a week at Padua, and the slightest allusion to what had happened had never been made by either Lady Annabel or her child. It was only by her lavish testimonies of affection that Lady Annabel conveyed to Venetia how deeply she sympathised with her, and how unhappy she was herself. She had, indeed, never quitted for a moment the side of her daughter, and witnessed each day, with renewed anguish, her deplorable condition; for Venetia continued in a state which, to those unacquainted with her, might have been mistaken for insensibility, but her mother knew too well that it was despair. She never moved, she never sighed, nor wept; she took no notice of anything that occurred; she sought relief in no resources. Books, and drawings, and music, were quite forgotten by her; nothing amused, and nothing annoyed her; she was not even fretful; she had, apparently, no physical ailment; she remained pale and silent, plunged in an absorbing paroxysm of overwhelming woe.

The unhappy Lady Annabel, at a loss how to act, at length thought it might be advisable to cross over to Venice. She felt assured now, that it would be a long time, if ever, before her child could again endure the fatigue of travel; and she thought that for every reason, whether for domestic comfort or medical advice, or those multifarious considerations which interest the invalid, a capital was by far the most desirable residence for them. There was a time when a visit to the city that had given her a name had been a favourite dream of Venetia; she had often sighed to be within

The sea-born city's walls; the graceful towers
Loved by the bard.

Those lines of her father had long echoed in her ear; but now the proposition called no light to her glazed eye, nor summoned for an instant the colour back to her cheek. She listened to her mother's suggestion, and expressed her willingness to do whatever she desired. Venice to her was now only a name; for, without the presence and the united love of both her parents, no spot on earth could interest, and no combination of circumstances affect her. To

Venice, however, they departed, having previously taken care that every arrangement should be made for their reception. The English ambassador at the Ducal court was a relative of Lady Annabel, and therefore no means or exertions were spared to study and secure the convenience and accommodation of the invalid. The barge of the ambassador met them at Fusina; and when Venetia beheld the towers and cupolas of Venice, suffused with a golden light and rising out of the bright blue waters, for a moment her spirit seemed to lighten. It is indeed a spectacle as beautiful as rare, and one to which the world offers few, if any, rivals. Gliding over the great Lagune, the buildings, with which the pictures at Cherbury had already made her familiar, gradually rose up before her: the mosque-like Church of St. Marc, the tall Campanile red in the sun, the Moresco Palace of the Doges, the deadly Bridge of Sighs, and the dark structure to which it leads.

Venice had not then fallen. The gorgeous standards of the sovereign republic, and its tributary kingdoms, still waved in the Place of St. Marc; the Bucentaur was not rotting in the Arsenal, and the warlike galleys of the state cruised without the Lagune; a busy and picturesque population swarmed in all directions; and the Venetian noble, the haughtiest of men, might still be seen proudly moving from the council of state, or stepping into a gondola amid a bowing crowd. All was stirring life, yet all was silent; the fantastic architecture, the glowing sky, the flitting gondolas, and the brilliant crowd gliding about with noiseless step, this city without sound, it seemed a dream!

CHAPTER VIII

The ambassador had engaged for Lady Annabel a palace on the Grand Canal, belonging to Count Manfrini. It was a structure of great size and magnificence, and rose out of the water with a flight of marble steps. Within was a vast gallery, lined with statues and busts on tall pedestals; suites of spacious apartments, with marble floors and hung with satin; ceilings painted by Tintoretto and full of Turkish trophies; furniture alike sumptuous and massy; the gilding, although of two hundred years' duration, as bright and burnished as if it had but yesterday been touched with the brush; sequin gold, as the Venetians tell you to this day with pride. But even their old furniture will soon not be left to them, as palaces are now daily broken up like old ships, and their colossal spoils consigned to Hanway Yard and Bond Street, whence, re-burnished and vamped up, their Titantic proportions in time appropriately figure in the boudoirs of May Fair and the miniature saloons of St. James'. Many a fine lady now sits in a doge's chair, and many a dandy listens to his doom from a couch that has already witnessed the less inexorable decrees of the Council of Ten.

Amid all this splendour, however, one mournful idea alone pervaded the tortured consciousness of Lady Annabel Herbert. Daily the dark truth stole upon her with increased conviction, that Venetia had come hither only to die. There seemed to the agitated ear of this distracted mother a terrible omen even in the very name of her child; and she could not resist the persuasion that her final destiny would, in some degree, be connected with her fanciful appellation. The physicians, for hopeless as Lady Annabel could not resist esteeming their interference, Venetia was now surrounded with physicians, shook their heads, prescribed different remedies and gave contrary opinions; each day, however, their patient became more languid, thinner and more thin, until she seemed like a beautiful spirit gliding into the saloon, leaning on her mother's arm, and followed by Pauncefort, who had now learnt the fatal secret from, her mistress, and whose heart was indeed almost broken at the prospect of the calamity that was impending over them.

At Padua, Lady Annabel, in her mortified reveries, outraged as she conceived by her husband, and anxious about her daughter, had schooled herself into visiting her fresh calamities on the head of the unhappy Herbert, to whose intrusion and irresistible influence she ascribed all the illness of her child; but, as the indisposition of Venetia gradually, but surely, increased, until at length it assumed so alarming an aspect that Lady Annabel, in the distraction of her mind, could no longer refrain from contemplating the most fatal result, she had taught herself bitterly to regret the failure of that approaching reconciliation which now she could not but believe would, at least, have secured her the life of Venetia. Whatever might be the risk of again uniting herself with her husband, whatever might be the mortification and misery which it might ultimately, or even speedily, entail upon her, there was no unhappiness that she could herself experience, which for one moment she could put in competition with the existence of her child. When that was the question, every feeling that had hitherto impelled her conduct assumed a totally different complexion. That conduct, in her view, had been a systematic sacrifice of self to secure the happiness of her daughter; and the result of all her exertions was, that not only her happiness was destroyed, but her life was fast vanishing away. To save Venetia, it now appeared to Lady Annabel that there was no extremity which she would not endure; and if it came to a question, whether Venetia should survive, or whether she should even be separated from her mother, her maternal heart now assured her that she would not for an instant hesitate in preferring an eternal separation to the death of her child. Her terror now worked to such a degree upon her character, that she even, at times, half resolved to speak to Venetia upon the subject, and contrive some method of communicating her wishes to her father; but pride, the habitual repugnance of so many years to converse upon the topic, mingled also, as should be confessed, with an indefinite apprehension of the ill consequences of a conversation of such a character on the nervous temperament of her daughter, restrained her.

'My love!' said Lady Annabel, one day to her daughter, 'do you think you could go out? The physicians think it of great importance that you should attempt to exert yourself, however slightly.'

'Dear mother, if anything could annoy me from your lips, it would be to hear you quote these physicians,' said Venetia. 'Their daily presence and inquiries irritate me. Let me be at peace. I wish to see no one but you.'

'But Venetia,' said Lady Annabel, in a voice of great emotion, 'Venetia—,' and here she paused; 'think of my anxiety.'

'Dear mother, it would be ungrateful for me ever to forget that. But you, and you alone, know that my state, whatever it may be, and to whatever it may be I am reconciled, is not produced by causes over which these physicians have any control, over which no one has control—now,' added Venetia, in a tone of great mournfulness.

For here we must remark that so inexperienced was Venetia in the feelings of others, and so completely did she judge of the strength and purity of their emotions from her own, that reflection, since the terrible adventure of Rovigo, had only convinced her that it was no longer in her mother's power to unite herself again with her other parent. She had taught herself to look upon her father's burst of feeling towards Lady Annabel as the momentary and inevitable result of a meeting so unexpected and overpowering, but she did not doubt that the stranger whose presence had ultimately so fatally clouded that interview of promise, possessed claims upon Marmion Herbert which he would neither break, nor, upon reflection, be desirous to question. It was then the conviction that a reconciliation between her parents was now impossible, in which her despair originated, and she pictured to herself her father once more at Arquâ disturbed, perhaps, for a day or two, as he naturally must be, by an interview so sudden and so harassing; shedding a tear, perhaps, in secret to the wife whom he had injured, and the child whom he had scarcely seen; but relapsing, alike from the force of habit and inclination, into those previous and confirmed feelings, under whose influence, she was herself a witness, his life had been so serene, and even so laudable. She was confirmed in these opinions by the circumstance of their never having heard since from him. Placed in his situation, if indeed an irresistible influence were not controlling him, would he have hesitated for a moment to have prevented even their departure, or to have pursued them; to have sought at any rate some means of communicating with them? He was plainly reconciled to his present position, and felt that under these circumstances silence on his part was alike kindest and most discreet. Venetia had ceased, therefore, to question the justice or the expediency, or even the abstract propriety, of her mother's conduct. She viewed their condition now as the result of stern necessity. She pitied her mother, and for herself she had no hope.

There was then much meaning in that little monosyllable with which Venetia concluded her reply to her mother. She had no hope 'now.' Lady Annabel, however, ascribed it to a very different meaning; she only believed that her daughter was of opinion that nothing would induce her now to listen to the overtures of her father. Prepared for any sacrifice of self, Lady Annabel replied, 'But there is hope, Venetia; when your life is in question, there is nothing that should not be done.'

'Nothing can be done,' said Venetia, who, of course, could not dream of what was passing in her mother's mind.

Lady Annabel rose from her seat and walked to the window; apparently her eye watched only the passing gondolas, but indeed she saw them not; she saw only her child stretched perhaps on the couch of death.

'We quitted, perhaps, Rovigo too hastily,' said Lady Annabel, in a choking voice, and with a face of scarlet. It was a terrible struggle, but the words were uttered.

'No, mother,' said Venetia, to Lady Annabel's inexpressible surprise, 'we did right to go.'

'Even my child, even Venetia, with all her devotion to him, feels the absolute necessity of my conduct,' thought Lady Annabel. Her pride returned; she felt the impossibility of making an overture to Herbert; she looked upon their daughter as the last victim of his fatal career.

CHAPTER IX.

How beautiful is night in Venice! Then music and the moon reign supreme; the glittering sky reflected in the waters, and every gondola gliding with sweet sounds! Around on every side are palaces and temples, rising from the waves which they shadow with their solemn forms, their costly fronts rich with the spoils of kingdoms, and softened with the magic of the midnight beam. The whole city too is poured forth for festival. The people lounge on the quays and cluster on the bridges; the light barks skim along in crowds, just touching the surface of the water, while their bright prows of polished iron gleam in the moonshine, and glitter in the rippling wave. Not a sound that is not graceful: the tinkle of guitars, the sighs of serenaders, and the responsive chorus of gondoliers. Now and then a laugh, light, joyous, and yet musical, bursts forth from some illuminated coffee-house, before which a buffo disports, a tumbler stands on his head, or a juggler mystifies; and all for a sequin!

The Place of St. Marc, at the period of our story, still presented the most brilliant spectacle of the kind in Europe. Not a spot was more distinguished for elegance, luxury, and enjoyment. It was indeed the inner shrine of the temple of pleasure, and very strange and amusing would be the annals of its picturesque arcades. We must not, however, step behind their blue awnings, but content ourselves with the exterior scene; and certainly the Place of St. Marc, with the variegated splendour of its Christian mosque, the ornate architecture of its buildings, its diversified population, a tribute from every shore of the midland sea, and where the noble Venetian, in his robe of crimson silk, and long white peruque, might be jostled by the Sclavonian with his target, and the Albanian in his kilt, while the Turk, sitting cross-legged on his Persian carpet, smoked his long chibouque with serene gravity, and the mild Armenian glided by him with a low reverence, presented an aspect under a Venetian moon such as we shall not easily find again in Christendom, and, in spite of the dying glory and the neighbouring vice, was pervaded with an air of romance and refinement, compared with which the glittering dissipation of Paris, even in its liveliest and most graceful hours, assumes a character alike coarse and commonplace.

It is the hour of love and of faro; now is the hour to press your suit and to break a bank; to glide from the apartment of rapture into the chamber of chance. Thus a noble Venetian contrived to pass the night, in alternations of excitement that in general left him sufficiently serious for the morrow's council. For more vulgar tastes there was the minstrel, the conjuror, and the story-teller, goblets of Cyprus wine, flasks of sherbet, and confectionery that dazzled like diamonds. And for every one, from the grave senator to the gay gondolier, there was an atmosphere in itself a spell, and which, after all, has more to do with human happiness than all the accidents of fortune and all the arts of government.

Amid this gay and brilliant multitude, one human being stood alone. Muffled in his cloak, and leaning against a column in the portico of St. Marc, an expression of oppressive care and affliction was imprinted on his countenance, and ill accorded with the light and festive scene. Had he been crossed in love, or had he lost at play? Was it woman or gold to which his anxiety and sorrow were attributable, for under one or other of these categories, undoubtedly, all the miseries of man may range. Want of love, or want of money, lies at the bottom of all our griefs.

The stranger came forward, and leaving the joyous throng, turned down the Piazzetta, and approached the quay of the Lagune. A gondolier saluted him, and he entered his boat.

'Whither, signor?' said the gondolier.

'To the Grand Canal,' he replied.

Over the moonlit wave the gondola swiftly skimmed! The scene was a marvellous contrast to the one which the stranger had just quitted; but it brought no serenity to his careworn countenance, though his eye for a moment kindled as he looked upon the moon, that was sailing in the cloudless heaven with a single star by her side.

They had soon entered the Grand Canal, and the gondolier looked to his employer for instructions. 'Row opposite to the Manfrini palace,' said the stranger, 'and rest upon your oar.'

The blinds of the great window of the palace were withdrawn. Distinctly might be recognised a female figure bending over the recumbent form of a girl. An hour passed away and still the gondola was motionless, and still the silent stranger gazed on the inmates of the palace. A servant now came forward and closed the curtain of the chamber. The stranger sighed, and waving his hand to the gondolier, bade him return to the Lagune.

CHAPTER X.

It is curious to recall our feelings at a moment when a great event is impending over us, and we are utterly unconscious of its probable occurrence. How often does it happen that a subject which almost unceasingly engages our mind, is least thought of at the very instant that the agitating suspense involved in its consideration is perhaps about to be terminated for ever! The very morning after the mysterious gondola had rested so long before the Manfrini Palace, Venetia rose for the first time since the flight from Rovigo, refreshed by her slumbers, and tranquil in her spirit. It was not in her power to recall her dreams; but they had left a vague and yet serene impression. There seemed a lightness in her heart, that long had been unusual with her, and she greeted her mother with a smile, faint indeed, yet natural.

Perhaps this beneficial change, slight but still delightful, might be attributed to the softness and the splendour of the morn. Before the approach of winter, it seemed that the sun was resolved to remind the Venetians that they were his children; and that, although his rays might be soon clouded for a season, they were not to believe that their parent had deserted them. The sea was like glass, a golden haze suffused the horizon, and a breeze, not strong enough to disturb the waters, was wafted at intervals from the gardens of the Brenta, fitful and sweet.

Venetia had yielded to the suggestion of her mother, and had agreed for the first time to leave the palace. They stepped into their gondola, and were wafted to an island in the Lagune where there was a convent, and, what in Venice was more rare and more delightful, a garden. Its scanty shrubberies sparkled in the sun; and a cypress flanked by a pine-tree offered to the eye unused to trees a novel and picturesque group. Beneath its shade they rested, watching on one side the distant city, and on the other the still and gleaming waters of the Adriatic. While they were thus sitting, renovated by the soft air and pleasant spectacle, a holy father, with a beard like a meteor, appeared and addressed them.

'Welcome to St. Lazaro!' said the holy father, speaking in English; 'and may the peace that reigns within its walls fill also your breasts!'

'Indeed, holy father,' said Lady Annabel to the Armenian monk, 'I have long heard of your virtues and your happy life.'

'You know that Paradise was placed in our country,' said the monk with a smile. 'We have all lost Paradise, but the Armenian has lost his country too. Nevertheless, with God's blessing, on this islet we have found an Eden, pure at least and tranquil.'

'For the pious, Paradise exists everywhere,' said Lady Annabel.

'You have been in England, holy father?' said Venetia.

'It has not been my good fortune,' replied the monk.

'Yet you speak our tongue with a facility and accent that surprise me.'

'I learnt it in America where I long resided,' rejoined the Armenian.

'This is for your eye, lady,' continued the monk, drawing a letter from his bosom.

Lady Annabel felt not a little surprised; but the idea immediately occurred to her that it was some conventual memorial appealing to her charity. She took the paper from the monk, who immediately moved away; but what was the agitation of Lady Annabel when she recognised the handwriting of her husband! Her first thought was to save Venetia from sharing that agitation. She rose quickly; she commanded herself sufficiently to advise her daughter, in a calm tone, to remain seated, while for a moment she refreshed herself by a stroll. She had not quitted Venetia many paces, when she broke the seal and read these lines:

'Tremble not, Annabel, when you recognise this handwriting. It is that of one whose only aspiration is to contribute to your happiness; and although the fulfilment of that fond desire may be denied him, it never shall be said, even by you, that any conduct of his should now occasion you annoyance. I am in Venice at the peril of my life, which I only mention because the difficulties inseparable from my position are the principal cause that you did not receive this communication immediately after our strange meeting. I have gazed at night upon your palace, and watched the forms of my wife and our child; but one word from you, and I quit Venice for ever, and it shall not be my fault if you are ever again disturbed by the memory of the miserable Herbert.

'But before I go, I will make this one appeal if not to your justice, at least to your mercy. After the fatal separation of a life, we have once more met: you have looked upon me not with hatred; my hand has once more pressed yours; for a moment I indulged the impossible hope, that this weary and exhausted spirit might at length be blessed. With agony I allude to the incident that dispelled the rapture of this vision. Sufficient for me most solemnly to assure you that four-and-twenty hours had not elapsed without that feeble and unhallowed tie being severed for ever! It vanished instantaneously before the presence of my wife and my child. However you decide, it can never again subsist: its utter and eternal dissolution was the inevitable homage to your purity.

'Whatever may have been my errors, whatever my crimes, for I will not attempt to justify to you a single circumstance of my life, I humble myself in the dust before you, and solicit only mercy; yet whatever may have been my career, ah! Annabel, in the infinite softness of your soul was it not for a moment pardoned? Am I indeed to suffer for that last lamentable intrusion? You are a woman, Annabel, with a brain as clear as your heart is pure. Judge me with calmness, Annabel; were there no circumstances in my situation to extenuate that deplorable connection? I will not urge them; I will not even intimate them; but surely, Annabel, when I kneel before you full of deep repentance and long remorse, if you could pardon the past, it is not that incident, however mortifying to you, however disgraceful to myself, that should be an impassable barrier to all my hopes!

'Once you loved me; I ask you not to love me now. There is nothing about me now that can touch the heart of woman. I am old before my time; bent with the blended influence of action and of thought, and of physical and moral suffering. The play of my spirit has gone for ever. My passions have expired like my hopes. The remaining sands of my life are few. Once it was otherwise: you can recall a different picture of the Marmion on whom you smiled, and of whom you were the first love. O Annabel! grey, feeble, exhausted, penitent, let me stagger over your threshold, and die! I ask no more; I will not hope for your affection; I will not even count upon your pity; but endure my presence; let your roof screen my last days!'

It was read; it was read again, dim as was the sight of Lady Annabel with fast-flowing tears. Still holding the letter, but with hands fallen, she gazed upon the shining waters before her in a fit of abstraction. It was the voice of her child that roused her.

'Mother,' said Venetia in a tone of some decision, 'you are troubled, and we have only one cause of trouble. That letter is from my father.'

Lady Annabel gave her the letter in silence.

Venetia withdrew almost unconsciously a few paces from her mother. She felt this to be the crisis of her life. There never was a moment which she believed required more fully the presence of all her energies. Before she had addressed Lady Annabel, she had endeavoured to steel her mind to great exertion. Yet now that she held the letter, she could not command herself sufficiently to read it. Her breath deserted her; her hand lost its power; she could not even open the lines on which perhaps her life depended. Suddenly, with a rapid effort, she glanced at the contents. The blood returned to her check; her eye became bright with excitement; she gasped for breath; she advanced to Lady Annabel. 'Ah! mother,' she exclaimed, 'you will grant all that it desires!'

Still gazing on the wave that laved the shore of the island with an almost inperceptible ripple, Lady Annabel continued silent.

'Mother,' said Venetia, 'my beloved mother, you hesitate.' She approached Lady Annabel, and with one arm round her neck, she grasped with the other her mother's hand. 'I implore you, by all that affection which you lavish on me, yield to this supplication. O mother! dearest mother! it has been my hope that my life has been at least a life of duty; I have laboured to yield to all your wishes. I have struggled to make their fulfilment the law of my being. Yes! mother, your memory will assure you, that when the sweetest emotions of my heart were the stake, you appealed to me to sacrifice them, and they were dedicated to your will. Have I ever murmured? I have sought only to repay your love by obedience. Speak to me, dearest mother! I implore you speak to me! Tell me, can you ever repent relenting in this instance? O mother! you will not hesitate; you will not indeed; you will bring joy and content to our long-harassed hearth! Tell me so; I beseech you tell me so! I wish, oh! how I wish, that you would comply from the mere impulse of your own heart! But, grant that it is a sacrifice; grant that it may be unwise; that it may be vain; I supplicate you to make it! I, your child, who never deserted you, who will never desert you, pledging my faith to you in the face of heaven; for my sake, I supplicate you to make it. You do not hesitate; you cannot hesitate; mother, you cannot hesitate. Ah! you would not if you knew all; if you knew all the misery of my life, you would be glad; you would be cheerful; you would look upon this as an interposition of Providence in favour of your Venetia; you would, indeed, dear mother!'

'What evil fortune guided our steps to Italy?' said Lady Annabel in a solemn tone, and as if in soliloquy.

'No, no, mother; not evil fortune; fortune the best and brightest,' exclaimed her daughter, 'We came here to be happy, and happiness we have at length gained. It is in our grasp; I feel it. It was not fortune, dear mother! it was fate, it was Providence, it was God. You have been faithful to Him, and He has brought back to you my father, chastened and repentant. God has turned his heart to all your virtues. Will you desert him? No, no, mother, you will not, you cannot; for his sake, for your own sake, and for your child's, you will not!'

'For twenty years I have acted from an imperious sense of duty,' said Lady Annabel, 'and for your sake, Venetia, as much as for my own. Shall the feelings of a moment—'

'O mother! dearest mother! say not these words. With me, at least, it has not been the feeling of a moment. It haunted my infancy; it harassed me while a girl; it has brought me in the prime of womanhood to the brink of the grave. And with you, mother, has it been the feeling of a moment? Ah! you ever loved him, when his name was never breathed by those lips. You loved him when you deemed he had forgotten you; when you pictured him to yourself in all the pride of health and genius, wanton and daring; and now, now that he comes to you penitent, perhaps dying, more like a remorseful spirit than a breathing being, and humbles himself before you, and appeals only to your mercy, ah! my mother, you cannot reject, you could not reject him, even if you were alone, even if you had no child!'

'My child! my child! all my hopes were in my child,' murmured Lady Annabel.

'Is she not by your side?' said Venetia.

'You know not what you ask; you know not what you counsel,' said Lady Annabel. 'It has been the prayer and effort of my life that you should never know. There is a bitterness in the reconciliation which follows long estrangement, that yields a pang more acute even than the first disunion. Shall I be called upon to mourn over the wasted happiness of twenty years? Why did he not hate us?'

'The pang is already felt, mother,' said Venetia. 'Reject my father, but you cannot resume the feelings of a month back. You have seen him; you have listened to him. He is no longer the character which justified your conduct, and upheld you under the trial. His image has entered your soul; your heart is softened. Bid him quit Venice without seeing you, and you will remain the most miserable of women.'

'On his head, then, be the final desolation,' said Lady Annabel; 'it is but a part of the lot that he has yielded me.'

'I am silent,' said Venetia, relaxing her grasp. 'I see that your child is not permitted to enter into your considerations.' She turned away.

'Venetia!' said her mother.

'Mother!' said Venetia, looking back, but not returning.

'Return one moment to me.'

Venetia slowly rejoined her. Lady Annabel spoke in a kind and gentle, though serious tone.

'Venetia,' she said, 'what I am about to speak is not the impulse of the moment, but has been long revolved in my mind; do not, therefore, misapprehend it. I express without passion what I believe to be truth. I am persuaded that the presence of your father is necessary to your happiness; nay, more, to your life. I recognise the mysterious influence which he has ever exercised over your existence. I feel it impossible for me any longer to struggle against a power to which I bow. Be happy, then, my daughter, and live. Fly to your father, and be to him as matchless a child as you have been to me.' She uttered these last words in a choking voice.

'Is this, indeed, the dictate of your calm judgment, mother?' said Venetia.

'I call God to witness, it has of late been more than once on my lips. The other night, when I spoke of Rovigo, I was about to express this.'

'Then, mother!' said Venetia, 'I find that I have been misunderstood. At least I thought my feelings towards yourself had been appreciated. They have not; and I can truly say, my life does not afford a single circumstance to which I can look back with content. Well will it indeed be for me to die?'

'The dream of my life,' said Lady Annabel, in a tone of infinite distress, 'was that she, at least, should never know unhappiness. It was indeed a dream.'

There was now a silence of several minutes. Lady Annabel remained in exactly the same position, Venetia standing at a little distance from her, looking resigned and sorrowful.

'Venetia,' at length said Lady Annabel, 'why are you silent?'

'Mother, I have no more to say. I pretend not to act in this life; it is my duty to follow you.'

'And your inclination?' inquired Lady Annabel.

'I have ceased to have a wish upon any subject,' said Venetia.

'Venetia,' said Lady Annabel, with a great effort, 'I am miserable.'

This unprecedented confession of suffering from the strong mind of her mother, melted Venetia to the heart. She advanced, and threw her arms round her mother's neck, and buried her weeping face in Lady Annabel's bosom.

'Speak to me, my daughter,' said Lady Annabel; 'counsel me, for my mind trembles; anxiety has weakened it. Nay, I beseech you, speak. Speak, speak, Venetia. What shall I do?'

'Mother, I will never say anything again but that I love you!'

'I see the holy father in the distance. Let us walk to him, my child, and meet him.'

Accordingly Lady Annabel, now leaning on Venetia, approached the monk. About five minutes elapsed before they reached him, during which not a word was spoken.

'Holy father,' said Lady Annabel, in a tone of firmness that surprised her daughter and made her tremble with anticipation, 'you know the writer of this letter?'

'He is my friend of many years, lady,' replied the Armenian; 'I knew him in America. I owe to him my life, and more than my life. There breathes not his equal among men.'

A tear started to the eye of Lady Annabel; she recalled the terms in which the household at Arquâ had spoken of Herbert. 'He is in Venice?' she inquired.

'He is within these walls,' the monk replied.

Venetia, scarcely able to stand, felt her mother start. After a momentary pause, Lady Annabel said, 'Can I speak with him, and alone?'

Nothing but the most nervous apprehension of throwing any obstacle in the way of the interview could have sustained Venetia. Quite pale, with her disengaged hand clenched, not a word escaped her lips. She hung upon the answer of the monk.

'You can see him, and alone,' said the monk. 'He is now in the sacristy. Follow me.'

'Venetia,' said Lady Annabel, 'remain in this garden. I will accompany this holy man. Stop! embrace me before I go, and,' she added, in a whisper, 'pray for me.'

It needed not the admonition of her mother to induce Venetia to seek refuge in prayer, in this agony of her life. But for its salutary and stilling influence, it seemed to her that she must have forfeited all control over her mind. The suspense was too terrible for human aid to support her. Seated by the seaside, she covered her face with her hands, and invoked the Supreme assistance. More than an hour passed away. Venetia looked up. Two beautiful birds, of strange form and spotless plumage, that perhaps had wandered from the Aegean, were hovering over her head, bright and glancing in the sun. She accepted their appearance as a good omen. At this moment she heard a voice, and, looking up, observed a monk in the distance, beckoning to her. She rose, and with a trembling step approached him. He retired, still motioning to her to follow him. She entered, by a low portal, a dark cloister; it led to an antechapel, through which, as she passed, her ear caught the solemn chorus of the brethren. Her step faltered; her sight was clouded; she was as one walking in a dream. The monk opened a door, and, retiring, waved his hand, as for her to enter. There was a spacious and lofty chamber, scantily furnished, some huge chests, and many sacred garments. At the extreme distance her mother was reclined on a bench, her head supported by a large crimson cushion, and her father kneeling by her mother's side. With a soundless step, and not venturing even to breathe, Venetia approached them, and, she knew not how, found herself embraced by both her parents.

END OF BOOK V.

BOOK VI.

CHAPTER I.

In a green valley of the Apennines, close to the sea-coast between Genoa and Spezzia, is a marine villa, that once belonged to the Malaspina family, in olden time the friends and patrons of Dante. It is rather a fantastic pile, painted in fresco, but spacious, in good repair, and convenient. Although little more than a mile from Spezzia, a glimpse of the blue sea can only be caught from one particular spot, so completely is the land locked with hills, covered with groves of chestnut and olive orchards. From the heights, however, you enjoy magnificent prospects of the most picturesque portion of the Italian coast; a lofty, undulating, and wooded shore, with an infinite variety of bays and jutting promontories; while the eye, wandering from Leghorn on one side towards Genoa on the other, traces an almost uninterrupted line of hamlets and casinos, gardens and orchards, terraces of vines, and groves of olive. Beyond them, the broad and blue expanse of the midland ocean, glittering in the meridian blaze, or about to receive perhaps in its glowing waters the red orb of sunset.

It was the month of May, in Italy, at least, the merry month of May, and Marmion Herbert came forth from the villa Malaspina, and throwing himself on the turf, was soon lost in the volume of Plato which he bore with him. He did not move until in the course of an hour he was roused by the arrival of servants, who brought seats and a table, when, looking up, he observed Lady Annabel and Venetia in the portico of the villa. He rose to greet them, and gave his arm to his wife.

'Spring in the Apennines, my Annabel,' said Herbert, 'is a happy combination. I am more in love each day with this residence. The situation is so sheltered, the air so soft and pure, the spot so tranquil, and the season so delicious, that it realises all my romance of retirement. As for you, I never saw you look so well; and as for Venetia, I can scarcely believe this rosy nymph could have been our pale-eyed girl, who cost us such anxiety!'

'Our breakfast is not ready. Let us walk to our sea view,' said Lady Annabel. 'Give me your book to carry, Marmion.'

'There let the philosopher repose,' said Herbert, throwing the volume on the turf. 'Plato dreamed of what I enjoy.'

'And of what did Plato dream, papa?' said Venetia.

'He dreamed of love, child.'

Venetia took her father's disengaged arm.

They had now arrived at their sea view, a glimpse of the Mediterranean between two tall crags.

'A sail in the offing,' said Herbert. 'How that solitary sail tells, Annabel!'

'I feel the sea breeze, mother. Does not it remind you of Weymouth?' said Venetia.

'Ah! Marmion,' said Lady Annabel, 'I would that you could see Masham once more. He is the only friend that I regret.'

'He prospers, Annabel; let that be our consolation: I have at least not injured him.'

They turned their steps; their breakfast was now prepared. The sun had risen above the hill beneath whose shade they rested, and the opposite side of the valley sparkled in light. It was a cheerful scene. 'I have a passion for living in the air,' said Herbert; 'I always envied the shepherds in Don Quixote. One of my youthful dreams was living among mountains of rosemary, and drinking only goat's milk. After breakfast I will read you Don Quixote's description of the golden age. I have often read it until the tears came into my eyes.'

'We must fancy ourselves in Spain,' said Lady Annabel; 'it is not difficult in this wild green valley; and if we have not rosemary, we have scents as sweet. Nature is our garden here, Venetia; and I do not envy even the statues and cypresses of our villa of the lake.'

'We must make a pilgrimage some day to the Maggiore, Annabel,' said Herbert. 'It is hallowed ground to me now.'

Their meal was finished, the servants brought their work, and books, and drawings; and Herbert, resuming his natural couch, re-opened his Plato, but Venetia ran into the villa, and returned with a volume. 'You must read us the golden age, papa,' she said, as she offered him, with a smile, his favourite Don Quixote.

'You must fancy the Don looking earnestly upon a handful of acorns,' said Herbert, opening the book, 'while he exclaims, "O happy age! which our first parents called the age of gold! not because gold, so much adored in this iron age, was then easily purchased, but because those two fatal words, *meum* and *tuum*, were distinctions unknown to the people of those fortunate times; for all things were in common in that holy age: men, for their sustenance, needed only to lift their hands, and take it from the sturdy oak, whose spreading arms liberally invited them to gather the wholesome savoury fruit; while the clear springs, and silver rivulets, with luxuriant plenty, afforded them their pure refreshing water. In hollow trees, and in the clefts of rocks, the labouring and industrious bees erected their little commonwealths, that men might reap with pleasure and with ease the sweet and fertile harvest of their toils, The tough and strenuous cork-trees did, of themselves, and without other art than their native liberality, dismiss and impart their broad light bark, which served to cover those lowly huts, propped up with rough-hewn stakes, that were first built as a shelter against the inclemencies of the air. All then was union, all peace, all love and friendship in the world. As yet no rude ploughshare presumed with violence to pry into the pious bowels of our mother earth, for she without compulsion kindly yielded from every part of her fruitful and spacious bosom, whatever might at once satisfy, sustain, and indulge her frugal children. Then was the time when innocent, beautiful young sheperdesses went tripping over the hills and vales; their lovely hair sometimes plaited, sometimes loose and flowing, clad in no other vestment but what the modesty of nature might require. The Tyrian dye, the rich glossy hue of silk, martyred and dissembled into every colour, which are now esteemed so fine and magnificent, were unknown to the innocent simplicity of that age; yet, bedecked with more becoming leaves and flowers, they outshone the proudest of the vaindressing ladies of our times, arrayed in the most magnificent garbs and all the most sumptuous adornings which idleness and luxury have taught succeeding pride. Lovers then expressed the passion of their souls in the unaffected language of the heart, with the native plainness and sincerity in which they were conceived, and divested of all that artificial contexture which enervates what it labours to enforce. Imposture, deceit, and malice had not yet crept in, and imposed themselves unbribed upon mankind in the disguise of truth: justice, unbiassed either by favour or interest, which now so fatally pervert it, was equally and impartially dispensed; nor was the judge's fancy law, for then there were neither judges nor causes to be judged. The modest maid might then walk alone. But, in this degenerate age, fraud and a legion of ills infecting the world, no virtue can be safe, no honour be secure; while wanton desires, diffused into the hearts of men, corrupt the strictest watches and the closest retreats, which, though as intricate, and unknown as the labyrinth of Crete, are no security for chastity. Thus, that primitive innocence being vanished, the oppression daily prevailing, there was a necessity to oppose the torrent of violence; for which reason the order of knighthood errant was instituted, to defend the honour of virgins, protect widows, relieve orphans, and assist all that are distressed. Now I myself am one of this order, honest friends and though all people are obliged by the law of nature to be kind to persons of my character, yet since you, without knowing anything of this obligation, have so generously entertained me, I ought to pay you my utmost acknowledgment, and accordingly return you my most hearty thanks."

'There,' said Herbert, as he closed the book. 'In my opinion, Don Quixote was the best man that ever lived.'

'But he did not ever live,' said Lady Annabel, smiling.

'He lives to us,' said Herbert. 'He is the same to this age as if he had absolutely wandered over the plains of Castile and watched in the Sierra Morena. We cannot, indeed, find his tomb; but he has left us his great example. In his hero, Cervantes has given us the picture of a great and benevolent philosopher, and in his Sancho, a complete personification of the world, selfish and cunning, and yet overawed by the genius that he cannot comprehend: alive to all the material interests of existence, yet sighing after the ideal; securing his four young foals of the she-ass, yet indulging in dreams of empire.'

'But what do you think of the assault on the windmills, Marmion?' said Lady Annabel.

'In the outset of his adventures, as in the outset of our lives, he was misled by his enthusiasm,' replied Herbert, 'without which, after all, we can do nothing. But the result is, Don Quixote was a redresser of wrongs, and therefore the world esteemed him mad.'

In this vein, now conversing, now occupied with their pursuits, and occasionally listening to some passage which Herbert called to their attention, and which ever served as the occasion for some critical remarks, always as striking from their originality as they were happy in their expression, the freshness of the morning disappeared; the sun now crowned the valley with his meridian beam, and they re-entered the villa. The ladies returned to their cool saloon, and Herbert to his study.

It was there he amused himself by composing the following lines:

SPRING IN THE APENNINES.

I.

> Spring in the Apennine now holds her court
> Within an amphitheatre of hills,
> Clothed with the blooming chestnut; musical
> With murmuring pines, waving their light green cones
> Like youthful Bacchants; while the dewy grass,
> The myrtle and the mountain violet,
> Blend their rich odours with the fragrant trees,
> And sweeten the soft air. Above us spreads
> The purple sky, bright with the unseen sun
> The hills yet screen, although the golden beam
> Touches the topmost boughs, and tints with light
> The grey and sparkling crags. The breath of morn
> Still lingers in the valley; but the bee
> With restless passion hovers on the wing,
> Waiting the opening flower, of whose embrace

The sun shall be the signal. Poised in air,
The winged minstrel of the liquid dawn,
The lark, pours forth his lyric, and responds
To the fresh chorus of the sylvan doves,
The stir of branches and the fall of streams,
The harmonies of nature!

II

   Gentle Spring!
Once more, oh, yes! once more I feel thy breath,
And charm of renovation! To the sky
Thou bringest light, and to the glowing earth
A garb of grace: but sweeter than the sky
That hath no cloud, and sweeter than the earth
With all its pageantry, the peerless boon
Thou bearest to me, a temper like thine own;
A springlike spirit, beautiful and glad!
Long years, long years of suffering, and of thought
Deeper than woe, had dimmed the eager eye
Once quick to catch thy brightness, and the ear
That lingered on thy music, the harsh world
Had jarred. The freshness of my life was gone,
And hope no more an omen in thy bloom
Found of a fertile future! There are minds,
Like lands, but with one season, and that drear
Mine was eternal winter!

III.

   A dark dream
Of hearts estranged, and of an Eden lost
Entranced my being; one absorbing thought
Which, if not torture, was a dull despair
That agony were light to. But while sad
Within the desert of my life I roamed,
And no sweet springs of love gushed for to greet
My wearied heart, behold two spirits came
Floating in light, seraphic ministers,
The semblance of whose splendour on me fell
As on some dusky stream the matin ray,
Touching the gloomy waters with its life.
And both were fond, and one was merciful!
And to my home long forfeited they bore
My vagrant spirit, and the gentle hearth.

I reckless fled, received me with its shade
And pleasant refuge. And our softened hearts
Were like the twilight, when our very bliss
Calls tears to soothe our rapture; as the stars
Steal forth, then shining smiles their trembling ray
Mixed with our tenderness; and love was there
In all his manifold forms; the sweet embrace,
And thrilling pressure of the gentle hand,
And silence speaking with the melting eye!

IV.

And now again I feel thy breath, O spring!
And now the seal hath fallen from my gaze,
And thy wild music in my ready ear
Finds a quick echo! The discordant world
Mars not thy melodies; thy blossoms now
Are emblems of my heart; and through my veins
The flow of youthful feeling, long pent up,
Glides like thy sunny streams! In this fair scene,
On forms still fairer I my blessing pour;
On her the beautiful, the wise, the good,
Who learnt the sweetest lesson to forgive;
And on the bright-eyed daughter of our love,
Who soothed a mother, and a father saved!

CHAPTER II.

Between the reconciliation of Lady Annabel Herbert with her husband, at the Armenian convent at Venice, and the spring morning in the Apennines, which we have just described, half a year had intervened. The political position of Marmion Herbert rendered it impossible for him to remain in any city where there was a representative of his Britannic Majesty. Indeed, it was scarcely safe for him to be known out of America. He had quitted that country shortly after the struggle was over, chiefly from considerations for his health. His energies had been fast failing him; and a retired life and change of climate had been recommended by his physicians. His own feelings induced him to visit Italy, where he had once intended to pass his life, and where he now repaired to await death. Assuming a feigned name, and living in strict seclusion, it is probable that his presence would never have been discovered; or, if detected, would not have been noticed. Once more united with his wife, her personal influence at the court of St. James', and her powerful connections, might secure him from annoyance; and Venetia had even indulged in a vague hope of returning to England. But Herbert could only have found himself again in his native country as a prisoner on parole. It would have been quite impossible for him to mix in the civil business of his native land, or enjoy any of the rights of citizenship. If a mild sovereign in his mercy had indeed accorded him a pardon, it must have been accompanied with rigorous and mortifying conditions; and his presence, in all probability, would have been confined to his country residence and its immediate neighbourhood. The pride of Lady Annabel herself recoiled from this sufferance; and although Herbert, keenly conscious of the sacrifice which a permanent estrangement from England entailed upon his wife and child, would have submitted to any restrictions, however humiliating, provided they were not inconsistent with his honour, it must be confessed that, when he spoke of this painful subject to his wife, it was with no slight self-congratulation that he had found her resolution to remain abroad under any circumstances was fixed with her habitual decision. She communicated both to the Bishop of —— and to her brother the unexpected change that had occurred in her condition, and she had reason to believe that a representation of what had happened would be made to the Royal family. Perhaps both the head of her house and her reverend friend anticipated that time might remove the barrier that presented itself to Herbert's immediate return to England: they confined their answers, however, to congratulations on the reconciliation, to their confidence in the satisfaction it would occasion her, and to the expression of their faithful friendship; and neither alluded to a result which both, if only for her sake, desired.

The Herberts had quitted Venice a very few days after the meeting on the island of St. Lazaro; had travelled by slow journeys, crossing the Apennines, to Genoa; and only remained in that city until they engaged their present residence. It combined all the advantages which they desired: seclusion, beauty, comfort, and the mild atmosphere that Venetia had seemed to require. It was not, however, the genial air that had recalled the rose to Venetia's cheek and the sunny smile to her bright eye, or had inspired again that graceful form with all its pristine elasticity. It was a heart content; a spirit at length at peace. The contemplation of the happiness of those most dear to her that she hourly witnessed, and the blissful consciousness that her exertions had mainly contributed to, if not completely occasioned, all this felicity, were remedies of far more efficacy than all the consultations and prescriptions of her physicians. The conduct of her father repaid her for all her sufferings, and realised all her dreams of domestic tenderness and delight. Tender, grateful, and affectionate, Herbert hovered round her mother like a delicate spirit who had been released by some kind mortal from a tedious and revolting thraldom, and who believed he could never sufficiently testify his devotion. There was so much respect blended with his fondness, that the spirit of her mother was utterly subdued by his irresistible demeanour. All her sadness and reserve, her distrust and her fear, had vanished; and rising confidence mingling with the love she had ever borne to him, she taught herself even to seek his opinion, and be guided by his advice. She could not refrain, indeed, from occasionally feeling, in this full enjoyment of his love, that she might have originally acted with too much precipitation; and that, had she only bent for a moment to the necessity of conciliation, and condescended to the excusable artifices of affection, their misery might have been prevented. Once when they were alone, her softened heart would have confessed to Herbert this painful conviction, but he was too happy and too generous to permit her for a moment to indulge in such a remorseful retrospect. All the error, he insisted, was his own; and he had been fool enough to have wantonly forfeited a happiness which time and experience had now taught him to appreciate.

'We married too young, Marmion,' said his wife.

'It shall be that then, love,' replied Herbert; 'but for all that I have suffered. I would not have avoided my fate on the condition of losing the exquisite present!'

It is perhaps scarcely necessary to remark, that Herbert avoided with the most scrupulous vigilance the slightest allusion to any of those peculiar opinions for which he was, unhappily, too celebrated. Musing over the singular revolutions which had already occurred in his habits and his feelings towards herself, Lady Annabel, indeed, did not despair that his once self-sufficient soul might ultimately bow to that blessed faith which to herself had ever proved so great a support, and so exquisite a solace. It was, indeed, the inexpressible hope that lingered at the bottom of her heart; and sometimes she even indulged in the delightful fancy that his mild and penitent spirit had, by the gracious mercy of Providence, been already touched by the bright sunbeam of conviction. At all events, his subdued and chastened temperament was no unworthy preparation for still greater blessings. It was this hallowed anticipation which consoled, and alone consoled, Lady Annabel for her own estrangement from the communion of her national church. Of all the sacrifices which her devotion to Herbert entailed upon her, this was the one which she felt most constantly and most severely. Not a day elapsed but the chapel at Cherbury rose before her; and when she remembered that neither herself nor her daughter might again kneel round the altar of their God, she almost trembled at the step which she had taken, and almost esteemed it a sacrifice of heavenly to earthly duty, which no consideration, perhaps, warranted. This apprehension, indeed, was the cloud in her life, and one which Venetia, who felt all its validity, found difficulty in combating.

Otherwise, when Venetia beheld her parents, she felt ethereal, and seemed to move in air; for her life, in spite of its apparent tranquillity, was to her all excitement. She never looked upon her father, or heard his voice, without a thrill. His society was as delightful as his heart was tender. It seemed to her that she could listen to him for ever. Every word he spoke was different from the language of other men; there was not a subject on which his richly-cultivated mind could not pour forth instantaneously a flood of fine fancies and deep intelligence. He seemed to have read every book in every language, and to have mused over every line he had read. She could not conceive how one, the tone of whose mind was so original that it suggested on every topic some conclusion that struck instantly by its racy novelty, could be so saturated with the learning and the views of other men. Although they lived in unbroken solitude, and were almost always together, not a day passed that she did not find herself musing over some thought or expression of her father, and which broke from his mind without effort, and as if by chance. Literature to Herbert was now only a source of amusement and engaging occupation. All thought of fame had long fled his soul. He cared not for being disturbed; and he would throw down his Plato for Don Quixote, or close his Aeschylus and take up a volume of Madame de Sévigné without a murmur, if reminded by anything that occurred of a passage which might contribute to the amusement and instruction of his wife and daughter. Indeed, his only study now was to contribute to their happiness. For him they had given up their country and society, and he sought, by his vigilant attention and his various accomplishments, to render their hours as light and pleasant as, under such circumstances, was possible. His muse, too, was only dedicated to the celebration of any topic which their life or themselves suggested. He loved to lie under the trees, and pour forth sonnets to Lady Annabel; and encouraged Venetia, by the readiness and interest with which he invariably complied with her intimations, to throw out every fancy which occurred to her for his verse. A life passed without the intrusion of a single evil passion, without a single expression that was not soft, and graceful, and mild, and adorned with all the resources of a most accomplished and creative spirit, required not the distractions of society. It would have shrunk from it, from all its artificial excitement and vapid reaction. The days of the Herberts flowed on in one bright, continuous stream of love, and literature, and gentle pleasures. Beneath them was the green earth, above them the blue sky. Their spirits were as clear, and their hearts as soft as the clime.

The hour of twilight was approaching, and the family were preparing for their daily walk. Their simple repast was finished, and Venetia held the verses which her father had written in the morning, and which he had presented to her.

'Let us descend to Spezzia,' said Herbert to Lady Annabel; 'I love an ocean sunset.'

Accordingly they proceeded through their valley to the craggy path which led down to the bay. After passing through a small ravine, the magnificent prospect opened before them. The sun was yet an hour above the horizon, and the sea was like a lake of molten gold; the colour of the sky nearest to the sun, of a pale green, with two or three burnished streaks of vapour, quite still, and so thin you could almost catch the sky through them, fixed, as it were, in this gorgeous frame. It was now a dead calm, but the sail that had been hovering the whole morning in the offing had made the harbour in time, and had just cast anchor near some coasting craft and fishing-boats, all that now remained where Napoleon had projected forming one of the arsenals of the world.

Tracing their way down a mild declivity, covered with spreading vineyards, and quite fragrant with the blossom of the vine, the Herberts proceeded through a wood of olives, and emerged on a terrace raised directly above the shore, leading to Spezzia, and studded here and there with rugged groups of aloes.

'I have often observed here,' said Venetia, 'about a mile out at sea; there, now, where I point; the water rise. It is now a calm, and yet it is more troubled, I think, than usual. Tell me the cause, dear father, for I have often wished to know.'

'It passes my experience,' said Herbert; 'but here is an ancient fisherman; let us inquire of him.'

He was an old man, leaning against a rock, and smoking his pipe in contemplative silence; his face bronzed with the sun and the roughness of many seasons, and his grey hairs not hidden by his long blue cap. Herbert saluted him, and, pointing to the phenomenon, requested an explanation of it.

"Tis a fountain of fresh water, signor, that rises in our gulf,' said the old fisherman, 'to the height of twenty feet.'

'And is it constant?' inquired Herbert.

"Tis the same in sunshine and in storm, in summer and in winter, in calm or in breeze,' said the old fisherman.

'And has it always been so?'

'It came before my time.'

'A philosophic answer,' said Herbert, 'and deserves a paul. Mine was a crude question. Adio, good friend.'

'I should like to drink of that fountain of fresh water, Annabel,' said Herbert. 'There seems to me something wondrous fanciful in it. Some day we will row there. It shall be a calm like this.'

'We want a fountain in our valley,' said Lady Annabel.

'We do,' said Herbert; 'and I think we must make one; we must inquire at Genoa. I am curious in fountains. Our fountain should, I think, be classical; simple, compact, with a choice inscription, the altar of a Naiad.'

'And mamma shall make the design, and you shall write the inscription,' said Venetia.

'And you shall be the nymph, child,' said Herbert.

They were now within a bowshot of the harbour, and a jutting cliff of marble, more graceful from a contiguous bed of myrtles, invited them to rest, and watch the approaching sunset.

'Say what they like,' said Herbert, 'there is a spell in the shores of the Mediterranean Sea which no others can rival. Never was such a union of natural loveliness and magical associations! On these shores have risen all that interests us in the past: Egypt and Palestine, Greece, Rome, and Carthage, Moorish Spain, and feodal Italy. These shores have yielded us our religion, our arts, our literature, and our laws. If all that we have gained from the shores of the Mediterranean was erased from the memory of man, we should be savages. Will the Atlantic ever be so memorable? Its civilisation will be more rapid, but will it be as refined? and, far more important, will it be as permanent? Will it not lack the racy vigour and the subtle spirit of aboriginal genius? Will not a colonial character cling to its society, feeble, inanimate, evanescent? What America is deficient in is creative intellect. It has no nationality. Its intelligence has been imported, like its manufactured goods. Its inhabitants are a people, but are they a nation? I wish that the empire of the Incas and the kingdom of Montezuma had not been sacrificed. I wish that the republic of the Puritans had blended with the tribes of the wilderness.'

The red sun was now hovering over the horizon; it quivered for an instant, and then sank. Immediately the high and undulating coast was covered with a crimson flush; the cliffs, the groves, the bays and jutting promontories, each straggling sail and tall white tower, suffused with a rosy light. Gradually that rosy tint became a bright violet, and then faded into purple. But the glory of the sunset long lingered in the glowing west, streaming with every colour of the Iris, while a solitary star glittered with silver light amid the shifting splendour.

'Hesperus rises from the sunset like the fountain of fresh water from the sea,' said Herbert. 'The sky and the ocean have two natures, like ourselves,'

At this moment the boat of the vessel, which had anchored about an hour back, put to shore.

'That seems an English brig,' said Herbert. 'I cannot exactly make out its trim; it scarcely seems a merchant vessel.'

The projection of the shore hid the boat from their sight as it landed. The Herberts rose, and proceeded towards the harbour. There were some rude steps cut in the rock which led from the immediate shore to the terrace. As they approached these, two gentlemen in sailors' jackets mounted suddenly. Lady Annabel and Venetia simultaneously started as they recognised Lord Cadurcis and his cousin. They were so close that neither party had time to prepare themselves. Venetia found her hand in that of Plantagenet, while Lady Annabel saluted George. Infinite were their mutual inquiries and congratulations, but it so happened that, with one exception, no name was mentioned. It was quite evident, however, to Herbert, that these were very familiar acquaintances of his family; for, in the surprise of the moment, Lord Cadurcis had saluted his daughter by her Christian name. There was no slight emotion, too, displayed on all sides. Indeed, independently of the agitation which so unexpected a rencounter was calculated to produce, the presence of Herbert, after the first moments of recognition, not a little excited the curiosity of the young men, and in some degree occasioned the embarrassment of all. Who was this stranger, on whom Venetia and her mother were leaning with such fondness? He was scarcely too old to be the admirer of Venetia, and if there were a greater disparity of years between them than is usual, his distinguished appearance might well reconcile the lady to her lot, or even justify her choice. Had, then, Cadurcis again met Venetia only to find her the bride or the betrothed of another? a mortifying situation, even an intolerable one, if his feelings remained unchanged; and if the eventful year that had elapsed since they parted had not replaced her image in his susceptible mind by another more cherished, and, perhaps, less obdurate. Again, to Lady Annabel the moment was one of great awkwardness, for the introduction of her husband to those with whom she was recently so intimate, and who were then aware that the name of that husband was never even mentioned in her presence, recalled the painful past with a disturbing vividness. Venetia, indeed, did not share these feelings fully, but she thought it ungracious to anticipate her mother in the announcement.

The Herberts turned with Lord Cadurcis and his cousin; they were about to retrace their steps on the terrace, when Lady Annabel, taking advantage of the momentary silence, and summoning all her energy, with a pale cheek and a voice that slightly faltered, said, 'Lord Cadurcis, allow me to present you to Mr. Herbert, my husband,' she added with emphasis.

'Good God!' exclaimed Cadurcis, starting; and then, outstretching his hand, he contrived to add, 'have I, indeed, the pleasure of seeing one I have so long admired?'

'Lord Cadurcis!' exclaimed Herbert, scarcely less surprised. 'Is it Lord Cadurcis? This is a welcome meeting.'

Everyone present felt overwhelmed with confusion or astonishment; Lady Annabel sought refuge in presenting Captain Cadurcis to her husband. This ceremony, though little noticed even by those more immediately interested in it, nevertheless served, in some degree, as a diversion. Herbert, who was only astonished, was the first who rallied. Perhaps Lord Cadurcis was the only man in existence whom Herbert wished to know. He had read his works with deep interest; at least, those portions which foreign journals had afforded him. He was deeply impressed with his fame and genius; but what perplexed him at this moment, even more than his unexpected introduction to him, was the singular, the very extraordinary circumstance, that the name of their most celebrated countryman should never have escaped the lips either of his wife or his daughter, although they appeared, and Venetia especially, to be on terms with him of even domestic intimacy.

'You arrived here to day, Lord Cadurcis?' said Herbert. 'From whence?'

'Immediately from Naples, where we last touched,' replied his lordship; 'but I have been residing at Athens.'

'I envy you,' said Herbert.

'It would be a fit residence for you,' said Lord Cadurcis. 'You were, however, in some degree, my companion, for a volume of your poems was one of the few books I had with me. I parted with all the rest, but I retained that. It is in my cabin, and full of my scribblement. If you would condescend to accept it, I would offer it to you.'

Mr. Herbert and Lord Cadurcis maintained the conversation along the terrace. Venetia, by whose side her old companion walked, was quite silent. Once her eyes met those of Cadurcis; his expression of mingled archness and astonishment was irresistible. His cousin and Lady Annabel carried on a more suppressed conversation, but on ordinary topics. When they had reached the olive-grove Herbert said, 'Here lies our way homeward, my lord. If you and your cousin will accompany us, it will delight Lady Annabel and myself.'

'Nothing, I am sure, will give George and myself greater pleasure,' he replied. 'We had, indeed, no purpose when you met us but to enjoy our escape from imprisonment, little dreaming we should meet our kindest and oldest friends,' he added.

'Kindest and oldest friends!' thought Herbert to himself. 'Well, this is strange indeed.'

'It is but a slight distance,' said Lady Annabel, who thought it necessary to enforce the invitation. 'We live in the valley, of which yonder hill forms a part.'

'And there we have passed our winter and our spring,' added Venetia, 'almost as delightfully as you could have done at Athens.'

'Well,' thought Cadurcis to himself, 'I have seen many of the world's marvels, but this day is a miracle.'

When they had proceeded through the olive-wood, and mounted the acclivity, they arrived at a path which permitted the ascent of only one person at a time. Cadurcis was last, and followed Venetia. Unable any longer to endure the suspense, he was rather irritated that she kept so close to her father; he himself loitered a few paces behind, and, breaking off a branch of laurel, he tossed it at her. She looked round and smiled; he beckoned to her to fall back. 'Tell me, Venetia,' he said, 'what does all this mean?'

'It means that we are at last all very happy,' she replied. 'Do you not see my father?'

'Yes; and I am very glad to see him; but this company is the very last in which I expected to have that pleasure.'

'It is too long a story to tell now; you must imagine it.'

'But are you glad to see me?'

'Very.'

'I don't think you care for me the least.'

'Silly Lord Cadurcis!' she said, smiling.

'If you call me Lord Cadurcis, I shall immediately go back to the brig, and set sail this night for Athens.'

'Well then, silly Plantagenet!'

He laughed, and they ran on.

CHAPTER III.

'Well, I am not surprised that you should have passed your time delightfully here,' said Lord Cadurcis to Lady Annabel, when they had entered the villa; 'for I never beheld so delightful a retreat. It is even more exquisite than your villa on the lake, of which George gave me so glowing a description. I was almost tempted to hasten to you. Would you have smiled on me!' he added, rather archly, and in a coaxing tone.

'I am more gratified that we have met here,' said Lady Annabel.

'And thus,' added Cadurcis.

'You have been a great traveller since we last met?' said Lady Annabel, a little embarrassed.

'My days of restlessness are over,' said Cadurcis. 'I desire nothing more dearly than to settle down in the bosom of these green hills as you have done.'

'This life suits Mr. Herbert,' said Lady Annabel. 'He is fond of seclusion, and you know I am accustomed to it.'

'Ah! yes,' said Cadurcis, mournfully. 'When I was in Greece, I used often to wish that none of us had ever left dear Cherbury; but I do not now.'

'We must forget Cherbury,' said Lady Annabel.

'I cannot: I cannot forget her who cherished my melancholy childhood. Dear Lady Annabel,' he added in a voice of emotion, and offering her his hand, 'forget all my follies, and remember that I was your child, once as dutiful as you were affectionate.'

Who could resist this appeal? Lady Annabel, not without agitation, yielded him her hand, which he pressed to his lips. 'Now I am again happy,' said Cadurcis; 'now we are all happy. Sweetest of friends, you have removed in a moment the bitterness of years.'

Although lights were in the saloon, the windows opening on the portico were not closed. The evening air was soft and balmy, and though the moon had not risen, the distant hills were clear in the starlight. Venetia was standing in the portico conversing with George Cadurcis.

'I suppose you are too much of a Turk to drink our coffee, Lord Cadurcis,' said Herbert. Cadurcis turned and joined him, together with Lady Annabel.

'Nay,' said Lord Cadurcis, in a joyous tone, 'Lady Annabel will answer for me that I always find everything perfect under her roof.'

Captain Cadurcis and Venetia now re-entered the villa; they clustered round the table, and seated themselves.

'Why, Venetia,' said Cadurcis, 'George met me in Sicily and quite frightened me about you. Is it the air of the Apennines that has worked these marvels? for, really, you appear to me exactly the same as when we learnt the French vocabulary together ten years ago.'

'"The French vocabulary together, ten years ago!"' thought Herbert; 'not a mere London acquaintance, then. This is very strange.'

'Why, indeed, Plantagenet,' replied Venetia, 'I was very unwell when George visited us; but I really have quite forgotten that I ever was an invalid, and I never mean to be again.'

'"Plantagenet!"' soliloquised Herbert. 'And this is the great poet of whom I have heard so much! My daughter is tolerably familiar with him.'

'I have brought you all sorts of buffooneries from Stamboul,' continued Cadurcis; 'sweetmeats, and slippers, and shawls, and daggers worn only by sultanas, and with which, if necessary, they can keep "the harem's lord" in order. I meant to have sent them with George to England, for really I did not anticipate our meeting here.'

'"Sweetmeats and slippers,"' said Herbert to himself, '"shawls and daggers!" What next?'

'And has George been with you all the time?' inquired Venetia.

'Oh! we quarrelled now and then, of course. He found Athens dull, and would stay at Constantinople, chained by the charms of a fair Perote, to whom he wanted me to write sonnets in his name. I would not, because I thought it immoral. But, on the whole, we got on very well; a sort of Pylades and Orestes, I assure you; we never absolutely fought.'

'Come, come,' said George, 'Cadurcis is always ashamed of being amiable. We were together much more than I ever intended or anticipated. You know mine was a sporting tour; and therefore, of course, we were sometimes separated. But he was exceedingly popular with all parties, especially the Turks, whom he rewarded for their courtesy by writing odes to the Greeks to stir them up to revolt.'

'Well, they never read them,' said Cadurcis. 'All we, poor fellows, can do,' he added, turning to Herbert, 'is to wake the Hellenistic raptures of May Fair; and that they call fame; as much like fame as a toadstool is like a truffle.'

'Nevertheless, I hope the muse has not slumbered,' said Herbert; 'for you have had the happiest inspiration in the climes in which you have resided; not only are they essentially poetic, but they offer a virgin vein.'

'I have written a little,' replied Cadurcis; 'I will give it you, if you like, some day to turn over. Yours is the only opinion that I really care for. I have no great idea of the poetry; but I am very strong in my costume. I feel very confident about that. I fancy I know how to hit off a pasha, or touch in a Greek pirate now. As for all the things I wrote in England, I really am ashamed of them. I got up my orientalism from books, and sultans and sultanas at masquerades,' he added, archly. 'I remember I made my heroines always wear turbans; only conceive my horror when I found that a Turkish woman would as soon think of putting my hat on as a turban, and that it was an article of dress entirely confined to a Bond Street milliner.'

The evening passed in interesting and diverting conversation; of course, principally contributed by the two travellers, who had seen so much. Inspirited by his interview with Lady Annabel, and her gracious reception of his overtures, Lord Cadurcis was in one of those frolic humours, which we have before noticed was not unnatural to him. He had considerable powers of mimicry, and the talent that had pictured to Venetia in old days, with such liveliness, the habits of the old maids of Morpeth, was now engaged on more considerable topics; an interview with a pasha, a peep into a harem, a visit to a pirate's isle, the slave-market, the bazaar, the barracks of the janissaries, all touched with irresistible vitality, and coloured with the rich phrases of unrivalled force of expression. The laughter was loud and continual; even Lady Annabel joined zealously in the glee. As for Herbert, he thought Cadurcis by far the most hearty and amusing person he had ever known, and could not refrain from contrasting him with the picture which his works and the report of the world had occasionally enabled him to sketch to his mind's eye; the noble, young, and impassioned bard, pouring forth the eloquent tide of his morbid feelings to an idolising world, from whose applause he nevertheless turned with an almost misanthropic melancholy.

It was now much past the noon of night, and the hour of separation, long postponed, was inevitable. Often had Cadurcis risen to depart, and often, without regaining his seat, had he been tempted by his friends, and especially Venetia, into fresh narratives. At last he said, 'Now we must go. Lady Annabel looks good night. I remember the look,' he said, laughing, 'when we used to beg for a quarter of an hour more. O Venetia! do not you remember that Christmas when dear old Masham read Julius Caesar, and we were to sit up until it was finished. When he got to the last act I hid his spectacles. I never confessed it until this moment. Will you pardon me, Lady Annabel?' and he pressed his hands together in a mockery of supplication.

'Will you come and breakfast with us to-morrow?' said Lady Annabel.

'With delight,' he answered. 'I am used, you know, to walks before breakfast. George, I do not think George can do it, though. George likes his comforts;

he is a regular John Bull. He was always calling for tea when we were in Turkey!'

At this moment Mistress Pauncefort entered the room, ostensibly on some little affair of her mistress, but really to reconnoitre.

'Ah! Mistress Pauncefort; my old friend, Mistress Pauncefort, how do you do?' exclaimed his lordship.

'Quite well, my lord, please your lordship; and very glad to see your lordship again, and looking so well too.'

'Ah! Mistress Pauncefort, you always flattered me!'

'Oh! dear, my lord, your lordship, no,' said Mistress Pauncefort, with a simper.

'But you, Pauncefort,' said Cadurcis, 'why there must be some magic in the air here. I have been complimenting your lady and Miss Venetia; but really, you, I should almost have thought it was some younger sister.'

'Oh! my lord, you have such a way,' said Mistress Pauncefort, retreating with a slow step that still lingered for a remark.

'Pauncefort, is that an Italian cap?' said Lord Cadurcis; 'you know, Pauncefort, you were always famous for your caps.'

Mistress Pauncefort disappeared in a fluster of delight.

And now they had indeed departed. There was a pause of complete silence after they had disappeared, the slight and not painful reaction after the mirthful excitement of the last few hours. At length Herbert, dropping, as was his evening custom, a few drops of orange-flower into a tumbler of water, said, 'Annabel, my love, I am rather surprised that neither you nor Venetia should have mentioned to me that you knew, and knew so intimately, a man like Lord Cadurcis.'

Lady Annabel appeared a little confused; she looked even at Venetia, but Venetia's eyes were on the ground. At length she said, 'In truth, Marmion, since we met we have thought only of you.'

'Cadurcis Abbey, papa, is close to Cherbury,' said Venetia.

'Cherbury!' said Herbert, with a faint blush. 'I have never seen it, and now I shall never see it. No matter, my country is your mother and yourself. Some find a home in their country, I find a country in my home. Well,' he added, in a gayer tone, 'it has gratified me much to meet Lord Cadurcis. We were happy before, but now we are even gay. I like to see you smile, Annabel, and hear Venetia laugh. I feel, myself, quite an unusual hilarity. Cadurcis! It is very strange how often I have mused over that name. A year ago it was one of my few wishes to know him; my wishes, then, dear Annabel, were not very ambitious. They did not mount so high as you have since permitted them. And now I do know him, and under what circumstances! Is not life strange? But is it not happy? I feel it so. Good night, sweet wife; my darling daughter, a happy, happy night!' He embraced them ere they retired; and opening a volume composed his mind after the novel excitement of the evening.

CHAPTER IV.

Cadurcis left the brig early in the morning alone, and strolled towards the villa. He met Herbert half-way to Spezzia, who turned back with him towards home. They sat down on a crag opposite the sea; there was a light breeze, the fishing boats wore out, and the view was as animated as the fresh air was cheering.

'There they go,' said Cadurcis, smiling, 'catching John Dory, as you and I try to catch John Bull. Now if these people could understand what two great men were watching them, how they would stare! But they don't care a sprat for us, not they! They are not part of the world the three or four thousand civilised savages for whom we sweat our brains, and whose fetid breath perfumed with musk is fame. Pah!'

Herbert smiled. 'I have not cared much myself for this same world.'

'Why, no; you have done something, and shown your contempt for them. No one can deny that. I will some day, if I have an opportunity. I owe it them; I think I can show them a trick or two still.[A] I have got a Damascus blade in store for their thick hides. I will turn their flank yet.'

[Footnote A: I think I know a trick or two would turn Your flanks. *Don Juan.*]

'And gain a victory where conquest brings no glory. You are worth brighter laurels, Lord Cadurcis.'

'Now is not it the most wonderful thing in the world that you and I have met?' said Cadurcis. 'Now I look upon ourselves as something like, eh! Fellows with some pith in them. By Jove, if we only joined together, how we could lay it on! Crack, crack, crack; I think I see them wincing under the thong, the pompous poltroons! If you only knew how they behaved to me! By Jove, sir, they hooted me going to the House of Lords, and nearly pulled me off my horse. The ruffians would have massacred me if they could; and then they all ran away from a drummer-boy and a couple of grenadiers, who were going the rounds to change guard. Was not that good? Fine, eh? A brutish mob in a fit of morality about to immolate a gentleman, and then scampering off from a sentry. I call that human nature!'

'As long as they leave us alone, and do not burn us alive, I am content,' said Herbert. 'I am callous to what they say.'

'So am I,' said Cadurcis. 'I made out a list the other day of all the persons and things I have been compared to. It begins well, with Alcibiades, but it ends with the Swiss giantess or the Polish dwarf, I forget which. Here is your book. You see it has been well thumbed. In fact, to tell the truth, it was my cribbing book, and I always kept it by me when I was writing at Athens, like a gradus, a *gradus ad Parnassum*, you know. But although I crib, I am candid, and you see I fairly own it to you.'

'You are welcome to all I have ever written,' said Herbert. 'Mine were but crude dreams. I wished to see man noble and happy; but if he will persist in being vile and miserable, I must even be content. I can struggle for him no more.'

'Well, you opened my mind,' said Cadurcis. 'I owe you everything; but I quite agree with you that nothing is worth an effort. As for philosophy and freedom, and all that, they tell devilish well in a stanza; but men have always been fools and slaves, and fools and slaves they always will be.'

'Nay,' said Herbert, 'I will not believe that. I will not give up a jot of my conviction of a great and glorious future for human destinies; but its consummation will not be so rapid as I once thought, and in the meantime I die.'

'Ah, death!' said Lord Cadurcis, 'that is a botherer. What can you make of death? There are those poor fishermen now; there will be a white squall some day, and they will go down with those lateen sails of theirs, and be food for the very prey they were going to catch; and if you continue living here, you may eat one of your neighbours in the shape of a shoal of red mullets, when it is the season. The great secret, we cannot penetrate that with all our philosophy, my dear Herbert. "All that we know is, nothing can be known." Barren, barren, barren! And yet what a grand world it is! Look at this bay, these blue waters, the mountains, and these chestnuts, devilish fine! The fact is, truth is veiled, but, like the Shekinah over the tabernacle, the veil is of dazzling light!'

'Life is the great wonder,' said Herbert, 'into which all that is strange and startling resolves itself. The mist of familiarity obscures from us the miracle of our being. Mankind are constantly starting at events which they consider extraordinary. But a philosopher acknowledges only one miracle, and that is life. Political revolutions, changes of empire, wrecks of dynasties and the opinions that support them, these are the marvels of the vulgar, but these are only transient modifications of life. The origin of existence is, therefore, the first object which a true philosopher proposes to himself. Unable to discover it, he accepts certain results from his unbiassed observation of its obvious nature, and on them he establishes certain principles to be our guides in all social relations, whether they take the shape of laws or customs. Nevertheless, until the principle of life be discovered, all theories and all systems of conduct founded on theory must be considered provisional.'

'And do you believe that there is a chance of its being discovered?' inquired Cadurcis.

'I cannot, from any reason in my own intelligence, find why it should not,' said Herbert.

'You conceive it possible that a man may attain earthly immortality?' inquired Cadurcis.

'Undoubtedly.'

'By Jove,' said Cadurcis, 'if I only knew how, I would purchase an immense annuity directly.'

'When I said undoubtedly,' said Herbert, smiling, 'I meant only to express that I know no invincible reason to the contrary. I see nothing inconsistent with the existence of a Supreme Creator in the annihilation of death. It appears to me an achievement worthy of his omnipotence. I believe in the possibility, but I believe in nothing more. I anticipate the final result, but not by individual means. It will, of course, be produced by some vast and silent and continuous operation of nature, gradually effecting some profound and comprehensive alteration in her order, a change of climate, for instance, the great enemy of life, so that the inhabitants of the earth may attain a patriarchal age. This renovated breed may in turn produce a still more vigorous offspring, and so we may ascend the scale, from the threescore and ten of the Psalmist to the immortality of which we speak. Indeed I, for my own part, believe the operation has already commenced, although thousands of centuries may elapse before it is consummated; the threescore and ten of the Psalmist is already obsolete; the whole world is talking of the general change of its seasons and its atmosphere. If the origin of America were such as many profound philosophers suppose, viz., a sudden emersion of a new continent from the waves, it is impossible to doubt that such an event must have had a very great influence on the climate of the world. Besides, why should we be surprised that the nature of man should change? Does not everything change? Is not change the law of nature? My skin changes every year, my hair never belongs to me a month, the nail on my hand is only a passing possession. I doubt whether a man at fifty is the same material being that he is at five-and-twenty.'

'I wonder,' said Lord Cadurcis, 'if a creditor brought an action against you at fifty for goods delivered at five-and-twenty, one could set up the want of identity as a plea in bar. It would be a consolation to an elderly gentleman.'

'I am afraid mankind are too hostile to philosophy,' said Herbert, smiling, 'to permit so desirable a consummation.'

'Should you consider a long life a blessing?' said Cadurcis. 'Would you like, for instance, to live to the age of Methusalem?'

'Those whom the gods love die young,' said Herbert. 'For the last twenty years I have wished to die, and I have sought death. But my feelings, I confess, on that head are at present very much modified.'

'Youth, glittering youth!' said Cadurcis in a musing tone; 'I remember when the prospect of losing my youth frightened me out of my wits; I dreamt of nothing but grey hairs, a paunch, and the gout or the gravel. But I fancy every period of life has its pleasures, and as we advance in life the exercise of power and the possession of wealth must be great consolations to the majority; we bully our children and hoard our cash.'

'Two most noble occupations!' said Herbert; 'but I think in this world there is just as good a chance of being bullied by our children first, and paying their debts afterwards.'

'Faith! you are right,' said Cadurcis, laughing, 'and lucky is he who has neither creditors nor offspring, and who owes neither money nor affection, after all the most difficult to pay of the two.'

'It cannot be commanded, certainly,' said Herbert 'There is no usury for love.'

'And yet it is very expensive, too, sometimes, said Cadurcis, laughing. 'For my part, sympathy is a puzzler.'

'You should read Cabanis,' said Herbert, 'if indeed, you have not. I think I may find it here; I will lend it you. It has, from its subject, many errors, but it is very suggestive.'

'Now, that is kind, for I have not a book here, and, after all, there is nothing like reading. I wish I had read more, but it is not too late. I envy you your learning, besides so many other things. However, I hope we shall not part in a hurry; we have met at last,' he said, extending his hand, 'and we were always friends.'

Herbert shook his hand very warmly. 'I can assure you, Lord Cadurcis, you have not a more sincere admirer of your genius. I am happy in your society. For myself, I now aspire to be nothing better than an idler in life, turning over a page, and sometimes noting down a fancy. You have, it appears, known my family long and intimately, and you were, doubtless, surprised at finding me with them. I have returned to my hearth, and I am content. Once I sacrificed my happiness to my philosophy, and now I have sacrificed my philosophy to my happiness.'

'Dear friend!' said Cadurcis, putting his arm affectionately in Herbert's as they walked along, 'for, indeed, you must allow me to style you so; all the happiness and all the sorrow of my life alike flow from your roof!'

In the meantime Lady Annabel and Venetia came forth from the villa to their morning meal in their amphitheatre of hills. Marmion was not there to greet them as usual.

'Was not Plantagenet amusing last night?' said Venetia; 'and are not you happy, dear mother, to see him once more?'

'Indeed I am now always happy,' said Lady Annabel.

'And George was telling me last night, in this portico, of all their life. He is more attached to Plantagenet than ever. He says it is impossible for any one to have behaved with greater kindness, or to have led, in every sense, a more calm and rational life. When he was alone at Athens, he did nothing but write. George says that all his former works are nothing to what he has written now.'

'He is very engaging,' said Lady Annabel.

'I think he will be such a delightful companion for papa. I am sure papa must like him. I hope he will stay some time; for, after all, poor dear papa, he must require a little amusement besides our society. Instead of being with his books, he might be walking and talking with Plantagenet. I think, dearest mother, we shall be happier than ever!'

At this moment Herbert, with Cadurcis leaning on his arm, and apparently speaking with great earnestness, appeared in the distance. 'There they are,' said Venetia; 'I knew they would be friends. Come, dearest mother, let us meet them.'

'You see, Lady Annabel,' said Lord Cadurcis, 'it is just as I said: Mr. George is not here; he is having tea and toast on board the brig.'

'I do not believe it,' said Venetia, smiling.

They seated themselves at the breakfast-table.

'You should have seen our Apennine breakfasts in the autumn, Lord Cadurcis,' said Herbert. 'Every fruit of nature seemed crowded before us. It was indeed a meal for a poet or a painter like Paul Veronese; our grapes, our figs, our peaches, our mountain strawberries, they made a glowing picture. For my part, I have an original prejudice against animal food which I have never quite overcome, and I believe it is only to please Lady Annabel that I have relapsed into the heresy of cutlets.'

'Do you think I have grown fatter, Lady Annabel?' said Lord Cadurcis, starting up; 'I brought myself down at Athens to bread and olives, but I have been committing terrible excesses lately, but only fish.'

'Ah! here is George!' said Lady Annabel.

And Captain Cadurcis appeared, followed by a couple of sailors, bearing a huge case.

'George,' said Venetia, 'I have been defending you against Plantagenet; he said you would not come.'

'Never mind, George, it was only behind your back,' said Lord Cadurcis; 'and, under those legitimate circumstances, why even our best friends cannot expect us to spare them.'

'I have brought Venetia her toys,' said Captain Cadurcis, 'and she was right to defend me, as I have been working for her.'

The top of the case was knocked off, and all the Turkish buffooneries, as Cadurcis called them, made their appearance: slippers, and shawls, and bottles of perfumes, and little hand mirrors, beautifully embroidered; and fanciful daggers, and rosaries, and a thousand other articles, of which they had plundered the bazaars of Constantinople.

'And here is a Turkish volume of poetry, beautifully illuminated; and that is for you,' said Cadurcis giving it to Herbert. 'Perhaps it is a translation of one of our works. Who knows? We can always say it is.'

'This is the second present you have made me this morning. Here is a volume of my works,' said Herbert, producing the book that Cadurcis had before given him. 'I never expected that anything I wrote would be so honoured. This, too, is the work of which I am the least ashamed for my wife admired it. There, Annabel, even though Lord Cadurcis is here, I will present it to you; 'tis an old friend.'

Lady Annabel accepted the book very graciously, and, in spite of all the temptations of her toys, Venetia could not refrain from peeping over her mother's shoulder at its contents. 'Mother,' she whispered, in a voice inaudible save to Lady Annabel, 'I may read this!'

Lady Annabel gave it her.

'And now we must send for Pauncefort, I think,' said Lady Annabel, 'to collect and take care of our treasures.'

'Pauncefort,' said Lord Cadurcis, when that gentlewoman appeared, 'I have brought you a shawl, but I could not bring you a turban, because the Turkish ladies do not wear turbans; but if I had thought we should have met so soon, I would have had one made on purpose for you.'

'La! my lord, you always are so polite!'

CHAPTER V.

When the breakfast was over, they wandered about the valley, which Cadurcis could not sufficiently admire. Insensibly he drew Venetia from the rest of the party, on the pretence of showing her a view at some little distance. They walked along by the side of a rivulet, which glided through the hills, until they were nearly a mile from the villa, though still in sight.

'Venetia,' he at length said, turning the conversation to a more interesting topic, 'your father and myself have disburthened our minds to each, other this morning; I think we know each other now as well as if we were as old acquaintances as myself and his daughter.'

'Ah! I knew that you and papa must agree,' said Venetia; 'I was saying so this morning to my mother.'

'Venetia,' said Cadurcis, with a laughing eye, 'all this is very strange, is it not?'

'Very strange, indeed, Plantagenet; I should not be surprised if it appeared to you as yet even incredible.'

'It is miraculous,' said Cadurcis, 'but not incredible; an angel interfered, and worked the miracle. I know all.'

Venetia looked at him with a faint flush upon her cheek; she gathered a flower and plucked it to pieces.

'What a singular destiny ours has been, Venetia!' said Cadurcis. 'Do you know, I can sit for an hour together and muse over it.'

'Can you, Plantagenet?'

'I have such an extraordinary memory; I do not think I ever forgot anything. We have had some remarkable conversations in our time, eh, Venetia? Do you remember my visit to Cherbury before I went to Cambridge, and the last time I saw you before I left England? And now it all ends in this! What do you think of it, Venetia?'

'Think of what, Plantagenet?'

'Why, of this reconciliation?'

'Dear Plantagenet, what can I think of it but what I have expressed, that it is a wonderful event, but the happiest in my life.'

'You are quite happy now?'

'Quite.'

'I see you do not care for me the least.'

'Plantagenet, you are perverse. Are you not here?'

'Did you ever think of me when I was away?'

'You know very well, Plantagenet, that it is impossible for me to cease to be interested in you. Could I refrain from thinking of such a friend?'

'Friend! poh! I am not your friend; and, as for that, you never once mentioned my name to your father, Miss Venetia.'

'You might easily conceive that there were reasons for such silence,' said Venetia. 'It could not arise on my part from forgetfulness or indifference; for, even if my feelings were changed towards you, you are not a person that one would, or even could, avoid speaking of, especially to papa, who must have felt such interest in you! I am sure, even if I had not known you, there were a thousand occasions which would have called your name to my lips, had they been uncontrolled by other considerations.'

'Come, Venetia, I am not going to submit to compliments from you,' said Lord Cadurcis; 'no blarney. I wish you only to think of me as you did ten years ago. I will not have our hearts polluted by the vulgarity of fame. I want you to feel for me as you did when we were children. I will not be an object of interest, and admiration, and fiddlestick to you; I will not submit to it.'

'Well, you shall not,' said Venetia, laughing. 'I will not admire you the least; I will only think of you as a good little boy.'

'You do not love me any longer, I see that,' said Cadurcis.

'Yes I do, Plantagenet.'

'You do not love me so much as you did the night before I went to Eton, and we sat over the fire? Ah! how often I have thought of that night when I was at Athens!' he added in a tone of emotion.

'Dear Plantagenet,' said Venetia, 'do not be silly. I am in the highest spirits in the world; I am quite gay with happiness, and all because you have returned. Do not spoil my pleasure.'

'Ah, Venetia! I see how it is; you have forgotten me, or worse than forgotten me.'

'Well, I am sure I do not know what to say to satisfy you,' said Venetia. 'I think you very unreasonable, and very ungrateful too, for I have always been your friend, Plantagenet, and I am sure you know it. You sent me a message before you went abroad.'

'Darling!' said Lord Cadurcis, seizing her hand, 'I am not ungrateful, I am not unreasonable. I adore you. You were very kind then, when all the world was against me. You shall see how I will pay them off, the dogs! and worse than dogs, their betters far; dogs are faithful. Do you remember poor old Marmion? How we were mystified, Venetia! Little did we think then who was Marmion's godfather.'

Venetia smiled; but she said, 'I do not like this bitterness of yours, Plantagenet. You have no cause to complain of the world, and you magnify a petty squabble with a contemptible coterie into a quarrel with a nation. It is not a wise humour, and, if you indulge it, it will not be a happy one.'

'I will do exactly what you wish on every subject, said Cadurcis, 'if you will do exactly what I wish on one.'

'Well!' said Venetia.

'Once you told me,' said Cadurcis, 'that you would not marry me without the consent of your father; then, most unfairly, you added to your conditions the consent of your mother. Now both your parents are very opportunely at hand; let us fall down upon our knees, and beg their blessing.'

'O! my dear Plantagenet, I think it will be much better for me never to marry. We are both happy now; let us remain so. You can live here, and I can be your sister. Will not that do?'

'No, Venetia, it will not.'

'Dear Plantagenet!' said Venetia with a faltering voice, 'if you knew how much I had suffered, dear Plantagenet!'

'I know it; I know all,' said Cadurcis, taking her arm and placing it tenderly in his. 'Now listen to me, sweet girl; I loved you when a child, when I was unknown to the world, and unknown to myself; I loved you as a youth not utterly inexperienced in the world, and when my rising passions had taught me to speculate on the character of women; I loved you as a man, Venetia, with that world at my feet, that world which I scorn, but which I will command; I have been constant, Venetia; your heart assures you, of that. You are the only being in existence who exercises over me any influence; and the influence you possess is irresistible and eternal. It springs from some deep and mysterious sympathy of blood which I cannot penetrate. It can neither be increased nor diminished by time. It is entirely independent of its action. I pretend not to love you more at this moment than when I first saw you, when you entered the terrace-room at Cherbury and touched my cheek. From that moment I was yours. I declare to you, most solemnly I declare to you, that I know not what love is except to you. The world has called me a libertine; the truth is, no other woman can command my spirit for an hour. I see through them at a glance. I read all their weakness, frivolity, vanity, affectation, as if they were touched by the revealing rod of Asmodeus. You were born to be my bride. Unite yourself with me, control my destiny, and my course shall be like the sun of yesterday; but reject me, reject me, and I devote all my energies to the infernal gods; I will pour my lava over the earth until all that remains of my fatal and exhausted nature is a black and barren cone surrounded by bitter desolation.'

'Plantagenet; be calm!'

'I am perfectly calm, Venetia. You talk to me of your sufferings. What has occasioned them? A struggle against nature. Nature has now triumphed, and you are happy. What necessity was there for all this misery that has fallen on your house? Why is your father an exile? Do not you think that if your mother had chosen to exert her influence she might have prevented the most fatal part of his career? Undoubtedly despair impelled his actions as much as philosophy, though I give him credit for a pure and lofty spirit, to no man more. But not a murmur against your mother from me. She received my overtures of reconciliation last night with more than cordiality. She is your mother, Venetia, and she once was mine. Indeed, I love her; indeed, you would find that I would study her happiness. For after all, sweet, is there another woman in existence better qualified to fill the position of my mother-in-law? I could not behave unkindly to her; I could not treat her with neglect or harshness; not merely for the sake of her many admirable qualities, but from other considerations, Venetia, considerations we never can forget. By heavens! I love your mother; I do, indeed, Venetia! I remember so many things; her last words to me when I went to Eton. If she would only behave kindly to me, you would see what a son-in-law I should make. You would be jealous, that you should, Venetia. I can bear anything from you, Venetia, but, with others, I cannot forget who I am. It makes me bitter to be treated as Lady Annabel treated me last year in London: but a smile and a kind word and I recall all her maternal love; I do indeed, Venetia; last night when she was kind I could have kissed her!'

Poor Venetia could not answer, her tears were flowing so plenteously. 'I have told your father all, sweetest,' said Cadurcis; 'I concealed nothing.'

'And what said he?' murmured Venetia.

'It rests with your mother. After all that has passed, he will not attempt to control your fate. And he is right. Perhaps his interference in my favour might even injure me. But there is no cause for despair; all I wanted was to come to an understanding with you; to be sure you loved me as you always have done. I will not be impatient. I will do everything to soothe and conciliate and gratify Lady Annabel; you will see how I will behave! As you say, too, we are happy because we are together; and, therefore, it would be unreasonable not to be patient. I never can be sufficiently grateful for this meeting. I concluded you would be in England, though we were on our way to Milan to inquire after you. George has been a great comfort to me in all this affair,

Venetia; he loves you, Venetia, almost as much as I do. I think I should have gone mad during that cursed affair in England, had it not been for George. I thought you would hate me; but, when George brought me your message, I cared for nothing; and then his visit to the lake was so devilish kind! He is a noble fellow and a true friend. My sweet, sweet Venetia, dry your eyes. Let us rejoin them with a smile. We have not been long away, I will pretend we have been violet hunting,' said Cadurcis, stooping down and plucking up a handful of flowers. 'Do you remember our violets at home, Venetia? Do you know, Venetia, I always fancy every human being is like some object in nature; and you always put me in mind of a violet so fresh and sweet and delicate!'

CHAPTER VI.

'We have been exploring the happy valley,' said Lord Cadurcis to Lady Annabel, 'and here is our plunder,' and he gave her the violets.

'You were always fond of flowers,' said Lady Annabel.

'Yes, I imbibed the taste from you,' said Cadurcis, gratified by the gracious remark.

He seated himself at her feet, examined and admired her work, and talked of old times, but with such infinite discretion, that he did not arouse a single painful association. Venetia was busied with her father's poems, and smiled often at the manuscript notes of Cadurcis. Lying, as usual, on the grass, and leaning his head on his left arm, Herbert was listening to Captain Cadurcis, who was endeavouring to give him a clear idea of the Bosphorus. Thus the morning wore away, until the sun drove them into the villa.

'I will show you my library, Lord Cadurcis,' said Herbert.

Cadurcis followed him into a spacious apartment, where he found a collection so considerable that he could not suppress his surprise. 'Italian spoils chiefly,' said Herbert; 'a friend of mine purchased an old library at Bologna for me, and it turned out richer than I imagined: the rest are old friends that have been with me, many of them at least, at college. I brought them back with me from America, for then they were my only friends.'

'Can you find Cabanis?' said Lord Cadurcis.

Herbert looked about. It is in this neighbourhood, I imagine,' he said. Cadurcis endeavoured to assist him. 'What is this?' he said; 'Plato!'

'I should like to read Plato at Athens,' said Herbert. 'My ambition now does not soar beyond such elegant fortune.'

'We are all under great obligations to Plato,' said Cadurcis. 'I remember, when I was in London, I always professed myself his disciple, and it is astonishing what results I experienced. Platonic love was a great invention.'

Herbert smiled; but, as he saw Cadurcis knew nothing about the subject, he made no reply.

'Plato says, or at least I think he says, that life is love,' said Cadurcis. 'I have said it myself in a very grand way too; I believe I cribbed it from you. But what does he mean? I am sure I meant nothing; but I dare say you did.'

'I certainly had some meaning,' said Herbert, stopping in his search, and smiling, 'but I do not know whether I expressed it. The principle of every motion, that is of all life, is desire or love: at present; I am in love with the lost volume of Cabanis, and, if it were not for the desire of obtaining it, I should not now be affording any testimony of my vitality by looking after it.'

'That is very clear,' said Cadurcis, 'but I was thinking of love in the vulgar sense, in the shape of a petticoat. Certainly, when I am in love with a woman, I feel love is life; but, when I am out of love, which often happens, and generally very soon, I still contrive to live.'

'We exist,' said Herbert, 'because we sympathise. If we did not sympathise with the air, we should die. But, if we only sympathised with the air, we should be in the lowest order of brutes, baser than the sloth. Mount from the sloth to the poet. It is sympathy that makes you a poet. It is your desire that the airy children of your brain should be born anew within another's, that makes you create; therefore, a misanthropical poet is a contradiction in terms.'

'But when he writes a lampoon?' said Cadurcis.

'He desires that the majority, who are not lampooned, should share his hate,' said Herbert.

'But Swift lampooned the species,' said Cadurcis. 'For my part, I think life is hatred.'

'But Swift was not sincere, for he wrote the Drapier's Letters at the same time. Besides, the very fact of your abusing mankind proves that you do not hate them; it is clear that you are desirous of obtaining their good opinion of your wit. You value them, you esteem them, you love them. Their approbation causes you to act, and makes you happy. As for sexual love,' said Herbert, 'of which you were speaking, its quality and duration depend upon the degree of sympathy that subsists between the two persons interested. Plato believed, and I believe with him, in the existence of a spiritual antitype of the soul, so that when we are born, there is something within us which, from the instant we live and move, thirsts after its likeness. This propensity develops itself with the development of our nature. The gratification of the senses soon becomes a very small part of that profound and complicated sentiment, which we call love. Love, on the contrary, is an universal thirst for a communion, not merely of the senses, but of our whole nature, intellectual, imaginative, and sensitive. He who finds his antitype, enjoys a love perfect and enduring; time cannot change it, distance cannot remove it; the sympathy is complete. He who loves an object that approaches his antitype, is proportionately happy, the sympathy is feeble or strong, as it may be. If men were properly educated, and their faculties fully developed,' continued Herbert, 'the discovery of the antitype would be easy; and, when the day arrives that it is a matter of course, the perfection of civilisation will be attained.'

'I believe in Plato,' said Lord Cadurcis, 'and I think I have found my antitype. His theory accounts for what I never could understand.'

CHAPTER VII.

In the course of the evening Lady Annabel requested Lord Cadurcis and his cousin to take up their quarters at the villa. Independent of the delight which such an invitation occasioned him, Cadurcis was doubly gratified by its being given by her. It was indeed her unprompted solicitation; for neither Herbert nor even Venetia, however much they desired the arrangement, was anxious to appear eager for its fulfilment. Desirous of pleasing her husband and her daughter; a little penitent as to her previous treatment of Cadurcis, now that time and strange events had combined to soften her feelings; and won by his engaging demeanour towards herself, Lady Annabel had of mere impulse resolved upon the act; and she was repaid by the general air of gaiety and content which it diffused through the circle.

Few weeks indeed passed ere her ladyship taught herself even to contemplate the possibility of an union between her daughter and Lord Cadurcis. The change which had occurred in her own feelings and position had in her estimation removed very considerable barriers to such a result. It would not become her again to urge the peculiarity of his temperament as an insuperable objection to the marriage; that was out of the question, even if the conscience of Lady Annabel herself, now that she was so happy, were perfectly free from any participation in the causes which occasioned the original estrangement between Herbert and herself. Desirous too, as all mothers are, that her daughter should be suitably married, Lady Annabel could not shut her eyes to the great improbability of such an event occurring, now that Venetia had, as it were, resigned all connection with her native country. As to her daughter marrying a foreigner, the very idea was intolerable to her; and Venetia appeared therefore to have resumed that singular and delicate position which she occupied at Cherbury in earlier years, when Lady Annabel had esteemed her connection with Lord Cadurcis so fortunate and auspicious. Moreover, while Lord Cadurcis, in birth, rank, country, and consideration, offered in every view of the ease so gratifying an alliance, he was perhaps the only Englishman whose marriage into her family would not deprive her of the society of her child. Cadurcis had a great distaste for England, which he seized every opportunity to express. He continually declared that he would never return there; and his habits of seclusion and study so entirely accorded with those of her husband, that Lady Annabel did not doubt they would continue to form only one family; a prospect so engaging to her, that it would perhaps have alone removed the distrust which she had so unfortunately cherished against the admirer of her daughter; and although some of his reputed opinions occasioned her doubtless considerable anxiety, he was nevertheless very young, and far from emancipated from the beneficial influence of his early education. She was sanguine that this sheep would yet return to the fold where once he had been tended with so much solicitude. When too she called to mind the chastened spirit of her husband, and could not refrain from feeling that, had she not quitted him, he might at a much earlier period have attained a mood so full of promise and to her so cheering, she could not resist the persuasion that, under the influence of Venetia, Cadurcis might speedily free himself from the dominion of that arrogant genius to which, rather than to any serious conviction, the result of a studious philosophy, she attributed his indifference on the most important of subjects. On the whole, however, it was with no common gratification that Lady Annabel observed the strong and intimate friendship that arose between her husband and Cadurcis. They were inseparable companions. Independently of the natural sympathy between two highly imaginative minds, there were in the superior experience, the noble character, the vast knowledge, and refined taste of Herbert, charms of which Cadurcis was very susceptible Cadurcis had not been a great reader himself, and he liked the company of one whose mind was at once so richly cultured and so deeply meditative: thus he obtained matter and spirit distilled through the alembic of another's brain. Jealousy had never had a place in Herbert's temperament; now he was insensible even to emulation. He spoke of Cadurcis as he thought, with the highest admiration; as one without a rival, and in whose power it was to obtain an imperishable fame. It was his liveliest pleasure to assist the full development of such an intellect, and to pour to him, with a lavish hand, all the treasures of his taste, his learning, his fancy, and his meditation. His kind heart, his winning manners, his subdued and perfect temper, and the remembrance of the relation which he bore to Venetia, completed the spell which bound Cadurcis to him with all the finest feelings of his nature. It was, indeed, an intercourse peculiarly beneficial to Cadurcis, whose career had hitherto tended rather to the development of the power, than the refinement of his genius; and to whom an active communion with an equal spirit of a more matured intelligence was an incident rather to be desired than expected. Herbert and Cadurcis, therefore, spent their mornings together, sometimes in the library, sometimes wandering in the chestnut woods, sometimes sailing in the boat of the brig, for they were both fond of the sea: in these excursions, George was in general their companion. He had become a great favourite with Herbert, as with everybody else. No one managed a boat so well, although Cadurcis prided himself also on his skill in this respect; and George was so frank and unaffected, and so used to his cousin's habits, that his presence never embarrassed Herbert and Cadurcis, and they read or conversed quite at their ease, as if there were no third person to mar, by his want of sympathy, the full communion of their intellect. The whole circle met at dinner, and never again parted until at a late hour of night. This was a most agreeable life; Cadurcis himself, good humoured because he was happy, doubly exerted himself to ingratiate himself with Lady Annabel, and felt every day that he was advancing. Venetia always smiled upon him, and praised him delightfully for his delightful conduct.

In the evening, Herbert would read to them the manuscript poem of Cadurcis, the fruits of his Attic residence and Grecian meditations. The poet would sometimes affect a playful bashfulness on this head, perhaps not altogether affected, and amuse Venetia, in a whisper, with his running comments; or exclaim with an arch air, 'I say, Venetia, what would Mrs. Montague and the Blues give for this, eh? I can fancy Hannah More in decent ecstasies!'

CHAPTER VIII.

'It is an odd thing, my dear Herbert,' said Cadurcis to his friend, in one of these voyages, 'that destiny should have given you and me the same tutor.'

'Masham!' said Herbert, smiling. 'I tell you what is much more singular, my dear Cadurcis; it is, that, notwithstanding being our tutor, a mitre should have fallen upon his head.'

'I am heartily glad,' said Cadurcis. 'I like Masham very much; I really have a sincere affection for him. Do you know, during my infernal affair about those accursed Monteagles, when I went to the House of Lords, and was cut even by my own party; think of that, the polished ruffians! Masham was the only person who came forward and shook hands with me, and in the most marked manner. A bishop, too! and the other side! that was good, was it not? But he would not see his old pupil snubbed; if he had waited ten minutes longer, he might have had a chance of seeing him massacred. And then they complain of my abusing England, my mother country; a step-dame, I take it.'

'Masham is in politics a Tory, in religion ultra-orthodox,' Herbert. 'He has nothing about him of the latitudinarian; and yet he is the most amiable man with whom I am acquainted. Nature has given him a kind and charitable heart, which even his opinions have not succeeded in spoiling.'

'Perhaps that is exactly what he is saying of us two at this moment,' said Cadurcis. 'After all, what is truth? It changes as you change your clime or your country; it changes with the century. The truth of a hundred years ago is not the truth of the present day, and yet it may have been as genuine. Truth at Rome is not the truth of London, and both of them differ from the truth of Constantinople. For my part, I believe everything.'

'Well, that is practically prudent, if it be metaphysically possible,' said Herbert. 'Do you know that I have always been of opinion, that Pontius Pilate has been greatly misrepresented by Lord Bacon in the quotation of his celebrated question. 'What is truth?' said jesting Pilate, and would not wait for an answer. Let us be just to Pontius Pilate, who has sins enough surely to answer for. There is no authority for the jesting humour given by Lord Bacon. Pilate was evidently of a merciful and clement disposition; probably an Epicurean. His question referred to a declaration immediately preceding it, that He who was before him came to bear witness to the truth. Pilate inquired what truth?'

'Well, I always have a prejudice against Pontius Pilate,' said Lord Cadurcis; 'and I think it is from seeing him, when I was a child, on an old Dutch tile fireplace at Marringhurst, dressed like a burgomaster. One cannot get over one's early impressions; but when you picture him to me as an Epicurean, he assumes a new character. I fancy him young, noble, elegant, and accomplished; crowned with a wreath and waving a goblet, and enjoying his government vastly.'

'Before the introduction of Christianity,' said Herbert, 'the philosophic schools answered to our present religious sects. You said of a man that he was a Stoic or an Epicurean, as you say of a man now that he is a Calvinist or a Wesleyan.'

'I should have liked to have known Epicurus,' said Cadurcis.

'I would sooner have known him and Plato than any of the ancients,' said Herbert. 'I look upon Plato as the wisest and the profoundest of men, and upon Epicurus as the most humane and gentle.'

'Now, how do you account for the great popularity of Aristotle in modern ages?' said Cadurcis; 'and the comparative neglect of these, at least his equals? Chance, I suppose, that settles everything.'

'By no means,' said Herbert. 'If you mean by chance an absence of accountable cause, I do not believe such a quality as chance exists. Every incident that happens, must be a link in a chain. In the present case, the monks monopolised literature, such as it might be, and they exercised their intellect only in discussing words. They, therefore, adopted Aristotle and the Peripatetics. Plato interfered with their heavenly knowledge, and Epicurus, who maintained the rights of man to pleasure and happiness, would have afforded a dangerous and seducing contrast to their dark and miserable code of morals.'

'I think, of the ancients,' said Cadurcis; 'Alcibiades and Alexander the Great are my favourites. They were young, beautiful, and conquerors; a great combination.'

'And among the moderns?' inquired Herbert.

'They don't touch my fancy,' said Cadurcis. 'Who are your heroes?'

'Oh! I have many; but I confess I should like to pass a day with Milton, or Sir Philip Sidney.'

'Among mere literary men,' said Cadurcis; 'I should say Bayle.'

'And old Montaigne for me,' said Herbert.

'Well, I would fain visit him in his feudal chateau,' said Cadurcis. 'His is one of the books which give a spring to the mind. Of modern times, the feudal ages of Italy most interest me. I think that was a springtide of civilisation, all the fine arts nourished at the same moment.'

'They ever will,' said Herbert. 'All the inventive arts maintain a sympathetic connection between each other, for, after all, they are only various expressions of one internal power, modified by different circumstances either of the individual or of society. It was so in the age of Pericles; I mean the interval which intervened between the birth of that great man and the death of Aristotle; undoubtedly, whether considered in itself, or with reference to the effects which it produced upon the subsequent destinies of civilised man, the most memorable in the history of the world.'

'And yet the age of Pericles has passed away,' said Lord Cadurcis mournfully, 'and I have gazed upon the mouldering Parthenon. O Herbert! you are a great thinker and muse deeply; solve me the problem why so unparalleled a progress was made during that period in literature and the arts, and why that progress, so rapid and so sustained, so soon received a check and became retrograde?'

'It is a problem left to the wonder and conjecture of posterity,' said Herbert. 'But its solution, perhaps, may principally be found in the weakness of their political institutions. Nothing of the Athenians remains except their genius; but they fulfilled their purpose. The wrecks and fragments of their subtle and profound minds obscurely suggest to us the grandeur and perfection of the whole. Their language excels every other tongue of the Western world; their sculptures baffle all subsequent artists; credible witnesses assure us that their paintings were not inferior; and we are only accustomed to consider the painters of Italy as those who have brought the art to its highest perfection, because none of the ancient pictures have been preserved. Yet of all their fine arts, it was music of which the Greeks were themselves most proud. Its traditionary effects were far more powerful than any which we experience from the compositions of our times. And now for their poetry, Cadurcis. It is in poetry, and poetry alone, that modern nations have maintained the majesty of genius. Do we equal the Greeks? Do we even excel them?'

'Let us prove the equality first,' said Cadurcis. 'The Greeks excelled in every species of poetry. In some we do not even attempt to rival them. We have not a single modern ode, or a single modern pastoral. We have no one to place by Pindar, or the exquisite Theocritus. As for the epic, I confess myself a heretic as to Homer; I look upon the Iliad as a remnant of national songs; the wise ones agree that the Odyssey is the work of a later age. My instinct agrees with the result of their researches. I credit their conclusion. The Paradise Lost is, doubtless, a great production, but the subject is monkish. Dante is national, but he has all the faults of a barbarous age. In general the modern epic is framed upon the assumption that the Iliad is an orderly composition. They are indebted for this fallacy to Virgil, who called order out of chaos; but the Aeneid, all the same, appears to me an insipid creation. And now for the drama. You will adduce Shakspeare?'

'There are passages in Dante,' said Herbert, 'not inferior, in my opinion, to any existing literary composition, but, as a whole, I will not make my stand on him; I am not so clear that, as a lyric poet, Petrarch may not rival the Greeks. Shakspeare I esteem of ineffable merit.'

'And who is Shakspeare?' said Cadurcis. 'We know of him as much as we do of Homer. Did he write half the plays attributed to him? Did he ever write a single whole play? I doubt it. He appears to me to have been an inspired adapter for the theatres, which were then not as good as barns. I take him to have been a botcher up of old plays. His popularity is of modern date, and it may not last; it would have surprised him marvellously. Heaven knows, at present, all that bears his name is alike admired; and a regular Shaksperian falls into ecstasies with trash which deserves a niche in the Dunciad. For my part, I abhor your irregular geniuses, and I love to listen to the little nightingale of Twickenham.'

'I have often observed,' said Herbert, 'that writers of an unbridled imagination themselves, admire those whom the world, erroneously, in my opinion, and from a confusion of ideas, esteems correct. I am myself an admirer of Pope, though I certainly should not ever think of classing him among the great creative spirits. And you, you are the last poet in the world, Cadurcis, whom one would have fancied his votary.'

'I have written like a boy,' said Cadurcis. 'I found the public bite, and so I baited on with tainted meat. I have never written for fame, only for notoriety; but I am satiated; I am going to turn over a new leaf.'

'For myself,' said Herbert, 'if I ever had the power to impress my creations on my fellow-men, the inclination is gone, and perhaps the faculty is extinct. My career is over; perhaps a solitary echo from my lyre may yet, at times, linger about the world like a breeze that has lost its way. But there is a radical fault in my poetic mind, and I am conscious of it. I am not altogether void of the creative faculty, but mine is a fragmentary mind; I produce no whole. Unless you do this, you cannot last; at least, you cannot materially affect your species. But what I admire in you, Cadurcis, is that, with all the faults of youth, of which you will free yourself, your creative power is vigorous, prolific, and complete; your creations rise fast and fair, like perfect worlds.'

'Well, we will not compliment each other,' said Cadurcis; 'for, after all, it is a miserable craft. What is poetry but a lie, and what are poets but liars?'

'You are wrong, Cadurcis,' said Herbert, 'poets are the unacknowledged legislators of the world.'

'I see the towers of Porto Venere,' said Cadurcis directing the sail; 'we shall soon be on shore. I think, too, I recognise Venetia. Ah! my dear Herbert, your daughter is a poem that beats all our inspiration!'

CHAPTER IX.

One circumstance alone cast a gloom over this happy family, and that was the approaching departure of Captain Cadurcis for England. This had been often postponed, but it could be postponed no longer. Not even the entreaties of those kind friends could any longer prevent what was inevitable. The kind heart, the sweet temper, and the lively and companionable qualities of Captain Cadurcis, had endeared him to everyone; all felt that his departure would occasion a blank in their life, impossible to be supplied. It reminded the Herberts also painfully of their own situation, in regard to their native country, which they were ever unwilling to dwell upon. George talked of returning to them, but the prospect was necessarily vague; they felt that it was only one of those fanciful visions with which an affectionate spirit attempts to soothe the pang of separation. His position, his duties, all the projects of his life, bound him to England, from which, indeed, he had been too long absent. It was selfish to wish that, for their sakes, he should sink down into a mere idler in Italy; and yet, when they recollected how little his future life could be connected with their own, everyone felt dispirited.

'I shall not go boating to-day,' said George to Venetia; 'it is my last day. Mr. Herbert and Plantagenet talk of going to Lavenza; let us take a stroll together.'

Nothing can be refused to those we love on the last day, and Venetia immediately acceded to his request. In the course of the morning, therefore, herself and George quitted the valley, in the direction of the coast towards Genoa. Many a white sail glittered on the blue waters; it was a lively and cheering scene; but both Venetia and her companion were depressed.

'I ought to be happy,' said George, and sighed. 'The fondest wish of my heart is attained. You remember our conversation on the Lago Maggiore, Venetia? You see I was a prophet, and you will be Lady Cadurcis yet.'

'We must keep up our spirits,' said Venetia; 'I do not despair of our all returning to England yet. So many wonders have happened, that I cannot persuade myself that this marvel will not also occur. I am sure my uncle will do something; I have a secret idea that the Bishop is all this time working for papa; I feel assured I shall see Cherbury and Cadurcis again, and Cadurcis will be your home.'

'A year ago you appeared dying, and Plantagenet was the most miserable of men,' said Captain Cadurcis. 'You are both now perfectly well and perfectly happy, living even under the same roof, soon, I feel, to be united, and with the cordial approbation of Lady Annabel. Your father is restored to you.

Every blessing in the world seems to cluster round your roof. It is selfish for me to wear a gloomy countenance.'

'Ah! dear George, you never can be selfish,' said Venetia.

'Yes, I am selfish, Venetia. What else can make me sad?'

'You know how much you contribute to our happiness,' said Venetia, 'and you feel for our sufferings at your absence.'

'No, Venetia, I feel for myself,' said Captain Cadurcis with energy; 'I am certain that I never can be happy, except in your society and Plantagenet's. I cannot express to you how I love you both. Nothing else gives me the slightest interest.'

'You must go home and marry,' said Venetia, smiling 'You must marry an heiress.'

'Never,' said Captain Cadurcis. 'Nothing shall ever induce me to marry. No! all my dreams are confined to being the bachelor uncle of the family.'

'Well, now I think,' said Venetia, 'of all the persons I know, there is no one so qualified for domestic happiness as yourself. I think your wife, George, would be a very fortunate woman, and I only wish I had a sister, that you might marry her.'

'I wish you had, Venetia; I would give up my resolution against marriage directly.'

'Alas!' said Venetia, 'there is always some bitter drop in the cup of life. Must you indeed go, George?'

'My present departure is inevitable,' he replied; 'but I have some thoughts of giving up my profession and Parliament, and then I will return, never to leave you again.'

'What will Lord —— say? That will never do,' said Venetia. 'No; I should not be content unless you prospered in the world, George. You are made to prosper, and I should be miserable if you sacrificed your existence to us. You must go home, and you must marry, and write letters to us by every post, and tell us what a happy man you are. The best thing for you to do would be to live with your wife at the abbey; or Cherbury, if you liked. You see I settle everything.'

'I never will marry,' said Captain Cadurcis, seriously.

'Yes you will,' said Venetia.

'I am quite serious, Venetia. Now, mark my words, and remember this day. I never will marry. I have a reason, and a strong and good one, for my resolution.'

'What is it?'

'Because my marriage will destroy the intimacy that subsists between me and yourself, and Plantagenet,' he added.

'Your wife should be my friend,' said Venetia.

'Happy woman!' said George.

'Let us indulge for a moment in a dream of domestic bliss,' said Venetia gaily. 'Papa and mamma at Cherbury; Plantagenet and myself at the abbey, where you and your wife must remain until we could build you a house; and Dr. Masham coming down to spend Christmas with us. Would it not be delightful? I only hope Plantagenet would be tame. I think he would burst out a little sometimes.'

'Not with you, Venetia, not with you,' said George 'you have a hold over him which nothing can ever shake. I could always put him in an amiable mood in an instant by mentioning your name.'

'I wish you knew the abbey, George,' said Venetia. 'It is the most interesting of all old places. I love it. You must promise me when you arrive in England to go on a pilgrimage to Cadurcis and Cherbury, and write me a long account of it.'

'I will indeed; I will write to you very often.'

'You shall find me a most faithful correspondent, which, I dare say, Plantagenet would not prove.'

'Oh! I beg your pardon,' said George; 'you have no idea of the quantity of letters he wrote me when he first quitted England. And such delightful ones! I do not think there is a more lively letter-writer in the world! His descriptions are so vivid; a few touches give you a complete picture; and then his observations, they are so playful! I assure you there is nothing in the world more easy and diverting than a letter from Plantagenet.'

'If you could only see his first letter from Eton to me?' said Venetia. 'I have always treasured it. It certainly was not very diverting; and, if by easy you mean easy to decipher,' she added laughing, 'his handwriting must have improved very much lately. Dear Plantagenet, I am always afraid I never pay him sufficient respect; that I do not feel sufficient awe in his presence; but I cannot disconnect him from the playfellow of my infancy; and, do you know, it seems to me, whenever he addresses me, his voice and air change, and assume quite the tone and manner of childhood.'

'I have never known him but as a great man,' said Captain Cadurcis; 'but he was so frank and simple with me from the very first, that I cannot believe that it is not two years since we first met.'

'Ah! I shall never forget that night at Ranelagh,' said Venetia, half with a smile and half with a sigh. 'How interesting he looked! I loved to see the people stare at him, and to hear them whisper his name.'

Here they seated themselves by a fountain, overshadowed by a plane-tree, and for a while talked only of Plantagenet.

'All the dreams of my life have come to pass,' said Venetia. 'I remember when I was at Weymouth, ill and not very happy, I used to roam about the sands, thinking of papa, and how I wished Plantagenet was like him, a great man, a great poet, whom all the world admired. Little did I think that, before a year had passed, Plantagenet, my unknown Plantagenet, would be the admiration of England; little did I think another year would pass, and I should be living with my father and Plantagenet together, and they should be bosom friends. You see, George, we must never despair.'

'Under this bright sun,' said Captain Cadurcis, 'one is naturally sanguine, but think of me alone and in gloomy England.'

'It is indeed a bright sun,' said Venetia; 'how wonderful to wake every morning, and be sure of meeting its beam.'

Captain Cadurcis looked around him with a sailor's eye. Over the Apennines, towards Genoa, there was a ridge of dark clouds piled up with such compactness, that they might have been mistaken in a hasty survey for part of the mountains themselves.

'Bright as is the sun,' said Captain Cadurcis, 'we may have yet a squall before night.'

'I was delighted with Venice,' said his companion, not noticing his observation; 'I think of all places in the world it is one which Plantagenet would most admire. I cannot believe but that even his delicious Athens would yield to it.'

'He did lead the oddest life at Athens you can conceive,' said Captain Cadurcis. 'The people did not know what to make of him. He lived in the Latin convent, a fine building which he had almost to himself, for there are not half a dozen monks. He used to pace up and down the terrace which he had turned into a garden, and on which he kept all sorts of strange animals. He wrote continually there. Indeed he did nothing but write. His only relaxation was a daily ride to Piraeus, about five miles over the plain; he told me it was the only time in his life he was ever contented with himself except when he was at Cherbury. He always spoke of London with disgust.'

'Plantagenet loves retirement and a quiet life,' said Venetia; 'but he must not be marred with vulgar sights and common-place duties. That is the secret with him.'

'I think the wind has just changed,' said Captain Cadurcis. 'It seems to me that we shall have a sirocco. There, it shifts again! We shall have a sirocco for certain.'

'What did you think of papa when you first saw him?' said Venetia. 'Was he the kind of person you expected to see?'

'Exactly,' said Captain Cadurcis. 'So very spiritual! Plantagenet said to me, as we went home the first night, that he looked like a golden phantom. I think him very like you, Venetia; indeed, there can be no doubt you inherited your face from your father.'

'Ah! if you had seen his portrait at Cherbury, when he was only twenty!' said Venetia. 'That was a golden phantom, or rather he looked like Hyperion. What are you staring at so, George?'

'I do not like this wind,' muttered Captain Cadurcis. 'There it goes.'

'You cannot see the wind, George?'

'Yes, I can, Venetia, and I do not like it at all. Do you see that black spot flitting like a shade over the sea? It is like the reflection of a cloud on the water; but there is no cloud. Well, that is the wind, Venetia, and a very wicked wind too.'

'How strange! Is that indeed the wind?'

'We had better return home,' said Captain Cadurcis I wish they had not gone to Lavenza.'

'But there is no danger?' said Venetia.

'Danger? No! no danger, but they may get a wet jacket.'

They walked on; but Captain Cadurcis was rather distrait: his eye was always watching the wind; at last he said, 'I tell you, Venetia, we must walk quickly; for, by Jove, we are going to have a white squall.'

They hurried their pace, Venetia mentioned her alarm again about the boat; but her companion reassured her; yet his manner was not so confident as his words.

A white mist began to curl above the horizon, the blueness of the day seemed suddenly to fade, and its colour became grey; there was a swell on the waters that hitherto had been quite glassy, and they were covered with a scurfy foam.

'I wish I had been with them,' said Captain Cadurcis, evidently very anxious.

'George, you are alarmed,' said Venetia, earnestly. 'I am sure there is danger.'

'Danger! How can there be danger, Venetia? Perhaps they are in port by this time. I dare say we shall find them at Spezzia. I will see you home and run down to them. Only hurry, for your own sake, for you do not know what a white squall in the Mediterranean is. We have but a few moments.'

And even at this very instant, the wind came roaring and rushing with such a violent gush that Venetia could scarcely stand; George put his arm round her to support her. The air was filled with thick white vapour, so that they could no longer see the ocean, only the surf rising very high all along the coast.

'Keep close to me, Venetia,' said Captain Cadurcis; 'hold my arm and I will walk first, for we shall not be able to see a yard before us in a minute. I know where we are. We are above the olive wood, and we shall soon be in the ravine. These Mediterranean white squalls are nasty things; I had sooner by half be in a south-wester; for one cannot run before the wind in this bay, the reefs stretch such a long way out.'

The danger, and the inutility of expressing fears which could only perplex her guide, made Venetia silent, but she was terrified. She could not divest herself of apprehension about her father and Plantagenet. In spite of all he said, it was evident that her companion was alarmed.

They had now entered the valley; the mountains had in some degree kept off the vapour; the air was more clear. Venetia and Captain Cadurcis stopped a moment to breathe. 'Now, Venetia, you are safe,' said Captain Cadurcis. 'I will not come in; I will run down to the bay at once.' He wiped the mist off his face: Venetia perceived him deadly pale.

'George,' she said, 'conceal nothing from me; there is danger, imminent danger. Tell me at once.'

'Indeed, Venetia,' said Captain Cadurcis, 'I am sure everything will be quite right. There is some danger, certainly, at this moment; but of course, long ago, they have run into harbour. I have no doubt they are at Spezzia at this moment. Now, do not be alarmed; indeed there is no cause. God bless you!' he said, and bounded away. 'No cause,' thought he to himself, as the wind sounded like thunder, and the vapour came rushing up the ravine. 'God grant I may be right; but neither between the Tropics nor on the Line have I witnessed a severer squall than this! What open boat can live in this weather Oh! that I had been with them. I shall never forgive myself!'

CHAPTER X.

Venetia found her mother walking up and down the room, as was her custom when she was agitated. She hurried to her daughter. 'You must change your dress instantly, Venetia,' said Lady Annabel. 'Where is George?'

'He has gone down to Spezzia to papa and Plantagenet; it is a white squall; it comes on very suddenly in this sea. He ran down to Spezzia instantly, because he thought they would be wet,' said the agitated Venetia, speaking with rapidity and trying to appear calm.

'Are they at Spezzia?' inquired Lady Annabel, quickly.

'George has no doubt they are, mother,' said Venetia.

'No doubt!' exclaimed Lady Annabel, in great distress. 'God grant they may be only wet.'

'Dearest mother,' said Venetia, approaching her, but speech deserted her. She had advanced to encourage Lady Annabel, but her own fear checked the words on her lips.

'Change your dress, Venetia,' said Lady Annabel; 'lose no time in doing that. I think I will send down to Spezzia at once,'

'That is useless now, dear mother, for George is there.'

'Go, dearest,' said Lady Annabel; 'I dare say, we have no cause for fear, but I am exceedingly alarmed about your father, about them: I am, indeed. I do not like these sudden squalls, and I never liked this boating; indeed, I never did. George being with them reconciled me to it. Now go, Venetia; go, my love.'

Venetia quitted the room. She was so agitated that she made Pauncefort a confidant of her apprehensions.

'La! my dear miss,' said Mistress Pauncefort, 'I should never have thought of such a thing! Do not you remember what the old man said at Weymouth, "there is many a boat will live in a rougher sea than a ship;" and it is such an unlikely thing, it is indeed, Miss Venetia. I am certain sure my lord can manage a boat as well as a common sailor, and master is hardly less used to it than he. La! miss, don't make yourself nervous about any such preposterous ideas. And I dare say you will find them in the saloon when you go down again. Really I should not wonder. I think you had better wear your twill dress; I have put the new trimming on.'

They had not returned when Venetia joined her mother. That indeed she could scarcely expect. But, in about half an hour, a message arrived from Captain Cadurcis that they were not at Spezzia, but from something he had heard, he had no doubt they were at Sarzana, and he was going to ride on there at once. He felt sure, however, from what he had heard, they were at Sarzana. This communication afforded Lady Annabel a little ease, but Venetia's heart misgave her. She recalled the alarm of George in the morning, which it was impossible for him to disguise, and she thought she recognised in this hurried message and vague assurances of safety something of the same apprehension, and the same fruitless efforts to conceal it.

Now came the time of terrible suspense. Sarzana was nearly twenty miles distant from Spezzia. The evening must arrive before they could receive intelligence from Captain Cadurcis. In the meantime the squall died away, the heavens became again bright, and, though the waves were still tumultuous, the surf was greatly decreased. Lady Annabel had already sent down more than one messenger to the bay, but they brought no intelligence; she resolved now to go herself, that she might have the satisfaction of herself cross-examining the fishermen who had been driven in from various parts by stress of weather. She would not let Venetia accompany her, who, she feared, might already suffer from the exertions and rough weather of the morning. This was a most anxious hour, and yet the absence of her mother was in some degree a relief to Venetia; it at least freed her from the perpetual effort of assumed composure. While her mother remained, Venetia had affected to read, though her eye wandered listlessly over the page, or to draw, though the pencil trembled in her hand; anything which might guard her from conveying to her mother that she shared the apprehensions which had already darkened her mother's mind. But now that Lady Annabel was gone, Venetia, muffling herself up in her shawl, threw herself on a sofa, and there she remained without a thought, her mind a chaos of terrible images.

Her mother returned, and with a radiant countenance, Venetia sprang from the sofa. 'There is good news; O mother! have they returned?'

'They are not at Spezzia,' said Lady Annabel, throwing herself into a chair panting for breath; 'but there is good news. You see I was right to go, Venetia. These stupid people we send only ask questions, and take the first answer. I have seen a fisherman, and he says he heard that two persons, Englishmen he believes, have put into Lerici in an open boat.'

'God be praised!' said Venetia. 'O mother, I can now confess to you the terror I have all along felt.'

'My own heart assures me of it, my child,' said Lady Annabel weeping; and they mingled their tears together, but tears not of sorrow.

'Poor George!' said Lady Annabel, 'he will have a terrible journey to Sarzana, and be feeling so much for us! Perhaps he may meet them.'

'I feel assured he will,' said Venetia; 'and perhaps ere long they will all three be here again. Joy! joy!'

'They must never go in that boat again,' said Lady Annabel.

'Oh! they never will, dearest mother, if you ask them not,' said Venetia.

'We will send to Lerici,' said Lady Annabel.

'Instantly,' said Venetia; 'but I dare say they already sent us a messenger.'

'No!' said Lady Annabel; 'men treat the danger that is past very lightly. We shall not hear from them except in person.'

Time now flew more lightly. They were both easy in their minds. The messenger was despatched to Lerici; but even Lerici was a considerable distance, and hours must elapse before his return. Still there was the hope of seeing them, or hearing from them in the interval.

'I must go out, dear mother,' said Venetia. 'Let us both go out. It is now very fine. Let us go just to the ravine, for indeed it is impossible to remain here.'

Accordingly they both went forth, and took up a position on the coast which commanded a view on all sides. All was radiant again, and comparatively calm. Venetia looked upon the sea, and said, 'Ah! I never shall forget a white squall in the Mediterranean, for all this splendour.'

It was sunset: they returned home. No news yet from Lerici. Lady Annabel grew uneasy again. The pensive and melancholy hour encouraged gloom; but Venetia, who was sanguine, encouraged her mother.

'Suppose they were not Englishmen in the boat,' said Lady Annabel.

'It is impossible, mother. What other two persons in this neighbourhood could have been in an open boat? Besides, the man said Englishmen. You remember, he said Englishmen. You are quite sure he did? It must be they. I feel as convinced of it as of your presence.'

'I think there can be no doubt,' said Lady Annabel. 'I wish that the messenger would return.'

The messenger did return. No two persons in an open boat had put into Lerici; but a boat, like the one described, with every stitch of canvas set, had passed Lerici just before the squall commenced, and, the people there doubted not, had made Sarzana.

Lady Annabel turned pale, but Venetia was still sanguine. 'They are at Sarzana,' she said; 'they must be at Sarzana: you see George was right. He said he was sure they were at Sarzana. Besides, dear mother, he heard they were at Sarzana.'

'And we heard they were at Lerici,' said Lady Annabel in a melancholy tone.

And so they were, dear mother; it all agrees. The accounts are consistent. Do not you see how very consistent they are? They were seen at Lerici, and were off Lerici, but they made Sarzana; and George heard they were at Sarzana. I am certain they are at Sarzana. I feel quite easy; I feel as easy as if they were here. They are safe at Sarzana. But it is too far to return to-night. We shall see them at breakfast to-morrow, all three.'

'Venetia, dearest! do not you sit up,' said her mother. 'I think there is a chance of George returning; I feel assured he will send to-night; but late, of course. Go, dearest, and sleep.'

'Sleep!' thought Venetia to herself; but to please her mother she retired.

'Good-night, my child,' said Lady Annabel. 'The moment any one arrives, you shall be aroused.'

CHAPTER XI.

Venetia, without undressing, lay down on her bed, watching for some sound that might give her hope of George's return. Dwelling on every instant, the time dragged heavily along, and she thought that the night had half passed when Pauncefort entered her room, and she learnt, to her surprise, that only an hour had elapsed since she had parted from her mother. This entrance of Pauncefort had given Venetia a momentary hope that they had returned.

'I assure you, Miss Venetia, it is only an hour,' said Pauncefort, 'and nothing could have happened. Now do try to go to sleep, that is a dear young lady, for I am certain sure that they will all return in the morning, as I am here. I was telling my lady just now, I said, says I, I dare say they are all very wet, and very fatigued.'

'They would have returned, Pauncefort,' said Venetia, 'or they would have sent. They are not at Sarzana.'

'La! Miss Venetia, why should they be at Sarzana? Why should they not have gone much farther on! For, as Vicenzo was just saying to me, and Vicenzo knows all about the coast, with such a wind as this, I should not be surprised if they were at Leghorn.'

'O Pauncefort!' said Venetia, 'I am sick at heart!'

'Now really, Miss Venetia, do not take on so!' said Pauncefort; 'for do not you remember when his lordship ran away from the abbey, and went a gipsying, nothing would persuade poor Mrs. Cadurcis that he was not robbed and murdered, and yet you see he was as safe and sound all the time, as if he had been at Cherbury.'

'Does Vicenzo really think they could have reached Leghorn?' said Venetia, clinging to every fragment of hope.

'He is morally sure of it, Miss Venetia,' said Pauncefort, 'and I feel quite as certain, for Vicenzo is always right.'

'I had confidence about Sarzana,' said Venetia; 'I really did believe they were at Sarzana. If only Captain Cadurcis would return; if he only would return, and say they were not at Sarzana, I would try to believe they were at Leghorn.'

'Now, Miss Venetia,' said Pauncefort, 'I am certain sure that they are quite safe; for my lord is a very good sailor; he is, indeed; all the men say so; and the boat is as seaworthy a boat as boat can be. There is not the slightest fear, I do assure you, miss.'

'Do the men say that Plantagenet is a good sailor?' inquired Venetia.

'Quite professional!' said Mistress Pauncefort; 'and can command a ship as well as the best of them. They all say that.'

'Hush! Pauncefort, I hear something.'

'It's only my lady, miss. I know her step,'

'Is my mother going to bed?' said Venetia.

'Yes,' said Pauncefort, 'my lady sent me here to see after you. I wish I could tell her you were asleep.'

'It is impossible to sleep,' said Venetia, rising up from the bed, withdrawing the curtain, and looking at the sky. 'What a peaceful night! I wish my heart were like the sky. I think I will go to mamma, Pauncefort!'

'Oh! dear, Miss Venetia, I am sure I think you had better not. If you and my lady, now, would only just go to sleep, and forget every thing till morning, it would be much better for you. Besides, I am sure if my lady knew you were not gone to bed already, it would only make her doubly anxious. Now, really, Miss Venetia, do take my advice, and just lie down, again. You may be sure the moment any one arrives I will let you know. Indeed, I shall go and tell my lady that you are lying down as it is, and very drowsy;' and, so saying, Mistress Pauncefort caught up her candle, and bustled out of the room.

Venetia took up the volume of her father's poems, which Cadurcis had filled with his notes. How little did Plantagenet anticipate, when he thus expressed at Athens the passing impressions of his mind, that, ere a year had glided away, his fate would be so intimately blended with that of Herbert! It was impossible, however, for Venetia to lose herself in a volume which, under any other circumstances, might have compelled her spirit! the very associations with the writers added to the terrible restlessness of her mind. She paused each instant to listen for the wished-for sound, but a mute stillness reigned throughout the house and household. There was something in this deep, unbroken silence, at a moment when anxiety was universally diffused among the dwellers beneath that roof, and the heart of more than one of them was throbbing with all the torture of the most awful suspense, that fell upon Venetia's excited nerves with a very painful and even insufferable influence. She longed for sound, for some noise that might assure her she was not the victim of a trance. She closed her volume with energy, and she started at the sound she had herself created. She rose and opened the door of her chamber very softly, and walked into the vestibule. There were caps, and cloaks, and whips, and canes of Cadurcis and her father, lying about in familiar confusion. It seemed impossible but that they were sleeping, as usual, under the same roof. And where were they? That she should live and be unable to answer that terrible question! When she felt the utter helplessness of all her strong sympathy towards them, it seemed to her that she must go mad. She gazed around her with a wild and vacant stare. At the bottom of her heart there was a fear maturing into conviction too horrible for expression. She returned to her own chamber, and the exhaustion occasioned by her anxiety, and the increased coolness of the night, made her at length drowsy. She threw herself on the bed and slumbered.

She started in her sleep, she awoke, she dreamed they had come home. She rose and looked at the progress of the night. The night was waning fast; a grey light was on the landscape; the point of day approached. Venetia stole softly to her mother's room, and entered it with a soundless step. Lady Annabel had not retired to bed. She had sat up the whole night, and was now asleep. A lamp on a small table was burning at her side, and she held, firmly grasped in her hand, the letter of her husband, which he had addressed to her at Venice, and which she had been evidently reading. A tear glided down the cheek of Venetia as she watched her mother retaining that letter with fondness even in her sleep, and when she thought of all the misery, and heartaches, and harrowing hours that had preceded its receipt, and which Venetia believed that letter had cured for ever. What misery awaited them now? Why were they watchers of the night? She shuddered when these dreadful questions flitted through her mind. She shuddered and sighed. Her mother started, and woke.

'Who is there?' inquired Lady Annabel.

'Venetia.'

'My child, have you not slept?'

'Yes, mother, and I woke refreshed, as I hope you do.'

'I wake with trust in God's mercy,' said Lady Annabel. 'Tell me the hour.'

'It is just upon dawn, mother.'

'Dawn! no one has returned, or come.'

'The house is still, mother.'

'I would you were in bed, my child.'

'Mother, I can sleep no more. I wish to be with you;' and Venetia seated herself at her mother's feet, and reclined her head upon her mother's knee.

'I am glad the night has passed, Venetia,' said Lady Annabel, in a suppressed yet solemn tone. 'It has been a trial.' And here she placed the letter in her bosom. Venetia could only answer with a sigh.

'I wish Pauncefort would come,' said Lady Annabel; 'and yet I do not like to rouse her, she was up so late, poor creature! If it be the dawn I should like to send out messengers again; something may be heard at Spezzia.'

'Vicenzo thinks they have gone to Leghorn, mother.'

'Has he heard anything!' said Lady Annabel, eagerly.

'No, but he is an excellent judge,' said Venetia, repeating all Pauncefort's consolatory chatter. 'He knows the coast so well. He says he is sure the wind would carry them on to Leghorn; and that accounts, you know, mother, for George not returning. They are all at Leghorn.'

'Would that George would return,' murmured Lady Annabel; 'I wish I could see again that sailor who said they were at Lerici. He was an intelligent man.'

'Perhaps if we send down to the bay he may be there,' said Venetia.

'Hush! I hear a step!' said Lady Annabel.

Venetia sprung up and opened the door, but it was only Pauncefort in the vestibule.

'The household are all up, my lady,' said that important personage entering; "tis a beautiful morning. Vicenzo has run down to the bay, my lady; I sent him off immediately. Vicenzo says he is certain sure they are at Leghorn, my lady; and, this time three years, the very same thing happened. They were fishing for anchovies, my lady, close by, my lady, near Sarzana; two young men, or rather one about the same age as master, and one like my lord; cousins, my lady, and just in the same sort of boat, my lady; and there came on a squall, just the same sort of squall, my lady; and they did not return home; and everyone was frightened out of their wits, my lady, and their wives and families quite distracted; and after all they were at Leghorn; for this sort of wind always takes your open boats to Leghorn, Vicenzo says.'

The sun rose, the household were all stirring, and many of them abroad; the common routine of domestic duty seemed, by some general yet not expressed understanding, to have ceased. The ladies descended below at a very early hour, and went forth into the valley, once the happy valley. What was to be its future denomination? Vicenzo returned from the bay, and he contrived to return with cheering intelligence. The master of a felucca who, in consequence of the squall had put in at Lerici, and in the evening dropped down to Spezzia, had met an open boat an hour before he reached Sarzana, and was quite confident that, if it had put into port, it must have been, from the speed at which it was going, a great distance down the coast. No wrecks had been heard of in the neighbourhood. This intelligence, the gladsome time of day, and the non-arrival of Captain Cadurcis, which according to their mood was always a circumstance that counted either for good or for evil, and the sanguine feelings which make us always cling to hope, altogether reassured our friends. Venetia dismissed from her mind the dark thought which for a moment had haunted her in the noon of night; and still it was a suspense, a painful, agitating suspense, but only suspense that yet influenced them.

'Time! said Lady Annabel. 'Time! we must wait.'

Venetia consoled her mother; she affected even a gaiety of spirit; she was sure that Vicenzo would turn out to be right, after all; Pauncefort said he always was right, and that they were at Leghorn.

The day wore apace; the noon arrived and passed; it was even approaching sunset. Lady Annabel was almost afraid to counterorder the usual meals, lest Venetia should comprehend her secret terror; the very same sentiment influenced Venetia. Thus they both had submitted to the ceremony of breakfast, but when the hour of dinner approached they could neither endure the mockery. They looked at each other, and almost at the same time they proposed that, instead of dining, they should walk down to the bay.

'I trust we shall at least hear something before the night,' said Lady Annabel. 'I confess I dread the coming night. I do not think I could endure it.'

'The longer we do not hear, the more certain I am of their being at Leghorn,' said Venetia.

'I have a great mind to travel there to-night,' said Lady Annabel.

As they were stepping into the portico, Venetia recognised Captain Cadurcis in the distance. She turned pale; she would have fallen had she not leaned on her mother, who was not so advanced, and who had not seen him.

'What is the matter, Venetia!' said Lady Annabel, alarmed.

'He is here, he is here!'

'Marmion?'

'No, George. Let me sit down.'

Her mother tried to support her to a chair. Lady Annabel took off her bonnet. She had not strength to walk forth. She could not speak. She sat down opposite Venetia, and her countenance pictured distress to so painful a degree, that at any other time Venetia would have flown to her, but in this crisis of suspense it was impossible. George was in sight; he was in the portico; he was in the room.

He looked wan, haggard, and distracted. More than once he essayed to speak, but failed.

Lady Annabel looked at him with a strange, delirious expression. Venetia rushed forward and seized his arm, and gazed intently on his face. He shrank from her glance; his frame trembled.

CHAPTER XII.

In the heart of the tempest Captain Cadurcis traced his way in a sea of vapour with extreme danger and difficulty to the shore. On his arrival at Spezzia, however, scarcely a house was visible, and the only evidence of the situation of the place was the cessation of an immense white surf which otherwise indicated the line of the sea, but the absence of which proved his contiguity to a harbour. In the thick fog he heard the cries and shouts of the returning fishermen, and of their wives and children responding from the land to their exclamations. He was forced, therefore, to wait at Spezzia, in an agony of impotent suspense, until the fury of the storm was over and the sky was partially cleared. At length the objects became gradually less obscure; he could trace the outline of the houses, and catch a glimpse of the water half a mile out, and soon the old castles which guard the entrance of the strait that leads into the gulf, looming in the distance, and now and then a group of human beings in the vanishing vapour. Of these he made some inquiries, but in vain, respecting the boat and his friends. He then made the brig, but could learn nothing except their departure in the morning. He at length obtained a horse and galloped along the coast towards Lerici, keeping a sharp look out as he proceeded and stopping at every village in his progress for intelligence. When he had arrived in the course of three hours at Lerici, the storm had abated, the sky was clear, and no evidence of the recent squall remained except the agitated state of the waves. At Lerici he could hear nothing, so he hurried on to Sarzana, where he learnt for the first time that an open boat, with its sails set, had passed more than an hour before the squall commenced. From Sarzana he hastened on to Lavenza, a little port, the nearest sea-point to Massa, and where the Carrara marble is shipped for England. Here also his inquiries were fruitless, and, exhausted by his exertions, he dismounted and rested at the inn, not only for repose, but to consider over the course which he should now pursue. The boat had not been seen off Lavenza, and the idea that they had made the coast towards Leghorn now occurred to him. His horse was so wearied that he was obliged to stop some time at Lavenza, for he could procure no other mode of conveyance; the night also was fast coming on, and to proceed to Leghorn by this dangerous route at this hour was impossible. At Lavenza therefore he remained, resolved to hasten to Leghorn at break of day. This was a most awful night. Although physically exhausted, Captain Cadurcis could not sleep, and, after some vain efforts, he quitted his restless bed on which he had laid down without undressing, and walked forth to the harbour. Between anxiety for Herbert and his cousin, and for the unhappy women whom he had left behind, he was nearly distracted. He gazed on the sea, as if some sail in sight might give him a chance of hope. His professional experience assured him of all the danger of the squall. He could not conceive how an open boat could live in such a sea, and an instant return to port so soon as the squall commenced, appeared the only chance of its salvation. Could they have reached Leghorn? It seemed impossible. There was no hope they could now be at Sarzana, or Lerici. When he contemplated the full contingency of what might have occurred, his mind wandered, and refused to comprehend the possibility of the terrible conclusion. He thought the morning would never break.

There was a cavernous rock by the seashore, that jutted into the water like a small craggy promontory. Captain Cadurcis climbed to its top, and then descending, reclined himself upon an inferior portion of it, which formed a natural couch with the wave on each side. There, lying at his length, he gazed upon the moon and stars whose brightness he thought would never dim. The Mediterranean is a tideless sea, but the swell of the waves, which still set in to the shore, bore occasionally masses of sea-weed and other marine formations, and deposited them around him, plashing, as it broke against the shore, with a melancholy and monotonous sound. The abstraction of the scene, the hour, and the surrounding circumstances brought, however, no refreshment to the exhausted spirit of George Cadurcis. He could not think, indeed he did not dare to think; but the villa of the Apennines and the open boat in the squall flitted continually before him. His mind was feeble though excited, and he fell into a restless and yet unmeaning reverie. As long as he had been in action, as long as he had been hurrying along the coast, the excitement of motion, the constant exercise of his senses, had relieved or distracted the intolerable suspense. But this pause, this inevitable pause, overwhelmed him. It oppressed his spirit like eternity. And yet what might the morning bring? He almost wished that he might remain for ever on this rock watching the moon and stars, and that the life of the world might never recommence.

He started; he had fallen into a light slumber; he had been dreaming; he thought he had heard the voice of Venetia calling him; he had forgotten where he was; he stared at the sea and sky, and recalled his dreadful consciousness. The wave broke with a heavy plash that attracted his attention: it was, indeed, that sound that had awakened him. He looked around; there was some object; he started wildly from his resting-place, sprang over the cavern, and bounded on the beach. It was a corpse; he is kneeling by its side. It is the corpse of his cousin! Lord Cadurcis was a fine swimmer, and had evidently made strong efforts for his life, for he was partly undressed. In all the insanity of hope, still wilder than despair, George Cadurcis seized the body and bore it some yards upon the shore. Life had been long extinct. The corpse was cold and stark, the eyes closed, an expression of energy, however, yet lingering in the fixed jaw, and the hair sodden with the sea. Suddenly Captain Cadurcis rushed to the inn and roused the household. With a distracted air, and broken speech and rapid motion, he communicated the catastrophe. Several persons, some bearing torches, others blankets and cordials, followed him instantly to the fatal spot. They hurried to the body, they applied all the rude remedies of the moment, rather from the impulse of nervous excitement than with any practical purpose; for the case had been indeed long hopeless. While Captain Cadurcis leant over the body, chafing the extremities in a hurried frenzy, and gazing intently on the countenance, a shout was heard from one of the stragglers who had recently arrived. The sea had washed on the beach another corpse: the form of Marmion Herbert. It would appear that he had made no struggle to save himself, for his hand was locked in his waistcoat, where, at the moment, he had thrust the Phaedo, showing that he had been reading to the last, and was meditating on immortality when he died.

END OF BOOK VI.

BOOK VII

CHAPTER I.

It was the commencement of autumn. The verdure of summer still lingered on the trees; the sky, if not so cloudless, was almost as refulgent as Italy; and the pigeons, bright and glancing, clustered on the roof of the hall of Cherbury. The steward was in attendance; the household, all in deep mourning, were assembled; everything was in readiness for the immediate arrival of Lady Annabel Herbert.

"Tis nearly four years come Martinmas,' said the grey-headed butler, 'since my lady left us.'

'And no good has come of it,' said the housekeeper. 'And for my part I never heard of good coming from going to foreign parts.'

'I shall like to see Miss Venetia again,' said a housemaid. 'Bless her sweet face.'

'I never expected to see her Miss Venetia again from all we heard,' said a footman.

'God's will be done!' said the grey-headed butler; 'but I hope she will find happiness at home. 'Tis nigh on twenty years since I first nursed her in these arms.'

'I wonder if there is any new Lord Cadurcis,' said the footman. 'I think he was the last of the line.'

'It would have been a happy day if I had lived to have seen the poor young lord marry Miss Venetia,' said the housekeeper. 'I always thought that match was made in heaven.'

'He was a sweet-spoken young gentleman,' said the housemaid.

'For my part,' said the footman, 'I should like to have seen our real master, Squire Herbert. He was a famous gentleman by all accounts.'

'I wish they had lived quietly at home,' said the housekeeper.

'I shall never forget the time when my lord returned,' said the grey-headed butler. 'I must say I thought it was a match.'

'Mistress Pauncefort seemed to think so,' said the housemaid.

'And she understands those things,' said the footman.

'I see the carriage,' said a servant who was at a window in the hall. All immediately bustled about, and the housekeeper sent a message to the steward.

The carriage might be just discovered at the end of the avenue. It was some time before it entered the iron gates that were thrown open for its reception.

The steward stood on the steps with his hat off, the servants were ranged in order at the entrance. Touching their horses with the spur, and cracking their whips, the postilions dashed round the circular plot and stopped at the hall-door. Under any circumstances a return home after an interval of years is rather an awful moment; there was not a servant who was not visibly affected. On the outside of the carriage was a foreign servant and Mistress Pauncefort, who was not so profuse as might have been expected in her recognitions of her old friends; her countenance was graver than of yore. Misfortune and misery had subdued even Mistress Pauncefort. The foreign servant opened the door of the carriage; a young man, who was a stranger to the household, but who was in deep mourning, alighted, and then Lady Annabel appeared. The steward advanced to welcome her, the household bowed and curtseyed. She smiled on them for a moment graciously and kindly, but her countenance immediately reassumed a serious air, and whispering one word to the strange gentleman, she entered the hall alone, inviting the steward to follow her.

'I hope your ladyship is well; welcome home, my lady; welcome again to Cherbury; a welcome return, my lady; hope Miss Venetia is quite well; happy to see your ladyship amongst us again, and Miss Venetia too, my lady.' Lady Annabel acknowledged these salutations with kindness, and then, saying that Miss Herbert was not very well and was fatigued with her journey, she dismissed her humble but trusty friends. Lady Annabel then turned and nodded to her fellow-traveller.

Upon this Lord Cadurcis, if we must indeed use a title from which he himself shrank, carried a shrouded form in his arms into the hall, where the steward alone lingered, though withdrawn to the back part of the scene; and Lady Annabel, advancing to meet him, embraced his treasured burden, her own unhappy child.

'Now, Venetia! dearest Venetia!' she said, "tis past; we are at home.'

Venetia leant upon her mother, but made no reply.

'Upstairs, dearest,' said Lady Annabel: 'a little exertion, a very little.' Leaning on her mother and Lord Cadurcis, Venetia ascended the staircase, and they reached the terrace-room. Venetia looked around her as she entered the chamber; that scene of her former life, endeared to her by so many happy hours, and so many sweet incidents; that chamber where she had first seen Plantagenet. Lord Cadurcis supported her to a chair, and then, overwhelmed by irresistible emotion, she sank back in a swoon.

No one was allowed to enter the room but Pauncefort. They revived her; Lord Cadurcis holding her hand, and touching, with a watchful finger, her pulse. Venetia opened her eyes, and looked around her. Her mind did not wander; she immediately recognised where she was, and recollected all that had happened. She faintly smiled, and said, in a low voice 'You are all too kind, and I am very weak. After our trials, what is this, George?' she added, struggling to appear animated; 'you are at length at Cherbury.'

Once more at Cherbury! It was, indeed, an event that recalled a thousand associations. In the wild anguish of her first grief, when the dreadful intelligence was broken to her, if anyone had whispered to Venetia that she would yet find herself once more at Cherbury, she would have esteemed the intimation as mockery. But time and hope will struggle with the most poignant affliction, and their influence is irresistible and inevitable. From her darkened chamber in their Mediterranean villa, Venetia had again come forth, and crossed mountains, and traversed immense plains, and journeyed through many countries. She could not die, as she had supposed at first that she must, and therefore she had exerted herself to quit, and to quit speedily, a scene so terrible as their late abode. She was the very first to propose their return to England, and to that spot where she had passed her early life, and where she now wished to fulfil, in quiet and seclusion, the allotment of her remaining years; to meditate over the marvellous past, and cherish its sweet and bitter recollections. The native firmness of Lady Annabel, her long exercised control over her emotions, the sadness and subdued tone which the early incidents of her career had cast over her character, her profound sympathy with her daughter, and that religious consolation which never deserted her, had alike impelled and enabled her to bear up against the catastrophe with more fortitude than her child. The arrow, indeed, had struck Venetia with a double barb. She was the victim; and all the cares of Lady Annabel had been directed to soothe and support this stricken lamb. Yet perhaps these unhappy women must have sunk under their unparalleled calamities, had it not been for the devotion of their companion. In the despair of his first emotions, George Cadurcis was nearly plunging himself headlong into the wave that had already proved so fatal to his house. But when he thought of Lady Annabel and Venetia in a foreign land, without a single friend in their desolation, and pictured them to himself with the dreadful news abruptly communicated by some unfeeling stranger; and called upon, in the midst of their overwhelming agony, to attend to all the heart-rending arrangements which the discovery of the bodies of the beings to whom they were devoted, and in whom all their feelings were centred, must necessarily entail upon them, he recoiled from what he contemplated as an act of infamous desertion. He resolved to live, if only to preserve them from all their impending troubles, and with the hope that his exertions might tend, in however slight a degree, not to alleviate, for that was impossible; but to prevent the increase of that terrible woe, the very conception of which made his brain stagger. He carried the bodies, therefore, with him to Spezzia, and then prepared for that fatal interview, the commencement of which we first indicated. Yet it must be confessed that, though the bravest of men, his courage faltered as he entered the accustomed ravine. He stopped and looked down on the precipice below; he felt it utterly impossible to meet them; his mind nearly deserted him. Death, some great and universal catastrophe, an earthquake, a deluge, that would have buried them all in an instant and a common fate, would have been hailed by George Cadurcis, at that moment, as good fortune.

He lurked about the ravine for nearly three hours before he could summon up heart for the awful interview. The position he had taken assured him that no one could approach the villa, to which he himself dared not advance. At length, in a paroxysm of energetic despair, he had rushed forward, met them instantly, and confessed with a whirling brain, and almost unconscious of his utterance, that 'they could not hope to see them again in this world.'

What ensued must neither be attempted to be described, nor even remembered. It was one of those tragedies of life which enfeeble the most faithful memories at a blow shatter nerves beyond the faculty of revival, cloud the mind for ever, or turn the hair grey in an instant. They carried Venetia delirious to her bed. The very despair, and almost madness, of her daughter forced Lady Annabel to self-exertion, of which it was difficult to suppose that even she was capable. And George, too, was obliged to leave them. He stayed only the night. A few words passed between Lady Annabel and himself; she wished the bodies to be embalmed, and borne to England. There was no time to be lost, and there was no one to be entrusted except George. He had to hasten to Genoa to make all these preparations, and for two days he was absent from the villa. When he returned, Lady Annabel saw him, but Venetia was for a long time invisible. The moment she grew composed, she expressed a wish to her mother instantly to return to Cherbury. All the arrangements necessarily devolved upon George Cadurcis. It was his study that Lady Annabel should be troubled upon no point. The household were discharged, all the affairs were wound up, the felucca hired which was to bear them to Genoa, and in readiness, before he notified to them that the hour of departure had arrived. The most bitter circumstance was looking again upon the sea. It seemed so intolerable to Venetia, that their departure was delayed more than one day in consequence; but it was inevitable; they could reach Genoa in no other manner. George carried Venetia in his arms to the boat, with her face covered with a shawl, and bore her in the same manner to the hotel at Genoa, where their travelling carriage awaited them.

They travelled home rapidly. All seemed to be impelled, as it were, by a restless desire for repose. Cherbury was the only thought in Venetia's mind. She observed nothing; she made no remark during their journey; they travelled often throughout the night; but no obstacles occurred, no inconveniences. There was one in this miserable society whose only object in life was to support Venetia under her terrible visitation. Silent, but with an eye that never slept, George Cadurcis watched Venetia as a nurse might a child. He read her thoughts, he anticipated her wishes without inquiring them; every arrangement was unobtrusively made that could possibly consult her comfort.

They passed through London without stopping there. George would not leave them for an instant; nor would he spare a thought to his own affairs, though they urgently required his attention. The change in his position gave him no consolation; he would not allow his passport to be made out with his title; he shuddered at being called Lord Cadurcis; and the only reason that made him hesitate about attending them to Cherbury was its contiguity to his ancestral seat, which he resolved never to visit. There never in the world was a less selfish and more single-hearted man than George Cadurcis. Though the death of his cousin had invested him with one of the most ancient coronets in England, a noble residence and a fair estate, he would willingly have sacrificed his life to have recalled Plantagenet to existence, and to have secured the happiness of Venetia Herbert.

CHAPTER II.

The reader must not suppose, from the irresistible emotion that overcame Venetia at the very moment of her return, that she was entirely prostrated by her calamities. On the contrary, her mind had been employed, during the whole of her journey to England, in a silent effort to endure her lot with resignation. She had resolved to bear up against her misery with fortitude, and she inherited from her mother sufficient firmness of mind to enable her to achieve her purpose. She came back to Cherbury to live with patience and submission; and though her dreams of happiness might be vanished for ever, to contribute as much as was in her power to the content of that dear and remaining relative who was yet spared to her, and who depended in this world only upon the affection of her child. The return to Cherbury was a pang, and it was over. Venetia struggled to avoid the habits of an invalid; she purposed resuming, as far as was in her power, all the pursuits and duties of her life; and if it were neither possible, nor even desirable, to forget the past, she dwelt upon it neither to sigh nor to murmur, but to cherish in a sweet and musing mood the ties and affections round which all her feelings had once gathered with so much enjoyment and so much hope.

She rose, therefore, on the morning after her return to Cherbury, at least serene; and she took an early opportunity, when George and her mother were engaged, and absent from the terrace-room, to go forth alone and wander amid her old haunts. There was not a spot about the park and gardens, which had been favourite resorts of herself and Plantagenet in their childhood, that she did not visit. They were unchanged; as green, and bright, and still as in old days, but what was she? The freshness, and brilliancy, and careless happiness of her life were fled for ever. And here he lived, and here he roamed, and here his voice sounded, now in glee, now in melancholy, now in wild and fanciful amusement, and now pouring into her bosom all his domestic sorrows. It was but ten years since he first arrived at Cherbury, and who could have anticipated that that little, silent, reserved boy should, ere ten years had passed, have filled a wide and lofty space in the world's thought; that his existence should have influenced the mind of nations, and his death eclipsed their gaiety! His death! Terrible and disheartening thought! Plantagenet was no more. But he had not died without a record. His memory was embalmed in immortal verse, and he had breathed his passion to his Venetia in language that lingered in the ear, and would dwell for ever on the lips, of his fellow-men.

Among these woods, too, had Venetia first mused over her father; before her rose those mysterious chambers, whose secret she had penetrated at the risk of her life. There were no secrets now. Was she happier? Now she felt that even in her early mystery there was delight, and that hope was veiled beneath its ominous shadow. There was now no future to ponder over; her hope was gone, and memory alone remained. All the dreams of those musing hours of her hidden reveries had been realised. She had seen that father, that surpassing parent, who had satisfied alike her heart and her imagination; she had been clasped to his bosom; she had lived to witness even her mother yield to his penitent embrace. And he too was gone; she could never meet him again in this world; in this world in which they had experienced such exquisite bliss; and now she was once more at Cherbury! Oh! give her back her girlhood, with all its painful mystery and harassing doubt! Give her again a future!

She returned to the hall; she met George on the terrace, she welcomed him with a sweet, yet mournful smile. 'I have been very selfish,' she said, 'for I have been walking alone. I mean to introduce you to Cherbury, but I could not resist visiting some old spots.' Her voice faltered in these last words. They re-entered the terrace-room together, and joined her mother.

'Nothing is changed, mamma,' said Venetia, in a more cheerful tone. 'It is pleasant to find something that is the same.'

Several days passed, and Lord Cadurcis evinced no desire to visit his inheritance. Yet Lady Annabel was anxious that he should do so, and had more than once impressed upon him the propriety. Even Venetia at length said to him, 'It is very selfish in us keeping you here, George. Your presence is a great consolation, and yet, yet, ought you not to visit your home?' She avoided the name of Cadurcis.

'I ought, dear Venetia.' said George, 'and I will. I have promised Lady Annabel twenty times, but I feel a terrible disinclination. To-morrow, perhaps.'

'To-morrow, and to-morrow, and to-morrow,' murmured Venetia to herself, 'I scarcely comprehend now what to-morrow means.' And then again addressing him, and with more liveliness, she said, 'We have only one friend in the world now, George, and I think that we ought to be very grateful that he is our neighbour.'

'It is a consolation to me,' said Lord Cadurcis, 'for I cannot remain here, and otherwise I should scarcely know how to depart.'

'I wish you would visit your home, if only for one morning,' said Venetia; 'if only to know how very near you are to us.'

'I dread going alone,' said Lord Cadurcis. 'I cannot ask Lady Annabel to accompany me, because—' He hesitated.

'Because?' inquired Venetia.

'I cannot ask or wish her to leave you.'

'You are always thinking of me, dear George,' said Venetia, artlessly. 'I assure you, I have come back to Cherbury to be happy. I must visit your home some day, and I hope I shall visit it often. We will all go, soon,' she added.

'Then I will postpone my visit to that day,' said George. 'I am in no humour for business, which I know awaits me there. Let me enjoy a little more repose at dear Cherbury.'

'I have become very restless of late, I think,' said Venetia, 'but there is a particular spot in the garden that I wish to see. Come with me, George.'

Lord Cadurcis was only too happy to attend her. They proceeded through a winding walk in the shrubberies until they arrived at a small and open plot of turf, where Venetia stopped. 'There are some associations,' she said, 'of this spot connected with both those friends that we have lost. I have a fancy that it should be in some visible manner consecrated to their memories. On this spot, George, Plantagenet once spoke to me of my father. I should like to raise their busts here; and indeed it is a fit place for such a purpose; for poets,' she added, faintly smiling, 'should be surrounded with laurels.'

'I have some thoughts on this head that I am revolving in my fancy myself,' said Lord Cadurcis, 'but I will not speak of them now.'

'Yes, now, George; for indeed it is a satisfaction for me to speak of them, at least with you, with one who understood them so well, and loved them scarcely less than I did.'

George tenderly put his arm into hers and led her away. As they walked along, he explained to her his plans, which yet were somewhat crude, but which greatly interested her; but they were roused from their conversation by the bell of the hall sounding as if to summon them, and therefore they directed their way immediately to the terrace. A servant running met them; he brought a message from Lady Annabel. Their friend the Bishop of —— had arrived.

CHAPTER III.

'Well, my little daughter,' said the good Masham, advancing as Venetia entered the room, and tenderly embracing her. The kind-hearted old man maintained a conversation on indifferent subjects with animation for some minutes; and thus a meeting, the anticipation of which would have cost Venetia hours of pain and anxiety, occurred with less uneasy feelings.

Masham had hastened to Cherbury the moment he heard of the return of the Herberts to England. He did not come to console, but to enliven. He was well aware that even his eloquence, and all the influence of his piety, could not soften the irreparable past; and knowing, from experience, how in solitude the unhappy brood over sorrow, he fancied that his arrival, and perhaps his arrival only, might tend in some degree at this moment to their alleviation and comfort. He brought Lady Annabel and Venetia letters from their relations, with whom he had been staying at their country residence, and who were anxious that their unhappy kinsfolk should find change of scene under their roof.

'They are very affectionate,' said Lady Annabel, 'but I rather think that neither Venetia nor myself feel inclined to quit Cherbury at present.'

'Indeed not, mamma,' said Venetia. 'I hope we shall never leave home again.'

'You must come and see me some day,' said the Bishop; then turning to George, whom he was glad to find here, he addressed him in a hearty tone, and expressed his delight at again meeting him.

Insensibly to all parties this arrival of the good Masham exercised a beneficial influence on their spirits. They could sympathise with his cheerfulness, because they were convinced that he sympathised with their sorrow. His interesting conversation withdrew their minds from the painful subject on which they were always musing. It seemed profanation to either of the three mourners when they were together alone, to indulge in any topic but the absorbing one, and their utmost effort was to speak of the past with composure; but they all felt relieved, though at first unconsciously, when one, whose interest in their feelings could not be doubted, gave the signal of withdrawing their reflections from vicissitudes which it was useless to deplore. Even the social forms which the presence of a guest rendered indispensable, and the exercise of the courtesies of hospitality, contributed to this result. They withdrew their minds from the past. And the worthy Bishop, whose tact was as eminent as his good humour and benevolence, evincing as much delicacy of feeling as cheerfulness of temper, a very few days had elapsed before each of his companions was aware that his presence had contributed to their increased content.

'You have not been to the abbey yet, Lord Cadurcis,' said Masham to him one day, as they were sitting together after dinner, the ladies having retired. 'You should go.'

'I have been unwilling to leave them,' said George, 'and I could scarcely expect them to accompany me. It is a visit that must revive painful recollections.'

'We must not dwell on the past,' said Masham; 'we must think only of the future.'

'Venetia has no future, I fear,' said Lord Cadurcis.

'Why not?' said Masham; 'she is yet a girl, and with a prospect of a long life. She must have a future, and I hope, and I believe, it will yet be a happy one.'

'Alas!' said Lord Cadurcis, 'no one can form an idea of the attachment that subsisted between Plantagenet and Venetia. They were not common feelings, or the feelings of common minds, my dear lord.'

'No one knew them both better than I did,' said Masham, 'not even yourself: they were my children.'

'I feel that,' said George, 'and therefore it is a pleasure to us all to see you, and to speak with you.'

'But we must look for consolation,' said Masham; 'to deplore is fruitless. If we live, we must struggle to live happily. To tell you the truth, though their immediate return to Cherbury was inevitable, and their residence here for a time is scarcely to be deprecated, I still hope they will not bury themselves here. For my part, after the necessary interval, I wish to see Venetia once more in the world.'

Lord Cadurcis looked very mournful, and shook his head.

'As for her dear mother, she is habituated to sorrow and disappointment,' said Masham. 'As long as Venetia lives Lady Annabel will be content. Besides, deplorable as may be the past, there must be solace to her in the reflection that she was reconciled to her husband before his death, and contributed to his happiness. Venetia is the stricken lamb, but Venetia is formed for happiness, and it is in the nature of things that she will be happy. We must not, however, yield unnecessarily to our feelings. A violent exertion would be unwise, but we should habituate ourselves gradually to the exercise of our duties, and to our accustomed pursuits. It would be well for you to go to Cadurcis. If I were you I would go to-morrow. Take advantage of my presence, and return and give a report of your visit. Habituate Venetia to talk of a spot with which ultimately she must renew her intimacy.'

Influenced by this advice, Lord Cadurcis rose early on the next morning and repaired to the seat of his fathers, where hitherto his foot had never trod. When the circle at Cherbury assembled at their breakfast table he was missing, and Masham had undertaken the office of apprising his friends of the cause of his absence. He returned to dinner, and the conversation fell naturally upon the abbey, and the impressions he had received. It was maintained at first by Lady Annabel and the Bishop, but Venetia ultimately joined in it, and with cheerfulness. Many a trait and incident of former days was alluded to; they talked of Mrs. Cadurcis, whom George had never seen; they settled the chambers he should inhabit; they mentioned the improvements which Plantagenet had once contemplated, and which George must now accomplish.

'You must go to London first,' said the Bishop; 'you have a great deal to do, and you should not delay such business. I think you had better return with me. At this time of the year you need not be long absent; you will not be detained; and when you return, you will find yourself much more at ease; for, after all, nothing is more harassing than the feeling, that there is business which must be attended to, and which, nevertheless, is neglected.'

Both Lady Annabel and Venetia enforced this advice of their friend; and so it happened that, ere a week had elapsed, Lord Cadurcis, accompanying Masham, found himself once more in London.

CHAPTER IV.

Venetia was now once more alone with her mother; it was as in old times. Their life was the same as before the visit of Plantagenet previous to his going to Cambridge, except indeed that they had no longer a friend at Marringhurst. They missed the Sabbath visits of that good man; for, though his successor performed the duties of the day, which had been a condition when he was presented to the living, the friend who knew all the secrets of their hearts was absent. Venetia continued to bear herself with great equanimity, and the anxiety which she observed instantly impressed on her mother's countenance, the moment she fancied there was unusual gloom on the brow of her child, impelled Venetia doubly to exert herself to appear resigned. And in truth, when Lady Annabel revolved in her mind the mournful past, and meditated over her early and unceasing efforts to secure the happiness of her daughter, and then contrasted her aspirations with the result, she could not acquit herself of having been too often unconsciously instrumental in forwarding a very different conclusion than that for which she had laboured. This conviction preyed upon the mother, and the slightest evidence of reaction in Venetia's tranquilised demeanour occasioned her the utmost remorse and grief. The absence of George made both Lady Annabel and Venetia still more finely appreciate the solace of his society. Left to themselves, they felt how much they had depended on his vigilant and considerate attention, and how much his sweet temper and his unfailing sympathy had contributed to their consolation. He wrote, however, to Venetia by every post, and his letters, if possible, endeared him still more to their hearts. Unwilling to dwell upon their mutual sorrows, yet always expressing sufficient to prove that distance and absence had not impaired his sympathy, he contrived, with infinite delicacy, even to amuse their solitude with the adventures of his life of bustle. The arrival of the post was the incident of the day; and not merely letters arrived; one day brought books, another music; continually some fresh token of his thought and affection reached them. He was, however, only a fortnight absent; but when he returned, it was to Cadurcis. He called upon them the next day, and indeed every morning found him at Cherbury; but he returned to his home at night; and so, without an effort, from their guest he had become their neighbour.

Plantagenet had left the whole of his property to his cousin: his mother's fortune, which, as an accessory fund, was not inconsiderable, besides the estate. And George intended to devote a portion of this to the restoration of the abbey. Venetia was to be his counsellor in this operation, and therefore there were ample sources of amusement for the remainder of the year. On a high ridge, which was one of the beacons of the county, and which, moreover, marked the junction of the domains of Cherbury and Cadurcis, it was his intention to raise a monument to the united memories of Marmion Herbert and Plantagenet Lord Cadurcis. He brought down a design with him from London, and this was the project which he had previously whispered to Venetia. With George for her companion, too, Venetia was induced to resume her rides. It was her part to make him acquainted with the county in which he was so important a resident. Time therefore, at Cherbury, on the whole, flowed on in a tide of tranquil pleasure; and Lady Annabel observed, with interest and fondness, the continual presence beneath her roof of one who, from the first day she had met him, had engaged her kind feelings, and had since become intimately endeared to her.

The end of November was, however, now approaching, and Parliament was about to reassemble. Masham had written more than once to Lord Cadurcis, impressing upon him the propriety and expediency of taking his seat. He had shown these letters, as he showed everything, to Venetia, who was his counsellor on all subjects, and Venetia agreed with their friend.

'It is right,' said Venetia; 'you have a duty to perform, and you must perform it. Besides, I do not wish the name of Cadurcis to sink again into obscurity. I shall look forward with interest to Lord Cadurcis taking the oaths and his seat. It will please me; it will indeed.'

'But Venetia,' said George, 'I do not like to leave this place. I am happy, if we may be happy. This life suits me. I am a quiet man. I dislike London. I feel alone there.'

'You can write to us; you will have a great deal to say. And I shall have something to say to you now. I must give you a continual report how they go on at the abbey. I will be your steward, and superintend everything.'

'Ah!' said George, 'what shall I do in London without you, without your advice? There will be something occurring every day, and I shall have no one to consult. Indeed I shall feel quite miserable; I shall indeed.'

'It is quite impossible that, with your station, and at your time of life, you should bury yourself in the country,' said Venetia. 'You have the whole world before you, and you must enjoy it. It is very well for mamma and myself to lead this life. I look upon ourselves as two nuns. If Cadurcis is an abbey, Cherbury is now a convent.'

'How can a man wish to be more than happy? I am quite content here,' said George, 'What is London to me?'

'It may be a great deal to you, more than you think,' said Venetia. 'A great deal awaits you yet. However, there can be no doubt you should take your seat. You can always return, if you wish. But take your seat, and cultivate dear

Masham. I have the utmost confidence in his wisdom and goodness. You cannot have a friend more respectable. Now mind my advice, George.'

'I always do, Venetia.'

CHAPTER V.

Time and Faith are the great consolers, and neither of these precious sources of solace were wanting to the inhabitants of Cherbury. They were again living alone, but their lives were cheerful; and if Venetia no longer indulged in a worldly and blissful future, nevertheless, in the society of her mother, in the resources of art and literature, in the diligent discharge of her duties to her humble neighbours, and in cherishing the memory of the departed, she experienced a life that was not without its tranquil pleasures. She maintained with Lord Cadurcis a constant correspondence; he wrote to her every day, and although they were separated, there was not an incident of his life, and scarcely a thought, of which she was not cognisant. It was with great difficulty that George could induce himself to remain in London; but Masham, who soon obtained over him all the influence which Venetia desired, ever opposed his return to the abbey. The good Bishop was not unaware of the feelings with which Lord Cadurcis looked back to the hall of Cherbury, and himself of a glad and sanguine temperament, he indulged in a belief in the consummation of all that happiness for which his young friend, rather sceptically, sighed. But Masham was aware that time could alone soften the bitterness of Venetia's sorrow, and prepare her for that change of life which he felt confident would alone ensure the happiness both of herself and her mother. He therefore detained Lord Cadurcis in London the whole of the sessions that, on his return to Cherbury, his society might be esteemed a novel and agreeable incident in the existence of its inhabitants, and not be associated merely with their calamities.

It was therefore about a year after the catastrophe which had so suddenly changed the whole tenor of their lives, and occasioned so unexpected a revolution in his own position, that Lord Cadurcis arrived at his ancestral seat, with no intention of again speedily leaving it. He had long and frequently apprised his friends of his approaching presence, And, arriving at the abbey late at night, he was at Cherbury early on the following morning.

Although no inconsiderable interval had elapsed since Lord Cadurcis had parted from the Herberts, the continual correspondence that had been maintained between himself and Venetia, divested his visit of the slightest embarrassment. They met as if they had parted yesterday, except perhaps with greater fondness. The chain of their feelings was unbroken. He was indeed welcomed, both by Lady Annabel and her daughter, with warm affection; and his absence had only rendered him dearer to them by affording an opportunity of feeling how much his society contributed to their felicity. Venetia was anxious to know his opinion of the improvements at the abbey, which she had superintended; but he assured her that he would examine nothing without her company, and ultimately they agreed to walk over to Cadurcis.

It was a summer day, and they walked through that very wood wherein we described the journey of the child Venetia, at the commencement of this very history. The blue patches of wild hyacinths had all disappeared, but there were flowers as sweet. What if the first feelings of our heart fade, like the first flowers of spring, succeeding years, like the coming summer, may bring emotions not less charming, and, perchance, far more fervent!

'I can scarcely believe,' said Lord Cadurcis, 'that I am once more with you. I know not what surprises me most, Venetia, that we should be walking once more together in the woods of Cherbury, or that I ever should have dared to quit them.'

'And yet it was better, dear George,' said Venetia. 'You must now rejoice that you have fulfilled your duty, and yet you are here again. Besides, the abbey never would have been finished if you had remained. To complete all our plans, it required a mistress.'

'I wish it always had one,' said George. 'Ah, Venetia! once you told me never to despair.'

'And what have you to despair about, George?'

'Heigh ho!' said Lord Cadurcis, 'I never shall be able to live in this abbey alone.'

'You should have brought a wife from London,' said Venetia.

'I told you once, Venetia, that I was not a marrying man,' said Lord Cadurcis; 'and certainly I never shall bring a wife from London.'

'Then you cannot accustom yourself too soon to a bachelor's life,' said Venetia.

'Ah, Venetia!' said George, 'I wish I were clever; I wish I were a genius; I wish I were a great man.'

'Why, George?'

'Because, Venetia, perhaps,' and Lord Cadurcis hesitated, 'perhaps you would think differently of me? I mean perhaps your feelings towards me might; ah, Venetia! perhaps you might think me worthy of you; perhaps you might love me.'

'I am sure, dear George, if I did not love you, I should be the most ungrateful of beings: you are our only friend.'

'And can I never be more than a friend to you, Venetia?' said Lord Cadurcis, blushing very deeply.

'I am sure, dear George, I should be very sorry for your sake, if you wished to be more,' said Venetia.

'Why?' said Lord Cadurcis.

'Because I should not like to see you unite your destiny with that of a very unfortunate, if not a very unhappy, person.'

'The sweetest, the loveliest of women!' said Lord Cadurcis. 'O Venetia! I dare not express what I feel, still less what I could hope. I think so little of myself, so highly of you, that I am convinced my aspirations are too arrogant for me to breathe them.'

'Ah! dear George, you deserve to be happy,' said Venetia. 'Would that it were in my power to make you!'

'Dearest Venetia! it is, it is,' exclaimed Lord Cadurcis; then checking himself, as if frightened by his boldness, he added in a more subdued tone, 'I feel I am not worthy of you.'

They stood upon the breezy down that divided the demesnes of Cherbury and the abbey. Beneath them rose, 'embosomed in a valley of green bowers,' the ancient pile lately renovated under the studious care of Venetia.

'Ah!' said Lord Cadurcis, 'be not less kind to the master of these towers, than to the roof that you have fostered. You have renovated our halls, restore our happiness! There is an union that will bring consolation to more than one hearth, and baffle all the crosses of adverse fate. Venetia, beautiful and noble-minded Venetia, condescend to fulfil it!'

Perhaps the reader will not be surprised that, within a few months of this morning walk, the hands of George, Lord Cadurcis, and Venetia Herbert were joined in the chapel at Cherbury by the good Masham. Peace be with them.

Milton Keynes UK
Ingram Content Group UK Ltd.
UKHW031954281024
450365UK00009B/534